Swift Programming
The Big Nerd Ranch Guide

Mikey Ward

Big Nerd Ranch

Swift Programming: The Big Nerd Ranch Guide

by Mikey Ward

Big Nerd Ranch
200 Arizona Ave NE, Suite 200
Atlanta, GA 30307

(770) 817-6373
http://www.bignerdranch.com/
book-comments@bignerdranch.com

The 10-gallon hat is a trademark of Big Nerd Ranch.

Exclusive worldwide distribution of the English edition of this book by

Pearson Technology Group
800 East 96th Street
Indianapolis, IN 46240 USA
http://www.informit.com

ISBN-10 0135264200
ISBN-13 978-0135264201

Third edition, first printing, September 2020

Dedication

For Matt Mathias and John Gallagher; I stand on their shoulders. For Aaron Hillegass, who took a chance on hiring me. And for my parents, for their eternal loving support.

— M.W.

Acknowledgments

Writing a book is a team effort, and thanks are due.

First and foremost, thanks to Matt Mathias and John Gallagher, who wrote the the first two editions of this book. Their vision and creativity are still evident in its pages. Thank you Matt and John for all of the heart and soul that you poured into it.

Thank you also to Jacob Bullock, Juan Pablo Claude, Chris Downie, Nicole Hinckley, Chris Morris, and Zachary Waldowski, who went above and beyond in their contributions to this edition. Their words and wisdom have markedly improved its quality.

Over time, many colleagues have contributed to the continuous evolution of this book and our Swift training materials. They have provided a wealth of thoughtful suggestions and feedback. Thank you, Pouria Almassi, Matt Bezark, Amit Bijlani, Nate Chandler, Step Christopher, Kynerd Coleman, Matthew Compton, Mark Dalrymple, Joseph Dixon, Robert Edwards, Sean Farrell, Drew Fitzpatrick, Brian Hardy, Florian Harr, Tom Harrington, Gabe Hoffman, David House, Jeremiah Jessel, Bolot Kerimbaev, Christian Keur, Jake Kirshner, Drew Kreuzman, JJ Manton, Bill Monk, Chris Morris, Adam Preble, Kevin Randrup, Scott Ritchie, Jeremy Sherman, Steve Sparks, Rod Strougo, TJ Usiyan, Thomas Ward, Michael Williams, and Mike Zornek.

Colleagues in operations, marketing, and sales have provided instrumental support. Classes would literally never be scheduled without their work. Thank you Holly Avila, CJ Best, Nick Gravino, Mathew Jackson, Shannon Kroll, Anja McKinley, Thomas Moore, Q. Elle Mosley, Rodrigo Velasco, Don Wedington, Eric Wilson, and Madison Witzler.

And, of course, thank you to the many talented honorary Big Nerds who worked on the book.

Liz Holaday, editor extraordinaire, worked tirelessly to help refine, transform, and crystallize these ideas into prose. Your voice is integral to the quality of our work.

Anna Bentley jumped in to copyedit, correcting errors and inconsistencies. Thank you for your eagle eye and for accommodating the schedule crunch as the book raced toward completion.

Ellie Volckhausen designed the the cover; thanks for that rad skateboard!

Chris Loper designed and produced the print book and the EPUB and Kindle versions. Your hard work in the unglamorous part of production is extremely appreciated.

Finally, from all of us at Big Nerd Ranch, thank you to our students. We learn with you and for you. Teaching is part of the greatest thing that we do, and it has been a pleasure working with you. We hope that the quality of this book matches your enthusiasm and determination.

Table of Contents

Introduction

Learning Swift

Apple introduced the Swift language for the development of iOS and macOS applications in 2014. It was a dramatic shift from Objective-C, the previous development language for Apple's platforms. There is a lot to learn in a relatively new language, and this is especially true for Swift.

Swift continues to evolve even six years after its release. As new features are added, Swift users can collaboratively determine its best practices. You can be part of this conversation, and your work with this book will start you on your way to becoming a contributing member of the Swift community.

Why Swift?

You may be wondering why Apple released a new language. After all, developers had been producing high-quality apps for OS X and iOS for years. Apple had a few things in mind.

First, the syntax of Objective-C dates back to 1984, before the rise in the 1990s of prominent scripting languages that popularized more streamlined and elegant syntax (like JavaScript, Python, PHP, Ruby, and others). As a result, Objective-C syntax is not as accessible or familiar to developers as more modern languages. Also, while the language pioneered many ideas in object-oriented programming and allowed a lot of flexibility for programs to change their behavior while running, a tradeoff was that fewer bugs were discoverable during development. Instead, bugs often revealed themselves as crashes once a program was in the hands of its users.

In addition to adopting more modern patterns and paradigms, Swift is designed to be more safe by strictly requiring that developers follow certain safety rules that, in Objective-C, are only suggestions. Objective-C did not aim to be unsafe, of course, but industry best practices have changed quite a bit since it was released. For example, the Swift compiler aims to minimize undefined behavior and save the developer time debugging code that failed at runtime.

Another goal of Swift is to be a suitable replacement for the C family of languages (C, C++, and Objective-C). That means Swift has to be fast. Indeed, Swift's performance is comparable to these languages in most cases.

Swift gives you safety and performance, all in a clean, modern syntax. The language is quite expressive; developers can write code that feels natural. This feature makes Swift a joy to write and easy to read, which makes it great for collaborating on larger projects.

Last, Apple wants Swift to be a general-purpose programming language. In December 2015, it open-sourced Swift and its compiler, inviting developer involvement to help the language progress and making it easier for developers to port the language to systems beyond macOS and iOS. Apple hopes that developers will use Swift to write apps for a variety of mobile and desktop platforms and to develop back-end web applications as well.

What About Objective-C?

So do you still need to know Objective-C to develop for Apple's platforms? The answer is "a little." Being familiar with it can be helpful for the same reason that knowing some history is helpful: So you understand why things are the way they are and what decisions went into the modern way of doing things. But also, many Apple frameworks that you will use are written in Objective-C; even if you interact with them using Swift, the error messages that they produce will have an Objective-C "accent," so debugging will be easier if you understand that language. And Apple has made it easy to mix and match Objective-C with Swift in the same project, so as you become a more advanced developer for Apple's platforms, you might encounter Objective-C.

But do you need to know Objective-C to learn Swift or to write robust, useful apps? Not at all. At the end of this book, you will write a command-line tool and a task list app for iOS and macOS – entirely in Swift. Swift coexists and interoperates with Objective-C, but it is its own language. If you do not know Objective-C, it will not hinder you in learning Swift or starting your development career.

Prerequisites

This book was written for all types of macOS and iOS developers, from platform experts to first-timers. Having some development experience will be helpful, but it is not necessary to have a good experience with this book. For readers just starting software development, this book highlights and implements best practices for Swift and programming in general. Its strategy is to teach you the fundamentals of programming while learning Swift.

For more experienced developers, this book will serve as a helpful introduction to the language. Depending on the platform you are coming from, some of the fundamentals of Swift might already be familiar. The section called *How to Use This Book*, below, lists some chapters that you might only need to skim – and some that you should not skim.

How This Book Is Organized

This book is organized in six parts. Each is designed to help you accomplish a specific set of goals. By the end of the book, you will have built your knowledge of Swift from that of a beginner to a more advanced developer.

Getting Started	This part of the book focuses on the tools that you will need to write Swift code and introduces Swift's syntax.
The Basics	*The Basics* introduces the fundamental data types that you will use every day as a Swift developer. This part of the book also covers Swift's *control flow* features that will help you to control the order your code executes in.
Collections and Functions	You will often want to gather related data in your application. Once you do, you will want to operate on that data. This part of the book covers the *collections* and *functions* Swift offers to help with these tasks.

Enumerations, Structures, and Classes	This part of the book covers how you will model data in your own development. You will examine the differences between Swift's *enumerations*, *structures*, and *classes* and see some recommendations on when to use each.
Advanced Swift	Swift provides advanced features that enable you to write elegant, readable, and effective code. This part of the book discusses how to use these features to write idiomatic code that will set you apart from more casual Swift developers.
Writing Applications	This part of the book walks you through writing your first real applications for iOS and macOS.

How to Use This Book

Programming can be tough, and this book is here to make it easier. It does not focus on abstract concepts and theory; instead, it favors a practical approach. It uses concrete examples to unpack the more difficult ideas and also to show you best practices that make code more fun to write, more readable, and easier to maintain. To get the most out of it, follow these steps:

- Read the book. Really! Do not just browse it nightly before going to bed.

- Type out the examples as you read along. Part of learning is muscle memory. If your fingers know where to go and what to type without too much thought on your part, then you are on your way to becoming a more effective developer.

- Make mistakes! In our experience, the best way to learn how things work is to first figure out what makes them not work. Break our code examples and then make them work again.

- Experiment as your imagination sees fit. Whether that means tinkering with the code you find in the book or going off in your own direction, the sooner you start solving your own problems with Swift, the sooner you will become a better developer.

- Do the challenges at the end of each chapter. Again, it is important to begin solving problems with Swift as soon as possible. Doing so will help you to start thinking like a developer.

Remember that learning new things takes time. Dedicate some time to going through this book when you are able to avoid distractions. You will get more out of the text if you can give it your undivided attention.

More experienced developers coming to Swift from another language might not need to go through some of the earlier parts of the book. The tools and concepts introduced in *Getting Started* and *The Basics* might be very familiar to some developers – but you should still skim them, as Swift's strong and strict type system means that certain problems are solved differently than in other languages.

In the *Collections and Functions* section, do not skip or skim the chapter on optionals. They are at the heart of Swift, and in many ways they embody what is special about the language.

Other chapters in *Collections and Functions* and *Enumerations, Structures, and Classes* might seem like they will not present anything new to the practiced developer. But Swift's approach to topics on topics like arrays, dictionaries, functions, enumerations, structs, and classes is unique enough that every reader should at least skim these chapters.

Challenges and For the More Curious

Most of the chapters in this book conclude with *Challenge* sections. These are exercises for you to work through on your own and provide opportunities for you to challenge yourself. In our experience, true learning happens when you solve problems in your own way.

There are also *For the More Curious* sections at the end of many chapters. These sections address questions that may have occurred to the curious reader while working through the chapter. Sometimes they discuss how a language feature's underlying mechanics work or explore a programming concept not quite related to the heart of the chapter.

Typographical Conventions

You will be writing a lot of code as you work through this book. To make things easier, this book uses a couple of conventions to identify what code is old, what should be added, and what should be removed. For example, in the function implementation below, you are deleting `print("Hello")` and adding `print("Goodbye")`. The line reading `func talkToMe() {` and the final brace `}` were already in the code. They are shown to help you locate the changes.

```
func talkToMe() {
    print("Hello")
    print("Goodbye")
}
```

Necessary Hardware and Software

To build and run the applications in this book, you will need a Mac running macOS Catalina (macOS 10.15.6) or newer. Screen captures in the book are taken using macOS Big Sur (macOS 11). You will also need to install Xcode, Apple's *integrated development environment* (IDE), which is available on the Mac App Store. Xcode includes the Swift compiler as well as other development tools you will use throughout the book.

Swift is still under rapid development. This book is written for Swift 5.3 and Xcode 12. Many of the examples will not work as written with older versions of Xcode. If you are using a newer version of Xcode, there may have been changes in the language that will cause some examples to fail.

If future versions of Xcode do cause problems, take heart – the vast majority of what you learn will continue to be applicable to future versions of Swift even though there may be changes in syntax or names. You can check out our book forums at `forums.bignerdranch.com` for help.

Before You Begin

Swift is an elegant language, and it is fun to make applications for the Apple ecosystem. While writing code can be extremely frustrating, it can also be gratifying. There is something magical and exhilarating about solving a problem – not to mention the joy that comes from making an app that helps people and brings them happiness.

The best way to improve at anything is with practice. If you want to be a developer, then let's get started! If you find that you do not think you are very good at it, who cares? Keep at it and you will surprise yourself. Your next steps lie ahead. Onward!

Part I
Getting Started

This part of the book introduces Xcode, the Swift developer's primary development tool. You will begin by exploring Xcode's playgrounds, which provide a lightweight environment for trying out code. These initial chapters will also help you become familiar with some of Swift's most basic concepts, like constants and variables, to set the stage for the deeper understanding of the language you will build throughout this book.

1
Getting Started

In this chapter, you will set up your environment and take a small tour of some of the tools you will use every day as an iOS and macOS developer. Additionally, you will get your hands dirty with some code to help you get better acquainted with Swift and Xcode.

Getting Started with Xcode

If you have not already done so, download and install the latest version of Xcode available for macOS on the App Store.

When you have Xcode installed, launch it. The welcome screen appears; close it. It has options that are not relevant right now.

You are going to create a document called a *playground*.

Playgrounds provide an interactive environment for rapidly developing and evaluating Swift code and have become a useful prototyping tool. A playground does not require that you compile and run a complete project. Instead, playgrounds evaluate your Swift code on the fly, so they are ideal for testing and experimenting with the Swift language in a lightweight environment.

You will be using playgrounds frequently throughout this book to get quick feedback on your Swift code. In addition to playgrounds, you will create native command-line tools and even an app for iOS and macOS in later chapters. Why not just use playgrounds? You would miss out on a lot of Xcode's features and would not get as much exposure to the IDE. You will be spending a lot of time in Xcode, and it is good to get comfortable with it as soon as possible.

From Xcode's File menu, open the New submenu and select Playground... (Figure 1.1).

Figure 1.1 Creating a new playground

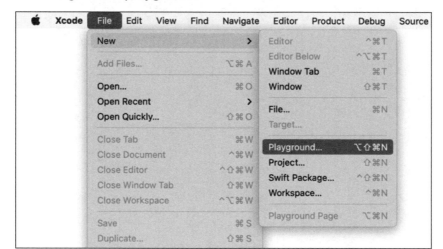

In the configuration window that appears, you have some options to choose from. For the platform (iOS, macOS, or tvOS), select macOS, even if you are an iOS developer (Figure 1.2). The Swift features you will be exploring are common to both platforms. Select the Blank document template from this group and click Next.

Figure 1.2 Picking a playground template

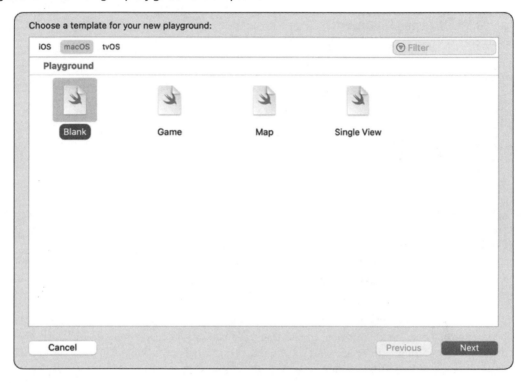

Finally, you are prompted to save your playground. As you work through this book, it is a good idea to put all your work in one folder. Choose a location that works for you and click Create (Figure 1.3).

Figure 1.3 Saving a playground

Playing in a Playground

Figure 1.4 shows a new Swift playground. It opens with three sections. On the left is the navigator area. In the middle, you have the Swift code editor. And on the right is the results sidebar. The code in the editor is evaluated and run, if possible, every time the source changes. The results of the code are displayed in the results sidebar.

Figure 1.4 Your new playground

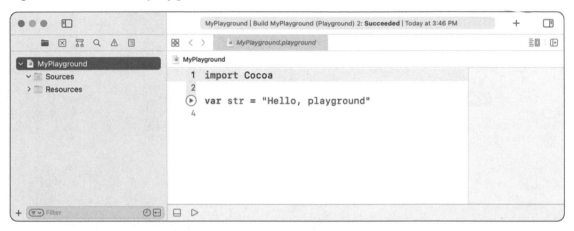

For the most part, you will not be using the navigator area in the playgrounds you create as you work through this book. You can close it with the ⬛ button just above it in the window toolbar.

Let's take a look at the code in your new playground. At the top, the playground imports the Cocoa framework. This import statement means that your playground has complete access to all the application programming interfaces (APIs) in the Cocoa framework. (An API is similar to a prescription – or set of definitions – for how a program can be written.)

Below the import statement is a line that reads `var str = "Hello, playground"`. The equals sign, which is called the *assignment operator*, assigns the result of code on its righthand side to a constant or variable on its lefthand side. In this case, on the lefthand side of the equals sign is the text `var str`. Swift's keyword `var` is used to declare a variable. This is an important concept that you will see in greater detail in the next chapter. For now, a variable represents some value that you expect to change or vary.

On the righthand side of the assignment operator, you have `"Hello, playground"`. In Swift, the quotation marks indicate a **String**, an ordered collection of characters. The template named this new variable `str`, but variables can be named almost anything. Of course, there are some limitations. Swift reserves certain words for its own use. What would happen if you changed the name `str` to be `var`? Try it and see; be sure to change the name back to `str` before moving on.

Running Your Code

A playground is a place for you to write and experiment with Swift code on your terms. You get to choose when the code you write will actually be run by Xcode. By default, a new playground will only execute code when you tell it to.

Notice the small play button (⊙) in the lefthand gutter next to your code (Figure 1.4). This symbol means that the playground is currently paused at this line and has not executed it. If you move your cursor up and down the gutter (without clicking), the button will follow you. Clicking the play button next to any line in the playground will execute all the code up to that line.

Click the play button next to the line var str = "Hello, playground" (Figure 1.5). The playground evaluates the declaration of str, which will make its value appear in the righthand sidebar.

Figure 1.5 Executing instructions

Manually executing some or all of your code is a convenient feature of playgrounds when you are exploring on your own, but it can become cumbersome when working through a book like this one. Good news: You can tell Xcode to automatically run your playground every time you make changes.

Click and hold the play button in the bottom-left of the playground window (Figure 1.6). (It may be a square if you just ran your playground.) In the pop-up, select Automatically Run. This will cause Xcode to reevaluate your whole playground every time you make changes, so that you do not have to do it yourself.

Figure 1.6 Automatically running your playground

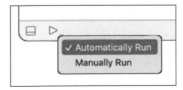

Enable Automatically Run on every playground you create for this book.

Troubleshooting Playgrounds

Xcode is an app like any other. Sometimes it has bugs and other strange behavior. At the time of this writing, a playground may sometimes "hang" – stop running or updating the sidebar. If this happens to you, one of these troubleshooting steps might help:

- Close and reopen your playground.

- Quit and relaunch Xcode.

- Switch the playground back to Manually Run and use the play button in the gutter to periodically run your code up to the selected line.

- Copy your code into a new playground.

These steps might also be useful if you encounter a different problem with a playground.

Varying Variables and Printing to the Console

String is a *type*, and we say that the str variable is "an instance of the **String** type." Types describe a particular structure for representing data. Swift has many types, which you will meet throughout this book. Each type has specific abilities (what the type can do with data) and limitations (what it cannot do with data). For example, the **String** type is designed to work with an ordered collection of characters and defines a number of functions to work with that ordered collection of characters.

Recall that str is a variable. That means you can change str's value. Let's append an exclamation point to the end of the string. (Whenever new code is added in this book, it will be shown in bold. Deletions will be struck through.)

Listing 1.1 Proper punctuation

```
import Cocoa

var str = "Hello, playground"
str += "!"
```

To add the exclamation point, you are using the += *addition assignment operator*. The addition assignment operator combines the addition (+) and assignment (=) operations in a single operator. You will learn more about operators in Chapter 3.

You should see a new line in the results sidebar showing str's new value, complete with an exclamation point (Figure 1.7).

Figure 1.7 Varying str

From now on, we will show the sidebar results on the righthand side of code listings.

Next, add some code to print the value of the variable str to the *console*. In Xcode, the console displays text messages that you create and want to log as things occur in your program. Xcode also uses the console to display warnings and errors as they occur.

To print to the console, you will use the **print()** *function*. Functions are groupings of related code that send instructions to the computer to complete a specific task. **print()** prints a value to the console (followed by a line break). Unlike playgrounds, Xcode projects do not have a results sidebar – but the console is always available. So you will use the **print()** function frequently when you are writing fully featured apps.

One thing the console is useful for is checking the current value of a variable. Use **print()** to check the value of str:

Listing 1.2 Printing to the console

```
import Cocoa

var str = "Hello, playground"          "Hello, playground"
str += "!"                             "Hello, playground!"
print(str)                             "Hello, playground!\n"
```

After you enter this new line and the playground executes the code, the console will open at the bottom of the Xcode screen. (If it does not, you can open the *debug area* to see it. Click on View → Debug Area → Show Debug Area, as shown in Figure 1.8. You can also type Shift-Command-Y, as the menu shows, to open the debug area.)

Figure 1.8 Showing the debug area

Now that you have your debug area open, you should see something like Figure 1.9.

Figure 1.9 Your first Swift code

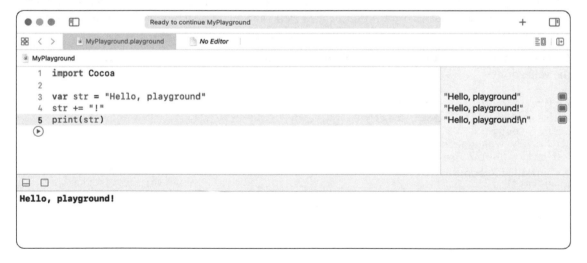

Adding Comments

Sometimes you want to include text in your project code that is not part of the program, such as an explanation of what is happening in nearby code.

Insert a new line above `print(str)` and add the following explanatory text:

Listing 1.3 Adding invalid text

```
import Cocoa

var str = "Hello, playground"                    "Hello, playground"
str += "!"                                        "Hello, playground!"
Print the string to the console
print(str)
```

Xcode will indicate an error in this line, because it does not contain valid Swift code. (The error is also shown in the console.) Now, add two slashes `//` to the beginning of the line:

Listing 1.4 Using a comment

```
import Cocoa

var str = "Hello, playground"                    "Hello, playground"
str += "!"                                        "Hello, playground!"
//Print the string to the console
print(str)                                        "Hello, playground!\n"
```

The error disappears. The slashes signify to the compiler that the whole line is a *comment*: text for the developer's benefit that should be ignored by the compiler.

Developers use comments to leave notes for themselves (or collaborators) about what is going on in the surrounding code. You can also turn code into a comment to temporarily remove it from your program without deleting it completely.

With the cursor still in the line with the comment, press Command-/. The slashes disappear. Use the same keyboard shortcut to toggle them back. (If you just installed Xcode and Command-/ does not work, restart your computer and try again.)

You Are on Your Way!

Let's review what you have accomplished so far. You have:

- installed Xcode

- created and gotten acquainted with a playground

- used a variable and modified it

- learned about the **String** type

- used a function to print to the console

That is a lot! You will be making your own apps in no time.

Bronze Challenge

Many of the chapters in this book end with one or more challenges. The challenges are for you to work through on your own to deepen your understanding of Swift and get a little extra experience. Your first challenge is below.

You learned about the **String** type and printing to the console using **print()**. Use your new playground to create a new instance of the **String** type. Set the value of this instance to be equal to your last name. Print its value to the console.

2

Types, Constants, and Variables

This chapter will introduce you to Swift's basic data types, constants, and variables. These elements are the fundamental building blocks of any program. You will use constants and variables to store values and to pass data around in your applications. Types describe the nature of the data held by the constant or variable. There are important differences between constants and variables, as well as each of the data types, that shape their uses.

Types

Variables and constants have a data type. The type describes the nature of the data and provides information to the compiler on how to handle the data. Based on the type of a constant or variable, the compiler knows how much memory to reserve and will also be able to help with *type checking*, a feature of Swift that helps prevent you from assigning the wrong kind of data to a variable.

Let's see this in action. Create a new macOS playground. From within Xcode, choose File → New → Playground.... Choose the blank template and name the playground Variables.

Do not forget to set the playground to Automatically Run as you make changes (Figure 2.1).

Figure 2.1 Automatically running your playground

Suppose you want to model a small town in your code. You might want a variable for the number of stoplights. Remove the code that came with the template, create a variable called numberOfStoplights, and give it a value. (Remember that code you are to delete is shown struck through.)

Listing 2.1 Assigning a string to a variable

```
import Cocoa

var str = "Hello, playground"
var numberOfStoplights = "Four"                              "Four"
```

13

Swift uses *type inference* to determine the data type of a variable. In this case, the compiler knows the variable `numberOfStoplights` is of the **String** type because the value on the right side of the assignment operator is an instance of **String**. How does it know that "Four" is an instance of **String**? Because the quotation marks indicate that it is a **String** literal.

Now add the integer 2 to your variable, using += as you did in the last chapter.

Listing 2.2 Adding "Four" and 2

```
import Cocoa

var numberOfStoplights = "Four"                          "Four"
numberOfStoplights += 2
```

The compiler gives you an error telling you that this operation does not make sense. You get this error because you are trying to add a number to a variable that is an instance of a different type: **String**. What would it mean to add the number 2 to a string? Does it put "2" on the end and give you "Four2"? Hard to say.

If you are thinking that it does not make sense to have `numberOfStoplights` be of type **String** in the first place, you are right. Because this variable represents the *number* of stoplights in your theoretical town, it makes sense to use a *numerical* type. Swift provides an **Int** type to represent whole integers that is perfect for your variable. Change your code to use **Int** instead.

Listing 2.3 Using a numerical type

```
import Cocoa

var numberOfStoplights = "Four"
var numberOfStoplights: Int = 4                          4
numberOfStoplights += 2                                  6
```

Before, the compiler relied on type inference to determine the data type of the variable `numberOfStoplights`. Now, you are explicitly declaring the variable to be of the **Int** type using Swift's *type annotation* syntax, indicated by the colon followed by the type name.

Note that type annotation does not mean that the compiler is no longer paying attention to what is on each side of the =. What if the type you specify is incompatible with the value that you assign? Try changing the explicit type of `numberOfStoplights` from **Int** to **String**.

Listing 2.4 Using the wrong type

```
import Cocoa

var numberOfStoplights: Int String = 4                   4
numberOfStoplights += 2                                  6
```

This produces an error: Cannot convert value of type Int to specified type String. Swift is telling you "I see that 4 is an Int, but you are asking me to store it in a String variable. I cannot do that."

You can add explicit type annotations when you think they will make your code more readable, but Swift checks your variable types whether or not it infers them.

Revert the type back to **Int** to fix the error.

Swift has a host of frequently used data types. You will learn more about numeric types in Chapter 4 and strings in Chapter 7. Other commonly used types represent collections of data; you will see those beginning in Chapter 8.

Now that you have changed numberOfStoplights to be an **Int** with an initial value of 4, the errors have disappeared. It makes sense to add one integer to another, and in fact it is something you will do quite often in your code.

Recall from Chapter 1 that you used += to put two strings together. Here you use it to add two integers. Swift knows how to apply this operator to most of its built-in types.

Constants vs Variables

We said that types describe the nature of the data held by a constant or variable. What, then, are constants and variables? Up to now, you have only seen variables. Variables' values can vary: You can assign them a new value, as you have seen.

Often, however, you will want to create instances with values that do not change. Use *constants* for these cases. As the name indicates, the value of a constant cannot be changed.

A good rule of thumb is to use variables for instances that must vary and constants for instances that will not. For example, if you did not expect the value of numberOfStoplights to ever change, it would be better to make it a constant.

Swift has different syntax for declaring constants and variables. As you have seen, you declare a variable with the keyword var. You use the let keyword to declare a constant.

Change numberOfStoplights to a constant to fix the number of stoplights in your small town.

Listing 2.5 Declaring a constant

```
import Cocoa

var numberOfStoplights: Int = 4
let numberOfStoplights: Int = 4                          4
numberOfStoplights += 2
```

You declare numberOfStoplights to be a constant via the let keyword. Unfortunately, this change causes the compiler to issue an error. You still have code that attempts to change the number of stoplights: numberOfStoplights += 2. Because constants cannot change, the compiler gives you an error when you try to change it.

Fix the problem by removing the addition and assignment code.

Listing 2.6 Constants do not vary

```
import Cocoa

let numberOfStoplights: Int = 4                          4
numberOfStoplights += 2
```

Now, create an **Int** to represent the town's population.

Listing 2.7 Declaring population

```
import Cocoa

let numberOfStoplights: Int = 4                          4
var population: Int
```

Your town's population is likely to change over time, so you declare population with the var keyword to make this instance a variable. You also declare population to be an instance of type **Int**, because a town's population is represented by a number. But you did not *initialize* population with any value. It is therefore an *uninitialized* **Int**.

Swift will not allow you to use any variable or constant without first assigning it a value. Use the assignment operator to give population its starting value.

Listing 2.8 Giving population a value

```
import Cocoa

let numberOfStoplights: Int = 4                          4
var population: Int
population = 5422                                         5422
```

String Interpolation

Every town needs a name. Your town is fairly stable, so it will not be changing its name any time soon. Make the town name a constant of type **String**.

Listing 2.9 Giving the town a name

```
import Cocoa

let numberOfStoplights: Int = 4                          4
var population: Int
population = 5422                                         5422
let townName: String = "Knowhere"                        "Knowhere"
```

It would be nice to have a short description of the town that the Tourism Council could use. The description is going to be a constant **String**, but you will be creating it a bit differently than the constants and variables you have created so far. The description will include all the data you have entered, and you are going to create it using a Swift feature called *string interpolation*.

String interpolation lets you combine constant and variable values into a new string. You can then assign the string to a new variable or constant or just print it to the console. You are going to print the town description to the console.

(Because of the limitations of the printed page, we have broken the string assigned to townDescription onto multiple lines. You should enter it on one line.)

Listing 2.10 Crafting the town description

```
import Cocoa

let numberOfStoplights: Int = 4                          4
var population: Int
population = 5422                                         5422
let townName: String = "Knowhere"                        "Knowhere"
let townDescription =                                    "Knowhere has a populat...
    "\(townName) has a population of \(population)
    and \(numberOfStoplights) stoplights."
print(townDescription)                                   "Knowhere has a populat...
```

We have truncated the sidebar results to make them fit. Xcode also truncates sidebar results to fit the window; you can drag the divider between the editor pane and the sidebar left or right to see more or less of the results.

The \() syntax represents a placeholder in the **String** literal that accesses an instance's value and places it (or "interpolates" it) within the new **String**. For example, \(townName) accesses the constant townName's value and places it within the new **String** instance.

The result of the new code is shown in Figure 2.2.

Figure 2.2 Knowhere's short description

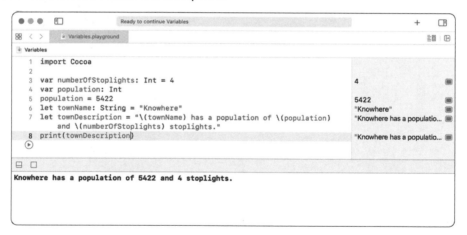

Bronze Challenge

Add a new variable to your playground representing Knowhere's elevation. Which data type should you use? Give this variable a value and update townDescription to use this new information.

Part II
The Basics

Programs execute code in a specific order. Writing software means having control over the order that code executes in. Programming languages provide *control flow statements* to help developers organize the execution of their code. This part of the book introduces the concepts of conditionals and loops to accomplish this task.

The chapters in this part of the book will also show you how Swift represents numbers and text in code. These types of data are the building blocks of many applications.

Conditionals

In previous chapters, your code led a relatively simple life: You declared some constants and variables and then assigned them values. But of course, an application really comes to life – and programming becomes a bit more challenging – when the application makes decisions based on the contents of its variables. For example, a game may let players leap a tall building *if* they have eaten a power-up. You use conditional statements to help applications make decisions like these.

if/else

if/else statements execute code based on a specific logical condition. You have a relatively simple either/or situation, and depending on the result one branch of code or another (but not both) runs.

Consider Knowhere, your small town from the previous chapter, and imagine that you need to buy stamps. Either Knowhere has a post office or it does not. If it does, you will buy stamps there. If it does not, you will need to drive to the next town to buy stamps. Whether there is a post office is your logical condition. The different behaviors are "get stamps in town" and "get stamps out of town."

Some situations are more complex than a binary yes/no. You will see a more flexible mechanism called switch in Chapter 5. But for now, let's keep it simple.

Create a new blank macOS playground and name it Conditionals. Set it to Automatically Run. Enter the code below, which shows the basic syntax for an if/else statement:

Listing 3.1 Big or small?

```
import Cocoa

var str = "Hello, playground"
let population: Int = 5422                                    5422
let message: String

if population < 10000 {
    message = "\(population) is a small town!"        "5422 is a small town!"
} else {
    message = "\(population) is pretty big!"
}
print(message)                                       "5422 is a small town!\n"
```

You first declare population as an instance of the **Int** type and assign it a value of 5,422. You also declare a constant called message that is of the **String** type. You leave this declaration uninitialized at first, meaning that you do not assign it a value. Swift requires you to assign it a value before you can use it, but that assignment can be in a separate step.

Next comes the conditional `if`/`else` statement. This is where `message` is assigned a value based on whether the "if" statement evaluates to true. (Notice that you use string interpolation to put the population into the `message` string.)

Figure 3.1 shows what your playground should look like.

Figure 3.1 Conditionally describing a town's population

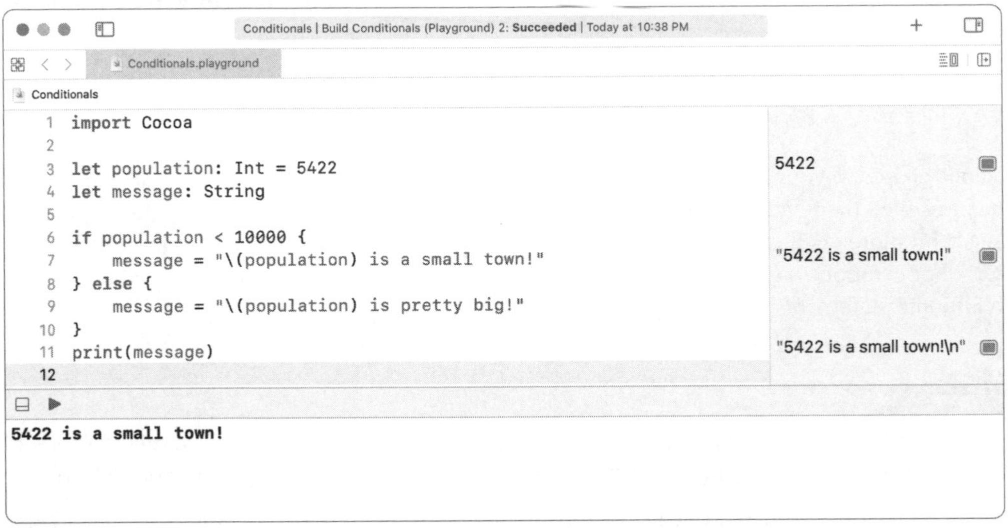

The condition in the `if`/`else` statement tests whether your town's population is less than 10,000 via the `<` *comparison operator*. If the condition evaluates to true, then the value of `message` is set to the first string literal (`"X is a small town!"`). If the condition evaluates to false – if the population is 10,000 or greater – then the value of `message` is set to the second string literal (`"X is pretty big!"`). In this case, the town's population is less than 10,000, so `message` is set to `"5422 is a small town!"`.

Table 3.1 lists Swift's comparison operators.

Table 3.1 Comparison operators

Operator	Description
`<`	Evaluates whether the value on the left is less than the value on the right.
`<=`	Evaluates whether the value on the left is less than or equal to the value on the right.
`>`	Evaluates whether the value on the left is greater than the value on the right.
`>=`	Evaluates whether the value on the left is greater than or equal to the value on the right.
`==`	Evaluates whether the value on the left is equal to the value on the right.
`!=`	Evaluates whether the value on the left is not equal to the value on the right.
`===`	Evaluates whether the two references point to the same instance.
`!==`	Evaluates whether the two references do not point to the same instance.

You do not need to understand all the operators' descriptions right now. You will see many of them in action as you move through this book, and they will become clearer as you use them. Refer back to this table as a reference if you have questions.

Sometimes you want to execute code if a certain condition is met and do nothing if it is not. Enter the code below to see an example. (Notice that new code, shown in bold, appears in two places. Also, we will no longer show the line import Cocoa unless it is needed to help you position new code.)

Listing 3.2 Is there a post office?

```
let population: Int = 5422                              5422
let message: String
let hasPostOffice: Bool = true                         true

if population < 10000 {
    message = "\(population) is a small town!"          "5422 is a small town!"
} else {
    message = "\(population) is pretty big!"
}
print(message)                                         "5422 is a small town!\n"

if !hasPostOffice {
    print("Where do we buy stamps?")
}
```

Here, you add a new variable called hasPostOffice. This variable has the type **Bool**, short for "Boolean." Boolean types can take one of two values: true or false. In this case, the Boolean hasPostOffice variable keeps track of whether the town has a post office. You set it to true, meaning that it does.

The ! is a *logical operator* known as *logical NOT*. It tests whether hasPostOffice is false. The ! returns the opposite of a Boolean value. So if a Boolean's value is true, the ! operator returns a value of false, and vice versa.

So in the code above, after setting the value of hasPostOffice, you ask whether it is false. If hasPostOffice is false, you do not know where to buy stamps, so you ask. If hasPostOffice is true, you know where to buy stamps and do not have to ask, so nothing happens.

Because hasPostOffice was initialized to true, the condition !hasPostOffice is false. That is, it is *not* the case that hasPostOffice is false. Therefore, the **print()** function never gets called.

Table 3.2 lists Swift's logical operators.

Table 3.2 Logical operators

Operator	Description
&&	Logical AND: true if and only if both are true (false otherwise).
||	Logical OR: true if either is true (false only if both are false).
!	Logical NOT: evaluates whether a condition is false (returns true for a false operand and vice versa).

Ternary Operator

The *ternary operator* is very similar to an `if`/`else` statement, but it has the more concise syntax
`a ? b : c`. In English, the ternary operator reads something like, "If a is true, then do b. Otherwise, do c."

Rewrite the town population check to use the ternary operator instead.

Listing 3.3 Using the ternary operator

```
...
if population < 10000 {
    message = "\(population) is a small town!"
} else {
    message = "\(population) is pretty big!"
}

message = population < 10000 ?                              "5422 is a small town!"
                    "\(population) is a small town!" :
                    "\(population) is pretty big!"
...
```

Your result is unchanged: `message` is still set to `"5422 is a small town!"`

The ternary operator can be a source of controversy: Some programmers love it; some programmers
loathe it. We come down somewhere in the middle. This particular usage is not very elegant. The
ternary operator is great for concise statements, but if your statement starts wrapping to the next line,
we think you should use `if`/`else` instead.

Hit Command-Z to undo, removing the ternary operator and restoring your `if`/`else` statement.

Listing 3.4 Restoring `if`/`else`

```
...
message = population < 10000 ?
                    "\(population) is a small town!" :
                    "\(population) is pretty big!"
if population < 10000 {
    message = "\(population) is a small town!"              "5422 is a small town!"
} else {
    message = "\(population) is pretty big!"
}
...
```

Nested ifs

You can nest `if` statements for scenarios with more than two possibilities. You do this by writing an if/else statement inside the curly braces of another if/else statement. To see this, nest an if/else statement within the `else` block of your existing if/else statement.

Listing 3.5 Nesting conditionals

```
let population: Int = 5422                              5422
let message: String
let hasPostOffice: Bool = true                         true

if population < 10000 {
    message = "\(population) is a small town!"          "5422 is a small town!"
} else {
    if population >= 10000 && population < 50000 {
        message = "\(population) is a medium town!"
    } else {
        message = "\(population) is pretty big!"
    }
}
print(message)                                         "5422 is a small town!\n"

if !hasPostOffice {
    print("Where do we buy stamps?")
}
```

Your nested `if` clause uses the >= *comparator* (that is, the comparison operator) and the && logical operator to check whether `population` is within the range of 10,000 to 50,000. Because your town's `population` does not fall within that range, your `message` is set to `"5422 is a small town!"`, as before.

Try bumping up the population to exercise the other branches.

Nested `if`/`else` statements are common in programming. You will find them out in the wild, and you will be writing them as well. There is no limit to how deeply you can nest these statements. However, the danger of nesting them too deeply is that it makes the code harder to read. One or two levels are fine, but beyond that your code becomes less readable and maintainable.

There are ways to avoid nested statements. Next, you are going to *refactor* the code that you have just written to make it a little easier to follow. Refactoring means changing code so that it does the same work but in a different way. It may be more efficient, be easier to understand, or just look prettier.

25

else if

The else if conditional lets you chain multiple conditional statements together. else if allows you to check against multiple cases and conditionally executes code depending on which clause evaluates to true. You can have as many else if clauses as you want. Only one condition will match.

To make your code a little easier to read, extract the nested if/else statement to be a standalone clause that evaluates whether your town is of medium size.

Listing 3.6 Using else if

```
let population: Int = 5422                               5422
let message: String
let hasPostOffice: Bool = true                          true

if population < 10000 {
    message = "\(population) is a small town!"           "5422 is a small town!"
} else if population >= 10000 && population < 50000 {
    message = "\(population) is a medium town!"
}   else {
    if population >= 10000 && population < 50000 {
        message = "\(population) is a medium town!"
    } else {
    message = "\(population) is pretty big!"
    }
}
print(message)                                          "5422 is a small town!\n"

if !hasPostOffice {
    print("Where do we buy stamps?")
}
```

You are using one else if clause, but you can chain many more. This block of code is an improvement over the nested if/else above. As we mentioned, you will see another Swift feature that allows you to cover multiple conditional possibilities later in this book – switch, described in Chapter 5.

Bronze Challenge

Add an additional else if statement to the town-sizing code to see if your town's population is very large. Choose your own population thresholds. Set the message variable accordingly.

4

Numbers

Numbers are the fundamental language of computers. They are also a staple of software development. Numbers are used to keep track of temperature, count the letters in a sentence, and track the number of zombies infesting a town. Numbers come in two basic flavors: integers and floating-point numbers.

Integers

You have worked with integers already, but we have not yet defined them. An integer is a number that does not have a decimal point or fractional component – a whole number. Integers are frequently used to represent a count of "things," such as the number of pages in a book.

A difference between integers used by computers and numbers you use elsewhere is that an integer type on a computer takes up a fixed amount of memory. Therefore, integers cannot represent all possible whole numbers – they have a minimum and maximum value.

We could tell you those minimum and maximum values, but we are going to let Swift tell you instead. Create a new macOS playground, name it Numbers, set it to Automatically Run, and enter the following code.

Listing 4.1 Maximum and minimum values for **Int**

```
import Cocoa

var str = "Hello, playground"

print("The maximum Int value is \(Int.max).")
print("The minimum Int value is \(Int.min).")
```

The sidebar results are too long to show on this page. In the console, you should see the following output:

```
    The maximum Int value is 9223372036854775807.
    The minimum Int value is -9223372036854775808.
```

Why are those numbers the minimum and maximum **Int** values? Computers store integers in binary form with a fixed number of bits. A bit is a single 0 or 1. Each bit position represents a power of 2; to compute the value of a binary number, add up each of the powers of 2 whose bit is a 1.

For example, the binary representations of 38 and -94 using an 8-bit signed integer are shown in Figure 4.1. (Note that the bit positions are read from right to left. *Signed* means that the integer can represent positive and negative values. More about signed integers in a moment.)

Figure 4.1 Binary numbers

$$\boxed{0}\ \boxed{0}\ \boxed{1}\ \boxed{0}\ \boxed{0}\ \boxed{1}\ \boxed{1}\ \boxed{0} = 2^1 + 2^2 + 2^5 = 2 + 4 + 32 = 38$$
$$-2^7\ 2^6\ 2^5\ 2^4\ 2^3\ 2^2\ 2^1\ 2^0$$

$$\boxed{1}\ \boxed{0}\ \boxed{1}\ \boxed{0}\ \boxed{0}\ \boxed{0}\ \boxed{1}\ \boxed{0} = 2^1 + 2^5 - 2^7 = 2 + 32 - 128 = -94$$
$$-2^7\ 2^6\ 2^5\ 2^4\ 2^3\ 2^2\ 2^1\ 2^0$$

Modern versions of iOS and macOS only support 64-bit software, so on these operating systems **Int** is a 64-bit integer. That means it has 2^{64} possible values. Imagine Figure 4.1, only 64 bits wide instead of 8. The power of 2 represented by the top (left-most) bit would be -2^{63} = -9,223,372,036,854,775,808, which is the value you see for Int.min in your playground. And, if you were to add up 2^0, 2^1, ..., 2^{62}, you would arrive at 9,223,372,036,854,775,807 – the value you see for Int.max.

If you need to know the exact size of an integer, you can use one of Swift's explicitly sized integer types. For example, **Int32** is Swift's 32-bit signed integer type. Use **Int32** to see the minimum and maximum value for a 32-bit integer.

Listing 4.2 Maximum and minimum values for **Int32**

```
...
print("The maximum Int value is \(Int.max).")
print("The minimum Int value is \(Int.min).")
print("The maximum value for a 32-bit integer is \(Int32.max).")
print("The minimum value for a 32-bit integer is \(Int32.min).")
```

Also available are **Int8**, **Int16**, and **Int64**, for 8-bit, 16-bit, and 64-bit signed integer types. You use the sized integer types when you need to know the size of the underlying integer, such as for some algorithms (common in cryptography) or to exchange integers with another computer (such as sending data across the internet). You will not use these types much; good Swift style is to use an **Int** for most use cases.

All the integer types you have seen so far are signed, which means they can represent both positive and negative numbers. Swift also has unsigned integer types to represent whole numbers greater than or equal to 0. Every signed integer type (**Int**, **Int16**, etc.) has a corresponding unsigned integer type (**UInt**, **UInt16**, etc.). The difference between signed and unsigned integers at the binary level is that the power of 2 represented by the top-most bit (2^7 for 8-bit integers) is positive and negative, respectively. For example, Figure 4.2 shows the same bit pattern (1010 0110) represented as an 8-bit signed integer and an 8-bit unsigned integer.

Figure 4.2 Signed vs unsigned integers

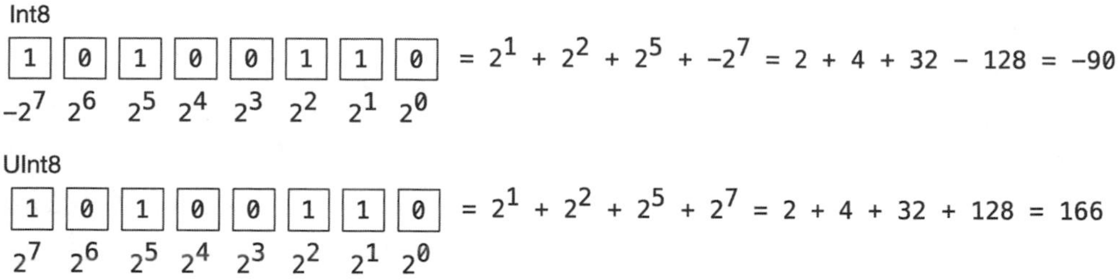

Int8

$$\boxed{1}\,\boxed{0}\,\boxed{1}\,\boxed{0}\,\boxed{0}\,\boxed{1}\,\boxed{1}\,\boxed{0} = 2^1 + 2^2 + 2^5 + -2^7 = 2 + 4 + 32 - 128 = -90$$
$$-2^7 \quad 2^6 \quad 2^5 \quad 2^4 \quad 2^3 \quad 2^2 \quad 2^1 \quad 2^0$$

UInt8

$$\boxed{1}\,\boxed{0}\,\boxed{1}\,\boxed{0}\,\boxed{0}\,\boxed{1}\,\boxed{1}\,\boxed{0} = 2^1 + 2^2 + 2^5 + 2^7 = 2 + 4 + 32 + 128 = 166$$
$$2^7 \quad 2^6 \quad 2^5 \quad 2^4 \quad 2^3 \quad 2^2 \quad 2^1 \quad 2^0$$

Test a couple of unsigned integer types.

Listing 4.3 Maximum and minimum values for unsigned integers

```
...
print("The maximum Int value is \(Int.max).")
print("The minimum Int value is \(Int.min).")
print("The maximum value for a 32-bit integer is \(Int32.max).")
print("The minimum value for a 32-bit integer is \(Int32.min).")

print("The maximum UInt value is \(UInt.max).")
print("The minimum UInt value is \(UInt.min).")
print("The maximum value for a 32-bit unsigned integer is \(UInt32.max).")
print("The minimum value for a 32-bit unsigned integer is \(UInt32.min).")
```

Like **Int**, **UInt** is a 64-bit integer on modern iOS and macOS. The minimum value for all unsigned types is 0. The maximum value for an N-bit unsigned type is 2^N - 1. For example, the maximum value for a 64-bit unsigned type is 2^{64} - 1, which equals 18,446,744,073,709,551,615.

Some quantities seem like they would naturally be represented by an unsigned integer. For example, it does not make sense for the count of a number of objects to ever be negative. However, Swift style is to prefer **Int** for all integer uses (including counts) unless an unsigned integer is required by the algorithm or code you are writing. The explanation for this involves topics we are going to cover later in this chapter, so we will return to the reasons behind consistently preferring **Int** soon.

Creating Integer Instances

You created instances of **Int** in Chapter 2, where you learned that you can declare a type explicitly or implicitly. Refresh your memory by declaring a couple more **Int**s in your playground:

Listing 4.4 Declaring **Int** explicitly and implicitly

```
...
let numberOfPages: Int = 10                        10
let numberOfChapters = 3                           3
```

The compiler always assumes that implicit declarations with integer values are of type **Int**, so both numberOfPages and numberOfChapters are **Int**s. However, you can create instances of the other integer types using explicit type declarations.

Listing 4.5 Declaring other integer types explicitly

```
...
let numberOfPages: Int = 10                                 10
let numberOfChapters = 3                                    3

let numberOfPeople: UInt = 40                               40
let volumeAdjustment: Int32 = -1000                         -1000
```

What happens if you try to create an instance with an invalid value? What if, for example, you try to create a **UInt** with a negative value, or an **Int8** with a value greater than 127? Try it and find out.

Listing 4.6 Declaring integer types with invalid values

```
...
let numberOfPeople: UInt = 40                               40
let volumeAdjustment: Int32 = -1000                        -1000

let badValue: UInt = -1
```

The console output will indicate an error (Figure 4.3).

Figure 4.3 Integer overflow error

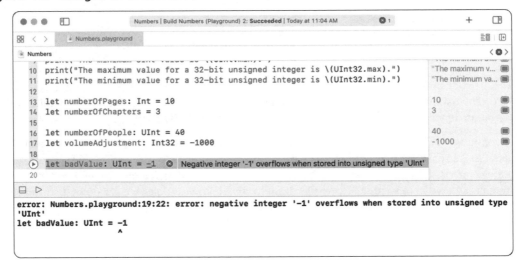

The compiler reports that the value you have typed in "overflows when stored into" a constant of type **UInt**. "Overflows when stored into…" means that when the compiler tried to store your number in the type you specified, the number did not fit in the type's allowed range of values.

All numerical types have limits on the numbers that they can store, dictated by their size in bits. An **Int8**, for example, can hold values from -128 to 127; 200 is outside that range, so trying to store 200 into an **Int8** overflows. The highest signed **Int64** is over 9 quintillion, though, so it is unlikely that this limitation will ever be a problem for you.

Remove the problematic code.

Listing 4.7 No more bad value

```
...
let badValue: UInt = -1
```

Operations on Integers

Swift allows you to perform basic mathematical operations on integers using the familiar operators + (add), − (subtract), and * (multiply). You can include these operations in your code; in a playground, you can also just enter them to see the result. Try it.

Listing 4.8 Performing basic operations

```
...
let numberOfPeople: UInt = 40                           40
let volumeAdjustment: Int32 = -1000                     -1000

10 + 20                                                 30
30 - 5                                                  25
5 * 6                                                   30
```

A quick aside: Usually, the whitespace in your code (like the number of spaces you indent or any blank lines you leave) does not matter. If you prefer more or less indentation or blank lines than this book shows, that is fine. But occasionally whitespace *does* matter, and now is one of those times. When you are using an operator like + or * that takes two operands (also called a *binary operator*), you can include space between the operator and its operands or not, but you have to make the same choice on both sides.

For example, your last print statement could be print(5 * 6) or print(5*6), but not print(5 *6). If you tried that, the compiler would think you were giving the multiplication operator only one operand – and, since * requires two, the compiler would give up. It is stylish to put spaces on both sides of a binary operator, so we will do that in this book.

Back to operations on integers. The compiler respects the mathematical principles of precedence and associativity, which define the order of operations when there are multiple operators in a single expression. For example:

Listing 4.9 Order of operations

```
...
10 + 20                                                 30
30 - 5                                                  25
5 * 6                                                   30

10 + 2 * 5                                              20
30 - 5 - 5                                              20
```

Both of these expressions above result in 20. In 10 + 2 * 5, 2 * 5 is evaluated first; in 30 - 5 - 5, 30 - 5 is evaluated first. You could memorize the rules governing precedence and associativity. However, we recommend taking the easy route and using parentheses to make your intentions explicit, because parentheses are always evaluated first.

Listing 4.10 Parentheses are your friends

```
...
10 + 2 * 5                                              20
30 - 5 - 5                                              20
(10 + 2) * 5                                            60
30 - (5 - 5)                                            30
```

Integer division

What is the value of the expression 11 / 3? You might (reasonably) expect 3.66666666667, but try it out.

Listing 4.11 Integer division can give unexpected results

```
...
(10 + 2) * 5                                            60
30 – (5 – 5)                                            30

11 / 3                                                  3
```

The result of any operation between two integers is always another integer of the same type; 3.66666666667 is not a whole number and cannot be represented as an integer. Swift truncates the fractional part, leaving just 3. If the result is negative, such as –11 / 3, the fractional part is still truncated, giving a result of -3. Integer division always rounds toward 0.

It is occasionally useful to get the remainder of a division operation. The *remainder operator*, %, returns exactly that. (If you are familiar with the modulo operator in math and some other programming languages, be warned: The remainder operator is not the same, and using it on a negative integer may not return what you expect.)

Listing 4.12 Remainders

```
...
11 / 3                                                  3
11 % 3                                                  2
–11 % 3                                                 –2
```

Of course, Swift also provides a way to work with numbers that include fractional values, which you will see shortly.

Operator shorthand

All the operators that you have seen so far return a new value. There are also versions of all these operators that modify a variable in place. For example, a common operation in programming is to increase or decrease the value of an integer by another integer. You can use the += operator, which combines addition and assignment, or the −= operator, which combines subtraction and assignment. Try them out.

Listing 4.13 Combining addition or subtraction and assignment

```
...
11 % 3                                      2
-11 % 3                                     -2

var x = 10                                  10
x += 10                                     20
x -= 5                                      15
```

As the results in the sidebar show, the expression x += 10 is equivalent to x = x + 10, and x −= 5 is equivalent to x = x − 5.

There are also shorthand operation-and-assignment combination operators for the other basic math operations: *=, /=, and %=, each of which assigns the result of the operation to the value on the lefthand side of the operator.

Overflow operators

What do you think the value of z will be in the following code? (Think about it for a minute before you type it in to find out for sure.)

Listing 4.14 Solving for z

```
...
let y: Int8 = 120                           120
let z = y + 10
```

If you thought the value of z would be 130, you are not alone. But type it in, and you will find that instead Xcode is showing you an error. Click on it to see a more detailed message (Figure 4.4).

Figure 4.4 Execution interrupted when adding to an **Int8**

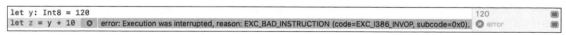

```
let y: Int8 = 120                                                          120
let z = y + 10   ⊗  error: Execution was interrupted, reason: EXC_BAD_INSTRUCTION (code=EXC_I386_INVOP, subcode=0x0).   ⊗ error
```

What does "Execution was interrupted" mean? Let's break down what is happening:

1. y is an **Int8**, so the compiler assumes y + 10 must be an **Int8**, too.

2. Therefore, the compiler infers the type of z to be **Int8**.

3. When your playground runs, Swift adds 10 to y, resulting in 130.

4. Before storing the result back into z, Swift checks that 130 is a valid value for an **Int8**.

But **Int8** can only hold values from -128 to 127; 130 is too big! Your playground therefore hits a *trap*, which stops the program from running. We will discuss traps in more detail in Chapter 23. For now, know that a trap results in your program stopping immediately and noisily, which indicates a serious problem you need to examine.

Swift provides *overflow operators* that have different behaviors when the value is too big (or too small). Instead of trapping the program, they "wrap around." To see what that means, try it now. The overflow addition operator is &+. Substitute it into your code:

Listing 4.15 Using an overflow operator

```
...
let y: Int8 = 120                                          120
let z = y + 10
let z = y &+ 10                                            -126
```

The result of overflow-adding 120 + 10 and storing the result into an **Int8** is -126. Was that what you expected?

Probably not. (And that is OK!) To understand the logic of this result, think about incrementing y one at a time. Because y is an **Int8**, once you get to 127 you cannot go any higher. Instead, incrementing one more time wraps around to -128. So 120 + 8 = -128, 120 + 9 = -127, and 120 + 10 = -126.

There are also overflow versions of the subtraction and multiplication operators: &- and &*. It should be apparent why there is an overflow version of the multiplication operator, but what about subtraction? Subtraction clearly cannot overflow, but it can *underflow*. For example, trying to subtract 10 from an **Int8** currently holding -120 would result in a value too negative to be stored in an **Int8**. Using &- would cause this underflow to wrap back around and give you positive 126.

Integer operations overflowing or underflowing unexpectedly can be a source of serious and hard-to-find bugs. Swift is designed to prioritize safety and minimize these errors.

Swift's default behavior of trapping on overflow calculations may come as a surprise to you if you have programmed in another language. Most other languages default to the wraparound behavior that Swift's overflow operators provide.

The philosophy of the Swift language is that it is better to trap (even though this may result in a program crashing) than potentially have a security hole. There are some use cases for wrapping arithmetic, so these special operators are available if you need them.

Converting Between Integer Types

So far, all the operations you have seen have been between two values with exactly the same type. What happens if you try to operate on numbers with different types? See for yourself:

Listing 4.16 Adding values of different types

```
...
let a: Int16 = 200                                    200
let b: Int8 = 50                                      50
let c = a + b
```

This is a compile-time error. You cannot add a and b, because they are not of the same type. Some languages will automatically convert types for you to perform operations like this. Swift does not. Instead, you have to manually convert types to get them to match.

You could either convert a to an **Int8** or convert b to an **Int16** – but only one of these will succeed. (Reread the previous section if you are not sure why.)

Listing 4.17 Converting type to allow addition

```
...
let a: Int16 = 200                                    200
let b: Int8 = 50                                      50
let c = a + b
let c = a + Int16(b)                                  250
```

Requiring you, the programmer, to decide how to convert variables in order to do math between different types is another feature that distinguishes Swift from other languages. Again, this requirement is in favor of safety and correctness.

The C programming language, for example, will convert numbers of different types in order to perform math between them, but the conversions it performs are sometimes "lossy" – you may lose information in the conversion. Swift code that requires math between numbers of different types will be more verbose, but it will be more clear about what conversions are taking place. The increase in verbosity will make it easier for you to reason about and maintain the code.

We can now return to the recommendation to stick with **Int** for almost all integer needs in Swift, even for values that might naturally only make sense as positive values (like a count of "things"). Swift's default type inference for literals is **Int**, and you cannot typically perform operations between different integer types without converting one of them. Using **Int** consistently throughout your code will greatly reduce the need for you to convert types, and it will allow you to use type inference for integers freely.

Floating-Point Numbers

To represent a number that has a decimal point, like 3.2, you use a *floating-point number*.

Bear in mind that floating-point numbers are often imprecise because of how they are stored in memory. There are many numbers that cannot be stored with perfect accuracy in a floating-point number. The computer will store a very close approximation to the number you expect. (More on that in a moment.)

Swift has two basic floating-point number types: **Float**, which is a 32-bit floating-point number, and **Double**, which is a 64-bit floating-point number. The different bit sizes of **Float** and **Double** do not determine a simple minimum and maximum value range as they do for integers. Instead, the bit sizes determine how much precision the numbers have. **Double** has more precision than **Float**, which means it is able to store more accurate approximations.

The default inferred type for floating-point numbers in Swift is **Double**. As with different types of integers, you can also declare **Float**s and **Double**s explicitly:

Listing 4.18 Declaring floating-point number types

```
...
let d1 = 1.1                                  1.1
let d2: Double = 1.1                          1.1
let f1: Float = 100.3                         100.3
```

All the same numeric operators work on floating-point numbers (except the remainder operator, which is only used on integers).

Listing 4.19 Operations on floating-point numbers

```
...
let d1 = 1.1                                  1.1
let d2: Double = 1.1                          1.1
let f1: Float = 100.3                         100.3

10.0 + 11.4                                   21.4
11.0 / 3.0                                    3.6666666666666667
```

The fact that floating-point numbers are inherently imprecise is an important difference from integer numbers that you should keep in mind. Let's see an example. Recall the == operator from Chapter 3, which determines whether two values are equal to each other. Try it out to compare two floating-point numbers.

Listing 4.20 Comparing two floating-point numbers

```
...
let d1 = 1.1                                             1.1
let d2: Double = 1.1                                     1.1
let f1: Float = 100.3                                    100.3

10.0 + 11.4                                              21.4
11.0 / 3.0                                               3.6666666666666667

if d1 == d2 {
    print("d1 and d2 are the same!")                    "d1 and d2 are the same!"
}
```

d1 and d2 were both initialized with a value of 1.1. So far, so good. Now, let's add 0.1 to d1. You would expect that to result in 1.2, so compare the result to that value. The result you get may be surprising.

Listing 4.21 Unexpected results

```
...
if d1 == d2 {
    print("d1 and d2 are the same!")                    "d1 and d2 are the same!"
}

print("d1 + 0.1 is \(d1 + 0.1)")                        "d1 + 0.1 is 1.20...02\n"
if d1 + 0.1 == 1.2 {
    print("d1 + 0.1 is equal to 1.2")
}
```

The **print()** inside the if statement does not run. Why not? Isn't 1.2 equal to 1.2?

Well, sometimes it is, and sometimes it is not.

As we said before, many numbers – including 1.2 – cannot be represented exactly in a floating-point number. Instead, the computer stores a very close approximation to 1.2. As the sidebar indicates, when you add 1.1 and 0.1 the result is really something like 1.2000000000000002. The value stored when you typed the literal 1.2 is really something like 1.1999999999999999. Swift will round both of those to 1.2 when you print them. But they are not technically equal, so the **print()** inside the if statement does not execute.

All the gory details behind floating-point arithmetic are outside the scope of this book. The moral of this story is just to be aware that there are some potential pitfalls with floating-point numbers. One consequence is that you should never use floating-point numbers for values that must be exact (such as calculations dealing with money). There are other tools available for those purposes.

Ranges of Numbers

Sometimes you want to represent a range of numbers. Imagine that you are handing out 1,000 numbered raffle tickets, and you want to represent the collection of ticket numbers. The *closed-range* operator (...) lets you do just that:

Listing 4.22 Defining a range of integers

```
...
let ticketCount = 1_000                                 1000
let ticketNumbers = 1 ... ticketCount                   {lowerBound 1, upperBoun...
```

The sidebar results represent the value of ticketNumbers as {lowerBound 1, upperBound 1000}. A closed range includes a lower bound, an upper bound, and everything in between, so ticketNumbers includes 1, 2, 3, … 998, 999, and 1,000.

What if you want to create a range that represents the numbers up to – but not including – the upper bound? You *could* do that by subtracting 1 from the upper bound:

```
        let ticketNumbers = 1 ... ticketCount - 1
```

You *could*. But it would not be stylish. Instead, use the *half-open range* operator (..<) to exclude the upper bound from your range:

Listing 4.23 Make that 999 tickets

```
...
let ticketCount = 1_000                                 1000
let ticketNumbers = 1 ... ticketCount
let ticketNumbers = 1 ..< ticketCount                   {lowerBound 1, upperBoun...
```

The sidebar results show that the ticketNumbers has the same lower and upper bounds ({lowerBound 1, upperBound 1000}). But the upper bound is now excluded from the range, so ticketNumbers includes 1, 2, 3, … 997, 998, and 999 – but not 1,000.

You will see how useful ranges can be starting in Chapter 5.

Bronze Challenge

Set down your computer and grab a pencil and paper for this challenge. What is the binary representation of -1 using an 8-bit signed integer?

If you took that same bit pattern and interpreted it as an 8-bit unsigned integer, what would the value be?

For the More Curious: Numeric Literals

Earlier in the chapter we looked at a few examples of creating both integer and floating-point instances with a literal value. Each of those examples involved creating numeric instances with base-10 (also known as decimal) numbers. You will typically create numeric types using the base-10 numeral system, because it is the numeral system most people are accustomed to using.

Computers actually store information in base-2. But if you try to use a binary number like 10100110 in your code, Swift will infer it as an **Int**. However, by prefixing a value with 0b, you can create a binary literal that can then be represented as another numeric type.

Listing 4.24 Binary literals

```
let binaryFail = 10100110                                10100110
let binaryInt = 0b10100110                               166
```

There is also literal syntax in Swift for scientific notation, which begins with the mantissa followed by the character e and finally the exponent. As with other numeric values, you can let Swift infer the appropriate type or declare the type explicitly.

Listing 4.25 Scientific notation in numeric literals

```
let scientificInt = 1.66e5                               166000
let fractionalFloat: Float = 1.66e-2                     0.0166
```

Swift has support for one additional literal format that comes in handy. Base-16, or hexadecimal, is a numeral system that has 16 symbols for each position value. The first 10 symbols are the digits 0 through 9, and the letters a through f are the final six.

Hex, as it is sometimes called, can be thought of as a compromise between humans and computers. Binary, which computers use to store data, can be overly verbose and cumbersome to read as a human. But decimal, which we are used to reading, is a poor fit for displaying computers' bit-based data. Hex is the best of both: succinct (for humans) and accurate when represented in bits (for computers).

For example, these three numbers represent the same value:

- 255 (decimal)
- 1111 1111 (binary)
- FF (hexadecimal)

And these three numbers also represent the same value:

- 2,343,432,205 (decimal)
- 1000 1011 1010 1101 1111 0000 0000 1101 (binary)
- 8BAD F00D (hexadecimal)

The syntax for working with hexadecimal values in Swift is similar to the binary literal syntax you just saw: Hex literals are prefixed with `0x`.

Listing 4.26 Hexadecimal literals

```
let hexLiteral = 0xff                                    255
let hexSpeak = 0x8BADF00D                                2343432205
```

Whatever number base you are using, you can separate groups of digits with underscores to make large numbers more legible in code. The program completely ignores underscores used this way; they are just for you.

Listing 4.27 Large numbers

```
let lightSpeed = 299_792_458 // m/s                      299792458
```

5

Switch

In Chapter 3, you saw one sort of conditional statement: `if/else`. Along the way, we mentioned that `if/else` is not great for scenarios that have more than a few conditions. This chapter looks at the `switch` statement, which is ideal for handling multiple conditions. As you will see, Swift's `switch` statement is a flexible and powerful feature of the language.

`if/else` statements execute code based on whether the condition under consideration evaluates to `true`. `switch` statements consider a particular value and attempt to match it against a number of expressions, called *cases*. If there is a match, the `switch` executes the code associated with that case. In this chapter, you will explore the use of `switch` statements for evaluating an expression against multiple possible matching values.

Switch Syntax

Create a new macOS playground called Switch that is set to Automatically Run and write your first switch to see how its syntax works. (From this point forward, we will only show sidebar results when they are helpful and fit on the page.)

Listing 5.1 Your first switch

```
import Cocoa

var str = "Hello, playground"

var statusCode: Int = 404
var errorString: String

switch statusCode {
case 401:
    errorString = "Unauthorized"

case 403:
    errorString = "Forbidden"

case 404:
    errorString = "Not found"

default:
    errorString = "None"
}
```

Whether or not you have ever worked with HTTP status codes directly, you have undoubtedly encountered pages that say something like "404 Not Found" while browsing the web. There are many status codes that web servers send to their clients (such as apps or web browsers) to indicate the success or failure of a request. Your switch statement compares statusCode, an **Int** variable representing an HTTP status code, against four cases to assign a **String** instance describing the error. To keep this example from getting too complex, this exercise will focus only on codes that represent errors.

The type in each of the cases must match the type being compared against. Here, the **Int** value of statusCode is compared to 401, 403, and 404, in that order. If statusCode matches any of the comparison cases, then the body of that case will be executed. Usually, the switch will then be done, and no more cases will be checked (though you will see an exception to this later in this chapter).

Because case 404 matches statusCode, errorString is assigned the value "Not found", as you can see in the sidebar.

Notice the default case, which is executed when the comparison value does not match any of the other cases. Switch cases must be exhaustive – every possible value of the input type must match at least one case. So it is sometimes necessary to use a default case to ensure the exhaustiveness of the switch.

Try changing the value of statusCode to see the other results. When you are done, set it back to 404.

Suppose you want to use a switch statement to build up the text description of an error. Update your code to do that.

Listing 5.2 `switch` cases can have multiple values

```
var statusCode: Int = 404
var errorString: String = "The request failed: "

switch statusCode {
case 401:
    errorString = "Unauthorized"

case 403:
    errorString = "Forbidden"

case 404:
    errorString = "Not found"

default:
    errorString = "None"
case 401, 403, 404:
    errorString += "There was something wrong with the request."
    fallthrough
default:
    errorString += " Please review the request and try again."
}
```

There is now only one case for all the error status codes (which are listed and separated by commas). If the `statusCode` matches any of the values in the case, the text `"There was something wrong with the request."` is added to the `errorString`.

You have also added a *control transfer statement* called `fallthrough`. Control transfer statements let you modify the order of execution in a control flow by transferring control from one chunk of code to another.

`fallthrough` tells the `switch` statement to "fall through" the bottom of a case to the next one. If a matching case has a `fallthrough` statement at its end, it will execute its code and then transfer control to the case immediately below. That case will execute its code – whether or not it matches the value being checked against. If it also has a `fallthrough` statement at the end, it will hand off control to the next case, and so on.

In other words, `fallthrough` statements allow you to enter a case and execute its code without having to match against it.

Without the `fallthrough` keyword, the `switch` statement would have ended execution after the first match. Because of the `fallthrough`, the `switch` statement does not stop, even though the first case matches. Instead, it proceeds to the `default` case, which adds a recommendation to the `errorString`. The use of `fallthrough` in this example allows you to build up `errorString` without having to use strange logic that would guarantee that the comparison value matched all the cases of interest.

The end result of this `switch` statement is that `errorString` is set to `"The request failed: There was something wrong with the request. Please review the request and try again."`. If the status code provided had not matched any of the values in the case, `errorString` would have been set to `"The request failed: Please review the request and try again."`. (Try it and see.)

If you are familiar with other languages like C or Objective-C, you will see that Swift's `switch` statement works differently. `switch` statements in those languages automatically fall through from one case to the next. Those languages require a `break` control transfer statement at the end of the case's code to break out of the switch. Swift's switch works in the opposite manner. If you match on a case, the case executes its code and the switch stops running.

Ranges

You have seen a switch statement in which the cases had single values to check against the comparison value and another with a case that had multiple values. switch statements can also compare to a range of values using the syntax valueX...valueY. Update your code to see this in action.

Listing 5.3 Cases can match ranges of values

```
var statusCode: Int = 404
var errorString: String = "The request failed with the error: "

switch statusCode {
case 401, 403, 404:
    errorString += "There was something wrong with the request."
    fallthrough
default:
    errorString += " Please review the request and try again."
case 401:
    errorString += "Unauthorized"

case 400...417:
    errorString += "Client error, 4xx."

case 500...505:
    errorString += "Server error, 5xx."

default:
    errorString = "Unknown status. Please review the request and try again."
}
```

The switch statement above takes advantage of the ... syntax of *range matching* to create inclusive ranges for categories of HTTP status codes. 400...417 is a range that includes 400, 417, and everything in between. And 500...505 is a range that includes 500, 505, and everything in between.

You also have a case with a single HTTP status code (case 401) and a default case. These are formed in the same way as the cases you saw before. All the case syntax options can be combined in a switch statement.

You may have noticed that a status code of 401 would match more than one case: both case 401 and case 400...417. Since a switch evaluates cases in the order that they are written, the switch will execute the first case that matches and then exit, unless the matched case has a fallthrough. So, if the statusCode were 401, then case 401 would be executed and case 400...417 would not – not because case 401 is more specific, but because case 401 comes first.

The result of this switch statement is that errorString is set to "The request failed with the error: Client error, 4xx." Again, try changing the value of statusCode to see the other results. Be sure to set it back to 404 before continuing.

Value binding

Suppose you want to include the actual numerical status codes in your errorString, whether the status code is recognized or not. You can build on your previous switch statement to include this information using string interpolation, which you learned about in Chapter 2, and Swift's *value binding* feature.

Value binding allows you to *bind* the matching value in a case to a local constant or variable. The constant or variable is available to use only within the matching case's body. Update your switch to use value binding:

Listing 5.4 Using value binding

```
...
switch statusCode {
case 401:
    errorString += "Unauthorized"

case 400...417:
    errorString += "Client error, 4xx."
    errorString += "Client error, \(statusCode)."

case 500...505:
    errorString += "Server error, 5xx."
    errorString += "Server error, \(statusCode)."

default:
    errorString = "Unknown status. Please review the request and try again."

case let code:
    errorString = "\(code) is not a known error code."
}
```

Here you use string interpolation to pass statusCode into the errorString in each case. Your result now reads "The request failed with the error: Client error, 404."

Take a closer look at the last case. When the statusCode does not match any of the values provided in the cases above, you create a temporary constant, called code, and bind it to the value of statusCode. For example, if statusCode had a value of 444, then your switch would set errorString to "444 is not a known error code.".

Notice also that a default case is not needed for this switch. Because code's value was bound from statusCode, it is guaranteed to match, so the switch cases are exhaustive.

This example shows you the syntax of value binding, but it does not really add much. You will see where value binding shines shortly. In this case, the standard default case can produce the same result.

Replace the final case with a `default` case.

Listing 5.5 Reverting to the `default` case

```
...
switch statusCode {
case 401:
    errorString += "Unauthorized."

case 400...417:
    errorString += "Client error, \(statusCode)."

case 500...505:
    errorString += "Server error, \(statusCode)."

case let code:
    errorString = "\(code) is not a known error code."

default:
    errorString = "\(statusCode) is not a known error code."
}
```

where clauses

The code above is fine, but it is not great. Every possible value of **Int** has to be handled by the switch statement, but some **Int** values do not correspond to status codes at all. In fact, status codes only range from 100 to 599.

Right now, a statusCode value like 13 (which is not a possible error code) produces the same result as a value like 418 (which is a status code, but not one you want to handle). You might want to treat status codes that you do not handle differently from status codes that do not exist. For example, if the server sent a status code of 13, you would know there was a problem with the server.

To fix this, use value binding and a where clause to make sure the value being checked is not out of bounds. where allows you to check for additional conditions that must be met for the case to match and the value to be bound. This feature creates a sort of dynamic filter within the switch.

Listing 5.6 Using where to create a filter

```
var statusCode: Int = 404 13
var errorString: String = "The request failed with the error: "

switch statusCode {
case 401:
    errorString += "Unauthorized."

case 400...417:
    errorString += "Client error, \(statusCode)."

case 500...505:
    errorString += "Server error, \(statusCode)."

case let code where code < 100 || code >= 600:
    errorString = "\(code) is an illegal status code."

default:
    errorString = "\(statusCode) is not a known error code."
    errorString = "Unexpected error encountered."
}
```

Recall that || is the logical OR operator, so your new case sets the value of code to equal the value of statusCode if the value is less than 100 or greater than 599. You can represent the where clause's expression more simply, but this example illustrates that you can use complex Boolean expressions in a where clause.

Value bindings are especially useful when combined with where clauses to say "I do not have a value to compare, but as long as this other expression is true, go ahead and match this case." Unlike the previous example involving value binding, this case is not exhaustive, since it only matches if the clause is true. But this is not a problem, because you also have a default case.

When statusCode's value is 13, errorString is set to "13 is an illegal status code.".

Change statusCode to exercise the other cases and confirm that it works as expected.

Tuples and Pattern Matching

Now that you have your `statusCode` and `errorString`, it would be helpful to pair those two pieces. Although they are logically related, they are currently stored in independent variables. A *tuple* can be used to group them.

A tuple groups values as a single, compound value. The result is an ordered list of elements. The elements can be of the same type or of different types.

Create your first Swift tuple that groups `statusCode` and `errorString`.

Listing 5.7 Creating a tuple

```
var statusCode: Int = 13 418
var errorString: String = "The request failed with the error: "

switch statusCode {
    ...
}

let error = (statusCode, errorString)
```

You made a tuple by grouping `statusCode` and `errorString` within parentheses and assigned the result to the constant `error`. The sidebar shows its value: (`.0 418`, `.1 "Unexpected error encountered."`).

The `.0` and `.1` in the value of your tuple are the elements' indices, which you can use to access the elements:

Listing 5.8 Accessing the elements of a tuple

```
...
let error = (statusCode, errorString)
error.0
error.1
```

It is not very easy to keep track of what values are represented by `error.0` and `error.1`. You can also assign names to the elements of a Swift tuple to make your code more readable. Change your tuple to use more informative element names.

Listing 5.9 Naming the tuple's elements

```
...
let error = (statusCode, errorString)
error.0
error.1
let error = (code: statusCode, msg: errorString)
error.code
error.msg
```

Now you can access your tuple's elements by using their related names: `code` for `statusCode` and `msg` for `errorString`.

You have already seen an example of pattern matching when you used ranges in the `switch` statement's cases. That form of pattern matching is called *interval matching*, because each case attempts to match a given interval against the comparison value. Tuples are also helpful in matching patterns.

Imagine, for example, that you have an application that is making multiple web requests. You save the HTTP status code that comes back with the server's response each time. Later, you would like to see which requests, if any, failed with the status code 404 (the "requested resource not found" error). Using a tuple in the `switch` statement's cases enables you to match against very specific patterns.

Add the following code to create and switch on a new tuple. (Do not split the strings in the new cases; enter them each on a single line.)

Listing 5.10 Pattern matching in tuples

```
...
let error = (code: statusCode, msg: errorString)
error.code
error.msg

let firstErrorCode = 404
let secondErrorCode = 418
let errorCodes = (firstErrorCode, secondErrorCode)

switch errorCodes {
case (404, 404):
    print("Both error codes were 404.")
case (404, _):
    print("Only the 1st code is 404, and we don't care about the 2nd code.")
case (_, 404):
    print("Only the 2nd code is 404, and we don't care about the 1st code.")
default:
    print("Neither code is 404.")
}
```

You first add a few new constants. `firstErrorCode` and `secondErrorCode` represent the HTTP status codes associated with two web requests. `errorCodes` is a tuple that groups these codes.

The new `switch` statement matches against several cases to determine what combination of 404s the requests might have yielded. The underscore (_) in the second and third cases is a wildcard that matches anything, which allows these cases to focus on a specific request's error code.

The first case will match only if both of the requests failed with status code 404. The second case will match only if the first request failed with status code 404. The third case will match only if the second request failed with status code 404. Finally, if the switch has not found a match, that means none of the requests failed with the status code 404.

Because `firstErrorCode` did have the status code 404, you should see `"Only the 1st code is 404, and we don't care about the 2nd code."`.

switch vs if/else

`switch` statements are primarily useful for comparing a value against a number of potentially matching cases. `if/else` statements, on the other hand, are best for checking against a single condition. `switch` also offers a number of powerful features that allow you to match against ranges, bind values to local constants or variables, and match patterns in tuples – to name just a few features covered in this chapter.

Sometimes you might be tempted to use a `switch` statement on a value that could potentially match against any number of cases, but you really only care about one of them. For example, imagine checking an `age` constant when you are looking for a specific demographic: ages 18-35.

Go ahead and write a `switch` statement with a single case to accomplish this:

Listing 5.11 Single-case `switch`

```
...
let age = 25
switch age {
case 18...35:
    print("Cool demographic")
default:
    break
}
```

If `age` is in the range from 18 to 35, then `age` is in the desired demographic and some code is executed. Otherwise, `age` is not in the target demographic and the `default` case matches, which simply transfers the flow of execution outside the switch with the `break` control transfer statement.

Notice that you *had* to include a `default` case, because `switch` statements have to be exhaustive. You do not really want to do anything here, but every case must have at least one executable statement, so you fill the requirement with a `break`. This works, but it may not feel elegant.

Swift provides a better way. In Chapter 3, you learned about `if/else` statements. Swift also has an `if-case` statement that provides pattern matching similar to what a `switch` statement offers. Replace your `switch` with an `if-case` statement:

Listing 5.12 `if-case`

```
...
let age = 25
switch age {
case 18...35:
    print("Cool demographic")
default:
    break
}

if case 18...35 = age {
    print("Cool demographic")
}
```

This syntax is much more elegant. It simply checks to see whether `age` is in the given range. You did not have to write a `default` case that you did not care about. Instead, the syntax of the `if-case` allows you to focus on the single case of interest: when `age` is in the target range.

if-cases can also include more complicated pattern matching, just as with `switch` statements. Say, for example, you wanted to know if `age` was greater than or equal to 25.

Listing 5.13 `if-cases` with multiple conditions

```
...
let age = 25

if case 18...35 = age {
    print("Cool demographic")
}
if case 18...35 = age, age >= 25 {
    print("In cool demographic and can rent a car")
}
```

The new code adds something to the `if-case` statement: After the comma, it also checks to see whether age is 25 or greater. In the United States, this often means that the person in question can rent a car.

if-cases provide an elegant shorthand for `switch` statements with only one case to consider. They also enjoy all the pattern-matching power that make `switch` statements so wonderful. The choice between them is usually a stylistic one. With practice, you will discover which syntax you find most readable for your different comparison needs.

Bronze Challenge

Review the switch statement below. What will be logged to the console? After you have decided, enter the code in a playground to see whether you were right.

```
let point = (x: 1, y: 4)

switch point {
case let q1 where (point.x > 0) && (point.y > 0):
    print("\(q1) is in quadrant 1")

case let q2 where (point.x < 0) && point.y > 0:
    print("\(q2) is in quadrant 2")

case let q3 where (point.x < 0) && point.y < 0:
    print("\(q3) is in quadrant 3")

case let q4 where (point.x > 0) && point.y < 0:
    print("\(q4) is in quadrant 4")

case (_, 0):
    print("\(point) sits on the x-axis")

case (0, _):
    print("\(point) sits on the y-axis")

default:
    print("Case not covered.")
}
```

Silver Challenge

You can add more conditions to the if-case by supplying a comma-separated list. For example, you could check whether the person is: a) in the cool demographic, b) old enough to rent a car in the United States, and c) not in their thirties. Add another condition to Listing 5.13 to check whether age meets all three criteria.

6

Loops

Loops help with repetitive tasks. They execute a set of code repeatedly, either for a given number of iterations or for as long as a defined condition is met. Loops can save you from writing tedious and repetitive code, and you will use them a lot in your development.

In this chapter, you will use two sorts of loops:

- `for` loops
- `while` loops

`for` loops are ideal for iterating over the elements of an instance or collection of instances if the number of iterations to perform is either known or easy to derive. `while` loops, on the other hand, are well suited for tasks that execute repeatedly as long as a certain condition is met. Each type of loop has variations.

Let's start with a `for-in` loop, which performs a set of code for each item in a range, sequence, or collection.

for-in Loops

Create a new macOS playground called Loops and set it to Automatically Run. Create a loop as shown.

Listing 6.1 A `for-in` loop

```
import Cocoa

var str = "Hello, playground"

var myFirstInt: Int = 0                                     0

for i in 1...5 {
    myFirstInt += 1                                 (5 times)
    print(myFirstInt)                               (5 times)
}
```

Ignore the warning about an unused value for now; you will address it shortly.

First, you declare a variable called `myFirstInt` that is an instance of **Int** and is initialized with a value of 0. Next, you create a `for-in` loop. Let's look at the components of the loop.

The `for` keyword signals that you are writing a loop. You next declare an *iterator* called `i` that represents the current iteration of the loop. The iterator is constant within the body of the loop and only exists here; it is also managed for you by the compiler.

In the first iteration of the loop, its value is the first value in the range of the loop. Because you used `...` to create an inclusive range of 1 through 5, the first value of `i` is 1. In the second iteration, the value of `i` is 2, and so on. You can think of `i` as being replaced with a new constant set to the next value in the range at the beginning of each iteration.

Notice that `i` is not declared to be of the **Int** type. It could be, as in `for i: Int in 1...5`, but an explicit type declaration is not necessary. The type of `i` is inferred from its context (as is the `let`). In this example, `i` is inferred to be of type **Int** because the specified range contains integers.

Type inference is handy, and when you type less you make fewer typos. In general, we recommend that you take advantage of type inference whenever possible, and you will see many examples of it in this book. However, there are a few cases in which you need to specifically declare the type. We will highlight those when they come up.

The code inside the braces (`{}`) is executed at each iteration of the loop. For each iteration, you increment `myFirstInt` by 1. After incrementing `myFirstInt`, you print the variable's name to log its value to the console. These two steps – incrementing and logging – continue until `i` reaches the end of the range: 5. This loop is represented in Figure 6.1.

Figure 6.1 Looping over a range

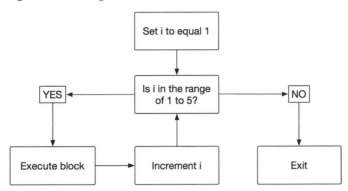

To see the results of your loop, find and click the Show Result button (▣) on the right edge of the results sidebar on the line with the code myFirstInt += 1 (Figure 6.2).

Figure 6.2 The Show Result button

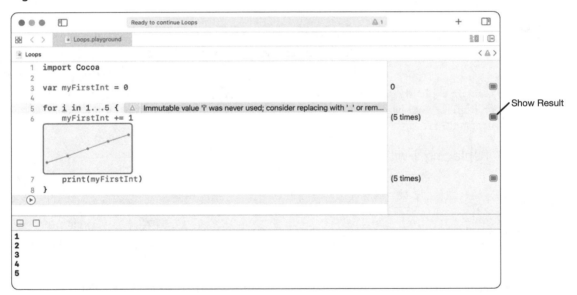

This opens a *results view* that displays the instance's value history. You can grow or shrink the graph window by clicking and dragging its edges.

Move your mouse pointer into this new window and you will see that you can select individual points on this plot. For example, if you click the middle point, the playground will tell you that the value of this point is 3 (Figure 6.3).

Figure 6.3 Selecting a value on the plot

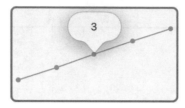

You can access i, the iterator you declared, inside each iteration of the loop. Change your output to show the value of i at each iteration.

Listing 6.2 Printing the changing value of i to the console

```
...
for i in 1...5 {
    myFirstInt += 1                                       (5 times)
    print(myFirstInt)
    print("myFirstInt = \(myFirstInt) at iteration \(i)")  (5 times)
}
```

If you do not want an explicitly declared iterator, you can ignore it by using _ to silence the warning you saw before. Replace your named constant with this wildcard and return your **print()** statement to its earlier implementation.

Listing 6.3 Replacing i with _

```
...
for i in 1...5 {
for _ in 1...5 {
    myFirstInt += 1                                       (5 times)
    print("myFirstInt = \(myFirstInt) at iteration \(i)")
    print(myFirstInt)                                     (5 times)
}
```

This implementation of the for-in loop ensures that a specific operation occurs a set number of times. But it does not check and report the value of the iterator in each pass of the loop over its range. Use the explicit iterator i if you want to refer to the iterator within your loop's code block or the wildcard _ if you do not.

where

Swift's for-in loop supports the use of where clauses similar to the ones you saw in Chapter 5. Using where allows for finer control over when the loop executes its code. The where clause provides a logical test that must be met to execute the loop's code. If the condition established by the where clause is not met, then the loop's code is not run.

For example, imagine that you want to write a loop that iterates over a range but only executes its code when the loop's iterator is a multiple of 3.

Listing 6.4 A for-in loop with a where clause

```
...
for _ in 1...5 {
    myFirstInt += 1                                    (5 times)
    print(myFirstInt)                                  (5 times)
}

for i in 1...100 where i % 3 == 0 {
    print(i)                                           (33 times)
}
```

As before, you create a local constant i that you can now use in the where clause's condition. Each integer in the range of 1 to 100 is bound to i. The where clause then checks to see whether i is divisible by 3. If the remainder is 0, the loop will execute its code. The result is that the loop will print out every multiple of 3 from 1 to 100.

Figure 6.4 demonstrates the flow of execution for this loop.

Figure 6.4 where clause loop diagram

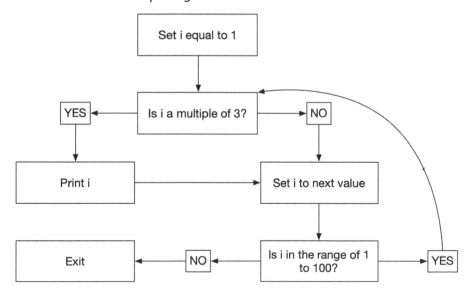

Imagine how you might accomplish this same result without the help of a where clause.

```
for i in 1...100 {
    if i % 3 == 0 {
        print(i)
    }
}
```

The code above does the same work as the loop with the where clause, but it is less elegant. There are more lines of code, and there is a nested conditional within the loop. Generally speaking, we prefer fewer lines of code, so long as the code is not overly complex to read. Swift's where clauses are very readable, so we typically choose this more concise solution.

while Loops

A while loop executes the code inside its body for as long as a specified condition is true. You can write while loops to do many of the same things you have seen in for loops above. Start with a while loop that replicates the for loop in Listing 6.1:

Listing 6.5 A while loop

```
...
var i = 1
while i < 6 {
    myFirstInt += 1                             (5 times)
    print(myFirstInt)                           (5 times)
    i += 1                                      (5 times)
}
```

Figure 6.5 shows the flow of execution in this code.

Figure 6.5 while loop diagram

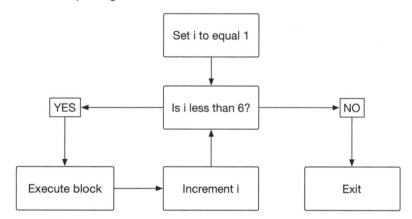

This while loop initializes a control variable (var i = 1), evaluates a condition (i < 6), executes code if the condition is valid (myFirstInt += 1, print(myFirstInt), i += 1), and then returns to the top of the while loop to determine whether the loop should continue iterating.

i is declared as a variable because the condition you evaluate (i < 6) must be able to change. Remember, the while loop will run as long as the condition it checks is true. If the condition never changes (or is always true), then the while loop will execute forever. Loops that never end are called *infinite loops*, and they are usually bugs.

while loops are best for circumstances in which the number of iterations the loop will pass through is unknown. For example, imagine a space shooter game with a spaceship that continuously fires its blasters as long as the spaceship has shields. Various external factors may lower or increase the ship's shields, so the exact number of iterations cannot be known. But if the shields have a value greater than 0, the blasters will keep shooting. The code snippet below illustrates a simplified implementation of this idea.

```
while shields > 0 {
    // Fire blasters!
    print("Fire blasters!")
}
```

repeat-while Loops

Swift also supports a type of `while` loop called the `repeat-while` loop. The `repeat-while` loop is called a do-while loop in other languages. The difference between `while` and `repeat-while` loops is *when* they evaluate their condition.

The `while` loop evaluates its condition before stepping into the loop. This means that the `while` loop may not ever execute, because its condition could be `false` when it is first evaluated. The `repeat-while` loop, on the other hand, executes its loop at least once and *then* evaluates its condition. The syntax for the `repeat-while` loop demonstrates this difference.

```
repeat {
    // Fire blasters!
    print("Fire blasters!")
} while shields > 0
```

In this `repeat-while` version of the space shooter game, the code block that contains the line `print("Fire blasters!")` is executed first. Then the `repeat-while` loop's condition is evaluated to determine whether the loop should continue iterating. Thus, the `repeat-while` loop ensures that the spaceship fires its blasters at least one time.

Control Transfer Statements in Loops

Let's revisit control transfer statements in the context of loops. Recall from Chapter 5 (where you used fallthrough and break) that control transfer statements change the typical order of execution. In the context of a loop, you can control whether execution iterates to the top of the loop or leaves the loop altogether.

Let's elaborate on the space shooter game to see how this works. You are going to use the continue control transfer statement to stop the loop where it is and begin again from the top.

Listing 6.6 Using continue

```
...
var shields = 5                                         5
var blastersOverheating = false                         false
var blasterFireCount = 0                                0
while shields > 0 {

    if blastersOverheating {
        print("Blasters overheated! Cooldown initiated.")  "Blasters overheated! ...
        sleep(5)
        print("Blasters ready to fire")
        sleep(1)
        blastersOverheating = false
        blasterFireCount = 0
    }

    if blasterFireCount > 100 {
        blastersOverheating = true                      true
        continue
    }

    // Fire blasters!
    print("Fire blasters!")                             101 times

    blasterFireCount += 1                               101 times
}
```

(We are showing the sidebar results as they appear the first time execution pauses. More about that in a moment.)

You have added a good bit of code, so let's break it down. First, you added some variables to keep track of certain information about the spaceship:

- shields is an **Int** that keeps track of the shield strength; it is initialized with a value of 5.

- blastersOverheating is a **Bool** that keeps track of whether the blasters need time to cool down; it is initialized to false.

- blasterFireCount is an **Int** that keeps track of the number of shots the spaceship has fired; it is initialized with a value of 0.

After creating your variables, you wrote two if statements, both contained in a while loop with a condition of shields > 0. The first if statement checks whether the blasters are overheating, and the second checks the fire count (which determines whether the blasters are overheating).

For the first, if the blasters are overheating, a number of code steps execute. You log information to the console, and the **sleep()** function tells the system to wait for 5 seconds, which models the blasters' cooldown phase. You next log that the blasters are ready to fire again, wait for 1 more second (simply because it makes it easier to see what logs to the console next), set blastersOverheating to false, and also reset blasterFireCount to 0.

With shields intact and blasters cooled down, the spaceship is ready to fire away.

The second if statement checks whether blasterFireCount is greater than 100. If this conditional evaluates to true, you set the Boolean for blastersOverheating to be true. At this point, the blasters are overheated, so you need a way to jump back up to the top of the loop so that the spaceship does not fire. You use continue to do this. Because the spaceship's blasters have overheated, the conditional in the first if statement will evaluate to true, and the blasters will shut down to cool off.

If the second conditional is evaluated to be false, you log to the console as before. Next, you increment the blasterFireCount by 1. After you increment this variable, the loop will jump back up to the top, evaluate the condition, and either iterate again or hand off the flow of execution to the line immediately after the closing brace of the loop. Figure 6.6 shows this flow of execution.

Figure 6.6 while loop diagram

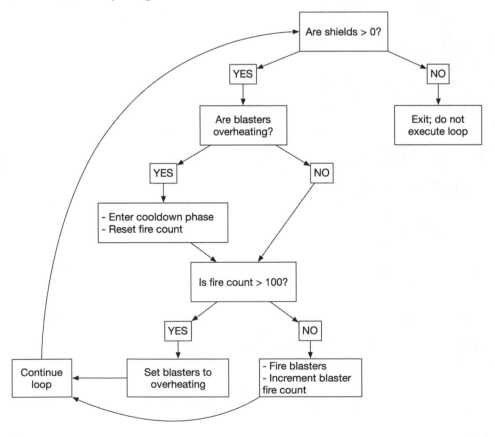

Note that this code will execute indefinitely – it is an infinite loop. There is nothing to change the value of shields, so while shields > 0 is always satisfied. If nothing changes, and your computer has enough power to run forever, the loop will continue to execute. In the time you have been reading this explanation, the sidebar results for the code in your loop have likely increased several times.

But all games must come to an end. Let's say that the game is over when the user has destroyed 500 space demons. To exit the loop, you will use the break control transfer statement.

Listing 6.7 Using break

```
...
var shields = 5                                              5
var blastersOverheating = false                              false
var blasterFireCount = 0                                     0
var spaceDemonsDestroyed = 0                                 0
while shields > 0 {

    if spaceDemonsDestroyed == 500 {
        print("You beat the game!")                          "You beat the game!\n"
        break
    }

    if blastersOverheating {
        print("Blasters overheated! Cooldown initiated.")    (4 times)
        sleep(5)                                             (4 times)
        print("Blasters ready to fire")                      (4 times)
        sleep(1)                                             (4 times)
        blastersOverheating = false                          (4 times)
        blasterFireCount = 0                                 (4 times)
    }

    if blasterFireCount > 100 {                              (4 times)
        blastersOverheating = true
        continue
    }

    // Fire blasters!
    print("Fire blasters!")                                  (500 times)

    blasterFireCount += 1                                    (500 times)
    spaceDemonsDestroyed += 1                                (500 times)
}
```

Here, you add a new variable called spaceDemonsDestroyed, which is incremented each time the blasters fire. (You are a pretty good shot, apparently.) Next, you add a new if statement that checks whether the value of spaceDemonsDestroyed is 500. If it is, you log victory to the console.

Note the use of break. The break control transfer statement will exit the while loop, and execution will pick up on the line immediately after the closing brace of the loop. The user has destroyed 500 space demons, and the game is won: The blasters do not need to fire anymore.

Now, your loop is no longer infinite. The sidebar results in Listing 6.7 show the final results.

Silver Challenge

Fizz Buzz is a game used to teach division. Create a version of the game that works like this: For every value in a given range, print out "FIZZ" if the current number is evenly divisible by 3. If the number is evenly divisible by 5, print out "BUZZ." If the number is evenly divisible by both 3 and 5, then print out "FIZZ BUZZ." If the number is not evenly divisible by 3 or 5, then simply print out the number.

For example, over the range of 1 through 10, playing Fizz Buzz should yield this: "1, 2, FIZZ, 4, BUZZ, FIZZ, 7, 8, FIZZ, BUZZ."

Computers love to play Fizz Buzz. The game is perfect for loops and conditionals. Loop over the range from 0 through 100 and print "FIZZ," "BUZZ," "FIZZ BUZZ," or the number appropriately for each number in the range.

For bonus points, solve Fizz Buzz with both an `if/else` conditional and a `switch` statement. When using the `switch` statement, make sure to match against a tuple in its various cases.

7

Strings

In programming, text content is represented by strings. You have seen and used strings already. "Hello, playground", for example, is a string that appears at the top of every newly created playground. In this chapter, you will see more of what strings can do.

Working with Strings

In Swift, you create strings with the **String** type. Create a new macOS playground called Strings and add the following new instance of the **String** type.

Listing 7.1 Hello, playground

```
import Cocoa

var str = "Hello, playground"
let playground = "Hello, playground"                    "Hello, playground"
```

You have created a **String** instance named playground using the string literal syntax, which encloses a sequence of text with quotation marks.

This instance was created with the let keyword, making it a constant. Recall that being a constant means that the instance cannot be changed. If you try to change it, the compiler will give you an error.

Create a new string, but make this instance mutable.

Listing 7.2 Creating a mutable string

```
let playground = "Hello, playground"                    "Hello, playground"
var mutablePlayground = "Hello, mutable playground"     "Hello, mutable playgro...
```

mutablePlayground is a mutable instance of the **String** type. In other words, you can change the contents of this string. Use the addition and assignment operator to add some final punctuation.

Listing 7.3 Adding to a mutable string

```
let playground = "Hello, playground"                    "Hello, playground"
var mutablePlayground = "Hello, mutable playground"     "Hello, mutable playgro...
mutablePlayground += "!"                                "Hello, mutable playgro...
```

You should see in the results sidebar that the instance has changed to "Hello, mutable playground!"

You have used the \() string interpolation syntax in previous chapters. The leading backslash is called an *escape character*, and it tells the compiler to treat the parentheses (and their contents) differently than it otherwise would. Together, the backslash and the specially treated text form an *escape sequence*.

There are several escape sequences you can use to insert different types of content into a string. Here some worth knowing:

- \() interpolates an expression into a string.
- \n inserts a new line when printing the string.
- \" inserts a quotation mark in a string (otherwise it would prematurely close the string).
- \\ inserts a backslash in a string (otherwise it would begin an escape sequence).

To see some of them in action, add this code to your playground:

Listing 7.4 Using escape sequences in a string

```
...
var mutablePlayground = "Hello, mutable playground"          "Hello, mutable playgro...
mutablePlayground += "!"                                     "Hello, mutable playgro...
let quote = "I wanted to \"say\":\n\(playground)"           "I wanted to "say":\nHe...
print(quote)
```

Run your playground and take a moment to examine the effect that each escape sequence has on the printed result:

```
I wanted to "say":
Hello, playground
```

The first two backslashes escape the quotation marks, so that they are taken as part of the string rather than terminating it. The third escape sequence, \n, creates a line break in the console output. The last escape sequence interpolates the value of another string instance, as you have used before. Feel free to experiment with the positioning and usage of these escape sequences.

Sometimes, you do not want the compiler to do anything at all to the contents of a string. No escaping, no string interpolation. Creating a *raw string* like this is as easy as wrapping it with hash symbols (#):

Listing 7.5 Creating a raw string

```
...
let quote = "I wanted to \"say\":\n\(playground)"
let quote = #"I wanted to \"say\":\n\(playground)"#          "I wanted to \\"say\\":...
print(quote)                                                 "I wanted to \\"say\\":...
```

This prints the string as you wrote it, with no processing:

```
I wanted to \"say\":\n\(playground)
```

In the sidebar, you can see the hidden truth: The compiler processes the string after all, but only to escape out your escape sequences, so that they are instead taken as parts of the string literal.

Characters

When talking about text, the term "string" is short for "string of characters," where a *character* is a single symbol or glyph – something that a reader would consider to be the smallest unit of written language. A, ȼ, ., 1, and © are all characters. In Swift, a **String** is a collection of instances of the **Character** type.

Loop through the `mutablePlayground` string to see its **Character** instances:

Listing 7.6 mutablePlayground's **Character**s

```
...
let quote = #"I wanted to \"say\":\n\(playground)"#        "I wanted to \\"say\\":...
print(quote)                                               "I wanted to \\"say\\":...
for c: Character in mutablePlayground {
    print("'\(c)'")                                        (26 times)
}
```

This loop iterates through every **Character** c in `mutablePlayground`. The explicit type annotation of **Character** is unnecessary. Swift's type inference knows that c is a **Character**. It knows this because Swift's **String** type conforms to a set of rules, a *protocol*, called **Collection**. (You will learn more about protocols in Chapter 19.) This protocol organizes a sequence's elements in terms of subscriptable indices.

The **Collection** protocol helps the **String** organize its contents as a collection of characters. This is how each iteration of the loop can access an individual character to log to the console. Every character is logged to the console on its own line because **print()** prints a line break after logging its content.

Your output should look like this:

```
'H'
'e'
'l'
'l'
'o'
','
' '
'm'
'u'
't'
'a'
'b'
'l'
'e'
' '
'p'
'l'
'a'
'y'
'g'
'r'
'o'
'u'
'n'
'd'
'!'
```

Unicode

Unicode is an international standard that encodes characters so they can be seamlessly processed and represented regardless of the platform. Unicode represents human language (and other forms of communication, like emoji) on computers. Every character in the Unicode standard is assigned a unique number.

Swift's **String** and **Character** types are built on top of Unicode, and they do the majority of the heavy lifting. Nonetheless, it is good to have an understanding of how these types work with Unicode. Having this knowledge will likely save you some time and frustration in the future.

Unicode scalars

At their heart, strings in Swift are composed of *Unicode scalars*. Unicode scalars are 21-bit numbers that represent a specific character in the Unicode standard. The text U+1F60E is the standard way of writing a Unicode character. (The 1F60E portion is a number written in hexadecimal.) For example, U+0061 represents the Latin small letter a. U+2603 represents a snowman.

Create a constant to see how to use specific Unicode scalars in Swift and the playground.

Listing 7.7 Using a Unicode scalar

```
...
for c: Character in mutablePlayground {
    print("'\(c)'")                              (26 times)
}

let snowman = "\u{2603}"                         "☃"
```

This time, you used a new syntax to create a string. The quotation marks are familiar, but what is inside them is not a string literal, as you have seen before. It does not match the results in the sidebar.

The \u{} syntax is an escape sequence that resolves to the Unicode scalar whose hexadecimal number appears between the braces. In this case, the value of snowman is the Unicode character of a snowman.

How does this relate to more familiar strings? Swift strings are composed of Unicode scalars. So why do they look unfamiliar? To explain, we need to discuss a few more concepts.

Every character in Swift is an *extended grapheme cluster*. Extended grapheme clusters are sequences of one or more Unicode scalars that combine to produce a single human-readable character. One Unicode scalar generally maps onto one fundamental character in a given language, but there are also *combining scalars*. For example, U+0301 represents the Unicode scalar for the combining acute accent: ´. This scalar is placed on top of – that is, combined with – the character that precedes it.

In your playground, use this scalar with the Latin small letter a to create the character á:

Listing 7.8 Using a combining scalar

```
...
let snowman = "\u{2603}"                         "☃"
let aAcute = "\u{0061}\u{0301}"                  "á"
```

Making characters extended grapheme clusters gives Swift flexibility in dealing with complex script characters.

Swift also provides a mechanism to see all the Unicode scalars in a string. For example, you can see all the Unicode scalars that Swift uses to create the instance of **String** named playground that you created earlier using the unicodeScalars property, which holds all the scalars that Swift uses to make the string. (Properties, which you will learn about in Chapter 16, are constants or variables that associate values with an instance of a type.)

Add the following code to your playground to see playground's Unicode scalars.

Listing 7.9 Revealing the Unicode scalars behind a string

```
...
let snowman = "\u{2603}"                              "☃"
let aAcute = "\u{0061}\u{0301}"                       "á"
for scalar in playground.unicodeScalars {
    print("\(scalar.value)")                         (17 times)
}
```

You should see the following output in the console: 72 101 108 108 111 44 32 112 108 97 121 103 114 111 117 110 100. What do all these numbers mean?

The unicodeScalars property holds on to data representing all the Unicode scalars used to create the string instance playground. Each number on the console corresponds to a Unicode scalar representing a single character in the string. But they are not the hexadecimal Unicode numbers. Instead, each is represented as an unsigned 32-bit integer. For example, the first, 72, corresponds to the Unicode scalar value of U+0048, or an uppercase H.

Canonical equivalence

While there is a role for combining scalars, Unicode also provides already combined forms for some common characters. For example, there is a specific scalar for á. You do not actually need to decompose it into its two parts, the letter and the accent. The scalar is U+00E1. Create a new constant string that uses this Unicode scalar.

Listing 7.10 Using a precomposed character

```
...
let aAcute = "\u{0061}\u{0301}"                          "á"
for scalar in playground.unicodeScalars {
    print("\(scalar.value) ")                            (17 times)
}

let aAcutePrecomposed = "\u{00E1}"                        "á"
```

As you can see, aAcutePrecomposed appears to have the same value as aAcute. Indeed, if you check whether these two characters are the same, you will find that Swift answers "yes."

Listing 7.11 Checking equivalence

```
...
let aAcute = "\u{0061}\u{0301}"                          "á"
for scalar in playground.unicodeScalars {
    print("\(scalar.value) ")                            (17 times)
}

let aAcutePrecomposed = "\u{00E1}"                        "á"

let b = (aAcute == aAcutePrecomposed)                    true
```

aAcute was created using two Unicode scalars, and aAcutePrecomposed only used one. Why does Swift say that they are equivalent? The answer is *canonical equivalence*.

Canonical equivalence refers to whether two sequences of Unicode scalars are the same *linguistically*. Two characters, or two strings, are considered equal if they have the same linguistic meaning and appearance, regardless of whether they are built from the same Unicode scalars. aAcute and aAcutePrecomposed are equal strings because both represent the Latin small letter a with an acute accent. The fact that they were created with different Unicode scalars does not affect this.

Counting elements

Canonical equivalence has implications for counting the elements of a string. You might think that
aAcute and aAcutePrecomposed would have different character counts. Write the following code to
check.

Listing 7.12 Counting characters

```
...
let aAcutePrecomposed = "\u{00E1}"                        "á"

let b = (aAcute == aAcutePrecomposed)                    true

aAcute.count                                             1
aAcutePrecomposed.count                                  1
```

You use the count property on **String** to determine the character count of these two strings. count
iterates over a string's Unicode scalars to determine its length. The results sidebar reveals that the
character counts are the same: Both are one character long.

Canonical equivalence means that whether you use a combining scalar or a precomposed scalar, the
result is treated as the same. aAcute uses two Unicode scalars; aAcutePrecomposed uses one. This
difference does not matter since both result in the same character.

Indices and ranges

Because strings are ordered collections of characters, if you have worked with collections in other languages, you might think that you can access a specific character in a string like so:

```
let playground = "Hello, playground"
let index = playground[3] // 'l'?
```

The code `playground[3]` uses the *subscript* syntax. In general, the brackets (`[]`) after a variable name indicate that you are using a subscript in Swift. Subscripts allow you to retrieve a specific value within a collection.

The 3 in this example is an *index* that is used to find a particular element within a collection. The code above suggests that you are trying to select the fourth character from the collection of characters making up the `playground` string (fourth, not third, because the first index is 0). And for other Swift collection types, subscript syntax like this would work. (You will learn more about subscripts below and will also see them in action in Chapter 8 on arrays and Chapter 10 on dictionaries.)

However, if you tried to use a subscript like this on a **String**, you would get an error: "'subscript' is unavailable: cannot subscript String with an Int." The Swift compiler will not let you access a specific character on a string via a subscript index.

This limitation has to do with the way Swift strings and characters are stored. You cannot index a string with an integer, because Swift does not know which Unicode scalar corresponds to a given index without stepping through every preceding character. This operation can be expensive. Therefore, Swift forces you to be more explicit.

Swift uses a type called **String.Index** to keep track of indices in string instances. (The period in **String.Index** just means that **Index** is a type that is defined on **String**. You will learn more about nested types like this in Chapter 16.)

As you have seen in this chapter, an individual character may be made up of multiple Unicode *code points* (another term for Unicode scalars). It is the job of the **Index** to represent these code points as a single **Character** instance and to combine these characters into the correct string.

Because **Index** is defined on **String**, you can ask the **String** to hand back indices that are meaningful. To find the character at a particular index, you begin with the **String** type's `startIndex` property. This property yields the starting index of a string as a **String.Index**. You then use this starting point in conjunction with the **index(_:offsetBy:)** method to move forward until you arrive at the position of your choosing. (A *method* is like a function; you will learn more about them in Chapter 12.)

Say you want to know the fifth character of the `playground` string that you created earlier.

Listing 7.13 Finding the fifth character

```
let playground = "Hello, playground"              "Hello, playground"
...
aAcute.count                                      1
aAcutePrecomposed.count                           1

let start = playground.startIndex                 String.Index
let end = playground.index(start, offsetBy: 4)    String.Index
let fifthCharacter = playground[end]              "o"
```

You use the startIndex property on the string to get the first index of the string. This property yields an instance of type **String.Index**. Next, you use the **index(_:offsetBy:)** method to advance from the starting point to your desired position. You tell the method to begin at the first index and then add 4 to advance to the fifth character.

The result of calling **index(_:offsetBy:)** is a **String.Index** that you assign to the constant end. Finally, you use end to subscript your playground string, which results in the character o being assigned to fifthCharacter.

Character ranges, like indices, depend upon the **String.Index** type. Suppose you wanted to grab the first five characters of playground. You can use the same start and end constants.

Listing 7.14 Pulling out a range

```
...
let start = playground.startIndex                  String.Index
let end = playground.index(start, offsetBy: 4)     String.Index
let fifthCharacter = playground[end]               "o"
let range = start...end                            {{_rawBits 1}, {_rawBit...
let firstFive = playground[range]                  "Hello"
```

The result of the syntax start...end is a constant named range. It has the type **ClosedRange<String.Index>**. A closed range, as you saw in Chapter 4, includes a lower bound, an upper bound, and everything in between. <String.Index> indicates the type of the elements along the range – the type that strings use for their indices. (In Chapter 4, the ranges you used were of type **Range<Int>** and **ClosedRange<Int>**.)

Your range's lower bound is start, which is a **String.Index** whose value you can think of as being 0. The upper bound is end, which is also a **String.Index** whose value you can think of as 4. (The actual values are more complicated, as the sidebar results hint at, and are outside the scope of this book.) Thus, range describes a series of indices within playground from its starting index up to and including the index offset by 4.

You used this new range as a subscript on the playground string. The subscript grabbed the first five characters from playground, making firstFive a constant equal to "Hello".

In addition to closed ranges and the half-open ranges you also saw in Chapter 4, there is a third type of range you can use in Swift: the *one-sided range*. Update your playground to use one:

Listing 7.15 Using a one-sided range

```
...
let start = playground.startIndex                  String.Index
let end = playground.index(start, offsetBy: 4)     String.Index
let fifthCharacter = playground[end]               "o"
let range = start...end
let range = ...end                                 PartialRangeThrough<Str...
let firstFive = playground[range]                  "Hello"
```

By removing the lower bound from your range, you tell the compiler that the range should begin with the lowest possible value; in this case, the beginning of the string. A one-sided range can be created with either the lower or upper bound removed and using either range operator (... or ..<).

Because strings are such a central part of communicating with your user, it is no surprise that they have so many features for examining and working with their contents.

Bronze Challenge

Create a new **String** instance called empty and give it an empty string (a string with no characters): let empty = "". It is useful to be able to tell if a string has any characters in it. For example, you may be designing a form for data input and want to prevent the user from submitting a blank entry. Use the startIndex and endIndex properties on empty to determine whether this string is truly empty.

Silver Challenge

Replace the "Hello" string with an instance created out of its corresponding Unicode scalars. You can find the appropriate codes on the internet.

For the More Curious: Substrings

In this chapter, you created a **ClosedRange** and used it to subscript the **String** playground. Doing so meant that you grabbed the word "Hello" from the **String** within the playground constant and assigned it to firstFive.

But here is a question: What is the type of firstFive? You might expect its type to be **String**, but it is not. Option-click firstFive. This opens a pop-up where you can see the variable's full declaration, including its type (Figure 7.1).

Figure 7.1 Substrings

firstFive is a **String.SubSequence**. What is that? Click SubSequence in the pop-up to open a page about the type in Apple's developer documentation (Figure 7.2).

Figure 7.2 **SubSequence** documentation

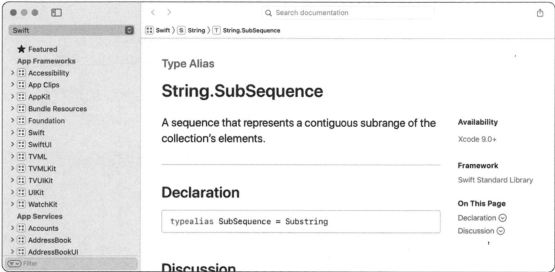

The documentation says that **SubSequence** is a *typealias* for something called **Substring**. (You can ignore what a typealias is for now. That will be covered in Chapter 20.) Click on **Substring** to see the documentation for this type.

Take some time to read through the documentation. You will find that `firstFive` is what is called a "slice" of the original **String** contained by the `playground` constant. A slice represents some subcomponent of the original sequence.

Since `firstFive` is a slice of `playground`, it is a substring carved out of the original "Hello, playground" **String**. Slicing a substring from an existing **String** does not create a new instance of that type. This is efficient, because it means that `firstFive` does not need its own storage. It shares its storage with `playground`. And **Substring** presents the same API as **String**, so you do not need to worry about loss of functionality.

Imagine that you need to subscript the `playground` **String** for the word "play." You would write code like this:

```
let startPlay = playground.index(playground.startIndex, offsetBy: 7)
let endPlay = playground.index(startPlay, offsetBy: 3)
let playRange = startPlay...endPlay
let play = playground[playRange]
```

You offset the start index of `playground` by 7 to get the index for the letter p. Next, you offset this index by 3 to get to the letter y. These indices formulate the **ClosedRange** that allows access to the word "play" within the source **String** named `playground`. With the range in hand, you subscript the `playground` to slice the word "play" from the original string.

Figure 7.3 shows the relationships and types of the five variables.

Figure 7.3 The layout of substrings

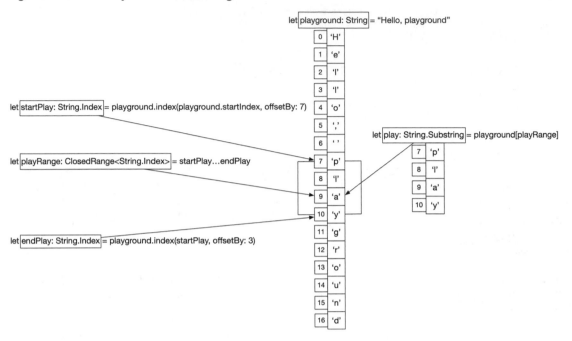

For the More Curious: Multiline Strings

You learned in Chapter 4 that sometimes the whitespace in your code (like spaces and line breaks) matters, such as when putting space on either side of a binary operator. Declaring a string is another situation where whitespace – in this case, line breaks – matters.

As you learned above, you can use the \n escape sequence to cause a string to insert a new line when printing to the console. But if you try to split a string across multiple lines in your code, you get a compiler error. For example, this code yields multiple errors:

```
let tale = "It was the best of times,
it was the worst of times."
print(tale)
```

The compiler sees an unterminated string on the first line, generating one error. And it does not realize that the second line is part of a string, so it tries to compile that line like any other code, generating more errors.

If you want to split a string across multiple lines in your code, use three quotation marks at the start and end of the string:

```
let tale = """
    It was the best of times,
    it was the worst of times.
    """
print(tale)
```

There are a couple important rules about multiline strings:

- The opening quotation marks must be followed by a new line and the first line of the string.

- The closing quotation marks must begin a new line.

The indentation level of the closing quotation marks establishes the leading margin of the text. The string above will be indented when printed to the console, because the text is indented relative to the closing quotation marks. The string below will not be indented when printed, since the text and closing quotation marks are aligned:

```
let tale = """
    It was the best of times,
    it was the worst of times.
    """
print(tale)
```

When you have a lot of text that you want to store in a **String**, using this multiline string syntax can save you some headaches (and lots of horizontal scrolling).

Part III
Collections and Functions

As a programmer, you will often have a collection of related values that you need to keep together. This part of the book will introduce you to Swift's collection types, which help you do this.

This part of the book also introduces the concept of *optionals* in Swift. Optionals play an important role in the language and provide a mechanism to represent the concept of *nothing* in a safe way. As you will see, how Swift deals with optionals highlights the language's approach to writing safe and reliable code.

Finally, these chapters describe how to use the system functions provided by Swift to transform and understand your data, as well as how to create your own functions to accomplish your goals.

8

Arrays

An important task in programming is to group together logically related values. For example, imagine that your application keeps lists of a user's friends, favorite books, travel locations, and so on. It is often necessary to be able to keep those values together and pass them around your code. *Collections* make these operations convenient.

Swift has a number of collection types. The first we will cover is called **Array**.

An array is an ordered collection of objects or values. Because it is ordered, each position in an array is identified by an index. Arrays are typically used when the order of the values is important or useful to know. The items in a Swift **Array** can be of any type – objects and values alike. And while all the elements of an array must be of the same type, they do not need to be unique; a value can appear multiple times in an array.

To get started, create a new macOS playground called Arrays.

Creating an Array

In this chapter, you will create an array that represents your bucket list: the things you would like to do in the future. Begin by declaring your first array.

Listing 8.1 Creating an array

```
import Cocoa

var str = "Hello, playground"

var bucketList: Array<String>
```

Here, you create a new variable called bucketList that is of the **Array** type. As you have seen, the var keyword means that bucketList is a variable. Arrays declared with var are called *mutable* – another way of saying they can be changed. There are also *immutable* arrays, which we will discuss later in this chapter.

The <String> part of the declaration tells the bucketList array what sort of instances it can accept. Arrays can hold instances of any type; bucketList will accept instances of **String**.

There is a shorthand syntax for declaring an array. Make the following change in your playground:

Listing 8.2 Changing the syntax

```
var bucketList: Array<String>
var bucketList: [String]
```

This syntax does the same work, but it is more convenient. Here, the brackets identify bucketList as an instance of **Array**, and the **String** syntax tells bucketList what sort of values it can accept.

Your bucketList is declared, which means you have made a place to put an array – but you have not yet created the array itself. If you were to try to put an item in your bucketList, you would get an error saying that you are trying to add something before your bucketList is initialized.

Initialize the array with your first bucket list goal:

Listing 8.3 Initializing the array

```
var bucketList: [String]
bucketList = ["Climb Mt. Everest"]                    ["Climb Mt. Everest"]
```

You use the assignment operator = in conjunction with the **Array** literal syntax ["Climb Mt. Everest"]. An **Array** literal is a shorthand syntax that initializes an array with whatever instances you include. In this case, you initialize bucketList with an array containing a single item: "Climb Mt. Everest".

By the way, you are not required to initialize your variable with an array that contains elements. If you did the bronze challenge in Chapter 7, you saw that you can create an empty string with no characters: var empty = "". You can also create an empty array using [] to represent a literal array with no elements. You would then have an initialized array variable, ready for use.

As you have seen previously, you can declare and initialize on the same line. Update your declaration to also provide a value for your bucketList.

Listing 8.4 Initializing the array alongside its declaration

```
var bucketList: [String] = ["Climb Mt. Everest"]                    ["Climb Mt. Everest"]
bucketList = ["Climb Mt. Everest"]
```

There is one more way you can simplify your declaration. As with other types, **Array** instances can be declared by taking advantage of Swift's type inference capabilities. Remove the type declaration from your code to use type inference.

Listing 8.5 Using type inference

```
var bucketList: [String] = ["Climb Mt. Everest"]                    ["Climb Mt. Everest"]
```

Your bucketList will still only accept instances of the **String** type, but now it infers the variable's type based on the type of the instance used to initialize it. If you were to try to add an integer to this array, you would see an error telling you that you cannot add an instance of **Int** to your array, because it is expecting instances of the **String** type. In this way, your variable is of a single, compound type: an array of strings.

Note that if you are initializing an empty array using literal syntax, the compiler cannot infer the type of instance that the array contains. You need to declare it explicitly, as in var emptyStringArray: [String] = []. You can also use Swift's *constructor syntax*, if you prefer: var emptyStringArray = [String]().

Now that you know how to create and initialize an array, it is time to learn how to access and modify your array's elements.

Accessing and Modifying Arrays

So, you have a bucket list? Great! Sadly, you do not have many ambitions in it yet. But you are an interesting person with a zest for life, so let's add some values to your bucketList. Update your list with another ambition.

Listing 8.6 Reading the classics

```
var bucketList = ["Climb Mt. Everest"]                    ["Climb Mt. Everest"]
bucketList.append("Read War and Peace")                   ["Climb Mt. Everest", "...
```

You are using **append(_:)** to add a value to bucketList. The **append(_:)** method takes an *argument* of whatever type an array accepts and makes it a new element in the array. Arguments are data given to a method for it to work with; you will learn more about them in Chapter 12.

The sidebar shows the value of bucketList, which now includes two strings.

Add more future adventures to your bucketList using the **append(_:)** function.

Listing 8.7 So many ambitions!

```
var bucketList = ["Climb Mt. Everest"]                    ["Climb Mt. Everest"]
bucketList.append("Read War and Peace")                   ["Climb Mt. Everest", "...
bucketList.append("Go on an Arctic expedition")           ["Climb Mt. Everest", "...
bucketList.append("Scuba dive in the Great Blue Hole")    ["Climb Mt. Everest", "...
bucketList.append("Find a triple rainbow")                ["Climb Mt. Everest", "...
```

An **Array** like bucketList can hold many items – as many as you can dream up. But it is easy to find out the number of items in an array. Arrays keep track of the number of items in them via the count property. Use this property to access the number of bucket list items.

Listing 8.8 Counting items in the array

```
...
bucketList.append("Scuba dive in the Great Blue Hole")    ["Climb Mt. Everest", "...
bucketList.append("Find a triple rainbow")                ["Climb Mt. Everest", "...
bucketList.count                                          5
```

What happens when you accomplish one of the items on your list and are ready to take it off? Because **Array**s are ordered, you can access specific items in an **Array** via their indices.

Suppose you worked your way through *War and Peace*. Remove that goal from your list with the function **remove(at:)**, specifying the index position of "Read War and Peace". Arrays are zero-indexed, so "Climb Mt. Everest" is at index 0 and "Read War and Peace" is at index 1.

Listing 8.9 Removing an item from the array

```
var bucketList = ["Climb Mt. Everest"]                    ["Climb Mt. Everest"]
bucketList.append("Read War and Peace")                   ["Climb Mt. Everest", "...
bucketList.append("Go on an Arctic expedition")           ["Climb Mt. Everest", "...
bucketList.append("Scuba dive in the Great Blue Hole")    ["Climb Mt. Everest", "...
bucketList.append("Find a triple rainbow")                ["Climb Mt. Everest", "...
bucketList.count                                          5
bucketList.remove(at: 1)                                  "Read War and Peace"
bucketList                                                ["Climb Mt. Everest", "...
```

To confirm that the value in the first index was removed from your bucketList, mouse over the sidebar next to the final line (bucketList) and click the Quick Look button (◉). The Quick Look window will appear (Figure 8.1).

Figure 8.1 Checking the Quick Look window

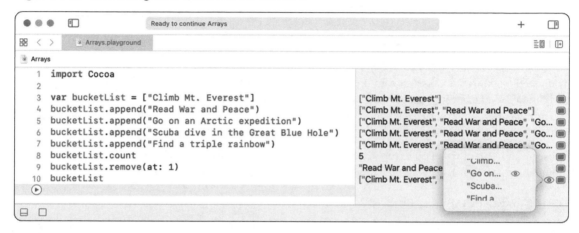

Scroll down in the Quick Look window to see that the count of items in your array is now four. The item formerly at the first index is gone. "Go on an Arctic expedition" now occupies the first index.

The ordered nature of arrays also means that you can use subscripting to get a handle on the values they contain. Print the first three items in your bucketList array:

Listing 8.10 Subscripting to find your top three items

```
...
bucketList.remove(at: 1)                                "Read War and Peace"
bucketList                                              ["Climb Mt. Everest", "...
print(bucketList[...2])                                 ["Climb Mt. Everest", "...
```

You have seen the subscripting bracket syntax before. Here, you use a half-open range to specify the first three items in the array, which print to the console. You could also have used a closed range, like bucketList[0...2], to access the same top three items or the basic subscripting syntax to log a single item, such as bucketList[2].

Subscripting is a powerful feature. You can also use it to change an item at a particular index (or range of indices). Add some detail to the second item in your `bucketList`:

Listing 8.11 Subscripting to append new information

```
...
bucketList                                      ["Climb Mt. Everest", "...
print(bucketList[...2])                          ["Climb Mt. Everest", "...
bucketList[1] += " with friends"
bucketList[1]                                   "Go on an Arctic expedi...
```

You use the addition and assignment operator (+=) to add some text to the item at index 1. This assignment works because the instance at index 1 is of the same type as the instance you added to it – "Go on an Arctic expedition" and " with friends" are both **String**s. As the sidebar shows, the value at index 1 is now "Go on an Arctic expedition with friends".

Subscripting also allows you to replace an item in an array. Suppose you decide to climb a different mountain, instead of Everest. You can replace the string at index 0 using the assignment operator:

Listing 8.12 Replacing an array item

```
...
print(bucketList[...2])                           ["Climb Mt. Everest", "...
bucketList[1] += " with friends"
bucketList[1]                                    "Go on an Arctic expedi...
bucketList[0] = "Climb Mt. Kilimanjaro"          "Climb Mt. Kilimanjaro"
bucketList                                        ["Climb Mt. Kilimanjaro...
```

Finally, suppose you decide on a new goal that is more important than going on an Arctic expedition but less important than climbing Kilimanjaro. You can use the **insert(_:at:)** function to add a new element to your array at a specified index.

Listing 8.13 Inserting a new ambition

```
...
bucketList[1]                                          "Go on an Arctic expedi...
bucketList[0] = "Climb Mt. Kilimanjaro"               "Climb Mt. Kilimanjaro"
bucketList.insert("Toboggan across Alaska", at: 1)    ["Climb Mt. Kilimanjaro...
bucketList                                             ["Climb Mt. Kilimanjaro...
```

The **insert(_:at:)** function has two arguments. The first argument takes the instance to add to the array. The second argument takes the index where the new element should be added. Use the Quick Look window (or the results sidebar) to confirm that your array now has five elements, with "Toboggan across Alaska" in the second position.

Combining Arrays

You added items to your array using `bucketList.append` (and `bucketList.insert`, when you wanted to add an element at a specific index). You can also add the contents of one array to another by looping over the contents and passing them, one by one, to **append(_:)**. Create a new list of adventures to add to your `bucketList`:

Listing 8.14 Using a loop to append items from one array to another

```
...
bucketList.insert("Toboggan across Alaska", at: 1)          ["Climb Mt. Kilimanjaro...
bucketList                                                  ["Climb Mt. Kilimanjaro...

var newItems = [                                            ["Bike across America",...
    "Bike across America",
    "Make a perfect souffle",
    "Solve Fermat's enigma"
]

for item in newItems {
    bucketList.append(item)                                 (3 times)
}
print(bucketList)                                           ["Climb Mt. Kilimanjaro...
```

You create an array for the bucket list items that you want to add, called `newItems`. Next, you make a `for-in` loop that iterates through each `item` in the array and appends it to your `bucketList`. You use the `item` variable in the local scope of the loop to append it to your `bucketList` array.

The console shows your complete array:

```
["Climb Mt. Kilimanjaro", "Toboggan across Alaska", "Go on an Arctic expedition
with friends", "Scuba dive in the Great Blue Hole", "Find a triple rainbow",
"Bike across America", "Make a perfect souffle", "Solve Fermat\'s enigma"]
```

This works, as the console shows, but it can be simplified. While there are times when looping over an array makes sense, in this case you really just want to add one array to another. And just as you can use `+=` to add one integer to another, you can use it to add one array to another.

Listing 8.15 Refactoring with the addition and assignment operator

```
...
var newItems = [                                            ["Bike across America",...
    "Bike across America",
    "Make a perfect souffle",
    "Solve Fermat's enigma"
]

for item in newItems {
    bucketList.append(item)
}
bucketList += newItems                                      ["Climb Mt. Kilimanjaro...
print(bucketList)                                           ["Climb Mt. Kilimanjaro...
```

The `+=` operator makes for an easy way to add your array of new items to your existing bucket list. Your console output should be unchanged.

Array Equality

You have seen that the equality operator == can be used to check whether two strings or two numeric values are equal. It can also be used to check the equality of two arrays. Create a new array and use == to compare it to newItems.

Listing 8.16 Checking two arrays for equality

```
...
var newItems = [                                    ["Bike across America",...
    "Bike across America",
    "Make a perfect souffle",
    "Solve Fermat's enigma"
]

bucketList += newItems                              ["Climb Mt. Kilimanjaro...
print(bucketList)                                   ["Climb Mt. Kilimanjaro...

var anotherList = [                                 ["Bike across America",...
    "Bike across America",
    "Solve Fermat's enigma",
    "Make a perfect souffle"
]

newItems == anotherList                             false
```

Because the contents of the two arrays are the same, you might expect this check to resolve to true. But the sidebar shows that it is false. Why?

Remember that arrays are ordered. That means two arrays that have the same values are not equal if the ordering is different, and anotherList reverses the order of the second and third items. Put the items in the same order to make the two lists equal.

Listing 8.17 Fixing anotherList

```
...
var anotherList = [                                 ["Bike across America",...
    "Bike across America",
    "Solve Fermat's enigma",
    "Make a perfect souffle",
    "Solve Fermat's enigma"
]

newItems == anotherList                             true
```

If you get an error, double-check the commas that separate the elements in your array. It is legal (but uncommon) to have a trailing comma after the last element, but it is illegal to be missing a comma between two elements.

Immutable Arrays

You have been doing a lot of tinkering with your bucket list array. As we mentioned early in this chapter, you can also create an array that cannot be changed – an immutable array. Here is how.

Let's say you are making an application that allows users to keep track of the lunches they eat each week. Users will log what they ate and generate reports at a later time. You decide to put these meals in an immutable array to generate the reports. After all, it does not make sense to change last week's lunches after they have been eaten.

Create an immutable array and initialize it with a week's worth of lunches.

Listing 8.18 An immutable array

```
...
let lunches = [                                         ["Cheeseburger", "Veggi...
    "Cheeseburger",
    "Veggie Pizza",
    "Chicken Caesar Salad",
    "Black Bean Burrito",
    "Falafel Wrap"
]
```

You use the let keyword to create an immutable array. If you were to try to modify the array in any way, the compiler would issue an error stating that you cannot mutate an immutable array. If you even try to reassign a new array to lunches, you would get an error from the compiler telling you that you cannot reassign an instance to a constant created via the let keyword.

Documentation

The documentation for any programming language is an indispensable resource, and Swift's is no exception. Open the documentation that shipped with Xcode by clicking Help → Developer Documentation at the top (Figure 8.2).

Figure 8.2 Help menu

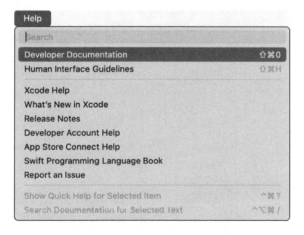

A new documentation window will open. In the search bar at the top, type in "Array" and wait just a moment. You will see some live search results populate, showing different documentation references (Figure 8.3).

Figure 8.3 Searching for "Array"

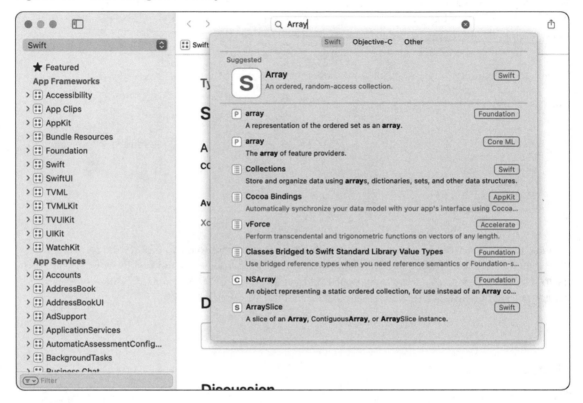

Select the suggested item, which comes from the Swift standard library (the set of features, types, and functions baked into the Swift language itself, as opposed to additional frameworks). This will open the documentation for Swift's **Array** type, as in Figure 8.4.

Figure 8.4 **Array** documentation

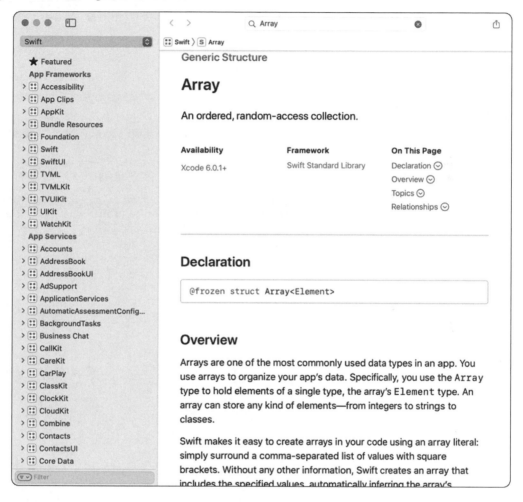

Take some time to explore the documentation for **Array**. Do not worry if you do not recognize or understand all the syntax you see here yet. Get to know the organization of the documentation to save yourself a lot of time in the future. You will be visiting these pages regularly.

Bronze Challenge

Look at the array below.

```
var toDoList = ["Take out the trash", "Pay bills", "Cross off finished items"]
```

Use the documentation to find a property defined on the **Array** type that will tell you whether toDoList contains any elements.

Silver Challenge

Enter the toDoList array from the bronze challenge in your playground. Use a loop to reverse the order of the elements of this array. Log the results to the console.

Then, examine the **Array** documentation to see whether there is a more convenient way to do this operation. (There is.)

Finally, use the **Array** documentation to find an easy way to rearrange the items in your toDoList into a random order.

9
Optionals

In Swift, it is illegal to use a variable before you have given it a value. And once a value has been set, it is impossible to take the value away; you can only assign another value of the same type. But sometimes you need to represent the absence of a value, or a value that might go away, without crashing your app.

If you ask someone "How many beans are in this jar?", you might expect an integer answer (and declare an `Int` variable to store it). But if they answer "I don't know," what should you put in your variable? 0? Some other number? If your variable can only store values of type `Int`, what do you do so that you can move on with your program and deal with the lack of an answer later?

You need a way to declare a variable that *might* have an `Int` or *might* be empty – or might become empty later, after a value has been assigned.

Swift has a type called `Optional` to represent the possible absence of a value. You can think of `Optional` as a small container type that can hold either a ready-for-use instance of another type or nothing at all. If an instance of type `Optional` has no value associated with it, we say that its value is *nil*.

This chapter covers how to declare optionals, how to use *optional binding* to extract the value from an optional that is not nil, and how to use *optional chaining* to query a sequence of optional values.

Optional Types

Create a new macOS playground and name it Optionals.

There is both a long-form syntax and a shorter, more convenient syntax for declaring and using an optional. In practice, developers exclusively use the shorthand syntax. You are going to start with the long form because it more clearly demonstrates how optionals work, and then you will switch to using the more convenient syntax for the rest of this book. Declare your first optional instance:

Listing 9.1 Declaring an optional instance

```
import Cocoa

var str = "Hello, playground"

var errorCodeString: Optional<String>
errorCodeString = Optional("404")                              "404"
```

Optional<String> indicates that your variable is of type **Optional**, and the angle bracket syntax – like in the declaration of an **Array** – indicates that it is designed to hold a value of the **String** type. This means your optional will contain either an instance of **String** or the value nil. The second line, errorCodeString = Optional("404"), creates an instance of the **Optional** type and stores the string "404" in it.

As with **Array** and other container types, there is a shorthand syntax for **Optional**s that is more stylish. Update your playground to use it:

Listing 9.2 Using shorthand optional syntax

```
var errorCodeString: Optional<String>
errorCodeString = Optional("404")
var errorCodeString: String?                                  nil
errorCodeString = "404"                                       "404"
```

This preferred syntax does exactly the same work as before, but it hides some of the details of what is really happening. The ? in String? tells the compiler that you want an **Optional** that will hold a **String** or nil.

A more surprising change has happened on the second line: The constructor syntax (Optional(...)) has disappeared. Now, the value of errorCodeString (which, remember, is of type **Optional**) is assigned to "404" – which is a **String**.

Normally, assigning a value of one type to a variable of a different type is a type mismatch and causes a compiler error. But the compiler has no problem with this assignment. Why is this case different?

Optionals are a common feature of Swift code. The creators of Swift knew that creating lots of optionals manually would be cumbersome for developers, so they *overloaded* the assignment operator (=) to allow an optional on the lefthand side and an instance of the optional's associated type (**String**, in this case) on the right. ("Overloading" means creating an additional implementation of an operator or function.)

The compiler takes care of the rest, creating the **Optional** instance and putting the assigned **String** in it. The result is that you have a much more concise and convenient way to create and use optionals.

When you need to store a value that may come and go, you should use **Optional**. When you see an optional in code, you know that the value is impermanent – and, as you will see, the compiler will force you to check for a value before trying to use it. This system of purpose-built types and forced checks helps make Swift an expressive, safe language.

Now that you have declared an optional and given it a value, log the value of the optional to the console.

Listing 9.3 Logging the value of the optional to the console

```
var errorCodeString: String?                              nil
errorCodeString = "404"                                   "404"
print(errorCodeString)                                    "Optional("404")\n"
```

(You can ignore the compiler warning that appears; you will see it again later in this book.)

Logging the value of errorCodeString to the console shows Optional("404"). What would happen if you did not give errorCodeString a value? Try it! Comment out the line assigning a value to errorCodeString. (Remember that you can use the keyboard shortcut Command-/ to toggle commenting on and off.)

Listing 9.4 Logging the nil value of the optional to the console

```
var errorCodeString: String?                              nil
// errorCodeString = "404"
print(errorCodeString)                                    "nil\n"
```

Checking the console, you will see that it has logged the value nil.

As you work through this chapter, you might find it helpful to comment this line out periodically so that you can see how variables with a nil value behave. Just be sure to uncomment the line before moving forward.

On its own, logging nil to the console is not very helpful. As a developer, you will often want to know when your variables are nil so that you can execute code based on whether there is a value. In those circumstances, you can use a conditional to check whether a variable's value is nil.

For example, let's say that if some operation generated an error, you would want to assign that error to a new variable and log it to the console. Add the following code to your playground.

Listing 9.5 Adding a condition

```
var errorCodeString: String?                              nil
// errorCodeString = "404"                                "404"
print(errorCodeString)
if errorCodeString != nil {
    let theError = errorCodeString!                       "404"
    print(theError)                                       "404\n"
}
```

You can compare an optional value to nil to determine whether it contains a value, and here you set up a conditional with code that executes if errorCodeString is not nil. (Remember that != means "is not equal to.")

In the body of the conditional, you create a new constant called `theError` to hold the value of `errorCodeString`. To do this, you append `!` to `errorCodeString`. The exclamation mark here does what is called *forced unwrapping*.

Forced unwrapping accesses the value stored inside the **Optional**, which allows you to grab `"404"` and assign it to the constant `theError`. It is called "forced" unwrapping because it tries to access the underlying value whether or not there is actually a value there at all. That is, the `!` assumes there is a value; if there is no value, unwrapping the value in this way would lead to a runtime error.

There can be danger in forced unwrapping. If there is no value inside the optional, your program will trap at runtime. In this case, you check to make sure that `errorCodeString` is not nil, so force-unwrapping it is not dangerous. Nonetheless, we suggest that you use forced unwrapping cautiously and sparingly.

Finally, you log this new constant's value to the console.

What would have happened if you had not unwrapped `errorCodeString`'s value but simply assigned the optional to the `theError` constant? The value of `theError` would still have been logged to the console correctly. So, why unwrap the optional's value and assign it to a constant? The answer requires a better understanding of the optional type.

If you had omitted the exclamation mark at the end of `errorCodeString`, you would have assigned `errorCodeString`, an optional **String**, to the constant `theError`. Both `errorCodeString` and `theError` would have been of type **String?**.

Try it yourself: Delete the exclamation mark, then Option-click `theError`. Observe its inferred type: **String?**. Replace the exclamation mark and Option-click `theError` again. Its inferred type is now just **String**.

So by using the exclamation mark to forcibly unwrap the optional, you are assigning the actual **String** value held by `errorCodeString` to `theError`. In your code, `errorCodeString`'s type is **String?**, and `theError`'s type is **String**. These are not the same types – if you have a **String** variable, you cannot set it to the value of a **String?** without unwrapping the optional.

Creating a constant inside the conditional is a little clunky. Fortunately, there is a better way to conditionally bind an optional's value to a constant. It is called *optional binding*.

Optional Binding

Optional binding is a useful pattern to detect whether an optional contains a value. If there is a value, you assign it to a temporary constant or variable and make it available within a conditional's first branch of execution. This can make your code more concise while also retaining its expressive nature. Here is the basic syntax:

```
if let temporaryConstant = anOptional {
    // Do something with temporaryConstant
} else {
    // There was no value in anOptional – anOptional is nil
}
```

With this syntax in hand, refactor the example above to use optional binding.

Listing 9.6 Optional binding

```
var errorCodeString: String?                          nil
errorCodeString = "404"                               "404"
if errorCodeString != nil {
    let theError = errorCodeString!
if let theError = errorCodeString {
    print(theError)                                   "404\n"
}
```

As you can see, the syntax for optional binding is more or less the same as the syntax that creates a constant within a conditional. The constant theError moves from the body of the conditional to its first line. This makes theError a temporary constant that is available within the first branch of the conditional. In other words, if there is a value within the optional, a temporary constant is made available for use in the block of code that is executed if the condition is evaluated as true.

(Note that you could have declared theError with the var keyword if you needed to manipulate the value inside the first branch of the conditional.)

Also, you no longer forcibly unwrap the optional. If the conversion is successful, then this operation is done for you, and the optional's value is made available in the temporary constant you declared.

Suppose you wanted to convert errorCodeString to its corresponding integer representation. You could accomplish this by nesting if let bindings.

Listing 9.7 Nesting optional binding

```
var errorCodeString: String?                          nil
errorCodeString = "404"                               "404"
if let theError = errorCodeString {
    print(theError)
    if let errorCodeInt = Int(theError) {
        print("\(theError): \(errorCodeInt)")         "404: 404\n"
    }
}
```

Notice that the second if let is within the first, which makes theError available to use in the second optional binding.

Here, you use Int(theError) to initialize a new **Int** instance with the value of theError. But initializing an **Int** from a **String** can fail; for example, the string "Hello!" does not naturally translate to an integer. Therefore, Int(theError) returns an optional, in case the string contains non-numeric characters.

The result of Int(theError) is unwrapped and assigned to errorCodeInt in the second binding, which makes the integer value available for use. You can then use both of these new constants in a call to **print()** to log them to the console.

Nesting optional binding can be convoluted. While it is not *too* bad with just a couple of optionals, you can imagine how complicated this strategy can get if you have several more optionals that need to be unwrapped. Programmers call deeply nested syntax the "Pyramid of Doom," a reference to the many indentation levels.

Thankfully, you can unwrap multiple optionals in a single if let binding. This feature helps you avoid the need for nesting multiple if let calls. Refactor your playground to unwrap both optionals in one line. (We have broken them across two lines to fit on the page.)

Listing 9.8 Unwrapping multiple optionals

```
var errorCodeString: String?                              nil
errorCodeString = "404"                                   "404"
if let theError = errorCodeString,
      let errorCodeInt = Int(theError) {
    if let errorCodeInt = Int(theError) {
    print("\(theError): \(errorCodeInt)")                 "404: 404\n"
    }
}
```

You now unwrap two optionals in a single line with if let theError = errorCodeString, let errorCodeInt = Int(theError). First, errorCodeString is unwrapped, and its value is given to theError. You use Int(theError) to try to convert theError into an **Int**. Because this results in an optional, you next unwrap that optional and bind its value to errorCodeInt.

If either of these bindings returns nil, then the success block of the conditional will not execute. In this case, errorCodeString *does* have a value and theError *can* be successfully unwrapped, because theError can be converted into an integer.

Optional binding can even perform additional checks that work very similarly to what you have already seen with standard if statements. Imagine that you only care about an error code if the value is 404.

Listing 9.9 Optional binding and additional checks

```
var errorCodeString: String?                              nil
errorCodeString = "404"                                   "404"
if let theError = errorCodeString,
      let errorCodeInt = Int(theError),
      errorCodeInt == 404 {
    print("\(theError): \(errorCodeInt)")                 "404: 404\n"
}
```

(Do not overlook the added comma in this code.)

Now, the conditional evaluates to true only if errorCodeInt is equal to 404. And the final clause (errorCodeInt == 404) is only executed if both optionals are successfully unwrapped. Because theError is "404", and that string can be converted to the integer 404, all conditions are met and 404: 404 is logged to the console.

Implicitly Unwrapped Optionals

At this point it is worth mentioning *implicitly unwrapped optionals*, though you will not use them much until we discuss classes and class initialization later in this book. Implicitly unwrapped optionals are like regular optional types, with one important difference: You do not need to unwrap them. How is that the case? It has to do with how you declare them. Take a look at the code below, which refactors the example above to work with an implicitly unwrapped optional.

```
var errorCodeString: String!
errorCodeString = "404"
print(errorCodeString)
```

Here, the optional is declared with !, which signifies that it is an implicitly unwrapped optional. The conditional is removed because using an implicitly unwrapped optional signifies a great deal more confidence than its more humble counterpart. Indeed, much of the power and flexibility associated with the implicitly unwrapped optional is related to the idea that you do not need to unwrap it to access its value.

But note that this power and flexibility comes with some danger: Accessing the value of an implicitly unwrapped optional will result in a runtime error if it does not have a value. For this reason, we suggest that you do not use an implicitly unwrapped optional if you believe that the instance has any chance of becoming nil. Indeed, implicitly unwrapped optionals are so unsafe that Swift will attempt to give you regular optionals if you are not specific about wanting an implicitly unwrapped optional.

Let's revisit the example above to see this in action. Suppose you set `errorCodeString` to be `nil`. What would happen if you declared a constant named `anotherErrorCodeString` with type **String** and tried to assign to it the contents (or lack thereof) of `errorCodeString`? If you were to assign `errorCodeString` to another instance, what type do you think Swift would infer for that new instance, if you were not explicit about the type?

```
var errorCodeString: String! = nil
let anotherErrorCodeString: String = errorCodeString // Will this work?
let yetAnotherErrorCodeString = errorCodeString // Optional? Implicitly unwrapped?
```

For the first question, you would see a trap. If `errorCodeString` is `nil`, assigning that value to `anotherErrorCodeString`, which is of type **String**, results in a runtime error. Why? Because `anotherErrorCodeString` cannot be optional, due to its explicitly declared type.

As for the second question, Swift will infer the safest thing possible: a regular optional. `yetAnotherErrorCodeString` would be a **String?** whose value is `nil`. You would have to unwrap the optional to access its value. This feature makes type inference safe by default – and therefore increases the safety of all your code.

If you want `yetAnotherErrorCodeString` to be an implicitly unwrapped optional, then the compiler requires you to be explicit. You need to declare that the type of optional that you want is implicitly unwrapped, as in `let yetAnotherErrorCodeString: String! = errorCodeString`.

Using implicitly unwrapped optionals is best limited to somewhat special cases. As we indicated, the primary case concerns class initialization, which we will discuss in detail in Chapter 17. For now, you know enough of the basics of implicitly unwrapped optionals to understand what is going on if you find them in the wild.

Optional Chaining

Like optional binding, *optional chaining* provides a mechanism for querying an optional to determine whether it contains a value. One important difference between the two is that optional chaining allows the programmer to chain numerous queries into an optional's value. If each optional in the chain contains a value, then the call to each succeeds, and the entire query chain will return an optional of the expected type. If any optional in the query chain is `nil`, then the entire chain will return `nil`.

Let's begin with a concise example. Imagine that your app has a custom error code. If you encounter a 404, you want to use your custom error code instead, as well as an error description you will display to the user. Add the following to your playground.

Listing 9.10 Optional chaining

```
var errorCodeString: String?                              nil
errorCodeString = "404"                                   "404"
var errorDescription: String?                             nil
if let theError = errorCodeString,
        let errorCodeInt = Int(theError),
        errorCodeInt == 404 {
    print("\(theError): \(errorCodeInt)")
    errorDescription =
            "\(errorCodeInt + 200): resource not found."   "604: resource not found."
}

var upCaseErrorDescription =
        errorDescription?.uppercased()                     "604: RESOURCE NOT FOUND."
```

You add a new `var` named `errorDescription`. Inside the `if let` success block, you create a new interpolated string and assign that instance to `errorDescription`. When you create the interpolated string, you increase 404 to your custom error code value of 604 using `\(errorCodeInt + 200)` (this is arbitrary and theoretically unique to your app). Last, you add some more informative text about the error.

Next, you use optional chaining to create a new instance of the error description in all uppercase text, perhaps to indicate its urgency. This instance is called `upCaseErrorDescription`.

The question mark appended to the end of `errorDescription` signals that this line of code initiates the optional chaining process. If there is no value in `errorDescription`, then there is no string to make uppercase. In that case, `upCaseErrorDescription` would be set to `nil`. (Remember: Optional chaining returns an optional.)

Because `errorDescription` does have a value in it, you made the description uppercase and reassigned that new value to `upCaseErrorDescription`. The results sidebar should display the updated value: `"604: RESOURCE NOT FOUND."`

Modifying an Optional in Place

You can also modify an optional "in place" so that you do not have to create a new variable or constant. Add a call to the **append(_:)** method on upCaseErrorDescription.

Listing 9.11 Modifying in place

```
...
var upCaseErrorDescription =
        errorDescription?.uppercased()                      "604: RESOURCE NOT FOUND."
upCaseErrorDescription?.append(" PLEASE TRY AGAIN.")        ()
upCaseErrorDescription                                      "604: RESOURCE NOT FOUN...
```

The sidebar result does not fit on the page, but it reads "604: RESOURCE NOT FOUND. PLEASE TRY AGAIN."

Modifying an optional in place can be extremely helpful. In this case, all you want to do is update a string inside an optional. You do not need anything returned. If there is a value inside the optional, then you want to add some text to the string. If there is no value, then you do not want to do anything.

This is exactly what modifying an optional in place does. The ? at the end of upCaseErrorDescription works similarly to optional chaining: It exposes the value of the optional if it exists. If upCaseErrorDescription were nil, then the optional would not have been modified because no value would exist to update.

It is worth mentioning that you can also use the ! operator in the code above. This operation would forcibly unwrap the optional – which can be dangerous, as you have learned. If upCaseErrorDescription were nil, then upCaseErrorDescription!.append(" PLEASE TRY AGAIN.") would lead to a runtime crash.

As we said earlier, it is best to use ? most of the time. The ! operator should be used only when you know that the optional will not be nil or that the *only* reasonable action to take if the optional is nil is to crash.

To observe how nil propagates through your program, comment out the assignment of errorCodeString: errorCodeString = "404". Try to understand each change that you see in the sidebar in the context of what you have learned so far. Which other values became nil, and why?

Uncomment the assignment before continuing.

The Nil Coalescing Operator

A common operation when dealing with optionals is to either get the value (if the optional contains a value) or to use some default value if the optional is nil. For example, when extracting the error information from errorDescription, you might want to default to "No error." if the string does not contain an error. You could accomplish this with optional binding.

Listing 9.12 Using optional binding to parse errorDescription

```
...
upCaseErrorDescription?.append(" PLEASE TRY AGAIN.")          ()
upCaseErrorDescription                                        "604: RESOURCE NOT FOUN...
let description: String
if let errorDescription = errorDescription {
    description = errorDescription                            "604: resource not found."
} else {
    description = "No error."
}
```

This is another good time to try commenting out errorCodeString = "404" to see the difference nil makes in the following code. Remember to uncomment the line before continuing.

This technique works, but it has a problem. You had to write a lot of code for what should be a simple operation: Get the value from the optional or use "No error." if the optional is nil. This can be solved via the *nil coalescing operator*: ??. Let's see what that looks like.

Listing 9.13 Using the nil coalescing operator

```
...
let description: String
if let errorDescription = errorDescription {
    description = errorDescription
} else {
    description = "No error."
}

let description = errorDescription ?? "No error."          "604: resource not found."
```

The lefthand side of ?? must be an optional – errorDescription, in this case, which is an optional **String**. The righthand side must be a value of type the optional holds – "No error.", in this case, which is a **String**. If the optional on the lefthand side is nil, ?? returns the value on the righthand side. If the optional is not nil, ?? returns the value contained in the optional.

Try changing errorDescription so that it does not contain an error and confirm that description gets the value "No error.".

Listing 9.14 Changing errorDescription

```
...
errorDescription = nil
let description = errorDescription ?? "No error"
```

Even if you are already a programmer, optionals may be an entirely new concept. Be patient with yourself if they feel strange – you will get lots of practice with them throughout the rest of this book. This chapter was fairly involved, and you learned a lot of new material.

Here is the bottom line: As a developer, you will often need to represent `nil` in an instance. Optionals help you keep track of whether instances are `nil` and provide a mechanism to respond appropriately. If optionals do not quite feel comfortable yet, do not worry. You will be seeing them quite a bit in future chapters.

Bronze Challenge

Optionals are best used for things that can literally be nil. That is, they are useful in representing the complete absence of something.

But nonexistence is not the same as zero. For example, if you are writing code to model a bank account and the user has no balance in a given account, the value `0` is more appropriate than `nil`. The user does not lack an account – what they are missing is money! Take a look at the examples below and select which type would model them best.

- A person's age: **Int** or **Int?**

- A person's middle name: **String** or **String?**

- A person's kids' names: **[String]** or **[String]?** or **[String?]**

Silver Challenge

Earlier in the chapter we told you that accessing an optional's value when it is `nil` will result in a runtime error. Make this mistake by force-unwrapping an optional when it is `nil`. Next, examine the error and understand what the error is telling you.

Gold Challenge

Open your playground from Chapter 8, `Arrays.playground`.

Consult the documentation to find a method on **Array** that will locate the index of `"Go on an Arctic expedition"` in your `bucketList`. This method will return an **Index?**. Unwrap that value and use it to compute the index that is two positions later in the array. Last, use this new index to find the **String** at that position within your `bucketList`.

Look at the documentation for the **String** and **Array** types. What other properties and methods work with optionals? Why?

10
Dictionaries

Chapter 8 introduced you to Swift's **Array** type. The **Array** type is a useful collection when the order of the elements in the collection is important.

But order is not always important. Sometimes you simply want to hold on to a set of information in a container and then retrieve the information as needed. That is what dictionaries are for.

A **Dictionary** is a collection type that organizes its content by *key-value* pairs. The keys in a dictionary map onto values. A key is like the ticket you give to the attendant at a coat check. You hand your ticket over, and the attendant uses it to find your coat. Similarly, you give a key to an instance of the **Dictionary** type, and it returns to you the value associated with that key.

The keys in a **Dictionary** must be unique. This requirement means that every key will uniquely map onto its value. To continue the coat check metaphor, a coat check might have several navy blue coats. So long as each coat has its own ticket, you can be sure that the attendant will be able to find *your* navy blue coat when you return with your ticket.

In this chapter, you will see how to:

- create and initialize a dictionary

- loop through dictionaries

- access and modify dictionaries via their keys

You will also learn more about keys and how they work, especially as they pertain to Swift. Last, you will see how to create arrays out of your dictionary's keys and values.

Creating a Dictionary

The general syntax to create a Swift dictionary is `var dict: Dictionary<Key, Value>`. This code creates a mutable instance of the **Dictionary** type called `dict`. The declarations for what types the dictionary's keys and values accept are inside the angle brackets (`<>`), denoted here by `Key` and `Value`.

The values stored in a dictionary can be of any type, just like the values in an array. The only type requirement for keys in a Swift **Dictionary** is that the type must be *hashable*. You will learn more about hashability in Chapter 25, but the basic concept is that each `Key` type must provide a mechanism to guarantee that its instances are unique. Swift's basic types, such as **String**, **Int**, **Float**, **Double**, and **Bool**, are all hashable.

Before you begin typing code, let's take a look at the different ways you can explicitly declare an instance of **Dictionary**:

```
var dict1: Dictionary<String, Int>
var dict2: [String:Int]
```

Both options yield the same result: an uninitialized **Dictionary** whose keys are **String** instances and whose values are of type **Int**. The second example uses the dictionary literal syntax (`[:]`).

As with Swift's other data types, you can also declare and initialize a dictionary in one line. In that case, you can explicitly declare the types of the keys and values or take advantage of type inference:

```
var companyZIPCode: [String:Int] = ["Big Nerd Ranch": 30307]
var sameCompanyZIPCode = ["Big Nerd Ranch": 30307]
```

Again, these two options yield the same result: a dictionary initialized with a single key-value pair consisting of a **String** key, `"Big Nerd Ranch"`, and an **Int** value, `30307`.

It is useful to take advantage of Swift's type-inference capabilities. Type inference creates code that is more concise but just as expressive. Accordingly, you will stick with type inference in this chapter.

Time to create your own dictionary. Start with a new macOS playground called Dictionary. Declare a dictionary called `movieRatings` and use type inference to initialize it with some data.

Listing 10.1 Creating a dictionary

```
import Cocoa

var str = "Hello, playground"                           ["Tron": 4, "WarGames":...

var movieRatings =
    ["Tron": 4, "WarGames": 5, "Sneakers": 4]
```

(Since dictionaries are not ordered, the sidebar result may show the key-value pairs in a different order each time your code executes.)

You created a mutable dictionary to hold movie ratings using the **Dictionary** literal syntax. Its keys are instances of **String** and represent individual movies. These keys map onto values that are instances of **Int** that represent the ratings of the movies.

As an aside, just as you can create an array literal with no elements using `[]`, you can create a dictionary with no keys or values using `[:]`. As with arrays, this syntax omits anything the compiler could use to infer the key and value types, so that information would have to be declared explicitly.

Accessing and Modifying Values

Now that you have a mutable dictionary, how do you work with it? You will want to read from and modify the dictionary. Begin by using count to get some useful information about your dictionary.

Listing 10.2 Using count

```
var movieRatings =                                      ["Tron": 4, "WarGames":...
        ["Tron": 4, "WarGames": 5, "Sneakers": 4]
movieRatings.count                                       3
```

Now, read a value from the movieRatings dictionary.

Listing 10.3 Reading a value from the dictionary

```
var movieRatings =                                      ["Tron": 4, "WarGames":...
        ["Tron": 4, "WarGames": 5, "Sneakers": 4]
movieRatings.count                                       3
let tronRating = movieRatings["Tron"]                    4
```

The brackets in movieRatings["Tron"] are the subscripting syntax you have seen before. But because dictionaries are not ordered, you do not use an index to find a particular value. Instead, you access values from a dictionary by supplying the key associated with the value you would like to retrieve. In the example above, you supply the key "Tron", so tronRating is set to 4 – the value associated with that key.

Option-click the tronRating instance to get more information (Figure 10.1).

Figure 10.1 Option-clicking tronRating

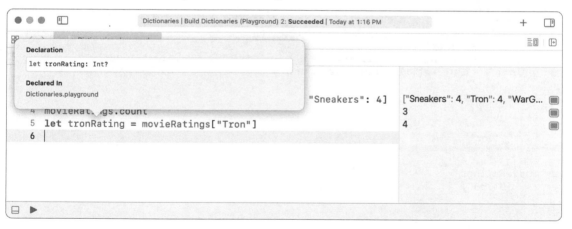

Xcode tells you that its type is **Int?**, but movieRatings has type **[String: Int]**. Why the discrepancy? When you subscript a **Dictionary** instance for a given key, the dictionary will return an optional matching the type of the **Dictionary**'s values. This is because the **Dictionary** type needs a way to tell you that the value you asked for is not present. For example, you have not rated *Primer* yet, so let primerRating = movieRatings["Primer"] would result in primerRating having type **Int?** and being set to nil.

A dictionary's keys are constants: They cannot be mutated. The informal contract a dictionary makes is something like "Give me a value, and a key to store it by, and I'll remember both. Come back with the key later, and I'll look up its value for you." If a key were able to mutate, that could break the dictionary's ability to find its related value later.

But values *can* be mutated. Modify a value in your dictionary of movie ratings:

Listing 10.4 Modifying a value

```
...
movieRatings.count                                         3
let tronRating = movieRatings["Tron"]                      4
movieRatings["Sneakers"] = 5                               5
movieRatings                                               ["Sneakers": 5, "WarGam...
```

As you can see, the value associated with the key "Sneakers" is now 5.

There is another useful way to update values associated with a dictionary's keys: the **updateValue(_:forKey:)** method. It takes two arguments: The first, value, takes the new value. The second, forKey, specifies the key whose value you would like to change.

There is one small caveat: **updateValue(_:forKey:)** returns an optional, because the key may not exist in the dictionary. But that actually makes this method more useful, because it gives you a handle on the last value to which the key mapped, using optional binding. Let's see this in action.

Listing 10.5 Updating a value

```
...
movieRatings["Sneakers"] = 5                               5
movieRatings                                               ["Sneakers": 5, "WarGam...
let oldRating: Int? =                                      4
      movieRatings.updateValue(5, forKey: "Tron")
if let lastRating = oldRating, let currentRating =
      movieRatings["Tron"] {
   print("old rating: \(lastRating)")                      "old rating: 4\n"
   print("current rating: \(currentRating)")               "current rating: 5\n"
}
```

Adding and Removing Values

Now that you have seen how to update a value, let's look at how you can add or remove key-value pairs. Begin by adding a value.

Listing 10.6 Adding a value

```
...
if let lastRating = oldRating, let currentRating =
        movieRatings["Tron"] {
    print("old rating: \(lastRating)")                    "old rating: 4\n"
    print("current rating: \(currentRating)")             "current rating: 5\n"
}
movieRatings["Hackers"] = 5                                5
```

Here, you add a new key-value pair to your dictionary using the syntax movieRatings["Hackers"] = 5. You use the assignment operator to associate a value (in this case, 5) with the new key ("Hackers").

Next, remove the entry for *Sneakers*.

Listing 10.7 Removing a value

```
...
if let lastRating = oldRating, let currentRating =
        movieRatings["Tron"] {
    ...
}
movieRatings["Hackers"] = 5                                5
movieRatings.removeValue(forKey: "Sneakers")              5
```

The method **removeValue(forKey:)** takes a key as an argument and removes the key-value pair that matches what you provide. Now, movieRatings has no entry for *Sneakers*.

Additionally, this method returns the value the key was associated with, if the key is found and removed successfully. In the example above, you could have typed let removedRating: Int? = movieRatings.removeValue(forKey: "Sneakers"). Because **removeValue(forKey:)** returns an optional of the type that was removed, removedRating would be an optional **Int**. Placing the old value in a variable or constant like this can be handy if you need to do something with the old value.

However, you do not have to assign the method's return value to anything. If the key is found in the dictionary, then the key-value pair is removed whether or not you assign the old value to a variable.

You can also remove a key-value pair by setting a key's value to nil.

Listing 10.8 Setting the key's value to nil

```
...
if let lastRating = oldRating, let currentRating =
        movieRatings["Tron"] {
    ...
}
movieRatings["Hackers"] = 5                                5
movieRatings.removeValue(forKey: "Sneakers")
movieRatings["Sneakers"] = nil                            nil
```

The result is essentially the same, but this strategy does not return the removed key's value.

Looping over a Dictionary

You can use for-in to loop through a dictionary. Swift's **Dictionary** type provides a convenient mechanism to loop through the key-value pairs for each entry. This mechanism breaks each entry into its constituent parts by providing temporary constants representing the key and the value. These constants are placed within a tuple that the for-in loop can access inside its body.

Listing 10.9 Looping through your dictionary

```
...
movieRatings["Hackers"] = 5                                    5
movieRatings["Sneakers"] = nil                                 nil
for (key, value) in movieRatings {
    print("The movie \(key) was rated \(value).")              (3 times)
}
```

Notice how you use string interpolation to combine the values of key and value into a single string. You should see that each movie and its rating was logged to the console.

You do not have to access both the key and the value of each entry. A **Dictionary** has properties for its keys and values that can be accessed separately if you only need the information from one.

Listing 10.10 Accessing just the keys

```
...
movieRatings["Sneakers"] = nil                                 nil
for (key, value) in movieRatings {
    print("The movie \(key) was rated \(value).")              (3 times)
}
for movie in movieRatings.keys {
    print("User has rated \(movie).")                          (3 times)
}
```

This new loop iterates through movieRatings's keys (in an unpredictable order, since dictionaries are unordered) and logs each movie the user has rated to the console.

Immutable Dictionaries

Creating an immutable dictionary works much the same as creating an immutable array. You use the let keyword to tell the Swift compiler that you do not want your instance of **Dictionary** to change. Convert movieRatings into an immutable dictionary by changing var to let in its declaration (you will change it back shortly).

Listing 10.11 Making the dictionary immutable

```
~~var~~ let movieRatings =                                    ["Tron": 4, "WarGames":...
        ["Tron": 4, "WarGames": 5, "Sneakers": 4]
...
```

The playground should now show an error on each line where a change has been made to the dictionary, regardless of the nature of the change. An immutable dictionary cannot be modified in any way.

Go ahead and change the declaration back to var to make the errors go away.

Listing 10.12 Making the dictionary mutable again

```
~~let~~ var movieRatings =                                    ["Tron": 4, "WarGames":...
        ["Tron": 4, "WarGames": 5, "Sneakers": 4]
...
```

Translating a Dictionary to an Array

Sometimes it is helpful to pull information out of a dictionary and put it into an array. Suppose, for example, that you want to list all the movies that have been rated (without their ratings).

In this case, it makes sense to create an instance of the **Array** type with the keys from your dictionary.

Listing 10.13 Sending keys to an array

```
...
for movie in movieRatings.keys {
    print("User has rated \(movie).")              (3 times)
}
let watchedMovies = Array(movieRatings.keys)       ["WarGames", "Tron", "H...
```

You use the Array() syntax to create a new **[String]** instance. This is not the first time that you have initialized a new instance of a type with a value of another type. You will learn how this works under the hood in Chapter 17, but for now it is enough to recognize that some types can be initialized by passing arguments into this parenthetical syntax.

In this case, inside the (), you pass the dictionary's keys. The result is that watchedMovies is a constant instance of the **Array** type representing all the movies a user has in the movieRatings dictionary.

Silver Challenge

It is not uncommon to place instances of the `Array` type inside a dictionary. Create a dictionary that represents a league of sports teams. Each dictionary key will be the name of an individual team (three teams is enough), and each value will be an array of the names of five players on that team. (You can make up the team and player names.)

Nesting data structures like this allows you to organize hierarchical data within a single object.

In the console, log only the dictionary's player names. Your result should look something like the output below. (We have formatted the array so that the names fit on the page. Your array of names may appear in a single long line.)

```
The NWSL has the following players: ["Jane", "Michaela", "Rachel", "Allysha",
    "Janine", "Sydney", "Toni", "Shelina", "Emily", "Chioma", "Kailen",
    "McKenzie", "Thaisa", "Shea", "Jen"]
```

Gold Challenge

Combine your knowledge of dictionaries with some of the previous lessons in this book.

Output the members of each team with formatting that looks like this:

```
Sky Blue FC members:
Kailen
McKenzie
Thaisa
Shea
Jen

Orlando Pride members:
Sydney
Toni
Shelina
Emily
Chioma

Houston Dash members:
Jane
Michaela
Rachel
Allysha
Janine
```

Each team's members should appear one per line, with no other punctuation. There should be an additional new line between teams. For added difficulty, make your solution work using only one `print()` statement (inside a loop is fine). Writing extremely concise code in this way often harms your ability to read the code later, but it can be fun and satisfying to flex your understanding in a playground environment like this.

Some hints: Search the documentation for how to represent special characters in `String` literals. (For example, how do you add a tab or new line in a string?) Also, look at the documentation for the `print()` function. There are different ways you can call the function to control its output. Lastly, look at the documentation for the `Array` type. What are the different ways you can make a single string from an array's elements?

11

Sets

Swift provides a third collection type called **Set**. **Set** is not frequently used, but we do not think that this should be the case. This chapter will introduce **Set** and show off some of its unique advantages.

What Is a Set?

A **Set** is an unordered collection of distinct instances. This definition sets it apart from an **Array**, which is ordered and can accommodate repeated values.

A **Set** has some similarities to a **Dictionary**, but it is also a little different. Like a dictionary, a set's values are unordered within the collection. Also, like a dictionary's keys, the values in a **Set** must be unique; a value can only be added to a set once. To ensure that elements are unique, **Set** requires that its elements follow the same rule as a dictionary's keys – being hashable (which you will learn about in Chapter 25).

However, while dictionary values are accessed via their corresponding key, a set only stores individual elements, not key-value pairs.

Table 11.1 summarizes Swift's three collection types.

Table 11.1 Comparing Swift's collections

Collection Type	Ordered?	Unique?	Stores
Array	Yes	No	Elements
Dictionary	No	Keys	Key-value pairs
Set	No	Elements	Elements

Getting a Set

Create a new macOS playground called Groceries and create an instance of **Set**.

Listing 11.1 Creating a set

```
import Cocoa

var str = "Hello, playground"

var groceryList = Set<String>(["Apples", "Oranges"])        {"Apples", "Oranges"}
```

Your sidebar results might show the elements of the set in a different order. That is fine – sets are unordered, so the order shown is irrelevant.

Here you make an instance of **Set** and declare that it will hold instances of the **String** type. It is a mutable **Set** called groceryList and has two elements: apples and oranges. You initialized your set with an array. (As with other types, a set can also be immutable, and you could have declared it uninitialized. Also, like many other types, you can initialize an empty set for later use.)

Set does not have its own literal syntax like **Array** and **Dictionary**. However, recall from learning about numbers in Chapter 4 that a value like 1.21 could be either a **Double** or a **Float**, and the compiler will infer it to be a **Double** unless you specify otherwise. Set can borrow array literal syntax in the same way. Update your playground to use an explicit **Set** type annotation with array literal syntax:

Listing 11.2 Creating a set using array literal syntax

```
var groceryList = Set<String>(["Apples", "Oranges"])
var groceryList: Set = ["Apples", "Oranges"]        {"Oranges", "Apples"}
```

This code explicitly declares groceryList to be a **Set**, then uses the **Array** literal syntax to create an instance of **Set**. The compiler would otherwise infer that a collection created with [] syntax was an **Array**. However, the compiler can still infer the type of instance that the set will contain: in this case, strings.

In earlier chapters, you relied heavily on type inference for your collection types. **Set** does not offer quite as much flexibility to use type inference, but you do have a few choices for how to declare your instances. Which form you choose to declare your collection type instances does not matter. Choose a style that you find comfortable and readable. It should be a goal of any developer to write code that they – and other developers they work with – can easily read and understand.

You can add groceries to your groceryList using the **insert(_:)** method.

Listing 11.3 Adding to a set

```
var groceryList: Set = ["Apples", "Oranges"]        {"Apples", "Oranges"}
groceryList.insert("Kiwi")                          (inserted true, memberA...
groceryList.insert("Pears")                         (inserted true, memberA...
```

The results sidebar shows something like (inserted true, memberAfterInsert "Pears") for each insertion into your groceryList. This is because **insert(_:)** returns a tuple including a Boolean (indicating whether the instance was successfully inserted into the set) and the instance that was (or was not) inserted.

Now `groceryList` has a few items in it. As with arrays and dictionaries, you can loop through a set to see its contents.

Listing 11.4 Looping through a set

```
var groceryList: Set = ["Apples", "Oranges"]              {"Apples", "Oranges"}
groceryList.insert("Kiwi")                                (inserted true, memberA...
groceryList.insert("Pears")                               (inserted true, memberA...

for food in groceryList {
    print(food)                                           (4 times)
}
```

Each item in your `groceryList` is logged to the console.

Seeing that console output, you might remember that you already have pears at home. You can remove them from your set with **remove()**:

Listing 11.5 Removing an element from a set

```
...
for food in groceryList {
    print(food)                                           (4 times)
}

groceryList.remove("Pears")                               "Pears"
```

Working with Sets

Now that you have an instance of **Set**, you might be wondering what to do with it. The **Set** offers a number of methods that allow you to work on sets alone or in combination with another set – or, sometimes, a different collection type. Some (but not all) of these operations are also available for arrays; most are not available for dictionaries. The features of the various types are streamlined for their most common use cases.

For example, you might want to know if your `groceryList` contains a particular item. The **Set** type provides a method called **contains(_:)** that looks inside a set instance for a particular item.

Listing 11.6 Has bananas?

```
...
for food in groceryList {
    print(food)                                           (3 times)
}

groceryList.remove("Pears")                               "Pears"
let hasBananas = groceryList.contains("Bananas")          false
```

`hasBananas` is `false`; your `groceryList` set does not have `"Bananas"` in it.

Unions

Often, you will want to compare one set to another set or an array. For example, suppose you bump into a friend while you are shopping. While talking about the things in your lists, you decide to compare them.

First, you wonder what you would have if you combined your separate grocery lists into a new one, leaving out the duplicate groceries. You can do that with **Set**'s **union(_:)** method:

Listing 11.7 Combining sets

```
...
for food in groceryList {
    print(food)                                    (3 times)
}

groceryList.remove("Pears")                        "Pears"
let hasBananas = groceryList.contains("Bananas")   false
let friendsGroceryList =                           {"Cereal", "Oranges", "...
        Set(["Bananas", "Cereal", "Milk", "Oranges"])
let sharedList = groceryList.union(friendsGroceryList)  {"Cereal", "Apples", "P...
```

You add a new constant **Set** instance representing your friend's grocery list and use the **union(_:)** method to combine the two sets. **union(_:)** takes a list of values as its argument and compares the list to its own values. The return value is a **Set** that includes the elements of both collections, less any duplicates.

So you can pass arrays and sets to **union(_:)** and get back a set with every element that appears in either of the input collections.

Here, sharedList is a **Set** that contains the unique elements of groceryList and friendsGroceryList. Figure 11.1 depicts the union of the two sets.

Figure 11.1 Union of two sets

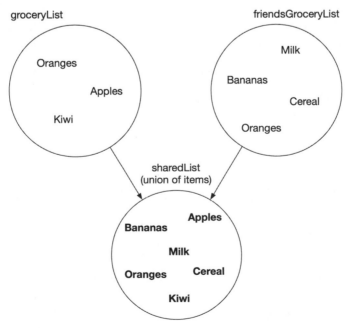

Intersections

The **union(_:)** method eliminates duplicates. What if, instead, you want a list of just the duplicates – the elements that appear in both sets? Compare your grocery list and your friend's list using the **intersection(_:)** method to identify the duplicate items.

Listing 11.8 Intersecting sets

```
...
let friendsGroceryList =                                  {"Cereal", "Oranges", "...
      Set(["Bananas", "Cereal", "Milk", "Oranges"])
let sharedList = groceryList.union(friendsGroceryList)    {"Cereal", "Apples", "P...

let duplicateItems =                                      {"Oranges"}
      groceryList.intersection(friendsGroceryList)
```

Set's **intersection(_:)** method identifies the items that are present in both collections and returns those duplicated items in a new **Set** instance. Figure 11.2 shows this relationship. In this case, you and your friend both have oranges in your grocery lists.

Figure 11.2 Intersecting sets

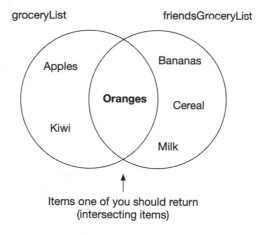

Items one of you should return
(intersecting items)

Disjoint

You have seen how to combine two sets into a new, all-inclusive set via the **union(_:)** method. You also used the **intersection(_:)** method to find the common elements of two sets and place them into a new set. What if you just want to know whether two sets contain any common elements?

The **isDisjoint(with:)** method checks whether two sets exclusively contain different items.

Listing 11.9 Detecting intersections in sets

```
...
let duplicateItems =                              {"Oranges"}
      groceryList.intersection(friendsGroceryList)

let disjoint =                                    false
      groceryList.isDisjoint(with: friendsGroceryList)
```

Set's **isDisjoint(with:)** method returns true if no members of the set (here, groceryList) are in the sequence provided to **isDisjoint(with:)**'s argument (here, friendsGroceryList) and false if there are any members in common. In this case, disjoint is false, because both sets include "Oranges".

There are other ways to compare grocery lists and other sets. For example, you could compute the **symmetricDifference(_:)**, which would tell you about all the items that appear in one and only one of your lists (Figure 11.3).

Figure 11.3 Two sets' symmetric difference

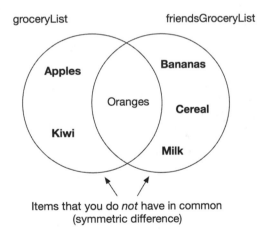

You make a note to look up the **Set** documentation for some light bedtime reading later, to find out what other interesting methods sets can use to compare their contents that arrays and dictionaries cannot. But for now, it is getting late, so you go home to enjoy your fruit salad.

Moving Between Types

As you have seen, each collection type has a feature set appropriate to the type's primary uses: arrays as ordered lists, dictionaries as key-value pairs, and sets modeling mathematical sets as bags of unique values. Some of these types can be initialized with data from the others. It will be especially common for you to want to compare the data from two arrays in a way that only sets support. The good news is that you can create sets from your arrays – but you must bear in mind the differences between those types.

For example, imagine playing some games with friends after you arrive home from your grocery trip. Create an array of players and an array to track who won each game:

Listing 11.10 Playing games

```
...
let players = ["Anna", "Vijay", "Jenka"]              ["Anna", "Vijay", "Jenka"]
let winners = ["Jenka", "Jenka", "Vijay", "Jenka"]   ["Jenka", "Jenka", "Vij...
```

Jenka won three games and Vijay has won one. Because values can repeated in arrays, an array is a suitable type for tracking who won each game.

Suppose you want to know who has not won any games yet. **Array** does not, on its own, have a good way to tell you that. But the **Set** type has a method, **subtracting(_:)**, that will give you a set that represents what is left when you subtract the values in one set from another set. So you could subtract the winners from the players to see who has not yet won a game.

But you don't have sets. You have arrays. No problem! Create two new arrays by initializing them with your sets:

Listing 11.11 Initializing sets using arrays

```
...
let players = ["Anna", "Vijay", "Jenka"]              ["Anna", "Vijay", "Jenka"]
let winners = ["Jenka", "Jenka", "Vijay", "Jenka"]   ["Jenka", "Jenka", "Vij...

let playerSet = Set(players)                          {"Jenka", "Vijay", "Anna"}
let winnerSet = Set(winners)                          {"Vijay", "Jenka"}
```

Here, you create two instances of **Set** and initialize them with the data from instances of **Array**. Because the source arrays were of type **Array<String>**, the compiler will infer the types of the new sets to be **Set<String>**. Notice that winnerSet only contains two values, because values in a set must be unique. Also, because sets are unordered, the names may appear in a different order in the playground results than they did in the source arrays.

Since the set is unordered and does not contain duplicates, winnerSet represents the list of players who have won at least one game, rather than the list of players who won *each* game.

Now, to find out who has not won any games yet, you can subtract the `winnerSet` from the `playerSet`:

Listing 11.12 Subtracting one set from another

```
...
let players = ["Anna", "Vijay", "Jenka"]                    ["Anna", "Vijay", "Jenka"]
let winners = ["Jenka", "Jenka", "Vijay", "Jenka"]          ["Jenka", "Jenka", "Vij...

let playerSet = Set(players)                                {"Jenka", "Vijay", "Anna"}
let winnerSet = Set(winners)                                {"Vijay", "Jenka"}

playerSet.subtracting(winnerSet)                            {"Anna"}
```

Anna, being the only value in the `playerSet` that is not also in the `winnerSet`, is the only player who has not won any games yet. Figure 11.4 illustrates the subtraction:

Figure 11.4 Subtracting sets

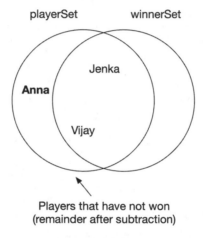

Players that have not won
(remainder after subtraction)

You can also go the other way, creating a set from an array using code like `let players2 = Array(playerSet)`. But note that if you do, the order of the items in the resulting array may be different every time you run your code, since values from the set will be copied to the array in no particular order.

You have now met the most commonly used data types in the Swift standard library. In the coming chapters, you will build your experience working with these types and the methods on them. You will also implement your own functions and methods – and then begin defining your own custom data types.

Bronze Challenge

Consider the following code that models the cities two people have visited as sets.

```
let myCities: Set = ["Atlanta", "Chicago", "Jacksonville", "New York", "Denver"]
let yourCities: Set = ["Chicago", "Denver", "Jacksonville"]
```

Find a method on **Set** that returns a **Bool** indicating whether myCities contains all the cities contained by yourCities. (Hint: This relationship would make myCities a *superset* of yourCities.)

Silver Challenge

In this chapter, you used methods like **union(_:)** and **intersection(_:)** to create new sets. Sometimes you may prefer to modify an existing instance instead of creating a new one.

Look through the **Set** documentation and rework the examples in the chapter for **union(_:)** and **intersection(_:)** using methods that mutate the set directly.

12
Functions

A function is a named set of code that is used to accomplish some specific task. The function's name describes the task the function performs. You have already used some functions, such as `print()`, which is a function provided to you by Swift. Other functions are created in code you write.

Functions execute code. Some functions define *arguments* that you can use to pass in data to help the function do its work. Some functions *return* something after they have completed their work. You might think of a function as a little machine. You turn it on and it chugs along, doing its work. You can feed it data and, if it is built to do so, it will return a new chunk of data that results from its work.

Functions are an extremely important part of programming. Indeed, a program is mostly a collection of related functions that combine to accomplish some purpose. So, there is a lot to cover in this chapter. Take your time and make sure that you are comfortable with each new concept before moving on.

Let's start with some examples.

A Basic Function

Create a new macOS playground called Functions and enter the code below.

Listing 12.1 Defining a function

```
import Cocoa

var str = "Hello, playground"

func printGreeting() {
    print("Hello, playground.")
}
printGreeting()
```

Here, you define a function with the `func` keyword followed by the name of the function: `printGreeting()`. The parentheses are empty because this function does not take any arguments. (More on arguments soon.)

The opening brace ({) denotes the beginning of the function's implementation. This is where you write the code that describes how the function will perform its work. When the function is called, the code inside the braces is executed.

The `printGreeting()` function is fairly simple. You have one line of code that uses `print()` to log the string `Hello, playground.` to the console.

Finally, you *call* the function to execute the code inside it. To do this, you enter its name, `printGreeting()`. Calling the function executes its code, and `Hello, playground.` is logged to the console.

Now that you have written and executed a simple function, it is time to move on to more sophisticated varieties.

Function Parameters

Functions take on more life when they have *parameters*. A function's parameters name the inputs that the function accepts, and the function takes the data passed to its parameters to execute a task or produce a result.

Create a function that prints a more personal greeting by using a parameter.

Listing 12.2 Using a parameter

```
func printGreeting() {
    print("Hello, playground.")
}
printGreeting()

func printPersonalGreeting(name: String) {
    print("Hello, \(name). Welcome to your playground.")
}
printPersonalGreeting(name: "Step")
```

printPersonalGreeting(name: String) has a single parameter, as indicated in the parentheses directly after the function name. The parameter is called name, and it is an instance of the **String** type. You specify the type after the : that follows the parameter's name, just as you specify the types of variables and constants. When it is called, the function will declare its own new constant called name to store a copy of the value provided by the caller.

When you call a function, you include the parameter name and a value of the correct type, called an *argument*. (By the way, although the terms "parameter" and "argument" technically have different meanings, people often use them interchangeably.) If you tried to pass an argument of some other type, the compiler would give you an error telling you that the type you passed in was incorrect. This is an example of type safety – the compiler's insistence that all uses of a variable agree on its type.

In this case, the argument passed to the parameter name must be an instance of **String**. That string value will be interpolated into the string that is logged to the console. Check it out: Your console should say Hello, Step. Welcome to your playground.

Functions can – and often do – take multiple arguments. Write a new function that does a little math.

Listing 12.3 A function for division

```
...
func printPersonalGreeting(name: String) {
    print("Hello, \(name). Welcome to your playground.")
}
printPersonalGreeting(name: "Step")

func divisionDescriptionFor(numerator: Double, denominator: Double) {
    print("\(numerator) divided by \(denominator) is \(numerator / denominator)")
}
divisionDescriptionFor(numerator: 9.0, denominator: 3.0)
```

The function **divisionDescriptionFor(numerator:denominator:)** describes some basic division constructed from the instances of the **Double** type that are supplied to the function's two parameters: numerator and denominator. Note that you did some math within the \() of the string printed to the console. You should see 9.0 divided by 3.0 is 3.0 logged to the console.

Parameter names

As you have seen, parameter names are included when you call the function and are available for use within the body of the function. Sometimes it is useful to have different parameter names for these two uses: one name for when you call the function, and a different name within the function's body. A parameter name used only when the function is called is known as an *external* parameter.

External parameters can make your functions more readable – provided you choose the names well. Your goal for all parameter names (as for all your code) should be to make them informative and readable. At the moment, the visible parameter name when you call `printPersonalGreeting(name:)` is informative, but it is not very readable. You should typically aim for your code to read like something you might say while speaking, but you probably would never say something like "Print personal greeting name Step."

Making your code readable and informative will make it easier to follow. For example, if a function is going to be used in some other file in your application's code base, and the function's implementation is not immediately visible or intuitive, it could be difficult to infer what values to give to the function's parameters. This would make the function less useful, so it can be helpful to use more descriptive external parameter names in your function.

Update `printPersonalGreeting(name:)` to have an external parameter name that is different from its internal parameter name to make calling the function more readable.

Listing 12.4 Using explicit parameter names

```
...
func printPersonalGreeting(name: String) {
func printPersonalGreeting(to name: String) {
    print("Hello, \(name). Welcome to your playground.")
}
printPersonalGreeting(name: "Step")
printPersonalGreeting(to: "Step")

func divisionDescriptionFor(numerator: Double, denominator: Double) {
    print("\(numerator) divided by \(denominator) is \(numerator / denominator)")
}
divisionDescriptionFor(numerator: 9.0, denominator: 3.0)
```

Now `printPersonalGreeting(to:)` has an external parameter, `to`, that you use when you call the function: `printPersonalGreeting(to: "Step")`. This parameter helps the function read more like you would speak: "Print personal greeting to Step."

Note that you still use `name` within the function's definition. `name` has a clearer meaning within the implementation of the function than `to` would. It would be a little confusing if your implementation read `print("Hello, \(to). Welcome to your playground.")`.

You may have noticed that there is a preposition at the end of **divisionDescriptionFor** and a preposition inside **printPersonalGreeting(to:)**. This is not accidental: Prepositions often make function names more readable. The Swift naming guidelines suggest that if a function has multiple parameters that formulate a single concept, then the preposition should be placed at the end of the function name.

This is the case with **divisionDescriptionFor(numerator:denominator:)**, because two inputs are combined in the division operation. On the other hand, **printPersonalGreeting(to:)** does not have multiple parameters, so the preposition should be placed within the parentheses as an external parameter name.

Naming functions and parameters can be tricky, and it is more art than science. As we said, it is advisable to choose function and parameter names that are readable and informative. You should also strive to formulate grammatical phrases with your code. Last, you should always consider how easy it is to type out and call your functions.

Default parameter values

All of a function's parameters must be provided with a value when the function is called. As the caller, you provide values by passing in arguments.

Swift's parameters can also take default values. If a parameter has a default value, you can omit that argument when calling the function (in which case, as you might expect, the function will use the parameter's default value).

Go ahead and add one to your division function. (Note that we have broken the call to **print()** across two lines to make it fit on the page. You should enter it on one line.)

Listing 12.5 Adding a default parameter value

```
...
func divisionDescriptionFor(numerator: Double, denominator: Double) {
    print("\(numerator) divided by \(denominator) is \(numerator / denominator)")
}
func divisionDescriptionFor(numerator: Double,
                            denominator: Double,
                            withPunctuation punctuation: String = ".") {

    print("\(numerator) divided by \(denominator) is
            \(numerator / denominator)\(punctuation)")
}
divisionDescriptionFor(numerator: 9.0, denominator: 3.0)
divisionDescriptionFor(numerator: 9.0, denominator: 3.0, withPunctuation: "!")
```

Now the function has three parameters:
divisionDescriptionFor(numerator:denominator:withPunctuation:). Notice the new code, punctuation: String = ".". You add a new parameter for punctuation, including its expected type, and also give it a default value via the = "." syntax. This means that the string created by the function will conclude with a period by default.

Your two function calls illustrate how the default value works. To use the default, as in your first function call, you can simply omit the final parameter. Or, as in your second function call, you can substitute a new punctuation mark for the default value by passing in a new argument. The first call to the **divisionDescriptionFor(numerator:denominator:withPunctuation:)** function logs the description with a period, and the second logs the description with an exclamation point (Figure 12.1).

Figure 12.1 Default and explicit punctuation

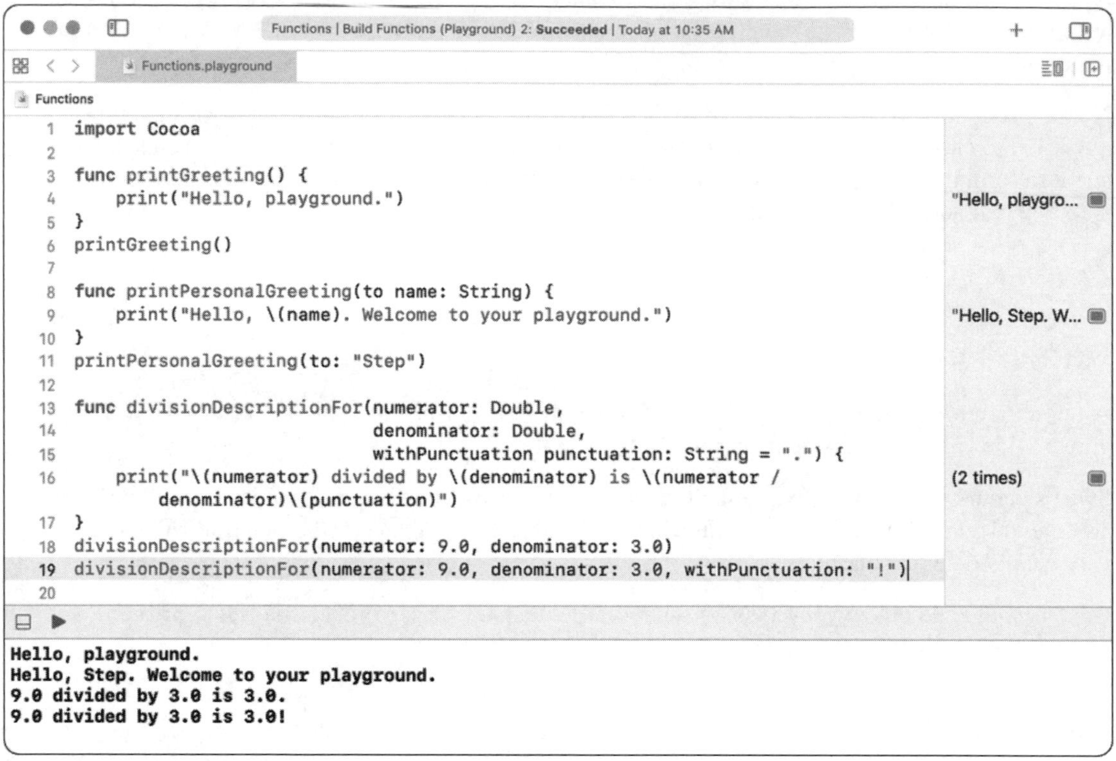

```
●  ●  ●    ▣                  Functions | Build Functions (Playground) 2: Succeeded | Today at 10:35 AM                    +      ⬚

▦   <  >      ▴ Functions.playground                                                                                      ≡▣ | ⊞

▴ Functions

  1   import Cocoa
  2
  3   func printGreeting() {
  4       print("Hello, playground.")                                                                        "Hello, playgro... ▣
  5   }
  6   printGreeting()
  7
  8   func printPersonalGreeting(to name: String) {
  9       print("Hello, \(name). Welcome to your playground.")                                               "Hello, Step. W... ▣
 10   }
 11   printPersonalGreeting(to: "Step")
 12
 13   func divisionDescriptionFor(numerator: Double,
 14                               denominator: Double,
 15                               withPunctuation punctuation: String = ".") {
 16       print("\(numerator) divided by \(denominator) is \(numerator /                                     (2 times)          ▣
             denominator)\(punctuation)")
 17   }
 18   divisionDescriptionFor(numerator: 9.0, denominator: 3.0)
 19   divisionDescriptionFor(numerator: 9.0, denominator: 3.0, withPunctuation: "!")|
 20

🗖  ▶

Hello, playground.
Hello, Step. Welcome to your playground.
9.0 divided by 3.0 is 3.0.
9.0 divided by 3.0 is 3.0!
```

In-out parameters

Sometimes there is a reason to have a function modify the value of an argument. *In-out parameters* allow a function's impact on a variable to live beyond the function's body.

Say you have a function that will take an error message as an argument and will append some information based on certain conditions. Enter this code in your playground.

Listing 12.6 An in-out parameter

```
...
var error = "The request failed:"
func appendErrorCode(_ code: Int, toErrorString errorString: inout String) {
    if code == 400 {
        errorString += " bad request."
    }
}
appendErrorCode(400, toErrorString: &error)
print(error)
```

The function **appendErrorCode(_:toErrorString:)** has two parameters. The first is the error code that the function will compare against, which expects an instance of **Int**. Notice that you gave this parameter an external name of _, which has a special meaning in Swift. Using _ in front of a parameter name will suppress the external name when calling the function. Because its name is already at the end of the function name, there is no reason for the parameter name to be used in the call.

The second is an inout parameter – denoted by the inout keyword – named toErrorString. This parameter expects an instance of **String** as its argument. toErrorString is an external parameter name used when calling the function, while errorString is an internal parameter name used within the function.

The inout keyword is added prior to **String** to express that the function expects to modify the original value. It does this by taking as its argument not a copy of the passed-in value, but a reference to the original. This way, any changes it makes to the string affect the original string, and those changes will remain after the function is done executing.

When you call the function, the variable you pass into the inout parameter must be preceded by an ampersand (&) to acknowledge that you are providing shared access to your variable instead of just a copy of it and that you understand that the variable's value may be directly modified by the function. Here, the function modifies errorString to read The request failed: bad request., which you should see printed to the console.

Note that in-out parameters cannot have default values. Also, in-out parameters are not the same as a function returning a value. Lastly, because in-out parameters grant shared access to a variable, you cannot pass a constant or literal value into an in-out parameter. If you want your function to produce something, there is a more elegant way to accomplish that goal.

Returning from a Function

Functions can give you information after they finish executing the code inside their implementation. This information is called the *return* of the function. In fact, this is often the purpose of a function: to do some work and return some data. Make your `divisionDescriptionFor(numerator:denominator:withPunctuation:)` function return an instance of the **String** type instead of simply printing a string to the console.

Listing 12.7 Returning a string

```
...
func divisionDescriptionFor(numerator: Double,
                            denominator: Double,
                            withPunctuation punctuation: String = ".") -> String {

    print("\(numerator) divided by \(denominator) is
          \(numerator / denominator)\(punctuation)")

    return "\(numerator) divided by \(denominator) is
           \(numerator / denominator)\(punctuation)"
}
divisionDescriptionFor(numerator: 9.0, denominator: 3.0)
divisionDescriptionFor(numerator: 9.0, denominator: 3.0, withPunctuation: "!")
...
```

The behavior of this new function is very similar to your earlier implementation, with an important twist: This new implementation returns a value to the code that called it. This *return value* is denoted by the -> syntax at the end of the function signature, which indicates that the function will return an instance of the type that follows the arrow.

Your function returns an instance of the **String** type. The return keyword tells the program "Stop executing this function and resume the calling code where it left off." If there is a value to the right of the return keyword, that value will be handed back to the calling code. The type of this value must be the same as the declared return type of the function.

When there is no value to return to the caller, a function will implicitly return at the end of its *scope* (at the closing curly brace that ends the function body – more on scope in just a moment). This is why your previous functions have not needed to explicitly return so far. You will learn more about implicit and explicit returns from functions in Chapter 13.

Because your `divisionDescriptionFor(numerator:denominator:withPunctuation:)` function no longer contains a call to **print()**, your calls to it no longer produce console output. But it returns a **String**, and **print()** accepts **String** arguments – so you can call your division function nested within a call to **print()** to log the string instance to the console.

Listing 12.8 Nesting function calls

```
...
print(divisionDescriptionFor(numerator: 9.0, denominator: 3.0))
print(divisionDescriptionFor(numerator: 9.0, denominator: 3.0, withPunctuation: "!"))
```

When one function call is nested within another like this, they are executed from the innermost function to the outermost. In this case, `divisionDescriptionFor(numerator:denominator:withPunctuation:)` will be executed by the program first, and then its `String` return value will be passed as the argument to `print()`.

Nested Function Definitions and Scope

Swift's function definitions can also be nested. Nested functions are declared and implemented within the definition of another function. The nested function is not available outside the enclosing function. This feature is useful when you need a function to do some work, but only within another function. Let's look at an example.

Listing 12.9 Nested functions

```
...
func areaOfTriangleWith(base: Double, height: Double) -> Double {
    let rectangle = base * height
    func divide() -> Double {
        return rectangle / 2
    }
    return divide()
}
print(areaOfTriangleWith(base: 3.0, height: 5.0))
```

The function `areaOfTriangleWith(base:height:)` takes two arguments of type `Double`: a base and a height. It also returns a `Double`. Inside this function's implementation, you declare and implement another function called `divide()`. This function takes no arguments and returns a `Double`. The `areaOfTriangleWith(base:height:)` function calls the `divide()` function and returns the result.

The `divide()` function above uses a constant called rectangle that is defined in `areaOfTriangleWith(base:height:)`. Why does this work?

Anything within a function's braces ({}) is said to be enclosed by that function's scope. In this case, both the rectangle constant and the `divide()` function are enclosed by the scope of `areaOfTriangleWith(base:height:)`.

A function's scope describes the visibility an instance or function will have. It is a sort of horizon. Anything defined within a function's scope will be visible to that function; anything that is not is past that function's field of vision. rectangle is visible to the `divide()` function because they share the same *enclosing scope*.

On the other hand, because the `divide()` function is defined within the `areaOfTriangleWith(base:height:)` function's scope, it is not visible outside it. The compiler will give you an error if you try to call `divide()` outside the enclosing function. Give it a try to see the error.

By the way, nearly any pair of braces in Swift defines a scope. For example, switches, loops, and conditionals define scopes of their own.

`divide()` is a very simple function. Indeed, `areaOfTriangleWith(base:height:)` could achieve the same result without it: return (base * height) / 2. The important point here is how scope works. You will see a more sophisticated example of nested functions in Chapter 13. Stay tuned!

Multiple Returns

Functions can only return one value – but they can *pretend* to return more than one value. To do this, a function can return an instance of the tuple data type to encapsulate multiple values into one.

Recall that a tuple is an ordered list of related values. To better understand how to use tuples, write a function that takes an array of integers and sorts it into arrays for even and odd integers.

Listing 12.10 Sorting evens and odds

```
...
func sortedEvenOddNumbers(_ numbers: [Int]) -> (evens: [Int], odds: [Int]) {
    var evens = [Int]()
    var odds = [Int]()
    for number in numbers {
        if number % 2 == 0 {
            evens.append(number)
        } else {
            odds.append(number)
        }
    }
    return (evens, odds)
}
```

Here, you first declare a function called **sortedEvenOddNumbers(_:)**. You specify this function to take an array of integers as its only argument. The function returns a *named tuple*, so called because its constituent parts are named: evens will be an array of integers, and odds will also be an array of integers.

Next, inside the implementation of the function, you initialize the evens and odds arrays to prepare them to store their respective integers. You then loop through the array of integers provided to the function's parameter, numbers. At each iteration through the loop, you use the % operator to see whether number is even. If the result is even, you append it to the evens array. If the result is not even, the integer is added to the odds array.

Now that your function is set up, call it and pass it an array of integers. (As usual, do not break the string passed to **print()** in your code.)

Listing 12.11 Calling **sortedEvenOddNumbers(_:)**

```
...
func sortedEvenOddNumbers(_ numbers: [Int]) -> (evens: [Int], odds: [Int]) {
    var evens = [Int]()
    var odds = [Int]()
    for number in numbers {
        if number % 2 == 0 {
            evens.append(number)
        } else {
            odds.append(number)
        }
    }
    return (evens, odds)
}

let aBunchOfNumbers = [10,1,4,3,57,43,84,27,156,111]
let theSortedNumbers = sortedEvenOddNumbers(aBunchOfNumbers)
print("The even numbers are: \(theSortedNumbers.evens);
        the odd numbers are: \(theSortedNumbers.odds)")
```

First, you create an instance of the **Array** type to house a number of integers. Second, you give that array to the **sortedEvenOddNumbers(_:)** function and assign the return value to a constant called theSortedNumbers. Because the return value was specified as (evens: [Int], odds: [Int]), this is the type the compiler infers for your newly created constant. Finally, you log the result to the console.

Notice that you use string interpolation in combination with a tuple. You can access a tuple's members by name if they are defined. So, theSortedNumbers.evens inserts the contents of the evens array into the string logged to the console. Your console output should be The even numbers are: [10, 4, 84, 156]; the odd numbers are: [1, 3, 57, 43, 27, 111].

Optional Return Types

Sometimes you want a function to return an optional. When a function might need to return nil but will have a value to return at other times, Swift allows you to use an optional return.

Imagine, for example, that you need a function that looks at a person's full name and pulls out and returns that person's middle name. For the purposes of this exercise, assume that everyone has a first name and a last name (though this is not an assumption you would necessarily make in a production app). But not all people have a middle name, so your function will need a mechanism to return the person's middle name if there is one and return nil otherwise. Use an optional to do just that.

Listing 12.12 Using an optional return

```
...
func grabMiddleName(fromFullName name: (String, String?, String)) -> String? {
    return name.1
}

let middleName = grabMiddleName(fromFullName: ("Alice", nil, "Ward"))
if let theName = middleName {
    print(theName)
}
```

Here, you create a function called **grabMiddleName(fromFullName:)**. This function looks a little different than what you have seen before. It takes one argument: a tuple of type (String, String?, String). The tuple's three **String** instances are for the first, middle, and last names, and the instance for the middle name is declared as an optional type.

The **grabMiddleName(fromFullName:)** function's one parameter is called name, which has an external parameter name called fromFullName. You access this parameter inside the implementation of the function using the index of the name that you want to return. Because the tuple is zero-indexed, you use 1 to access the middle name provided to the argument. And because the middle name might be nil, the return type of the function is optional.

You then call **grabMiddleName(fromFullName:)** and provide it a first, middle, and last name (feel free to change the names). Because you declared the middle name component of the tuple to be of type **String?**, you can pass nil to that portion of the tuple. You cannot do this for the first or last name portion of the tuple.

Nothing is logged to the console. Because the middle name provided is nil, the Boolean used in the optional binding does not evaluate to true and **print()** is not executed.

Try giving the middle name a valid **String** instance and note the result.

Exiting Early from a Function

You learned about Swift's conditional statements in Chapter 3, but there is one more to introduce: guard statements. Just like if/else statements, guard statements execute code depending on a Boolean value resulting from some expression. But guard statements are different from what you have seen before. A guard statement is used to exit early from a function if some condition is *not* met. As their name suggests, you can think of guard statements as a way to protect your code from running under improper conditions.

Following the example above, consider an example in which you want to write a function that greets a person by their middle name if they have one. If they do not have a middle name, you will use something more generic.

Listing 12.13 Early exits with guard statements

```
...
func greetByMiddleName(fromFullName name: (first: String,
                                           middle: String?,
                                           last: String)) {
    guard let middleName = name.middle else {
        print("Hey there!")
        return
    }
    print("Hey, \(middleName)")
}
greetByMiddleName(fromFullName: ("Alice", "Richards", "Ward"))
```

greetByMiddleName(fromFullName:) is similar to **grabMiddleName(fromFullName:)** in that it takes the same argument, but it differs in that it has no return value. Another difference is that the names of the elements in the tuple name match specific components of a person's name. As you can see, these element names are available inside the function.

The code guard let middleName = name.middle binds the value in middle to a constant called middleName. If there is no value in the optional, then the code in the guard statement's body is executed. This would result in a generic greeting being logged to the console that omits the middle name: Hey there!. After this, you must explicitly return from the function, which represents that the condition established by the guard statement was not met and the function needs to return early.

You can think of guard as protecting you from embarrassingly addressing somebody as "mumble-mumble" when you do not know their middle name. But if the tuple did get passed to the function with a middle name, then its value is bound to middleName and is available after the guard statement. This means that middleName is visible in the parent scope that encompasses the guard statement.

In your call to **greetByMiddleName(fromFullName:)**, however, you pass in a middle name to the tuple name. That means Hey, Richards! will be logged to the console. If nil were passed to the middle name element, then Hey there! would log to the console. (Go ahead and try it.)

Function Types

Each function has a specific type, just as pieces of data do. *Function types* are made up of the function's parameter and return types. Consider the **sortedEvenOddNumbers(_:)** function. This function takes an array of integers as an argument and returns a tuple with two arrays of integers. Thus, the function type for **sortedEvenOddNumbers(_:)** is expressed as ([Int]) -> ([Int], [Int]).

The function's parameters are listed inside the left parentheses, and the return type comes after the ->. You can read this function type as: "A function with one parameter that takes an array of integers and returns a tuple with two arrays containing integers." For comparison, a function with no arguments and no return has the type () -> ().

Function types are useful because you can assign them to variables. This feature will become particularly handy in Chapter 13, when you will use functions in the arguments and returns of other functions. For now, let's just take a look at how you can assign a function type to a constant:

```
let evenOddFunction: ([Int]) -> ([Int], [Int]) = sortedEvenOddNumbers
```

This code creates a constant of function type named evenOddFunction whose value is the body of the **sortedEvenOddNumbers(_:)** function. Pretty cool, right? Now you can pass this constant around just like any other. You can even use this constant to call the function; for example, evenOddFunction([1,2,3]) will sort the numbers in the array supplied to the function's sole argument into a tuple of two arrays – one each for even and odd integers.

You accomplished a lot in this chapter. There was a lot of material here, and it may make sense to go through it all a second time. Be sure to type out all the code in this chapter. In fact, try to extend the examples to different cases. Try to break the examples and then fix them.

If you are still a little fuzzy on functions, do not worry. They are also a major focus in the next chapter, so you will get lots more practice.

Bronze Challenge

Like if/else conditions, guard statements support the use of multiple clauses to perform additional checks. Using additional clauses with a guard statement gives you further control over the statement's condition. Refactor the **greetByMiddleName(fromFullName:)** function to have an additional clause in its guard statement. This clause should check whether the middle name is longer than 10 characters. If it is, then greet the person with their first name, their middle initial (the first letter of the middle name followed by a period), and their last name instead.

For example, if the name is Alois Rumpelstiltskin Chaz, the function should print Hey, Alois R. Chaz.

Silver Challenge

Write a function called **siftBeans(fromGroceryList:)** that takes a grocery list (as an array of strings) and "sifts out" the beans from the other groceries. The function should take one argument that has a parameter name called list, and it should return a named tuple of the type (beans: [String], otherGroceries: [String]).

Here is an example of how you should be able to call your function and what the result should be:

```
let result = siftBeans(fromGroceryList: ["green beans",
                                         "milk",
                                         "black beans",
                                         "pinto beans",
                                         "apples"])

result.beans == ["green beans", "black beans", "pinto beans"] // true
result.otherGroceries == ["milk", "apples"] // true
```

Hint: You may need to use a function on the **String** type called **hasSuffix(_:)**.

For the More Curious: Void

The first function you wrote in this chapter was **printGreeting()**. It took no arguments and returned nothing. Or did it?

Actually, functions that do not explicitly return something *do* have a return. They return something called **Void**. This return is inserted into the code for you by the compiler.

So, while you wrote **printGreeting()** like this:

```
func printGreeting() {
    print("Hello, playground.")
}
```

The compiler actually added something like this to your code:

```
func printGreeting() -> Void {
    print("Hello, playground.")
}
```

In other words, it added a return value of **Void** for you. Just what is **Void**? Go ahead and make **printGreeting** explicitly return **Void**, as shown above. Option-click the word Void, and Xcode will show you what it looks like in the standard library.

```
typealias Void = ()
```

Void is a typealias for (). You will read about typealiases in detail in Chapter 20. For now, think of typealiases as a way to tell the compiler that one thing is shorthand for another. In the excerpt above, the standard library is establishing that **Void** is another way of expressing ().

You have already seen the concept at play in Chapter 5. The () refers to what is called an empty tuple. If a tuple is a list of ordered elements, then an empty tuple is simply a list with nothing in it.

Given what you know now, you can see that these three implementations of **printGreeting()** are equivalent.

```
func printGreeting() {
    print("Hello, playground.")
}

func printGreeting() -> Void {
    print("Hello, playground.")
}

func printGreeting() -> () {
    print("Hello, playground.")
}
```

The first version above is what you originally wrote. The second is what the compiler inserts for you. And the third uses the empty parentheses, which is what the standard library maps **Void** to.

Knowing that **Void** maps to () should help you understand what is going on in a given function type. For example, the function type for **printGreeting()** is () -> Void. This is simply the type for a function that takes no arguments and returns an empty tuple, which is the implicit return type for all functions that do not explicitly have a return value.

For the More Curious: Variadic Parameters

The **print()** function has an interesting feature: You can pass it as many arguments as you want, in a comma-delimited list, and it will print all of them. Here are a couple examples:

```
print("Hello ", username)
print(thing1, thing2, thing3)
```

All the functions you have written so far accept a fixed list of inputs. If the caller passes too many or too few arguments, the compiler will emit an error. How can **print()** handle any number of arguments? By accepting a *variadic* parameter.

A variadic parameter takes zero or more input values for its argument. Here are the rules: A function can have only one variadic parameter, it cannot be marked with inout, and it should typically be the final parameter in the list. The values provided to the argument are made available within the function's body as an array.

To make a variadic parameter, use three periods after the parameter's type, like names: String.... In this example, names is available within the function's body and has the type **[String]**.

Consider a version of your **printPersonalGreeting(to:)** function designed to take multiple names and greet them all. You could accomplish this with a parameter that expects an array of strings:

```
func printPersonalGreetings(to names: [String]) {
    for name in names {
        print("Hello \(name), welcome to the playground.")
    }
}

printPersonalGreetings(to: ["Tessa", "Selah", "Aria", "Elijah"])
```

Or you could use a variadic parameter:

```
func printPersonalGreetings(to names: String...) {
    for name in names {
        print("Hello, \(name). Welcome to your playground.")
    }
}

printPersonalGreetings(to: "Tessa", "Selah", "Aria", "Elijah")
```

Even though the declared argument type is **String...**, the names instance inside the implementation is still a **[String]**. Using a variadic parameter changes nothing inside the implementation – only the way the parameter is declared.

In practice, most Swift developers write functions that accept array parameters rather than variadic parameters. This is because a caller can manually pack a list of objects into an array for a function that requires an array. But there is no way to unpack an array into a variadic list for a function with a variadic parameter. That said, variadic parameters are a convenient and expressive way to define a function for callers that will have in mind a discrete list of arguments they wish to provide.

13

Closures

Closures are discrete bundles of functionality that can be used in your application to accomplish specific tasks. Functions, which you learned about in the last chapter, are a special case of closures. You can think of a function as a named closure. Because functions are technically closures, Swift programmers sometimes use the two words interchangeably, despite the subtle distinction.

In Chapter 12, you worked primarily with global and nested functions. (Global functions are not defined on any specific type, and for this reason they are also called *free functions*.)

Closures differ from functions in that they have a more compact and lightweight syntax. They allow you to write a "function-like" construct without having to give it a name and a full function declaration. This makes closures easy to pass around in function arguments and returns.

Let's get started. Create a new macOS playground called Closures.

Closure Syntax

Imagine that you are a community organizer managing a number of organizations. You want to keep track of how many volunteers there are for each organization and have created an **Array** for this task.

Listing 13.1 Starting with an array

```
import Cocoa

var str = "Hello, playground"

let volunteerCounts = [1,3,40,32,2,53,77,13]
```

You entered the number of volunteers for each organization as they were provided to you. This means that the array is completely disorganized. It would be better if your array of volunteers were sorted from lowest to highest number.

Good news: Swift provides a method called **sorted(by:)** that allows you to sort an instance of **Array** based on criteria you specify.

(We have mentioned methods before but never explained the terminology. A function defined on a type, the way **sorted(by:)** is defined on **Array**, is also called a method. More on this topic in Chapter 15.)

sorted(by:) takes one argument: a closure that describes how the sorting should be done. The closure takes two arguments, whose types must match the type of the elements in the array, and returns a **Bool**. The two arguments are compared, and the return value indicates whether the first argument should be sorted before the second argument.

In the closure you pass to **sorted(by:)**, you use < in the comparison if you would like the elements in the array to be sorted in ascending fashion. Use > in the comparison if you would like the elements to be sorted in a descending fashion. (Like +, the < and > operators are available for use with many, but not all, Swift types. You will learn more about these operators and how to make them available to your custom types as well in Chapter 25.)

Because your array of volunteer counts is filled with integers, the function type for **sorted(by:)** will look like ((Int, Int) -> Bool) -> [Int] in your code. As you saw in Chapter 12, function types begin with the function's parameters, enclosed in parentheses. In this case, the single parameter is a closure, represented by its own function type.

So, in other words, **sorted(by:)** is a method that takes a closure. That closure, in turn, takes two values to compare and returns a Boolean value specifying whether the first value should come before the second in a sorted list. **sorted(by:)** calls the passed-in closure multiple times with different pairs of arguments from the source array to determine their overall order. **sorted(by:)** then returns the sorted array of values.

Add the following code to sort your array.

Listing 13.2 Sorting the array

```
let volunteerCounts = [1,3,40,32,2,53,77,13]

func isAscending(_ i: Int, _ j: Int) -> Bool {
    return i < j
}
let volunteersSorted = volunteerCounts.sorted(by: isAscending)
print(volunteersSorted)
```

First, you create a function called **isAscending(_:_:)** that has the required type to be **sorted(by:)**'s argument. It compares two integers and returns a Boolean that indicates whether integer i is less than integer j. is is a common prefix in the names of functions that return a Boolean, so the name **isAscending** implies that the function will be sorting two things. That being the case, you use _ to suppress the parameter names from being used in the call.

The function will return true if i is less than – and should be placed before – j. As this global function is a named closure (remember, all functions are closures), you can provide this function as the value of the argument in **sorted(by:)**.

Next, you call **sorted(by:)**, passing in **isAscending(_:_:)** for its argument. Because **sorted(by:)** returns a new array, you assign that result to a new constant array called volunteersSorted. This instance will serve as your new record for the organizations' volunteer counts, correctly sorted.

Look in the playground's console. You should see that the values in volunteersSorted are sorted from lowest to highest:

```
[1, 2, 3, 13, 32, 40, 53, 77]
```

Closure Expression Syntax

This works, but you can clean up your code. There is no need to declare a named function; you can create a closure to pass to **sorted(by:)** inline – right in the method call – using closure expression syntax, like:

```
{(parameters) -> return type in
    // Code
}
```

You write a closure expression inside braces ({}). The closure's parameters are listed in parentheses immediately after the opening brace. Its return type comes after the parameters and uses the regular syntax. The keyword in is used to separate the closure's parameters and return type from the statements in its body.

Refactor your code to use a closure expression, creating the closure inline instead of defining a separate function outside the **sorted(by:)** method.

Listing 13.3 Refactoring your sorting code

```
let volunteerCounts = [1,3,40,32,2,53,77,13]

func isAscending(_ i: Int, _ j: Int) -> Bool {
    return i < j
}
let volunteersSorted = volunteerCounts.sorted(by: isAscending)

let volunteersSorted = volunteerCounts.sorted(by: {
    (i: Int, j: Int) -> Bool in
    return i < j
})

print(volunteersSorted)
```

This code is a bit cleaner and more elegant than the first version. Instead of providing a function defined elsewhere in the playground, you define a closure inline in the **sorted(by:)** method's argument. The closure's parameters and their type are the same as before, as is the return type. In the closure's body, you provide the same logical test (is i less than j?) to determine the Boolean return value.

The result is just as before: The sorted array is assigned to volunteersSorted.

This refactoring is a step in the right direction, but it is still a little verbose. Closures can take advantage of Swift's type inference system, so you can clean up your closure even more by trimming out the type information.

Listing 13.4 Taking advantage of type inference

```
let volunteerCounts = [1,3,40,32,2,53,77,13]

let volunteersSorted = volunteerCounts.sorted(by: {
    (i: Int, j: Int) -> Bool in
    return i < j
})

let volunteersSorted = volunteerCounts.sorted(by: { i, j in i < j })

print(volunteersSorted)
```

There are three new developments here. First, you remove the type information for both the parameters and the return. The compiler can infer that the parameters have the same type as the elements in the input array. As for the return type, the compiler knows that checking i < j will return true or false – that is, a **Bool** value.

Second, you move the entire closure expression to be one line. Third, you remove the keyword return. Any function or closure with only one expression can implicitly return the value of that expression by omitting the return keyword.

Notice that the result in the console has not changed.

Your closure is getting fairly compact, but it can become even more succinct. Swift provides *positional variable names* that you can refer to in inline closure expressions. These shorthand names behave similarly to the explicitly declared arguments you have been using: They have the same types and values. The compiler's type inference capabilities help it know the number and types of arguments your closure takes, which means it is not necessary to name them.

For example, the compiler knows that **sorted(by:)** takes a closure, and it knows that the closure takes two parameters that are of the same type as the items in the array you pass into the method's argument. Because the closure has two arguments, whose values are compared to determine their order, you can refer to the arguments positionally using $0 for the first and $1 for the second.

(Notice that the positional variable names are zero-indexed. Also, for a closure with more than two arguments, you can use $2, $3, and so on.)

Adjust your code to take advantage of the shorthand syntax.

Listing 13.5 Using shorthand syntax for arguments

```
let volunteerCounts = [1,3,40,32,2,53,77,13]

let volunteersSorted = volunteerCounts.sorted(by: { i, j in i < j })

let volunteersSorted = volunteerCounts.sorted(by: { $0 < $1 })

print(volunteersSorted)
```

Now that your inline closure expression uses the positional argument syntax, you do not need to explicitly declare the parameters as you did for i and j. The compiler knows that the values in the closure's arguments are of the correct type and knows what to infer based on the < operator.

Before you think this closure could not possibly get any slimmer, just wait – there is more! Closures that appear at the end of the argument list can be written outside of and after the function's parentheses; this is called *trailing closure syntax*. If doing so would leave an empty pair of parentheses behind, you may remove them entirely.

Make this change.

Listing 13.6 Inline closure as the function's final argument

```
let volunteerCounts = [1,3,40,32,2,53,77,13]

let volunteersSorted = volunteerCounts.sorted(by: { $0 < $1 })

let volunteersSorted = volunteerCounts.sorted { $0 < $1 }

print(volunteersSorted)
```

Here, because no parameters remain after moving the closure argument outside the parentheses, the parentheses are deleted.

Notice that when the closure moves outside the parentheses, its argument label is removed from the call. If there are multiple trailing closures, this only applies to the first; subsequent trailing closures retain their argument labels. For example, a function whose signature looks like this:

```
func doAwesomeWork(on input: String,
                   using transformer: () -> Void,
                   then completion: () -> Void)
```

Would be called using trailing closure syntax like this:

```
doAwesomeWork(on: "My Project") {
    print("Doing work on \(input) in `transformer`")
} then: {
    print("Finishing up in `completion`")
}
```

In this example, the `using` parameter name is omitted, but `then` is not.

Truly, "Brevity is the soul of wit." The code in Listing 13.6 works just as well in this terse form as in the earlier, much more verbose version.

This trailing closure syntax adds complexity to the language, but it feels more stylish to many Swift developers as it helps remove clutter from the function call site.

Do not feel like you need to use all these code-condensing features to be an effective Swift developer. They are here for your convenience. The most important thing is to make sure that your code is as readable and understandable as possible.

Functions as Arguments

You initially sorted your `volunteerCounts` array using a named function passed as an argument to `sorted(by:)`. Although that particular task could be accomplished elegantly without the need for a named function, there are times when declaring a function and passing it as an argument to another function is the best solution.

Now you will write your own function that takes a closure to modify a collection. In the playground, add this incomplete function:

Listing 13.7 Formatting numbers as strings

```
...
func format(numbers: [Double], using formatter: (Double) -> String) -> [String] {
    var result = [String]()

    return result
}
```

That is a lot of parentheses! Do not be intimidated. Study the function's signature from beginning to end. The **format(numbers:using:)** function takes two arguments and returns an array of **String**s. The first argument is an array of **Double**s. The second is a closure that takes a **Double** and returns a **String**.

In other words, **format(numbers:using:)** takes an array of numbers and a closure that can format a single number into a string. The specifics of the formatting will be defined by the closure that is passed in to the second argument: It could take an array of seven-digit numbers and format them as phone numbers, make sure that each element in an array of dollar values has exactly two digits after the decimal point, and so on.

The next step is to apply the closure to each number in the array. Flesh out the body of the function to do exactly that:

Listing 13.8 The real work

```
...
func format(numbers: [Double], using formatter: (Double) -> String) -> [String] {
    var result = [String]()
    for number in numbers {
        let transformed = formatter(number)
        result.append(transformed)
    }
    return result
}
```

Now you can declare a closure that a caller of this function might provide for transforming a single **Double** into a **String**.

Recall from the beginning of this chapter that functions are closures with a slightly different syntax. You call a closure the same way you call a function: by its name, with a parenthetical argument list. Here, you call the passed-in `formatter` closure with `number` as its argument in `formatter(number)`.

Thinking back to the volunteers example, suppose you have been asked to report the average number of volunteers each organization sent to this year's major events. It might sound weird to say that an organization averaged 10.75 volunteers per event, so you want to round the averages to the nearest integer and drop the decimal point. Create a closure to accomplish this task.

Listing 13.9 Rounding and converting doubles

```
...
func format(numbers: [Double], using formatter: (Double) -> String) -> [String] {
    var result = [String]()
    for number in numbers {
        let transformed = formatter(number)
        result.append(transformed)
    }
    return result
}

let rounder: (Double) -> String = {
    (num: Double) -> String in
    return "\(Int(num.rounded()))"
}
```

Here, you define a **(Double) -> String** closure that returns the string interpolation of an integer rounded from a double. To round a **Double** to the nearest integral value, you use its **rounded()** method, which returns another **Double**, so 10.6 becomes 11.0. Then you initialize an **Int** from that value, which truncates any decimal portion – so, for example, 11.0 becomes 11.

Finally, you interpolate the integer into a string. (Remember, **format(numbers:using:)**'s formatter closure must return an array of strings.)

Now prepare your list of average volunteer counts, rounded and converted to strings:

Listing 13.10 Calling your format function

```
...
let volunteerAverages = [10.75, 4.2, 1.5, 12.12, 16.815]
let roundedAveragesAsStrings = format(numbers: volunteerAverages, using: rounder)
```

The values listed in the sidebar for roundedAveragesAsStrings should read ["11", "4", "2", "12", "17"].

What if the caller of your function does not want to have to provide a closure for the using argument? A reasonable default behavior for your **format(numbers:using:)** function would be to just convert the numbers to strings if no custom formatting is desired.

Update the declaration of **format(numbers:using:)**:

Listing 13.11 Default closure argument

```
...
func format(numbers: [Double],
            using formatter: (Double) -> String = {"\($0)"}) -> [String] {
    var result = [String]()
    for number in numbers {
        let transformed = formatter(number)
        result.append(transformed)
    }
    return result
}
...
```

Here you use a technique that you learned in Chapter 12 to add a default value for the formatter argument: a concise closure that merely returns its argument interpolated into a **String**.

Now, if the caller does not pass **format(numbers:using:)** a closure, the function will just use each number's `description` for the strings instead.

Verify that your updated function works by adding a call that omits the `using` parameter:

Listing 13.12 Using the default value

```
...
let volunteerAverages = [10.75, 4.2, 1.5, 12.12, 16.815]
let roundedAveragesAsStrings = format(numbers: volunteerAverages, using: rounder)
let exactAveragesAsStrings = format(numbers: volunteerAverages)
...
```

The sidebar should show the value of exactAveragesAsStrings as ["10.75", "4.2", "1.5", "12.12", "16.815"].

Closures Capture Their Enclosing Scope

Now that you have some experience with closures, it is time to examine an important feature of how they interact with the code around them.

To set the stage for this examination, you will want to have a few different scopes available. Any scope will do – conditionals, loops, and functions all define scopes. For this experiment, nest your `rounder` closure and its usage in the scope of a new function.

Listing 13.13 A scope in which to play

```
...
func format(numbers: [Double],
            using formatter: (Double) -> String = {"\($0)"}) -> [String] {
    var result = [String]()
    for number in numbers {
        let transformed = formatter(number)
        result.append(transformed)
    }
    return result
}

func experimentWithScopes() {
    let rounder: (Double) -> String = {
        (num: Double) -> String in
        return "\(Int(num.rounded()))"
    }

    let volunteerAverages = [10.75, 4.2, 1.5, 12.12, 16.815]
    let roundedAveragesAsStrings = format(numbers: volunteerAverages, using: rounder)
    let exactAveragesAsStrings = format(numbers: volunteerAverages)
}

experimentWithScopes()
```

The **experimentWithScopes()** function provides a nested scope so you can inspect the interactions between declarations in different scopes. After defining the function, you call it so that your code will execute when the playground updates.

Add a variable before your declaration of rounder and modify it within the closure:

Listing 13.14 Capturing enclosing scope

```
...
func format(numbers: [Double],
            using formatter: (Double) -> String = {"\($0)"}) -> [String] {
    var result = [String]()
    for number in numbers {
        let transformed = formatter(number)
        result.append(transformed)
    }
    return result
}

func experimentWithScopes() {
    var numberOfTransformations = 0

    let rounder: (Double) -> String = {
        (num: Double) -> String in
        numberOfTransformations += 1
        return "\(Int(num.rounded()))"
    }

    let volunteerAverages = [10.75, 4.2, 1.5, 12.12, 16.815]
    let roundedAveragesAsStrings = format(numbers: volunteerAverages, using: rounder)
    let exactAveragesAsStrings = format(numbers: volunteerAverages)
}
...
```

Here you set aside a variable to track the number of transformations you perform, which is equal to the number of times your closure runs. You increment that value each time rounder executes.

So far, this does not seem far-fetched. Recall from Chapter 12 that a function can use any of the variables defined in the same scope it is defined in (also called its enclosing scope), so it makes sense that rounder has access to numberOfTransformations. (Reread the explanation for Listing 12.9 if you need to review.) For the same reason, **experimentWithScopes()** could call **format(numbers:using:)** if you wanted it to.

However, a function cannot see into another nested scope. So, for example, result, which is declared in the *local scope* of **format(numbers:using:)**, is invisible to rounder.

A function or variable that is declared outside any other scope is considered to be in the *global scope*, and it is visible to any function or closure in the program. In the example above, **format(numbers:using:)** and **experimentWithScopes()** are declared in the global scope, but numberOfTransformations and rounder are in the local scope of **experimentWithScopes()**.

Now, print the value of numberOfTransformations after **format(numbers:using:)** is called with rounder as its closure argument:

Listing 13.15 Printing a closure-modified value

```
...
func experimentWithScopes() {
    var numberOfTransformations = 0

    let rounder: (Double) -> String = {
        (num: Double) -> String in
        numberOfTransformations += 1
        return "\(Int(num.rounded()))"
    }

    let volunteerAverages = [10.75, 4.2, 1.5, 12.12, 16.815]
    let roundedAveragesAsStrings = format(numbers: volunteerAverages, using: rounder)
    let exactAveragesAsStrings = format(numbers: volunteerAverages)
    print(numberOfTransformations)
}
...
```

The value printed to the console should be 5. The **format(numbers:using:)** function executed the rounder closure five times (one for each number in volunteerAverages), and each time rounder incremented the value of numberOfTransformations.

This means that rounder has access to numberOfTransformations even when it is passed to **format(numbers:using:)**. In fact, we say that a function not only has access to its enclosing scope but also *captures* it. When you define a function and then pass that function as an argument, it maintains its access to the variables that were in its enclosing scope when it was defined.

In this example, when the closure stored in rounder is passed into **format(numbers:using:)**, where it becomes the local variable named formatter, it is no longer in a scope that can access numberOfTransformations. The formatter closure can only access numberOfTransformations because the closure captured its enclosing scope when it was defined in **experimentWithScopes()**.

You will see other ways a closure's capture of its scope can impact your program when you learn about memory management in Chapter 24.

Now that you are done with your experiment, you can eliminate the **experimentWithScopes()** function scope and unindent its body. (Xcode will indent your code nicely for you. First, select the code you want to format. Then choose Editor → Structure → Re-Indent or use the keyboard shortcut Control-I.)

Listing 13.16 Removing **experimentWithScopes()**

```
...
func experimentWithScopes() {
var numberOfTransformations = 0

let rounder: (Double) -> String = {
    (num: Double) -> String in
    numberOfTransformations += 1
    return "\(Int(num.rounded()))"
}

let volunteerAverages = [10.75, 4.2, 1.5, 12.12, 16.815]
let roundedAveragesAsStrings = format(numbers: volunteerAverages, using: rounder)
let exactAveragesAsStrings = format(numbers: volunteerAverages)
print(numberOfTransformations)
}
experimentWithScopes()
```

Functional Programming

Programming languages are sometimes classified by characteristics they share. One such paradigm, or classification, is *functional programming*, from which Swift adopts some of its patterns. It is difficult to provide a concrete definition of functional programming because people use the phrase with different meanings and intentions, but typically it is understood to include:

- *First-class functions* – functions can be returned from and passed as arguments to other functions, can be stored in variables, etc.; they are just like any other type.

- *Pure functions* – functions have no side effects; functions, given the same input, always return the same output and do not modify other states elsewhere in the program. Most math functions like sin, cos, fibonacci, and factorial are pure.

- *Immutability* – mutability is de-emphasized, because it is more difficult to reason about data whose values can change.

- *Strong typing* – a strong type system increases the runtime safety of the code because the guarantees of the language's type system are checked at compile time.

Swift supports all these approaches.

Functional programming can make your code more concise and expressive. By emphasizing immutability and strong compile-time type checking, it can also make your code safer at runtime. These hallmarks of functional programming can also make code easier to reason about and maintain.

As you have seen, Swift's `let` keyword allows you to declare immutable instances in your code. And its strong type system helps you catch errors at compile time instead of waiting until runtime. Swift also provides several *higher-order functions* that are well known to developers fond of functional programming: `map(_:)`, `filter(_:)`, and `reduce(_:_:)`. These functions emphasize that Swift's functions are indeed first-class citizens.

Let's look at what these functions add to Swift's toolkit.

Higher-Order Functions

Higher-order functions are functions that can take another function as an argument or can return a function. You have already worked with higher-order functions in this chapter and even written your own, like `format(numbers:using:)`.

Let's take a look at three higher-order functions from the standard library – `map(_:)`, `filter(_:)`, and `reduce(_:_:)` – in the context of your imaginary volunteerism reports.

map(_:)

The Swift standard library provides an implementation of **map(_:)** as a method on the **Array** type. It is used to transform an array's contents. You *map* an array's contents from one value to another and put the new values into a new array. Because **map(_:)** is a higher-order function, you provide it with another function that tells it how to transform the array's contents.

Your current usage of **format(numbers:using:)** uses a closure that rounds the passed-in numbers before converting them to strings. Now you will do something similar using **map(_:)**, but you will skip the string-conversion step for simplicity.

At the bottom of your playground, use **map(_:)** to round the average volunteer counts per organization to the nearest number of actual humans:

Listing 13.17 Transforming values with **map(_:)**

```
...
let roundedAverages = volunteerAverages.map {
    (avg: Double) -> Int in
    return Int(avg.rounded())
}
```

First, notice that you used trailing-closure syntax to pass the closure argument to **map(_:)**. This is common in the Swift community.

Your closure will be called by the **map(_:)** function once for each value in the array, with the value as the closure's argument. The closure then transforms the value and returns it. By the time **map(_:)** is done, you have a new array with the modified versions of all the original array's values.

Next, look at the closure's signature. You are using **map(_:)** here not just to change a value but also to return a value of a different type. Since you passed in a closure that takes a **Double** and returns an **Int**, the **map(_:)** method assumes that it is operating on an **Array** of **Double**s and will return an **Array** of **Int**s. Your closure must take as its only argument a value of whatever the **Array**'s type is, but it can return anything.

You should see in the sidebar that roundedAverages equals [11, 4, 2, 12, 17].

filter(_:)

Now imagine that the mayor wants to throw a party for the organizations that had an average volunteer participation of 10 or higher, so she has asked you to produce a list of only those volunteer counts.

Where the `map(_:)` method expects a closure that will transform a value, the `filter(_:)` method expects a closure that will decide whether each value should be added to the result array. Your closure will receive each value, one at a time, and should return `true` if the value passes your test and `false` if it does not. The result array will contain a subset of the original array's items: only those for which your closure returns `true`.

Use the `filter(_:)` method to create a new array that only includes volunteer counts of 10 or higher:

Listing 13.18 Selecting desirable values with `filter(_:)`

```
...
let roundedAverages = volunteerAverages.map {
    (avg: Double) -> Int in
    return Int(avg.rounded())
}

let passingAverages = roundedAverages.filter {
    (avg: Int) -> Bool in
    return avg >= 10
}
```

As the sidebar shows, the organizations that will be invited to the party are the ones with these average counts: [11, 12, 17].

reduce(_:_:)

Now that the mayor knows which organizations to invite, she wants an estimate of how many attendees to expect at the party. She intends to invite five volunteers from her own staff plus each organization's average volunteer count.

You use the **reduce(_:_:)** method to produce a single representative value from an array of values. In other words, it *reduces* an array of values to just one value. The single value can be one of the values in the collection or any meaningful value derived from them, but it must be of the same type as the elements of the **Array**.

Use **reduce(_:_:)** to compute the sum of the volunteer counts, including the five volunteers from the mayor's staff:

Listing 13.19 Reducing

```
...
let roundedAverages = volunteerAverages.map {
    (avg: Double) -> Int in
    return Int(avg.rounded())
}

let passingAverages = roundedAverages.filter {
    (avg: Int) -> Bool in
    return avg >= 10
}

let estimatedParticipation = passingAverages.reduce(5) {
    (estimationSoFar: Int, currentOrgAverage: Int) -> Int in
    return estimationSoFar + currentOrgAverage
}
```

reduce(_:_:) differs from **map(_:)** and **filter(_:)** in an important way. In addition to taking one of the **Array**'s values, your closure takes an additional argument: the return value from the previous execution. In this way, **reduce(_:_:)** acts like an assembly line where each worker receives a partially completed product from the previous worker, adds something to it, and passes the result to the next worker until the line is complete and the final product is ready.

Each time your closure is executed, it receives both the corresponding value from the **Array** *and* the return value from the previous execution. It can then combine or process these values in some way, and its result is then passed as one of the arguments to the *next* execution.

The **reduce(_:_:)** function itself takes two arguments. In addition to your closure, it takes in an initial value to pass in as the aggregated value for the first execution of your closure.

This was a big chapter with many big ideas. Closures can take awhile to get used to, especially if you have not used features like them in another programming language before. You will see more examples of closures and their usefulness in the coming chapters, and you can return here later for review. For now, try out the challenges below and do not feel like you are behind if you need more time. This is hard stuff, and you are doing great.

Bronze Challenge

In this chapter, you sorted a collection by returning a new instance of **Array** with its integers sorted from smallest to largest. You can also sort collections in place – meaning modifying the existing collection, rather than returning a new one. Change the way you sort volunteerCounts to sort the array in place from smallest to largest.

Silver Challenge

You used **sorted(by:)** to sort a collection from smallest to largest. But if you just want to sort a collection in an ascending fashion, there is a simpler method to use. Use the documentation to find this method. Apply the method to your solution to the bronze challenge.

Gold Challenge

Use what you have learned about closure syntax in this chapter to perform all the calculations on the volunteerAverages array (the **map(_:)**, **filter(_:)**, and **reduce(_:_:)** calls) in as little code as possible. Your entire solution should fit in one (long) line.

Consider the balance of brevity and readability in your solution, and experiment with including and excluding different compiler-inferrable parts of the closure syntax to find a balance that you feel comfortable with.

Hint: You can chain method calls using dot syntax, so long as the return value of each method is of a type that has the *next* method available on it. For example:

```
let sortedRoundedAverages = startingArray.map(…).sorted(by:…)
```

sorted(by:) must be called on an **Array**. This works because **map(_:)** returns an **Array**, and **sorted(by:)** is being called on **map(_:)**'s return value.

For the More Curious: Functions as Return Types

You have worked with several higher-order functions now, but you have only worked with higher-order functions that take other functions as arguments. Higher-order functions can also *return* another function.

You already know that a function that takes an argument of, say, **Character** and returns an **Int** is of type **(Character) -> Int**. But what is the type of a function that takes a **Character** and returns a **(String) -> String** closure?

Let's explore this idea. Suppose you have a **String** and want to remove all occurrences of a particular **Character** from it. Now imagine that you need to do this multiple times, with multiple characters across multiple strings. Being a stylish developer, you decide to write a function to help out. Go ahead and enter it in your playground:

Listing 13.20 Functions begetting functions

```
func makeCharacterRemover(for character: Character) -> (String) -> String {
    func removeFrom(_ input: String) -> String {
        return input.filter { $0 != character }
    }
    return removeFrom
}
```

This function takes in a **Character** as its argument and returns a function that will strip all instances of the character from a passed-in **String**.

Recall that a **String** is a collection of **Character** instances. It has the **filter(_:)** method, just like the **Array** type does. The inner **removeFrom(_:)** function uses **filter(_:)** to filter out all instances of the character provided to the outer function. Notice that – since a function is a closure and captures its enclosing scope – **removeFrom(_:)** has access to the local variable character owned by the outer function.

Now you can use **makeCharacterRemover(for:)** to generate as many character-specific **removeFrom(_:)** functions as you want.

Listing 13.21 Using the returned function

```
func makeCharacterRemover(for character: Character) -> (String) -> String {
    func removeFrom(_ input: String) -> String {
        return input.filter { $0 != character }
    }
    return removeFrom
}

let removeLowerCaseLs = makeCharacterRemover(for: "l")
let strangeGreeting = removeLowerCaseLs("Hello, World!")

let removeLowerCaseOs = makeCharacterRemover(for: "o")
let strangerGreeting = removeLowerCaseOs(strangeGreeting)
```

You can see in the playground sidebar that removeLowerCaseLs and removeLowerCaseOs are both variables of type **(String) -> String**, and strangeGreeting and strangerGreeting are stripped strings emitted by them

Admittedly, this approach is a little overengineered. A more readable and concise approach might be to define a single function of type **(Character, String) -> String** to take in a string and a character to remove from it, returning the resulting string. Such a function might look like this:

```
func remove(_ character: Character, from string: String) -> String {
    return string.filter { $0 != character }
}

let britishGreeting = remove("H", from: "Hello, World!")
```

Since a function that returns another function can often be refactored into something simpler, you will not see it much in the wild. It is, however, an example of the flexibility and power of functions in Swift.

Part IV
Enumerations, Structures, and Classes

You will be defining your own custom types in this part of the book and studying how decisions you make while writing code impact your project later. You will be adding features to projects and changing them as the projects progress. This is part of writing code for real projects: Sometimes you start developing an application with one solution in mind and then have to modify your code when you learn a better pattern or need to accommodate a new or changed feature.

That does not mean the first code or tools were bad – just that they would be better for other circumstances. Projects often evolve and develop, and decisions that are ideal at one stage may become inadequate as requirements change. Learning to be flexible in the face of these changes is part of the trade.

14

Enumerations

Up to this point, you have been using Swift's built-in types, like integers, strings, arrays, and dictionaries. The next two chapters will show the capabilities the language provides to create your own types. The focus of this chapter is *enumerations* (or enums), which allow you to create instances that are one of a defined list of cases.

If you have used enumerations in other languages, much of this chapter will be familiar. But Swift's enums also have some advanced features that make them unique.

Basic Enumerations

Create a new macOS playground called Enumerations. Define an enumeration of possible text alignments.

Listing 14.1 Defining an enumeration

```
import Cocoa

var str = "Hello, playground"

enum TextAlignment {
    case left
    case right
    case center
}
```

You define an enumeration with the enum keyword followed by the name of the enumeration. The opening brace ({) opens the body of the enum, and it must contain at least one `case` statement that declares the possible values for the enum. Here, you include three.

As an aside, the names of types (including enums) begin with a capital letter by convention. If multiple words are needed, capitalize the first letter of each word (this is called *Pascal case*): **PascalCasedType**. The names of variables, functions, and enum cases use a similar case structure but with a lowercase first letter (called *camel case*): camelCasedVariable.

The name of the enumeration (here, **TextAlignment**) is now usable as a type, just like **Int** or **String** or the various other types you have used so far. That means that you can now create instances of that type:

Listing 14.2 Creating an instance of **TextAlignment**

```
enum TextAlignment {
    case left
    case right
    case center
}
```

var alignment: TextAlignment = TextAlignment.left

Although **TextAlignment** is a type that you have defined, the compiler can still infer the type for `alignment`. Therefore, you can omit the explicit type of the `alignment` variable:

Listing 14.3 Taking advantage of type inference

```
...
var alignment: TextAlignment = TextAlignment.left
```

The compiler's ability to infer the type of enumerations is not limited to variable declarations. If you have a variable known to be of a particular enum type, you can omit the type from the case statement when assigning a new value to the variable.

Listing 14.4 Inferring the enum type

```
...
var alignment = TextAlignment.left
alignment = .right
```

You have to specify the enum's type and value when initially creating the `alignment` variable, because that line gives `alignment` both its type and its value. In the next line, you can omit the type and simply reassign `alignment` to a different value within its type. You can also omit the enum type when passing its values to functions or comparing them.

Listing 14.5 Type inference when comparing values

```
...
alignment = .right

if alignment == .right {
    print("We should right-align the text!")
}
```

While enum values can be compared in `if` statements, `switch` statements are typically used to handle enum values. Use `switch` to print the alignment in a more human-readable way.

Listing 14.6 Switching to switch

```
...
alignment = .right

if alignment == .right {
    print("We should right align the text!")
}
switch alignment {
case .left:
    print("left aligned")

case .right:
    print("right aligned")

case .center:
    print("center aligned")
}
```

Recall from Chapter 5 that all `switch` statements must be exhaustive. Some of the `switch` statements you wrote in that chapter required a `default` case to meet that requirement. When switching on enumeration values, the compiler knows all possible values of the enumeration to check. If you include a case for each one, the switch is exhaustive and no `default` case is necessary.

You *could* include a `default` case when switching on an enum type:

Listing 14.7 Making center the default case

```
...
switch alignment {
case .left:
    print("left aligned")

case .right:
    print("right aligned")

case .center:
default:
    print("center aligned")
}
```

This code works, but we recommend avoiding `default` clauses when switching on enum types, because using a default is not as "future proof." Suppose, for example, you add another alignment option for justified text.

Listing 14.8 Adding a case

```
enum TextAlignment {
    case left
    case right
    case center
    case justify
}

var alignment = TextAlignment.left justify
alignment = .right
...
```

Your program still runs, but it now prints the wrong value. The `alignment` variable is set to `.justify`, but the `switch` statement prints `center aligned`. This is what we mean when we say that using a default is not future proof: It adds complication to modifying your code in the future.

Change your `switch` back to listing each case explicitly.

Listing 14.9 Returning to explicit cases

```
...
switch alignment {
case .left:
    print("left aligned")

case .right:
    print("right aligned")

default:
case .center:
    print("center aligned")
}
```

Now, instead of your program running and printing the wrong answer, you have a compile-time error that your `switch` statement is not exhaustive. It may seem odd to say that a compiler error is desirable, but that is exactly the situation here.

If you use a `default` clause when switching on an enum, your `switch` statement will always be exhaustive and satisfy the compiler. If you add a new case to the enum without updating the `switch`, the `switch` statement will use the `default` case when it encounters the new case. Your code will compile, but it might not do what you intended.

By listing each enum case in the `switch`, you ensure that the compiler will help you find all the places in your code that must be updated if you add cases to your enum. That is what is happening here: The compiler is telling you that your `switch` statement does not include all the cases defined in your enum.

Go ahead and fix that.

Listing 14.10 Including all cases

```
...
switch alignment {
case .left:
    print("left aligned")

case .right:
    print("right aligned")

case .center:
    print("center aligned")

case .justify:
    print("justified")
}
```

Now the compiler is satisfied *and* the desired value prints to the console.

Enumerations with Raw Values

If you have used enumerations in a language like C or C++, you may be surprised to learn that Swift enums do not have an underlying integer type. But you can get the same behavior by using what Swift calls a *raw value*. To use **Int** raw values for your text alignment enumeration, change the declaration of the enum.

Listing 14.11 Using raw values

```
enum TextAlignment: Int {
    case left
    case right
    case center
    case justify
}
...
```

Specifying a raw value type for **TextAlignment** gives a distinct raw value of that type (**Int**, here) to each case. The default behavior for integer raw values is that the first case gets raw value 0, the next case gets raw value 1, and so on. Confirm this by printing some interpolated strings.

Listing 14.12 Confirming the raw values

```
...
var alignment = TextAlignment.justify

TextAlignment.left.rawValue
TextAlignment.right.rawValue
TextAlignment.center.rawValue
TextAlignment.justify.rawValue
alignment.rawValue
...
```

You are not limited to the default behavior for raw values. If you prefer, you can specify the raw value for each case.

Listing 14.13 Specifying raw values

```
enum TextAlignment: Int {
    case left    = 20
    case right   = 30
    case center  = 40
    case justify = 50
}
...
```

When are raw values in an enumerations useful? The most common reason for using raw values is to store or transmit the enum to a system that does not know about your **TextAlignment** type. Instead of writing functions to transform a variable holding an enum, you can use rawValue to convert the variable to its raw value.

This brings up another question: If you have a raw value, how do you convert it back to the enum type? Every enum type with a raw value can be created with a rawValue argument, which returns an optional enum.

Listing 14.14 Converting raw values to enum types

```
...
TextAlignment.justify.rawValue
alignment.rawValue

// Create a raw value
let myRawValue = 20

// Try to convert the raw value into a TextAlignment
if let myAlignment = TextAlignment(rawValue: myRawValue) {
    // Conversion succeeded!
    print("successfully created \(myAlignment) from \(myRawValue)")
} else {
    // Conversion failed
    print("\(myRawValue) has no corresponding TextAlignment case")
}
...
```

You start with myRawValue, a variable of type **Int**. Then you try to convert that raw value into a **TextAlignment** case using **TextAlignment(rawValue:)**. Because **TextAlignment(rawValue:)** has a return type of **TextAlignment?**, you use optional binding to determine whether you get a **TextAlignment** value or nil back.

The raw value you used here corresponds to TextAlignment.left, so the conversion succeeds. Try changing myRawValue to a raw value that does not exist to see the message that conversion is not possible.

So far, you have been using **Int** as the type for your raw values. Swift also allows raw values to be **String**s, **Character**s, or instances of any numeric type. Create a new enum that uses **String** as its raw value type.

Listing 14.15 Creating an enum with strings

```
...
enum ProgrammingLanguage: String {
    case swift     = "swift"
    case objectiveC = "objective-c"
    case c         = "c"
    case cpp       = "c++"
    case java      = "java"
}

let myFavoriteLanguage = ProgrammingLanguage.swift
print("My favorite programming language is \(myFavoriteLanguage.rawValue)")
```

Here, you specify a corresponding raw **String** value for each case. However, just as the compiler will automatically provide integer raw values if you do not set them yourself, it will automatically use the name of a case as its string raw value. So once you have declared that an enum has string raw values, you do not need to assign values if they match the case names.

Modify **ProgrammingLanguage** to take out the unnecessary raw value assignments:

Listing 14.16 Using default string raw values

```
...
enum ProgrammingLanguage: String {
    case swift       = "swift"
    case objectiveC = "objective-c"
    case c           = "c"
    case cpp         = "c++"
    case java        = "java"
}

let myFavoriteLanguage = ProgrammingLanguage.swift
print("My favorite programming language is \(myFavoriteLanguage.rawValue)")
```

Your declaration of devotion to Swift does not change.

Methods

Recall that a method is a function that is associated with a type. In some languages, methods can only be associated with classes (which we will discuss in Chapter 15). In Swift, methods can also be associated with enums. Create a new enum that represents the state of a light bulb.

Listing 14.17 Light bulbs can be on or off

```
...
enum LightBulb {
    case on
    case off
}
```

Suppose you want to know the temperature of the light bulb. Add a method for computing the surface temperature. (For simplicity, this method ignores a lot of physics.)

Listing 14.18 Establishing temperature behaviors

```
...
enum LightBulb {
    case on
    case off

    func surfaceTemperature(forAmbientTemperature ambient: Double) -> Double {
        switch self {
        case .on:
            return ambient + 150.0

        case .off:
            return ambient
        }
    }
}
```

Here, you add a function inside the definition of the **LightBulb** enumeration. Because **surfaceTemperature(forAmbientTemperature:)** is defined with the enum, it is now a method associated with the **LightBulb** type. We would call it "a method on **LightBulb**."

The function appears to take a single argument (`ambient`) – but, because it is a method, it also takes an implicit argument named `self` of type **LightBulb**. All Swift methods have a `self` argument, which is used to access the instance on which the method is called – in this case, the instance of **LightBulb**.

Create a variable to represent a light bulb and call your new method.

Listing 14.19 Turning on the light

```
...
enum LightBulb {
    case on
    case off

    func surfaceTemperature(forAmbientTemperature ambient: Double) -> Double {
        switch self {
        case .on:
            return ambient + 150.0

        case .off:
            return ambient
        }
    }
}

var bulb = LightBulb.on
let ambientTemperature = 77.0

var bulbTemperature = bulb.surfaceTemperature(forAmbientTemperature:
                                              ambientTemperature)
print("the bulb's temperature is \(bulbTemperature)")
```

First you create `bulb`, an instance of the **LightBulb** type. When you have an instance of the type, you can call methods on that instance using the syntax `instance.methodName(arguments)`. You do exactly that here when you call `bulb.surfaceTemperature(forAmbientTemperature: ambientTemperature)`.

You store the result of the method call, a **Double**, in the `bulbTemperature` variable. Finally, you print a string with the bulb's temperature to the console.

The **Bool** type has a **toggle()** method that flips the variable to the opposite value (true to false and vice versa). It would be handy for your **LightBulb** type to have a **toggle()** method as well. To toggle the light bulb, you need to modify self to change it from on to off or off to on. Add a **toggle()** method that takes no arguments and does not return anything.

Listing 14.20 Trying to toggle

```
...
enum LightBulb {
    case on
    case off

    func surfaceTemperature(forAmbientTemperature ambient: Double) -> Double {
        switch self {
        case .on:
            return ambient + 150.0

        case .off:
            return ambient
        }
    }

    func toggle() {
        switch self {
        case .on:
            self = .off

        case .off:
            self = .on
        }
    }
}
...
```

When you enter this, you will get a compiler error that states that you cannot assign to self inside a method. In Swift, an enumeration is a *value type*, and, by default, methods on value types are not allowed to make changes to self.

If you want to allow a method on a value type to change self, you need to mark the method as *mutating*, which makes the implicit self argument mutable. You will learn more about value types and the mutating keyword in Chapter 15. For now, add this to your code:

Listing 14.21 Making **toggle()** a mutating method

```
...
mutating func toggle() {
    switch self {
    case .on:
        self = .off

    case .off:
        self = .on
    }
}
...
```

Now you can toggle your light bulb and see what the temperature is when the bulb is off.

Listing 14.22 Turning off the light

```
...
var bulbTemperature = bulb.surfaceTemperature(forAmbientTemperature:
                                             ambientTemperature)
print("the bulb's temperature is \(bulbTemperature)")

bulb.toggle()
bulbTemperature = bulb.surfaceTemperature(forAmbientTemperature: ambientTemperature)
print("the bulb's temperature is \(bulbTemperature)")
```

Associated Values

Everything you have done so far with enumerations falls into the same general category of defining static cases that enumerate possible values or states. Swift also offers a much more powerful flavor of enumeration: cases with associated values. Associated values allow you to attach data to instances of an enumeration, and different cases can have different types of associated values.

Create an enumeration to track the dimensions of a couple of basic shapes. Each kind of shape has different properties. To represent a square, you need a single value (the length of one side). To represent a rectangle, you need two values: a width and a height.

Listing 14.23 Setting up **ShapeDimensions**

```
...
enum ShapeDimensions {
    // square's associated value is the length of one side
    case square(side: Double)

    // rectangle's associated value defines its width and height
    case rectangle(width: Double, height: Double)
}
```

You define a new enumeration type, **ShapeDimensions**, with two cases. The `square` case has an associated value of type **(side: Double)**. The `rectangle` case has an associated value of type **(width: Double, height: Double)**. Both of these are named tuples (first seen in Chapter 12).

To create instances of **ShapeDimensions**, you must specify both the case and an appropriate associated value for the case.

Listing 14.24 Creating shapes

```
...
enum ShapeDimensions {
    // square's associated value is the length of one side
    case square(side: Double)

    // rectangle's associated value defines its width and height
    case rectangle(width: Double, height: Double)
}

var squareShape = ShapeDimensions.square(side: 10.0)
var rectShape = ShapeDimensions.rectangle(width: 5.0, height: 10.0)
```

Here, you create a square with sides 10 units long and a rectangle that is 5 units by 10 units.

You can use a switch statement to unpack and use an associated value. Add a method to **ShapeDimensions** that computes the area of a shape.

Listing 14.25 Using associated values to compute area

```
...
enum ShapeDimensions {
    // square's associated value is the length of one side
    case square(side: Double)

    // rectangle's associated value defines its width and height
    case rectangle(width: Double, height: Double)

    func area() -> Double {
        switch self {
        case let .square(side: side):
            return side * side

        case let .rectangle(width: w, height: h):
            return w * h
        }
    }
}
...
```

In your implementation of **area()**, you switch on self just as you did earlier in the chapter. Here, the switch cases use Swift's pattern matching to bind self's associated value with a new variable (or variables).

Call the **area()** method on the instances you created earlier to see it in action.

Listing 14.26 Computing areas

```
...
var squareShape = ShapeDimensions.square(side: 10.0)
var rectShape = ShapeDimensions.rectangle(width: 5.0, height: 10.0)

print("square's area = \(squareShape.area())")
print("rectangle's area = \(rectShape.area())")
```

Not all enum cases need to have associated values. For example, you could add a `point` case. Geometric points do not have any dimensions. Add a `point` to your enum with no associated value and update the **area()** method to include its area.

Listing 14.27 Setting up a **point**

```
...
enum ShapeDimensions {
    // point has no associated value - it is dimensionless
    case point

    // square's associated value is the length of one side
    case square(side: Double)

    // rectangle's associated value defines its width and height
    case rectangle(width: Double, height: Double)

    func area() -> Double {
        switch self {
        case .point:
            return 0

        case let .square(side: side):
            return side * side

        case let .rectangle(width: w, height: h):
            return w * h
        }
    }
}
...
```

Now, create an instance of a point and confirm that **area()** works as expected.

Listing 14.28 What is the area of a point?

```
...
var squareShape = ShapeDimensions.square(side: 10.0)
var rectShape = ShapeDimensions.rectangle(width: 5.0, height: 10.0)
var pointShape = ShapeDimensions.point

print("square's area = \(squareShape.area())")
print("rectangle's area = \(rectShape.area())")
print("point's area = \(pointShape.area())")
```

In this chapter, you saw how to define custom data structures to represent one of a discrete list of values, sometimes with associated data. The Swift standard library has a wide range of types available for modeling different kinds of data, but the ability to directly model custom data using your own type in this way is extremely powerful.

In the next chapter, you will learn how to define more complex data structures to drive your applications.

Bronze Challenge

Add a `perimeter()` method to the `ShapeDimensions` enum. This method should compute the perimeter of a shape (the sum of the length of all its edges). Make sure you handle all the cases!

Silver Challenge

Add another case to the `ShapeDimensions` enum for a right triangle. You can ignore the orientation of the triangle. Just keep track of the lengths of its three sides. Adding a new case will cause your playground to give you an error in the `area()` method. Fix the error.

For the More Curious: Recursive Enumerations

You now know how to attach associated values to enum cases. This brings up a curious question. Can you attach an associated value of an enum's own type to one of its cases? (Perhaps this question brings up another: Why would you want to?)

A data structure that comes up frequently in computer science is a tree. Most hierarchical data can naturally be represented as a tree. Think of a genealogical family tree: It contains people (the "nodes" of the tree) and ancestral relationships (the "edges" of the tree). The family tree branching stops when you reach an ancestor you do not know, as in Figure 14.1.

Figure 14.1 A family tree

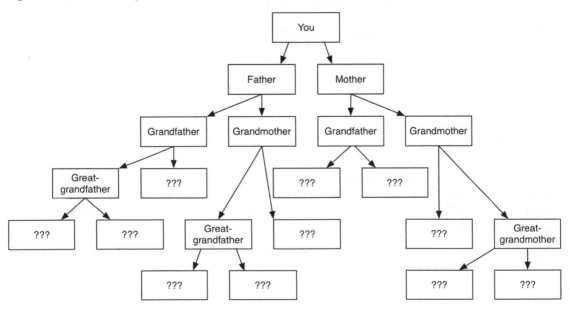

Modeling a family tree can be difficult because for any given person, you may know zero, one, or both of their biological parents. If you know one or both parents, you would like to keep track of their ancestors as well. Consider an enum that might let you build up as much of your family tree as you know.

```
enum FamilyTree {
    case noKnownParents
    case oneKnownParent(name: String, ancestors: FamilyTree)
    case twoKnownParents(fatherName: String,
                         paternalAncestors: FamilyTree,
                         motherName: String,
                         maternalAncestors: FamilyTree)
}
```

Unfortunately, this is will not compile. **FamilyTree** is *recursive*, because its cases have an associated value that is also of type **FamilyTree**, and Swift treats recursive enumerations specially.

To understand why, you need to know a little bit about how enumerations work under the hood. The Swift compiler has to know how much memory every instance of every type in your program will occupy. You do not (usually) have to worry about this, as the compiler figures it all out for you when it builds your program.

Enumerations are a little different. The compiler knows that any instance of an enum will only ever store one case at a time, although it may change cases as your program runs. Therefore, when the compiler is deciding how much memory an instance of enum requires, it will look at each case and figure out which case requires the most memory. The instance will require that much memory (plus a little bit more that the compiler will use to keep track of which case is currently assigned).

Look back at your **ShapeDimensions** enum. The point case has no associated data, so it requires no extra memory. The square case has an associated **Double**, so it requires one **Double**'s worth of memory (8 bytes). The rectangle case has two associated **Double**s, so it requires 16 bytes of memory. The actual size of an instance of **ShapeDimensions** is 17 bytes: enough room to store rectangle, if necessary, plus 1 byte to keep track of which case the instance actually is.

Now consider the **FamilyTree** enum. How much memory is required for the oneKnownParent case? Enough memory for a **String** plus enough memory for an instance of **FamilyTree**. See the problem? The compiler cannot determine how big a **FamilyTree** is without knowing how big a **FamilyTree** is. Looking at it another way, **FamilyTree** would require an infinite amount of memory!

To solve this issue, Swift can introduce a layer of indirection. Instead of deciding how much memory oneKnownParent will require (which would lead to infinite recursion), you can use the keyword indirect to instruct the compiler to instead store the enum's data behind a pointer. We do not discuss the details of pointers in this book, because Swift does not make you deal with them.

Here, all you have to do is opt in to making **FamilyTree** use pointers under the hood. Adding the indirect keyword allows cases to be recursive:

```
indirect enum FamilyTree {
    case noKnownParents
    case oneKnownParent(name: String, ancestors: FamilyTree)
    case twoKnownParents(fatherName: String,
                         paternalAncestors: FamilyTree,
                         motherName: String,
                         maternalAncestors: FamilyTree)
}
```

How does using a pointer solve the "infinite memory" problem? The compiler now knows to store a pointer to the associated data, putting the data somewhere else in memory rather than making the instance of **FamilyTree** big enough to hold the data. The size of an instance of **FamilyTree** is now 8 bytes on a 64-bit architecture – the size of one pointer.

It is worth noting that you do not have to mark the entire enumeration as indirect: You can also mark individual recursive cases as indirect:

```
enum FamilyTree {
    case noKnownParents
    indirect case oneKnownParent(name: String, ancestors: FamilyTree)
    indirect case twoKnownParents(fatherName: String,
                                  paternalAncestors: FamilyTree,
                                  motherName: String,
                                  maternalAncestors: FamilyTree)
}
```

Using indirect cases, a family tree can be constructed:

```
let fredAncestors = FamilyTree.twoKnownParents(
        fatherName: "Fred Sr.",
        paternalAncestors: .oneKnownParent(name: "Beth",
                                           ancestors: .noKnownParents),
        motherName: "Marsha",
        maternalAncestors: .noKnownParents)
```

This code is represented graphically by Figure 14.2.

Figure 14.2 Fred's family tree

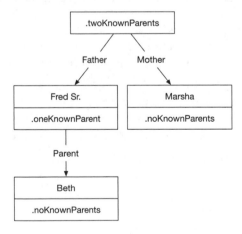

fredAncestors is a recursive enumeration that represents Fred's known family tree, with each node in the tree representing an instance of the same enumeration. As you can see, this sort of enumeration models nested information quite well.

15

Structs and Classes

You learned that an enum can be a powerful way to model custom data, such as the state of a light bulb. Using associated values, you were able to attach some arbitrary data to your enum cases, which made them even more flexible for data modeling. But while enums are great for representing a singular value with some associated contextual data, they are not designed for modeling large or complex systems.

For that, you use a structure (commonly just called a *struct*) or a *class*. These types are syntactically similar, which is why we will introduce them together. Over the next several chapters, you will learn about the important similarities, differences, and uses for these types.

For the next few chapters, you will be working in a *command-line tool* rather than a playground. Your command-line tool project will model a town undergoing a serious monster infestation. You will use both structs and classes to model these entities and will give them properties to store data and functions so that these entities can do some work.

A New Project

In Xcode, click File → New → Project... (Figure 15.1).

Figure 15.1 Creating a new project instead of a playground

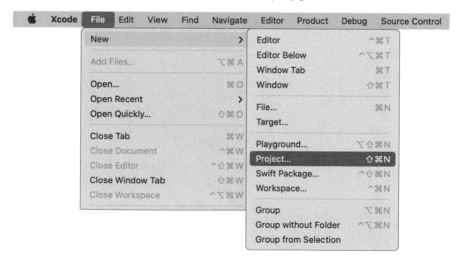

Next, you will select a project *template* (Figure 15.2). A template formats your project with a number of presets and configurations common to a given style of application. Along the top of the window, notice that there are several options: Multiplatform, iOS, macOS, watchOS, tvOS, and Other. Select macOS. Next, in the Application area of the window, choose the Command Line Tool template and click Next. This template will create a very basic project.

Figure 15.2 Choosing a template

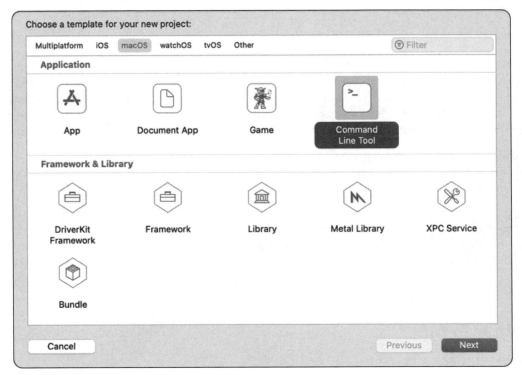

Now you will choose options for your project, including a name (Figure 15.3). In the Product Name field, enter MonsterTown. Enter BigNerdRanch (or whatever you would like) for the project's Organization Identifier. The Bundle Identifier, used to uniquely identify your app to the OS and to the App Store, fills in for you. (Do not worry about the Team item or adding an account; that feature is used for signing and distributing your application.)

Select Swift for the Language option and click Next.

Figure 15.3 Naming your project

Last, Xcode asks you where to save the project. You can ignore the Source Control, Add to, and Group fields. Select a good location on your Mac to save the project and click Create.

Your project opens in Xcode with the project file selected, as shown in Figure 15.4. This file allows you to manage various settings for your application. For example, you can sign your application for deployment, link to frameworks to use in your development, and much more.

Figure 15.4 The project file

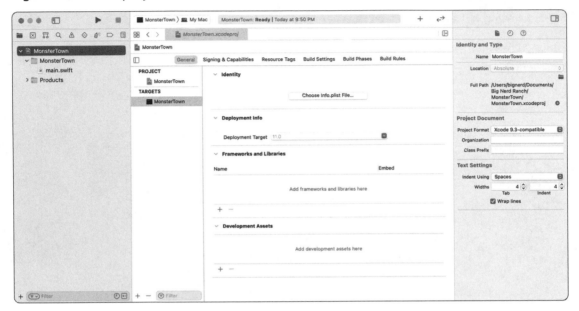

Let's take a moment to look at the organization of the Xcode application window (Figure 15.5).

Figure 15.5 Organization of Xcode

The pane on the far left is the *navigator area*. It provides several views that encapsulate how your project is organized. The view that opens by default is the *project navigator*. In the project navigator, you see a listing of your files, which at the moment only includes main.swift.

Moving one section to the right, you see the *editor area*. This is where you will add, view, and edit the code in a selected file.

On the far right is the *inspector area*. The inspector area provides several inspectors that allow you to get more information, such as the *file inspector*, which gives information about a file's location, name, and so on.

At the bottom of the Xcode window is the *debug area*, which includes the variable view and the console. You will use this area to debug your code when there are problems. (The debug area may not open by default; we will explain how to open it later.)

At the top of the window is the toolbar, which has play and stop buttons you will use to run and stop your programs, among other tools.

In the project navigator on the far left side, click the main.swift file to open it in the editor area (Figure 15.6).

Figure 15.6 main.swift

In a command-line tool, main.swift represents the entry point of your program. Like a playground, main.swift executes top to bottom. After the last line of code in this file executes, the program is complete and exits.

To let main.swift define the procedural story of your program, you define custom types and functions in other files and then use them in main.swift. For example, you will create a Town.swift file to hold a definition of a struct called **Town**. Then you will create an instance of **Town** in main.swift.

This strategy of defining each new type in its own file helps organize an application's source code, making it easier to find and debug code in large projects.

Notice that the `main.swift` file already has some code:

```
import Foundation

print("Hello, World!")
```

`import Foundation` brings the Foundation *framework* into the `main.swift` file. A framework is a precompiled collection of types and functions you can use in your program. There are frameworks published by Apple and others to give you the building blocks for programs that do anything from presenting rich user interfaces to communicating with web servers.

The Foundation framework is provided by Apple and consists of a number of classes primarily designed to do work in and with Objective-C. In the future, we will ignore this line of code unless you need it for context in the code listing or for using one of the types it provides.

The `print("Hello, World!")` code should look familiar. It logs the string `Hello, World!` to the console.

Build and run your program. There are several ways to do this:

- In the Xcode menu bar, click **Product**, then select **Run**.

- Click the triangular play button in Xcode's upper-left corner.

- Press Command-R.

When you run your program, the debug area opens, if it was not open already. `Hello, World!` is logged to the console, along with information from the compiler about how the program ended.

That is great, but you have seen strings logged to the console before. Let's make your program more interesting by creating custom structs and classes. Before you move on, delete `print("Hello, World!")`; you will not need it.

Listing 15.1 Removing "Hello, World!" (`main.swift`)

```
import Foundation

print("Hello, World!")
```

Structures

A struct is a type that groups a set of related chunks of data together in memory. You use structs when you would like to group data together under a common type. You are going to create a struct called **Town** to model a town with a monster problem, along with its size, population, and region.

In previous chapters, you modeled a town in a playground. Because the example was relatively small, this was not all that limiting. Playgrounds use a streamlined approach to code management to facilitate quick prototyping of code, but app development requires a more robust set of tools for code organization. It is better to encapsulate the definition of the town within its own type, in its own file.

Add a new file to your project using File → New → File.... You can also press Command-N. A window like the one shown in Figure 15.7 prompts you to select a template for your new file. With macOS selected at the top, choose Swift File from the Source section and click Next.

Figure 15.7 Adding a Swift file

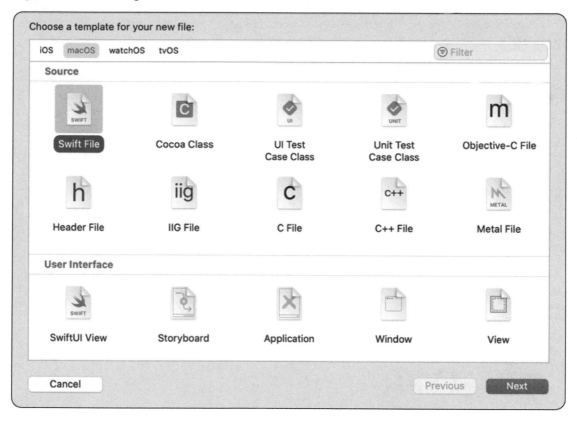

Next you are asked to name the new file and set its location. Call the file Town and make sure the box is checked to add it to the MonsterTown target (Figure 15.8). Click Create.

Figure 15.8 Town.swift

Your new file opens automatically. (If it does not, select Town.swift in the project navigator.) It is nearly blank: just the comments at the top and the import Foundation line.

Start declaring your **Town** struct.

Listing 15.2 Declaring a struct (Town.swift)

```
import Foundation

struct Town {

}
```

The keyword struct signals that you are declaring a struct, in this case named **Town**. You will add code between the braces ({}) to define the behavior of this struct. For example, you are about to add variables to your new struct so that it can hold on to some data that will help model the characteristics of your town.

Technically, these variables are called *properties*, which is the subject of Chapter 16. Properties can be variable or constant, using the var and let keywords you have seen before. Add some properties to your struct.

Listing 15.3 Adding properties (Town.swift)

```
struct Town {
    var population = 5_422
    var numberOfStoplights = 4
}
```

Here, you add two properties to **Town**: population and numberOfStoplights. Both of these properties are mutable – this makes sense, because a town's population and number of stoplights are likely to change over time. These properties also have default values, for the sake of simplicity. When a new instance of the **Town** struct is made, it will default to having a population of 5,422 and 4 stoplights.

Switch to your `main.swift` file and create a new instance of **Town** to see your struct in action. (As always, do not break the string in your code.)

Listing 15.4 Creating an instance of **Town** (`main.swift`)

```
var myTown = Town()
print("Population: \(myTown.population);
        number of stoplights: \(myTown.numberOfStoplights)")
```

You accomplish three things with this code. First, you create an instance of the **Town** type. You do this by entering the name of the type (here, **Town**) followed by empty parentheses `()`. Including the empty parentheses calls the default initializer for **Town** (more on initialization in Chapter 17).

Second, you assign this instance to a variable you call `myTown`.

Third, you use string interpolation to print the values of the **Town** struct's two properties to the console. Notice that you use dot syntax (like `myTown.population`) to access the properties' values.

Run your program. The output reads `Population: 5422; number of stoplights: 4.`

Instance Methods

The **print()** function is a fine way to print a description of myTown. But a town should know how to describe itself. Create a function on the **Town** struct that prints the values of its properties to the console. Navigate to your Town.swift file and add the following function definition.

Listing 15.5 Letting **Town** describe itself (Town.swift)

```
struct Town {
    var population = 5_422
    var numberOfStoplights = 4

    func printDescription() {
        print("Population: \(population);
                number of stoplights: \(numberOfStoplights)")
    }
}
```

Warning! By default, your files can see each other's code. (You will learn about code privacy in Chapter 23.) If you copied the **print()** function call above from main.swift, then it will incorrectly print myTown.population and myTown.numberOfStoplights (properties of the myTown instance declared in main.swift) instead of the properties declared above. Make sure your code matches the snippet shown here.

printDescription() is a method, because it is a function that is associated with a particular type. It takes no arguments and returns nothing. Its purpose is to log a description of a town's properties to the console. That makes **printDescription()** an *instance method*, because it is called on a specific instance of **Town**.

To use your new instance method, you need to call it on an instance of **Town**. Navigate back to main.swift and replace the **print()** function with your new instance method.

Listing 15.6 Calling your new instance method (main.swift)

```
var myTown = Town()
print("Population: \(myTown.population);
            number of stoplights: \(myTown.numberOfStoplights)")
myTown.printDescription()
```

You use dot syntax to call a function on an instance, as in myTown.printDescription(). Run your program. The console output is the same as before.

Mutating methods

Your `printDescription()` method is great for displaying your town's current information. But what if you need a function that *changes* your town's information? If an instance method on a struct changes any of the struct's properties, it must be marked with the `mutating` keyword. In `Town.swift`, add a mutating method to the **Town** type to increase a town instance's population.

Listing 15.7 Adding a mutating method to increase population (`Town.swift`)

```
struct Town {
    var population = 5_422
    var numberOfStoplights = 4

    func printDescription() {
        print("Population: \(population);
                number of stoplights: \(numberOfStoplights)")
    }

    mutating func changePopulation(by amount: Int) {
        population += amount
    }
}
```

Note that you mark the instance method **changePopulation(by:)** with the `mutating` keyword. As you saw with enumerations in Chapter 14, this means that the method can change the values in the struct. Both structures and enumerations require the `mutating` keyword on methods that change the value of an instance's properties.

Recall from Chapter 12 that a value passed in to a function is copied into the function. The function cannot modify the original variable's value unless the argument is marked `inout`. You also learned in Chapter 14 that instance methods take an implicit first argument, `self`, containing the value that the method has been called on.

The `mutating` keyword asks the compiler to make the implicit `self` argument `inout`, so that the instance method can make changes to the original value the method was called on, instead of a copy. You will learn more about this behavior, and a major exception to it, later on.

Your method has one explicit parameter, `amount`, which is an **Int**. You use this parameter to increase the town's population in the line `population += amount`. Switch over to `main.swift` to exercise this function:

Listing 15.8 Increasing the population (`main.swift`)

```
var myTown = Town()
myTown.changePopulation(by: 500)
myTown.printDescription()
```

As before, you use dot syntax to call the function on your town. Build and run the program; you will see that `myTown`'s population has been increased by 500 and the console reads `Population: 5922; number of stoplights: 4`.

185

Classes

Like structs, classes are used to model related data under a common type. You will use classes in MonsterTown to model various types of monsters that will be terrorizing your town. Classes differ from structs in a few very important ways, and this section will begin to highlight those differences.

A Monster class

Now that you have a struct representing a town, it is time to make things a little more interesting. Your town is, unfortunately, infested with monsters. This is not good for property values.

Create a new Swift file called `Monster.swift`: As before, click File → New → File... or press Command-N. Select the Swift File template from the Source section under macOS.

This file will contain the definition for a **Monster** class that will be used to model a monster's properties and town-terrorizing activities. Start by creating a new class:

Listing 15.9 Monster setup (`Monster.swift`)

```
import Foundation

class Monster {

}
```

The syntax to define a new class type is nearly identical to the syntax used to define a new struct type. You begin with the keyword `class`, followed by the name you are assigning to your new class. And, as before, the definition of the class takes place between the braces: {}.

For reasons relating to inheritance (discussed in the next section), the class **Monster** is defined in very general terms. This means that the **Monster** class will describe the general behavior of a monster. Later you will create different kinds of monsters that will have specific behaviors.

Listing 15.10 Defining the **Monster** class (`Monster.swift`)

```
class Monster {
    var town: Town?
    var name = "Monster"

    func terrorizeTown() {
        if town != nil {
            print("\(name) is terrorizing a town!")
        } else {
            print("\(name) hasn't found a town to terrorize yet...")
        }
    }
}
```

It is well known that monsters do one thing very well: They terrorize towns. The **Monster** class has a property for the town that a given monster is terrorizing. Because the monster may or may not have found a town to terrorize yet, the `town` property is an optional (**Town?**), and it starts out `nil`. You also create a property for the **Monster**'s name and give it a generic default value.

Next, you define a basic stub for a method called **terrorizeTown()**. This method will be called on an instance of **Monster** to represent the monster terrorizing a town.

Notice that you check whether the instance has a town using if town != nil. If it does, then **terrorizeTown()** will log to the console the name of the monster wreaking havoc. If the instance does not have a town yet, then the method will log that information.

As different sorts of monsters terrorize towns in different ways, *subclasses* will provide their own implementation of this function. You will learn about subclasses in the next section.

Switch to main.swift to exercise the **Monster** class. Add an instance of this type, give it a town, and call the **terrorizeTown()** function on it.

Listing 15.11 Setting a generic monster loose (main.swift)

```
var myTown = Town()
myTown.changePopulation(by: 500)
myTown.printDescription()

let genericMonster = Monster()
genericMonster.town = myTown
genericMonster.terrorizeTown()
```

First, you create an instance of the **Monster** class called genericMonster. This instance is declared as a constant because there is no need for it to be mutable. Next, you assign myTown to genericMonster's town property. Finally, you call the **terrorizeTown()** method on the **Monster** instance. Run the program, and Monster is terrorizing a town! logs to the console.

Inheritance

One of the main features of classes that structures and enumerations do not have is *inheritance*. Inheritance is a relationship in which one class, a *subclass*, is defined in terms of another, a *superclass*. The subclass *inherits* the properties and methods of its superclass. In a sense, inheritance defines the genealogy of class types.

The fact that classes can take advantage of inheritance is the primary reason you made the **Monster** type a class. You are going to create a subclass of the **Monster** class, **Zombie**, to represent a particular kind of monster. (In a more complex program, you could create subclasses for werewolves, chupacabras, and any other kind of monster you can imagine - and, in fact, for this chapter's silver challenge you will create a **Vampire** subclass with its own behaviors.)

A Zombie subclass

Create a new Swift file called `Zombie.swift`, following the same steps as you did to create `Town.swift` and `Monster.swift`. Add the following class declaration to see how the **Zombie** subclass inherits from the **Monster** class.

Listing 15.12 Zombie creation (`Zombie.swift`)

```
import Foundation

class Zombie: Monster {
    var walksWithLimp = true

    override func terrorizeTown() {
        town?.changePopulation(by: -10)
        super.terrorizeTown()
    }
}
```

Your new **Zombie** class inherits from the **Monster** type, which is indicated by the colon (`:`) and superclass name (`Monster`) after `Zombie`. Inheriting from **Monster** means that **Zombie** has all **Monster**'s properties and methods, like the `town` property and the **terrorizeTown()** method used here.

Zombie also adds a new property. The property is called `walksWithLimp` and is of type **Bool** (inferred from the property's default value: `true`).

Finally, **Zombie** *overrides* the **terrorizeTown()** method. Overriding a method means that a subclass provides its own definition of a method that is defined on its superclass. Note the use of the `override` keyword. Failing to use this keyword when overriding a method will result in a compiler error.

Figure 15.9 shows **Zombie**'s relationship to **Monster**.

Figure 15.9 **Zombie** inheritance

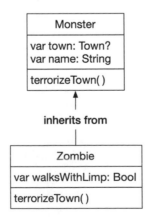

Zombie inherits the properties `town` and `name` from the **Monster** class. It also inherits the **terrorizeTown()** method, but it provides an override, which is why it is listed in both areas in the figure. Last, **Zombie** adds a property of its own: `walksWithLimp`.

Inheritance hierarchies can be as deep as you want. You could add a **ShamblingZombie** class that subclasses **Zombie**, for example. Perhaps a shambling zombie would have a smaller impact on a town's population because it does not move as fast.

Notice the line super.terrorizeTown() in Listing 15.12. super is a prefix used to access a superclass's implementation of a method. In this case, you use super to call the **Monster** class's implementation of **terrorizeTown()**.

Because super is a feature of inheritance, it is not available to enums or structs, which do not support inheritance. It is invoked to borrow or override functionality from a superclass.

Recall that **Zombie**'s town property, inherited from the **Monster** class, is an optional of type **Town?**. You need to make sure that an instance of **Zombie** has a town to terrorize before calling any methods on the town.

One possible solution might have been to use optional binding, like this:

```
if let terrorTown = town {
    // Do something to terrorTown
}
```

In the code above, if the **Zombie** instance has a town, then the value in the optional is unwrapped and put into the constant terrorTown. After that, this value is ready to be terrorized, but with an important caveat: terrorTown is not the same instance as the town instance. It is a copy, for reasons we will explain in the section called *Looking Ahead: What Is the Real Difference?* later in this chapter.

This means that any changes made on terrorTown will not be reflected in the **Zombie** instance's town property. They would be two different (albeit initially identical) instances of the **Town** type. In addition to this limitation, this code could also be more concise.

In short, this is not an ideal solution.

The optional chaining you use in Listing 15.12 (town?.changePopulation(by: −10)) allows a check like this to be done on a single line. It is just as expressive and is also more concise. If the optional town has a value, then the method **changePopulation(by:)** is called on that instance, and the population is decreased by 10 people. Furthermore, the copy problem described above is avoided, because town is changed directly.

In a moment, you will use optional chaining again to call **printDescription()** on a zombie's town.

Preventing overriding

Sometimes you want to prevent subclasses from being able to override methods or properties. The need to do this is rare in practice, but it does come up. In these cases, you use the `final` keyword to prevent a method or property from being overridden.

Imagine, for example, that you do not want subclasses of the **Monster** type to provide their own implementation of the `terrorizeTown()` function. In other words, all subclasses of **Monster** should terrorize their towns in the exact same way. Add the `final` keyword to this function's declaration. In a moment, you will see that this creates an error.

Listing 15.13 Preventing overriding of **terrorizeTown()** (Monster.swift)

```swift
class Monster {
    var town: Town?
    var name = "Monster"

    final func terrorizeTown() {
        if town != nil {
            print("\(name) is terrorizing a town!")
        } else {
            print("\(name) hasn't found a town to terrorize yet...")
        }
    }
}
```

Now, subclasses of the **Monster** class will not be able to override the `terrorizeTown()` method.

Try to build your program. You should see the following error on the line where you try to override the `terrorizeTown()` method in Zombie.swift: `Instance method overrides a 'final' instance method`. The error indicates that you cannot override `terrorizeTown()` because it is marked as `final` in the superclass.

The `final` keyword can also be used on a class declaration, just like a method declaration, if you want to prevent the class from being subclassed at all.

Undo your change before continuing:

Listing 15.14 Allowing overriding of **terrorizeTown()** again (Monster.swift)

```swift
class Monster {
    ...
    ~~final~~ func terrorizeTown() {
        ...
    }
}
```

The zombie problem

Now is a good time to exercise the **Zombie** type. Choose the main.swift file from the project navigator. Create an instance of the **Zombie** class. While you are there, delete the code that prints the town's description as well as the code that created a generic instance of the **Monster** type, which you no longer need.

Listing 15.15 Who's afraid of fredTheZombie? (main.swift)

```
var myTown = Town()
myTown.changePopulation(by: 500)
myTown.printDescription()

let genericMonster = Monster()
genericMonster.town = myTown
genericMonster.terrorizeTown()

let fredTheZombie = Zombie()
fredTheZombie.town = myTown
fredTheZombie.terrorizeTown()
fredTheZombie.town?.printDescription()
```

You first create a new instance of the **Zombie** type named fredTheZombie. Next, you assign your preexisting instance of the **Town** type, myTown, to the **Zombie** type's property town. At this point, fredTheZombie is free to terrorize myTown, which it will do with alacrity. (Or, at least, as much alacrity as a zombie can muster.)

After fredTheZombie has terrorized the townsfolk, you check the results with the **printDescription()**. As discussed earlier, because fredTheZombie's town property is an optional of type **Town?**, you have to unwrap it before you can call the **printDescription()** function on it. You do this with optional chaining: fredTheZombie.town?.printDescription(). This code ensures that fredTheZombie has a town before you try to use **printDescription()**.

The console output should read: Population: 5912; number of stoplights: 4.

Polymorphism and type casting

You have learned that a subclass has all the properties and methods of its superclass, and maybe more. You could say that every **Zombie** is also a **Monster**. This is an example of *polymorphism*, a term that means "having many forms."

You will explore polymorphism later in this book, but the short version for now is this: Because **Zombie** inherits from **Monster**, you can treat an instance of **Zombie** as though it were a **Monster**. *And*, in fact, vice versa. But only one of these things is safe to do.

Declare your fredTheZombie variable to be of type **Monster**.

Listing 15.16 Fred is a **Monster** (main.swift)

```
...
let fredTheZombie: Monster = Zombie()
fredTheZombie.town = myTown
fredTheZombie.terrorizeTown()
fredTheZombie.town?.printDescription()
```

Here you tell the compiler that you want a variable of type **Monster**, but then you store a value of type **Zombie** in it. The compiler uses the declared variable type to decide what you are allowed to do with the variable later. Because there is nothing you might do to a **Monster** that you could not also do to a **Zombie**, the compiler decides that this is OK - so long as you only want to do **Monster**-y things to your variable.

Run your program, and you will see that nothing at all has changed in the output. When the program runs, it is the type of instance actually stored in the variable, not the declared type of the variable, that matters. The declared variable type only matters to the compiler, so that it can check to make sure that you only access properties and methods that actually exist on that type.

So far you are accessing the town property and the **terrorizeTown()** method, both of which exist on both types. But what if you try to access a property that only exists on a **Zombie**? Try it:

Listing 15.17 Not all monsters walk with a limp (main.swift)

```
...
let fredTheZombie: Monster = Zombie()
fredTheZombie.town = myTown
fredTheZombie.terrorizeTown()
fredTheZombie.town?.printDescription()
fredTheZombie.walksWithLimp = true
```

This creates a compiler error. You know that when the program runs, fredTheZombie will contain an instance of **Zombie**, which has a walksWithLimp property. But the compiler complains that you said the variable might hold *any* **Monster**, so it cannot let you do **Zombie**-specific things to it.

You can instruct the compiler to treat a variable as though it were of a specific, related type. This is called *type casting* and is done with the as keyword. Note that type casting does not change the type of the variable itself - instead, it creates an expression that is of a different type than the variable. Try fixing the error by casting fredTheZombie back to its real type, **Zombie**.

Listing 15.18 Not actually fixing the error (main.swift)

```
...
(fredTheZombie as Zombie).walksWithLimp = true
```

This did not quite fix the error. Casting from a more general type (a superclass) to a more specific type (a subclass) is called *downcasting*, and it is unsafe. If the compiler let you cast a variable to a type with more properties but the instance actually stored in that variable did not have those properties, then the program would crash when you tried to access them.

You have two choices. You could force the cast to occur with the as! keyword. In that case, if you try to access a property that the instance does not have, the program will crash at the site of the cast. This is a bit like force-unwrapping an optional. It is only safe if you can guarantee that it will work.

Alternatively, you can perform a conditional cast with the as? keyword. In that case, if the cast fails at runtime, the casting expression will return nil. In most cases, this is the safer choice, just as optional binding is safer than force-unwrapping.

Perform the conditional cast:

Listing 15.19 Fred might be a **Zombie** after all (main.swift)

```
...
(fredTheZombie as? Zombie)?.walksWithLimp = true
```

Here you conditionally cast fredTheZombie back to type **Zombie**. Because the compiler does not know whether the cast will succeed at runtime, a conditional cast is an optional expression, so you use optional chaining to access the walksWithLimp property.

Two final notes about type casting: First, casting from a subclass to its superclass is called *upcasting* and is always safe; there is nothing a **Monster** can do that a **Zombie** cannot. Because it is safe, when you upcast, the unadorned as keyword works nicely.

Second, you can ask Swift whether you are correct about an instance's type at runtime with the is keyword, like this:

```
if fredTheZombie is Zombie {
    print("I knew it!")
}
```

The is expression will return true for the target type or any of its direct or indirect superclasses.

What you have learned here about type and polymorphism applies to functions as well: A function with a signature of **(Monster) -> Void** would be happy to accept an argument of type **Zombie**, but not the reverse, without potentially unsafe type casting.

Inheritance is only one form of polymorphism. You will see another in Chapter 19. The utility of type casting may not seem immediately obvious, but as you begin writing more complex programs for iOS and macOS, you will encounter scenarios where it will be required in order to use values as they move around your program in variables of different types.

But MonsterTown is not a complex program, and you do not want to have to cast fredTheZombie every time you use it. Go ahead and take out the explicit **Monster** declaration and walksWithLimp usage.

Listing 15.20 Rolling back the casting (main.swift)

```
...
let fredTheZombie: Monster = Zombie()
fredTheZombie.town = myTown
fredTheZombie.terrorizeTown()
fredTheZombie.town?.printDescription()
(fredTheZombie as? Zombie)?.walksWithLimp = true
```

Looking Ahead: What Is the Real Difference?

In this chapter, the biggest difference that you have encountered between classes and structs is that classes support inheritance and structs do not. That alone is not a compelling reason to have both structs and classes in the language, especially since the `final` keyword can be used to prevent a class from being subclassed where necessary.

The underlying difference between structs and classes is a bit more subtle, but it has crucial implications for how they are used. Here is a sneak peek at a feature of structs and classes that you will explore in much greater depth later in this book.

When you have a struct or enum variable, all the memory the instance needs to store its content is inside that variable. For example, a `Town` instance contains two `Int`s. Each `Int` is 64 bits (8 bytes) in size, so a variable that contains a `Town` takes up at least 16 bytes of memory. If you duplicate the variable, you duplicate the entire instance, copying its memory into the new variable.

Make this change to `main.swift`:

Listing 15.21 Value semantics (`main.swift`)

```
var myTown = Town()
var yourTown = myTown // Now there are two towns!
myTown.changePopulation(by: 500)
print("myTown has \(myTown.population) and yourTown has \(yourTown.population)")

let fredTheZombie = Zombie()
...
```

Run your program, and you will see that the change to `myTown`'s population does not affect `yourTown`. Setting `yourTown = myTown` made an entire copy of the struct in the `myTown` variable and stuffed that copy into the `yourTown` variable. Because a struct (or enum) variable stores the instance's entire value, we say that structs and enums are *value types* and that their instances follow *value semantics*.

You have also seen this behavior in the `Int`, `Float`, `Double`, `Bool`, etc. types. That is because they are also value types. In fact, they are implemented as structs in the Swift standard library.

Classes, on the other hand, only use a variable to store a *reference* to some other location in memory where the instance's actual content is stored. That other location is managed by the system. You manage and pass around copies of your reference, and the system will manage the lifetime of the memory your variable refers to.

In a modern program, a reference is always 64 bits (8 bytes) of memory, no matter how many bytes are used by the actual instance it refers to. A variable containing a reference to a class instance with 50 `Int` properties would still only be 8 bytes, even though the instance itself would be at least 400 bytes. This means it is possible for more than one variable to have a reference to a single shared bit of information.

At the bottom of `main.swift`, make another `Monster`:

Listing 15.22 Reference semantics (`main.swift`)

```
...
var frederickTheZombie = fredTheZombie // Still only one zombie!
frederickTheZombie.name = "Frederick"
print("Fred's name is \(fredTheZombie.name)")
```

Run now, and you will be told that `Fred's name is Frederick`.

A class variable does not store all the bytes that make up the instance of the class, like a struct variable does. Since a class variable only stores a reference to where the real bytes are, setting `frederickTheZombie = fredTheZombie` merely means that `frederickTheZombie` contains a reference to the same bytes in memory that `fredTheZombie` does. Both variables refer to the same actual **Zombie** in memory, and you can use either reference to access the instance's `name`.

(If you are familiar with the concept of *pointers* in other programming languages, this is the same idea but with a slightly different execution under the hood.)

Because class variables only hold references to bytes that are stored elsewhere, we say that classes are *reference types* and that their instances follow *reference semantics* when we use them. This memory is managed by a Swift feature that you will learn about in Chapter 24.

Add the following code to your **Zombie** class:

Listing 15.23 Classes can always mutate (Zombie.swift)

```
class Zombie: Monster {
    var walksWithLimp = true

    func regenerate() {
        walksWithLimp = false
    }

    override func terrorizeTown() {
        town?.changePopulation(by: -10)
        super.terrorizeTown()
        regenerate()
    }
}
```

terrorizeTown() now mutates a **Zombie**'s `walksWithLimp` property. It is not marked `mutating`, yet there is no error. Why?

Just as class types contain only a reference to the instance, and not the entire instance itself, the same is true for function arguments of class types - including the implicit `self` argument of class instance methods. Since `self` is already a reference to the instance, and not a copy of it, the `self` implicit argument does not need to be made `inout`, so the `mutating` keyword is not used with class instance methods.

It is OK if you feel a little fuzzy on the distinction between value types and reference types. You will get plenty of practice and learn much more about the nuance that value and reference types bring to the Swift language - as well as when to use them - in Chapter 18.

Before you move on, delete the code you added to main.swift in this section. It has served its purpose of illustrating some of the differences between value and reference types, and you will not need it again.

Listing 15.24 Cleaning up (main.swift)

```
var myTown = Town()
var yourTown = myTown // Now there are two towns!
myTown.changePopulation(by: 500)
print("myTown has \(myTown.population) and yourTown has \(yourTown.population)")

let fredTheZombie = Zombie()
fredTheZombie.town = myTown
fredTheZombie.terrorizeTown()
fredTheZombie.town?.printDescription()
var frederickTheZombie = fredTheZombie // Still only one zombie!
frederickTheZombie.name = "Frederick"
print("Fred's name is \(fredTheZombie.name)")
```

Bronze Challenge

Create a copy of your MonsterTown project, as you will continue to work on it in the next chapter and do not want your challenge solutions to get in the way.

There is currently a bug in the program. If a **Zombie** terrorizes a **Town** with a population less than 10, then the town's population will become negative. This result does not make sense. Fix this bug by changing the **changePopulation(by:)** method on **Town** to never have a negative population. That is, make sure that a town's population is set to 0 if the amount to decrement is greater than the current population.

Silver Challenge

Vampires are monsters that sometimes turn people into other vampires.

Create another subclass of the **Monster** type. Call this one **Vampire**. Give it a thralls property to hold an empty array of other **Vampire** instances.

In your new class, override the **terrorizeTown()** method to do everything that the superclass's implementation does *plus* capture one of the townspeople and make them into a vampire thrall. Do this by adding an instance of **Vampire** to its thralls array and decrementing the town's population by one.

Ensure that a thrall is only made (and the town's population changed) if the terrorized town had at least one person in it.

Exercise this **Vampire** type in main.swift by creating one and making it terrorize a town several times. Each time, print the changes to the vampire's thralls and the town's population to make sure it works.

For the More Curious: Type Methods

In this chapter, you defined some instance methods that were called on instances of a type. For example, **terrorizeTown()** is an instance method that you can call on instances of the **Monster** type. You can additionally define methods that are called on the type itself. These are called *type methods*. Type methods are useful for working with type-level information.

Imagine a struct named **Square**:

```
struct Square {
    static func numberOfSides() -> Int {
        return 4
    }
}
```

For value types, you indicate that you are defining a type method with the static keyword. The method **numberOfSides()** simply returns the number of sides a **Square** can have.

Type methods on classes use the `class` keyword. Here is a type method on the **Zombie** class that represents the universal zombie catchphrase.

```
class Zombie: Monster {
    class func makeSpookyNoise() -> String {
        return "Brains..."
    }
    ...
}
```

To use type methods, you simply call them on the type itself:

```
let sides = Square.numberOfSides() // sides is 4
let spookyNoise = Zombie.makeSpookyNoise() // spookyNoise is "Brains..."
```

One implication of making **makeSpookyNoise()** a `class` method is that subclasses can override that method to provide their own implementation.

```
class GiantZombie: Zombie {
    override class func makeSpookyNoise() -> String {
        return "ROAR!"
    }
}
```

Here, the **GiantZombie** class subclasses **Zombie** and provides its own implementation of the `class` method. But what if you have a class type with a `class` method that you do not want to be overridden? Perhaps you feel that all zombies should make the same spooky noise. Let's revisit the **Zombie** class.

```
class Zombie: Monster {
    static func makeSpookyNoise() -> String {
        return "Brains..."
    }
    ...
}
```

The `static` keyword tells the compiler that you do not want subclasses to provide their own version of the **makeSpookyNoise()** method.

You could also use `final class` in place of the `static` keyword. They are functionally equivalent.

```
class Zombie: Monster {
    final class func makeSpookyNoise() -> String {
        return "Brains..."
    }
    ...
}
```

Type methods can work with type-level information. This means that type methods can call other type methods and can even work with type properties, which we will discuss in Chapter 16. But type methods cannot call instance methods or work with any instance properties, because an instance is not available for use at the type level.

16
Properties

Chapter 15 introduced properties in a limited way. Its focus was on structures and classes, but you also gave your types some basic stored properties so that they had data to represent. This chapter discusses properties in detail and will deepen your understanding of how to use them with your custom types.

Properties model the characteristics of the entity that a type represents. They do this by associating values with the type. The values properties can take may be constant or variable values. Classes, structures, and enumerations can all have properties.

Properties have a lot of power and flexibility. Let's see what they can do.

Basic Stored Properties

Properties can either be *stored* or *computed*. Stored properties allocate memory to hold on to the property's value between accesses. A person's date of birth, for example, would be represented by a stored property, because it is a simple fact about a person that needs to be remembered. You can observe stored properties to execute code when the property's value changes.

Computed properties are like lightweight functions, using other properties, variables, and functions to calculate a new value each time they are accessed. A person's age would be represented by a computed property, because it is a value that changes over time and is based on the person's date of birth.

Most properties, including all the properties you have declared so far, are stored. To see how they work, you will expand the behavior of the types you developed in Chapter 15.

Open `Town.swift`. Take a look at the declaration of your `population` property: `var population = 5_422`. This code signifies three important items:

- `var` marks this property as variable, which means that it can be mutated.

- `population` has a default value of `5_422`.

- `population` is a stored property whose value can be read and set.

How can you tell that `population` is a stored property? Because it holds on to a piece of information – the town's population. That is what stored properties do: They store data.

`population` is a *read/write* property. You can both read the property's value *and* set the property's value. You can also make stored properties *read-only*, so that their values cannot be changed. Read-only properties are known by their more familiar name: constants.

Use `let` to create a read-only property storing information about the region that the town you are modeling is in. After all, towns cannot move, so they are always in the same region.

Listing 16.1 Adding a region constant (`Town.swift`)

```
struct Town {
    let region = "Middle"
    var population = 5_422
    var numberOfStoplights = 4

    func printDescription() {
        print("Population: \(population);
                number of stoplights: \(numberOfStoplights)")
    }

    mutating func changePopulation(by amount: Int) {
        population += amount
    }
}
```

This implementation of `region` is fine for now, but it does mean that all towns must exist in the Middle of the world. You will address this limitation in the next chapter.

Nested Types

Nested types are types that are defined within another enclosing type. They are often used to support the functionality of a type and are not intended to be used separately from that type. You have seen nested functions already, which are similar.

Enumerations are frequently nested. In Town.swift, create a new enumeration called **Size**. You will be using this enumeration, in coordination with another new property to be added later, to calculate whether the town can be designated as small, medium, or large. Make sure that you define the enum within the definition for the **Town** struct.

Listing 16.2 Setting up the **Size** enum (Town.swift)

```
struct Town {
    let region = "Middle"
    var population = 5_422
    var numberOfStoplights = 4

    enum Size {
        case small
        case medium
        case large
    }

    func printDescription() {
        print("Population: \(population);
                number of stoplights: \(numberOfStoplights)")
    }
    ...
}
```

Size will determine the size of the instance of the **Town** type. The instance of **Town** will need a value in its population property before this nested type is used. All the properties you have worked with so far have calculated the property's value when the instance was created. The next section introduces a new sort of property that delays the computation of its value until the necessary information is available.

Lazy Stored Properties

Sometimes a stored property's value cannot be assigned immediately. The necessary information may be available, but computing the values of a property immediately would be costly in terms of memory or time. Or, perhaps a property depends on factors external to the type that will be unknown until after the instance is created. These circumstances call for *lazy loading*.

In terms of properties, lazy loading means that the calculation of the property's value will not occur until the first time it is needed. This delay defers computation of the property's value until after the instance is initialized. This means that lazy properties must be declared with var, because their values will change.

Create a new lazy property called townSize. Make it of type **Size**, because its value will be an instance of the **Size** enum. Again, make sure to define this new property inside the **Town** type.

Listing 16.3 Setting up `townSize` (Town.swift)

```
struct Town {
    ...
    enum Size {
        case small
        case medium
        case large
    }

    lazy var townSize: Size = {
        switch population {
        case 0...10_000:
            return Size.small

        case 10_001...100_000:
            return Size.medium

        default:
            return Size.large
        }
    }()

    func printDescription() {
        print("Population: \(population);
                number of stoplights: \(numberOfStoplights)")
    }
    ...
}
```

townSize looks different than the properties that you have written before. You will not be setting the value of this property directly, as you have done with other properties. Instead, you will take advantage of the nested enum **Size** in coordination with a closure to calculate the town's size given its population.

First, you mark townSize as lazy and declare the type of the property as **Size**. Next, you set the value of townSize to the result returned by a closure (notice the opening brace: lazy var townSize: Size = {). Recall that functions and closures are first-class types and that properties can reference functions and closures.

A closure works well here because multiple steps must be performed to determine the town's size, and a closure can encapsulate that work. The closure switches over the instance's population to assign the correct size. The case bodies return an instance of the enum **Size** that matches the given population.

Notice that the closure for townSize ends with empty parentheses after the final brace: }(). With these parentheses, Swift will execute the closure and assign the value it returns to townSize. The lazy keyword ensures that this happens the first time the property is read, and only if a value has not already been assigned, rather than when the **Town** instance is created.

If you had omitted the parentheses, you would simply be assigning the closure itself to the townSize property, rather than storing the result of executing the closure.

Let's return to the need for townSize to be lazy. The closure implicitly references self to gain access to the instance's population property. For the closure to access self safely, the compiler requires that self (the town) is fully initialized and that all its properties have values (more on this in Chapter 17). This means that stored properties cannot access each other's values when setting their initial values, as doing so would unsafely reference self.

Marking townSize as lazy indicates to the compiler that this property does not need to have a value for self to be considered fully initialized and that its initial value should instead be assigned (in this case, by executing the closure) the first time it is read.

Switch to main.swift to exercise this lazy property.

Listing 16.4 Using the lazy townSize property (main.swift)

```
var myTown = Town()
let myTownSize = myTown.townSize
print(myTownSize)
myTown.changePopulation(by: 500)

let fredTheZombie = Zombie()
fredTheZombie.town = myTown
fredTheZombie.terrorizeTown()
fredTheZombie.town?.printDescription()
```

Here, you create a constant named myTownSize to hold myTown's size information. This line accesses the lazy property townSize and causes its closure to execute. After the closure switches over myTown's population, an instance of the **Size** enum is assigned to myTownSize. Next, you print the value of the myTownSize constant. As a result, when you run the program, small logs to the console.

It is important to note that properties marked with lazy are calculated only one time. This feature of lazy means that changing the value of myTown's population does not cause myTown's townSize to be recalculated. To see this, increase myTown's population by 1,000,000 and then check myTown's size by logging it to the console. Include myTown's population for comparison.

Listing 16.5 Changing myTown's population does not change townSize (main.swift)

```
var myTown = Town()
let myTownSize = myTown.townSize
print(myTownSize)
myTown.changePopulation(by: 500)(by: 1_000_000)
print("Size: \(myTown.townSize); population: \(myTown.population)")

let fredTheZombie = Zombie()
fredTheZombie.town = myTown
fredTheZombie.terrorizeTown()
fredTheZombie.town?.printDescription()
```

Run the program, and you will see in the console Size: small; population: 1005422. myTown's size has not changed, even though its population increased dramatically. This discrepancy is due to townSize's lazy nature. The property is only calculated when it is first accessed and is never recalculated.

This kind of discrepancy between myTown's population and townSize is undesirable. It seems that townSize should not be marked lazy, if lazy means that myTown will not be able to recalibrate its townSize to reflect population changes.

If you only needed to calculate the town's size once, a lazy stored property would be perfect. But since townSize needs to always reflect the current population, lazy loading is not the right tool for the job. A *computed property* is a better option.

Computed Properties

You can use computed properties with any class, struct, or enum that you define. Computed properties do not store values like the properties that you have been working with thus far. Instead, a computed property provides a *getter* and optional *setter* to retrieve or set the property's value. This difference allows the value of a computed property to change, unlike the value of a lazy stored property.

Replace your definition of the townSize property on the **Town** type with a computed read-only property. Unlike stored read-only properties, computed read-only properties are defined using var.

Listing 16.6 Using a computed property (Town.swift)

```
...
~~lazy var townSize: Size = {~~
var townSize: Size {
    switch population {
    case 0...10_000:
        return Size.small

    case 10_001...100_000:
        return Size.medium

    default:
        return Size.large
    }
}~~()~~
...
```

The changes here may look small. You delete the lazy keyword and the assignment operator (=) in the first line and delete the parentheses in the final line. That is all. But those small changes have a big impact.

townSize is now defined as a computed property declared, like all computed properties, with the var keyword. It provides a custom getter that uses the same switch statement that you used before. Notice that you explicitly declare the type of the computed property to be **Size**. You must provide computed properties with an explicit type annotation so that the compiler can verify that the computed value is of the correct type.

You access this property via dot syntax (myTown.townSize), so the code you already added to main.swift does not need to be changed. But now, accessing the property executes the getter for townSize every time, which results in using myTown's population to calculate the townSize. Run your program again. You will see Size: large; population: 1005422 logged to the console.

townSize is now a read-only computed property. In other words, townSize cannot be set directly. It can only retrieve and return a value based on the calculation you defined in the getter. A read-only property is perfect in this case because you want myTown to calculate its townSize based on the instance's population, which may change at runtime.

A getter and a setter

Computed properties can also be declared with both a getter and a setter. A getter allows you to *read* data from a property. A setter allows you to *write* data to the property. Properties with both a getter and a setter are called read/write. Open your `Monster.swift` file and add a computed property to the declaration for **Monster**.

Listing 16.7 Creating a computed `victimPool` property with a getter and a setter (`Monster.swift`)

```
class Monster {
    var town: Town?
    var name = "Monster"
    var victimPool: Int {
        get {
            return town?.population ?? 0
        }
        set(newVictimPool) {
            town?.population = newVictimPool
        }
    }

    func terrorizeTown() {
        if town != nil {
            print("\(name) is terrorizing a town!")
        } else {
            print("\(name) hasn't found a town to terrorize yet...")
        }
    }
}
```

Imagine that you need each instance of **Monster** to keep track of its potential pool of victims. This number will match the `population` of the town that the monster is terrorizing. Accordingly, `victimPool` is a new computed property with both a getter and a setter (collectively called *accessors*). As before, you declare the property to be mutable using `var` and give it explicit type information. In this case, `victimPool` is an **Int**.

Unlike your implementation of `townSize`, you explicitly annotate the getter with `get` and the setter with `set` so that the compiler knows which is which. This is required for read/write properties. The getter uses the `nil` coalescing operator to check whether the **Monster** instance has a town that it is currently terrorizing. If it does, then it returns the value of that town's population. If the instance has not yet found a town to terrorize, it simply returns 0.

The setter for the computed property is written within the `set` block. Notice the new syntax: `set(newVictimPool)`. Specifying `newVictimPool` within the parentheses lets you choose a name for the incoming value, just like a function's internal parameter name. If you had not explicitly named the new value, Swift would have provided a variable for you called `newValue` to hold on to the same information. You can refer to this variable within the setter's implementation. For example, you use optional chaining to ensure that the **Monster** instance has found a town, and then set that town's population to match `newVictimPool`.

Switch back to `main.swift` to use this new computed property. Add the code below to the bottom of the file.

Listing 16.8 Using `victimPool` (main.swift)

```
...
print("Victim pool: \(fredTheZombie.victimPool)")
fredTheZombie.victimPool = 500
print("Victim pool: \(fredTheZombie.victimPool);
        population: \(fredTheZombie.town?.population)")
```

The first new line exercises the getter for the computed property. Run the program and `Victim pool: 1005412` logs to the console. The next new line (`fredTheZombie.victimPool = 500`) uses the setter to change `fredTheZombie`'s `victimPool`. Last, you once again log the `victimPool` to the console via the property's getter. In the console, the `victimPool` should be updated to be `500`, and the town's population should match this change.

Notice that the output for the town's population is listed as `Optional(500)`. This looks different from the output for `victimPool`, because `fredTheZombie`'s `town` property is optional. If you are curious about what is causing this difference, Chapter 21 discusses how optionals are put together. The warning in your code is related, and you can ignore it for now.

Property Observers

Swift provides an interesting feature called *property observation*. Property observers watch for and respond to changes in a given property. Property observation is available to any stored property that you define and is also available to any property that you inherit. You cannot use property observers with computed properties that you define. (But you have full control over the definition of a computed property's setter and getter and can respond to changes there.)

Imagine that the citizens of your beleaguered town demand that the mayor do something to protect them from the monsters terrorizing them. The mayor's first action is to track the attacks on the townspeople. Property observers are perfect for this task.

You can observe changes to a property in one of two ways:

- when a property is about to change, via `willSet`

- when a property did change, via `didSet`

To keep track of monster attacks, the mayor decides to pay close attention to when the `population` of the town changes. Use a `didSet` observer in `Town.swift` to be notified right after the property receives a new value.

Listing 16.9 Observing population changes (`Town.swift`)

```
struct Town {
...
    var population = 5_422 {
        didSet(oldPopulation) {
            print("The population has changed to \(population)
                    from \(oldPopulation).")
        }
    }
    ...
}
```

The syntax for property observers looks similar to computed properties' getters and setters, but with different keywords. The `didSet` observer gives you a handle on the property's old value. In the example above, you create a custom parameter name for the old population: `oldPopulation`. If you had not specified a new name, Swift would have given you the parameter `oldValue` automatically.

(The `willSet` observer gives you a handle on the property's new value, and Swift generates a `newValue` parameter - which you can rename if you choose.)

The response to the change is defined within the braces. This property observer logs the town's `population` information to the console every time it changes, so you should see a log for the population change after `fredTheZombie` terrorizes the town. Run the program and take a look at the console. It should look like the output shown below, with a log for every time the `population` changes.

```
small
The population has changed to 1005422 from 5422.
Size: large; population: 1005422
The population has changed to 1005412 from 1005422.
Monster is terrorizing a town!
Population: 1005412; number of stoplights: 4
Victim pool: 1005412
The population has changed to 500 from 1005412.
Victim pool: 500; population: Optional(500)
Program ended with exit code: 0
```

Because you are logging changes to `population` with a property observer, you no longer need to log the population change in `main.swift` after you update the `victimPool`. Remove that code from the call to **print()** at the bottom of `main.swift`.

Listing 16.10 Removing population from **print()** (`main.swift`)

```
...
print("Victim pool: \(fredTheZombie.victimPool)")
fredTheZombie.victimPool = 500
print("Victim pool: \(fredTheZombie.victimPool)+
    population: \(fredTheZombie.town?.population)")
```

Note that if you define a `didSet` property observer on a `lazy` property, the property's initial value computation will be performed (such as the closure you wrote for `townSize` in Listing 16.3) to fill in the `didSet` observer's `oldValue`.

Type Properties

Up to now, you have been working with *instance properties*. When you create a new instance of a type, that instance gets its own properties that are distinct from other instances of that type. Instance properties are useful for storing and computing values on an instance of a type.

However, when you need to store a value that is common to all instances of a type, it is wasteful to store a copy of that value in memory for every instance. Instead, such properties can exist once, on the type itself, and are called *type properties*. For example, all instances of a **Square** type will have exactly four sides, so the number of sides for **Square** might be stored in a type property. If you create 1,000 instances of **Square** in your program, a type property for a square's number of sides will only exist once in memory, rather than 1,000 times.

Value types (structures and enumerations) can take both stored and computed type properties. As with type methods, type properties on value types begin with the static keyword.

For this version of your program, all towns will exist in the same world. Declare a static property on **Town** to hold this information.

Listing 16.11 Adding a stored type property (Town.swift)

```
struct Town {
    static let world = "Earth"
    ...
}
```

Stored type properties have to be given a default value. This requirement stems from the fact that types do not have initializers. You will learn about initialization in Chapter 17; for now, types not having initializers means that the stored type property has to have all the information it needs to vend its value to any caller. Here, world is given the value Earth.

Classes can also have stored and computed type properties, which use the same static syntax as structs. Subclasses cannot override a type property from their superclass. If you want a subclass to be able to provide its own implementation of the property, you use the class keyword instead.

In the section called *For the More Curious: Type Methods* in Chapter 15, we showed you a type method on the **Zombie** type to make a spooky noise:

```
class Zombie: Monster {
    class func makeSpookyNoise() -> String {
        return "Brains..."
    }
```

Notice that **makeSpookyNoise()** does not take any arguments. This makes it a great candidate for being a computed type property and not a method. Open Zombie.swift and add a computed type property for a zombie's catchphrase.

Listing 16.12 Creating the spookyNoise computed type property (Zombie.swift)

```
class Zombie: Monster {
    class var spookyNoise: String {
        return "Brains..."
    }
    var walksWithLimp = true
    ...
}
```

The definition of a type-level computed property is very similar to the definition of a type method. The main differences are that you use the var keyword, rather than func, and you do not use the parentheses.

One new aspect of the code above is that you use shorthand getter syntax. If you are not providing a setter for a computed property, you can omit the get block of the computed property's definition and simply return the computed value as needed.

Switch to main.swift. Add a line at the bottom of the file to print the **Zombie** type's spookyNoise property to the console.

Listing 16.13 "Brains..." (main.swift)

```
...
print("Victim pool: \(fredTheZombie.victimPool)")
fredTheZombie.victimPool = 500
print("Victim pool: \(fredTheZombie.victimPool)")
print(Zombie.spookyNoise)
```

Run the program. Spooky.

To see that class type properties can be overridden by subclasses, add a spookyNoise computed type property to **Monster**.

Listing 16.14 Generic **Monster** noise (Monster.swift)

```
class Monster {
    class var spookyNoise: String {
        return "Grrr"
    }
    var town: Town?
    var name = "Monster"
    ...
}
```

You may notice that the toolbar is indicating that there is a compiler error with a small red octagonal icon (see Figure 16.1). If you do not see the icon, try running the program.

Figure 16.1 Toolbar error

Switch back to Zombie.swift, and you will see the same error icon on the line that begins the definition of the spookyNoise class variable. If you click the red exclamation mark on the lefthand side of the editor area, the error will display (Figure 16.2).

Figure 16.2 Override error

```
class Zombie: Monster {
    class var spookyNoise: String {   ⊗  Overriding declaration requires an 'override' keyword
        return "Brains..."
    }
```

Zombie is now overriding a computed type property from its superclass. Because you used the class keyword for this type property, it is perfectly fine for subclasses to provide their own definition of spookyNoise. You just need to add the keyword override to **Zombie**'s definition of spookyNoise.

Make this change and the compiler error disappears.

Listing 16.15 Overriding spookyNoise (Zombie.swift)

```
class Zombie: Monster {
    override class var spookyNoise: String {
        return "Brains..."
    }
    var walksWithLimp = true
    ...
}
```

Build and run your program, and everything should work as it did before.

We mentioned that classes can have static properties at the type level. These properties work a bit differently than class properties on a type.

A defining characteristic of all monsters is that they are terrifying. Add a static property to the **Monster** class to represent this fact.

Listing 16.16 All **Monster**s are terrifying (Monster.swift)

```
class Monster {
    static let isTerrifying = true
    class var spookyNoise: String {
        return "Grrr"
    }
    ...
}
```

You add a new static property on **Monster** to represent the fact that all monsters are terrifying by definition. Because you added this property to **Zombie**'s superclass, **Monster**, it is also available on **Zombie**. Add the following to main.swift to see this in action.

Listing 16.17 Running away from **Zombie** (main.swift)

```
...
print(Zombie.spookyNoise)
if Zombie.isTerrifying {
    print("Run away!")
}
```

As you can see, you access the isTerrifying property on the **Zombie** via dot syntax. If the **Zombie** is terrifying, you run away.

Build and run your program. The console warns you to Run away!.

One of the major differences between static and class type properties is that static properties cannot be overridden by a subclass. Making this type property a static constant is very definitive: Monsters are terrifying, and subclasses cannot change that.

Access Control

You do not always want elements of your program's code to be visible to all other elements. In fact, you will frequently want to have much more granular control over your code's access. You can grant components of your code specific levels of access to other components of your code. This is called *access control*.

For example, you might want to hide or expose a method on a class. Suppose you have a property that is used only within a class's definition. It could be problematic if another, external type modified that property by mistake. With access control, you can manage the visibility of that property to hide it from other parts of the program. Doing so will encapsulate the property's data and prevent external code from meddling with it.

Access control is organized around two important and related concepts: *modules* and *source files*. In terms of your project's files and organization, these are the central building blocks of your application.

A module is code that is distributed as a unit. You probably recall seeing `import Cocoa` at the top of your playgrounds and `import Foundation` in your Swift files. These are frameworks, which bundle together a number of related types that perform a series of related tasks. For example, Cocoa is a framework designed to facilitate the development of macOS applications. Modules are brought into another module using Swift's `import` keyword, as suggested by the examples above.

Source files, on the other hand, are more discrete units. They represent a single file and live within a specific module. It is good practice to define a single type within a source file. This is not a requirement, but doing so helps keep your project organized.

Swift provides five levels of access (Table 16.1).

Table 16.1 Swift access control

Access level	Description	Visible to...	Subclassable within...
open	Entities are visible and subclassable to all files in the module and those that import the module.	defining module and importing modules	defining module and importing modules
public	Entities are visible to all files in the module and those that import the module.	defining module and importing modules	defining module
internal (the default)	Entities are visible to all files in the same module.	defining module	defining module
fileprivate	Entities are visible only within their defining source file.	defining file	defining file
private	Entities are visible only within their defining scope.	scope	scope

`open` access is the least restrictive access level, and `private` access is the most restrictive access level. In general, a type's access level must be consistent with the access levels of its properties and methods. A property cannot have a less restrictive level of access control than its type. For example, a property with an access control level of `internal` cannot be declared on a type with `private` access.

Likewise, the access control of a function cannot be less restrictive than the access control listed for its parameter types. If you violate these requirements, the compiler will issue an error to help you correct the mistake.

Swift specifies internal as the default level of access control for your app. Having a default level of access means that you do not need to declare access controls for every type, property, and method in your code. internal makes sense as a default, because you will typically be using the language to write Cocoa and iOS applications, both of which typically use a single module for the source code. Thus, you only need to declare a level of access control when you need to specify access that is more or less visible than internal.

Let's see the private level of access in action. Create an isFallingApart Boolean property defined on the **Zombie** type. Give it a default value of false. This property will keep track of an instance's physical integrity (zombies, after all, sometimes lose bits). This property really does not need to be exposed to the rest of the program, because it is an implementation detail of the **Zombie** class. Therefore, set it to private.

Listing 16.18 Falling apart is a private matter (Zombie.swift)

```
class Zombie: Monster {
    override class var spookyNoise: String {
        return "Brains..."
    }
    var walksWithLimp = true
    private var isFallingApart = false

    func regenerate() {
        walksWithLimp = false
    }

    override func terrorizeTown() {
        if !isFallingApart {
            town?.changePopulation(by: -10)
        }
        super.terrorizeTown()
        regenerate()
    }
}
```

After you create the property, you use it in the **terrorizeTown()** function: If isFallingApart is false, then the instance is free to terrorize its town. If the instance is falling apart, then it will not be able to terrorize its town.

isFallingApart is visible within **terrorizeTown()** because the property was declared as private. That means isFallingApart is accessible to any entity defined within the same scope. Because isFallingApart is a property on **Zombie**, any property or method defined at this same level will be able to access this new property. However, isFallingApart is *not* accessible outside the **Zombie** class. This property is a private implementation of the class.

Controlling getter and setter visibility

If a property has both a getter and a setter, you can control the visibility of the two independently. By default, however, the getter and setter have the same visibility. Here, isFallingApart has a private getter and a private setter.

However, you probably want other files in your project to be able to tell whether a **Zombie** is falling apart. You just do not want them to change its falling-apart-ness. Change the isFallingApart property to have an internal getter and a private setter.

Listing 16.19 Making the getter internal and the setter private (Zombie.swift)

```
class Zombie: Monster {
    ...
    private internal private(set) var isFallingApart = false
    ...
}
```

You use the syntax internal private(set) to specify that the getter should be internal and the setter should be private. You could use public, internal, or private for either, with one restriction: The setter cannot be more visible than the getter. That means, for example, that if you make the getter internal, you cannot use public(set), because public is more visible than internal.

Furthermore, the **Zombie** class is defaulting to internal, because you do not specify any level of access yourself. That means marking isFallingApart's getter or setter with public will prompt the compiler to remind you with a warning that its defining class has internal visibility.

You can clean this code up a little. If you leave off a modifier for the getter, the access control defaults to internal, which is what you want here. Refactor **Zombie** to use the default visibility for the getter (internal) and private visibility for the setter.

Listing 16.20 Using default getter visibility (Zombie.swift)

```
class Zombie: Monster {
    ...
    internal private(set) var isFallingApart = false
    ...
}
```

Using the default does not change anything except the amount of typing you have to do. The getter for isFallingApart is still visible to the other files in your project, and the setter is still visible only within the **Zombie** class.

This chapter introduced a lot of material. Take some time to let all the ideas sink in. You learned about:

- property syntax

- stored versus computed properties

- read-only and read/write properties

- lazy loading and lazy properties

- property observers

- type properties

- access control

Properties are a central concept in Swift programming. It is a good idea to get comfortable with all these ideas. The challenges below will help you master the important concepts.

Bronze Challenge

Your town's mayor is busy. Every birth and relocation does not require the mayor's attention. After all, the town is in crisis! Only log changes to the town's population if the new population is less than the old value.

Silver Challenge

Make a new type called **Mayor**. It should be a struct. The **Town** type should have a property called `mayor` that holds an instance of the **Mayor** type.

Have your town inform the `mayor` every time the property for `population` changes. If the town's `population` decreases, have the instance of the **Mayor** log this statement to the console: `I'm deeply saddened to hear about this latest tragedy. I promise that my office is looking into the nature of this rash of violence.` If the population increases, then the `mayor` should do nothing.

(Hint: You should define a new instance method on the **Mayor** type to complete this challenge.)

Gold Challenge

Mayors are people, too. An instance of the **Mayor** type will naturally get nervous whenever its town loses some `population` due to a **Zombie** attack. Create a stored instance property on the **Mayor** type called `anxietyLevel`. It should be of type **Int** and should start out with a default value of 0.

Increment the `anxietyLevel` property every time a **Mayor** instance is notified of a **Zombie** attack. Last, as a mayor will not want to outwardly display anxiety, use access control to protect this property. Verify that this property is not accessible from `main.swift`.

For the More Curious: Key Paths

Imagine you are building an index for a list of names. The first step to figuring out which section each name belongs to would be extracting the first character of each one:

```
let names = ["Almasi", "Haris", "Jun", "Kala"]
let firstLetters = names.compactMap({ $0.first })     // ["A", "H", "J", "K"]
```

As an aside, notice the use of **compactMap(_:)**, which is an **Array** method that behaves like **map(_:)** but omits results for which the provided closure returns nil. Since the first property of a **String** returns **Character?**, it is good to ensure that the resultant array does not contain any nil values.

In this example, it would be convenient to say, "Map this array of strings to their respective first properties without making me write a closure."

When you need an expression that refers to a specific property of a type, you can use a *key-path*. The **map(_:)** family of functions can take a key-path in place of a transforming closure, in which case the method will return a collection that has been transformed by extracting the specified property from each instance in the source collection:

```
let firstLetters = names.compactMap(\String.first)    // ["A", "H", "J", "K"]
```

A literal key-path begins with a backslash (\), followed by a type name and a property of that type, separated by a period (.). When the compiler can infer the type, it can be omitted:

```
let firstLetters = names.compactMap(\.first)          // ["A", "H", "J", "K"]
```

This concise syntax for referring to a property name has lots of uses that are outside the scope of this book, such as the Combine and SwiftUI frameworks that you will eventually encounter in your Swift journey. For now, it is worth knowing that this syntax offers a type-safe alternative to manually writing a closure for functions that support the **KeyPath** type as arguments.

17

Initialization

Initialization is the operation of setting up an instance of a type. It entails giving each stored property an initial value and may involve other preparatory work. After this process, the instance is prepared and available to use.

The types that you have been creating up to this point have all been created in more or less the same way: Properties were either given default stored values or their values were computed on demand. Initialization was not customized, and we did not give it much consideration.

It is very common to want control over how an instance of a type is created. For example, you have been giving default values to an instance's stored properties and then changing the properties' values after you create the instance. This strategy is inelegant. It would be ideal for the instance to have all the correct values in its properties immediately. *Initializers* help you create an instance with the appropriate values.

Initializer Syntax

Structures and classes are required to have initial values for their stored properties by the time initialization completes. This requirement explains why you have been giving all your stored properties default values. If you had not, the compiler would have given you errors saying that the type's properties were not ready to use. Defining an initializer on the type is another way to ensure that properties have values when the instance is created.

The syntax for writing an initializer is a little different from what you have already seen. Initializers are written with the `init` keyword. Even though they are methods on a type, initializers are not preceded with the `func` keyword. Initializer syntax looks like this:

```
struct CustomType {
    init(someValue: SomeType) {
        // Initialization code here...
    }
}
```

This general syntax does not differ among structures, enumerations, and classes. In the example above, the initializer has one parameter called `someValue` of type **SomeType**. While initializers typically have one or more parameters, they can also have zero parameters (in which case there is a set of empty parentheses after the `init` keyword).

The initializer's implementation is defined within the braces, just as you have been doing with regular functions and methods throughout this book. But unlike other methods, initializers do not return values. Instead, initializers are tasked with giving values to a type's stored properties.

Struct Initialization

Structures can have both default and custom initializers. When working with structs, you will typically want to take advantage of the default initializer provided, but there are some circumstances in which you will want to customize the initialization process.

Default initializers for structs

Remember how you have been getting instances of your **Town** type? You gave the type's stored properties default values. What you did not know is that you were taking advantage of an *empty initializer* (an initializer without parameters) provided to you by the Swift compiler automatically. If you could see its implementation, it would look like this:

```
init() {

}
```

When you entered code like `var myTown = Town()`, that syntax called the empty initializer and set the new instance's properties to the default values you specified.

Another form of default initializer is the *memberwise initializer*. A memberwise initializer has a parameter for each stored property on the instance, and it will use default parameter syntax to provide any default values you have declared on the type. This allows you to decide which parameters you wish to provide at the call site. The free memberwise initializer for **Town** looks like this:

```
init(population: Int = 5422, numberOfStoplights: Int = 4) {
    self.population = population
    self.numberOfStoplights = numberOfStoplights
}
```

(We call the empty and memberwise initializers "free" because they are synthesized for you by the Swift compiler – you do not need to define them yourself.)

At first, it seems like the empty initializer might just be a special case of the memberwise initializer, but the difference will become clearer when you study class initializers later in this chapter.

Remember, one of the principal goals of initialization is to give all the type's stored properties values so that the new instance is ready to use. The compiler will enforce the requirement that your new instance have values in its stored properties. If you do not provide an initializer for your custom struct, you must provide the necessary values through default values or memberwise initialization.

Make a copy of the MonsterTown project from the last chapter, so you have all the current code. Open the copy and navigate to `main.swift`.

In `main.swift`, change your use of the empty initializer on the **Town** type to a call to the free memberwise initializer. Give the town's properties values that are different from the default values provided in **Town**'s definition.

Listing 17.1 Using a memberwise initializer (`main.swift`)

```
var myTown = Town(population: 10_000, numberOfStoplights: 6)
myTown.printDescription()
...
```

Now run your program. myTown's description in the console reads `Population: 10_000; number of stoplights: 6`. The instance `myTown` is now created with the free memberwise initializer, and, as the console shows, the values you gave to the initializer replace the default values.

Notice that **Town**'s property names are used as external parameter names in the call to this initializer. Swift provides default external parameter names to every initializer automatically, one for each parameter given by the initializer. This convention is important because Swift's initializers all have the same name: `init`. Therefore, you cannot use the function name to identify which specific initializer should be called. The parameter names, and their types, help the compiler differentiate between initializers and know which initializer to call.

Free default memberwise initializers are a benefit of structs; they are not available on classes. Nonetheless, it is common that you will want to customize the initialization of your type. That is where custom initializers come in.

Custom initializers for structs

It is time to write your own initializer for the **Town** type. Custom initializers are powerful, and with great power comes great responsibility. When you write your own initializer, Swift will not give you any free initializers. You are responsible for ensuring that instances' properties are all given their appropriate values.

First, you need to do some housecleaning. You are going to remove all the default values you have given to properties. These were helpful before you knew about initializers, as they ensured that the properties for instances of your type had values when an instance was created. But now they do not really add value to the **Town** struct.

You will also add a new property for the town's `region` to the description that is logged by **printDescription**. It will be a constant, because towns do not move from region to region - but it will have no default value, because different town instances will have different `regions`.

Open the `Town.swift` file and make these changes. They will introduce errors, which you will fix in the next step.

Listing 17.2 Cleaning house (`Town.swift`)

```
struct Town {
    static let world = "Earth"
    let region = "Middle"
    var population = 5_422 {
        didSet(oldPopulation) {
            print("The population has changed to \(population)
                    from \(oldPopulation).")
        }
    }
    var numberOfStoplights = 4
    ...
    func printDescription() {
        print("Population: \(population); number of stoplights:
                \(numberOfStoplights); region: \(region)")
    }
    ...
}
```

219

When you delete the properties' default values, the compiler issues an error in three places, all indicating Type annotation missing in pattern. Previously, you took advantage of type inference for these properties, which worked well with the default values you gave them. Without the default values, you need to explicitly declare their types.

Listing 17.3 Declaring types (Town.swift)

```
struct Town {
    static let world = "Earth"
    let region: String
    var population: Int {
        didSet(oldPopulation) {
            print("The population has changed to \(population)
                    from \(oldPopulation).")
        }
    }
    var numberOfStoplights: Int
    ...
}
```

Now it is time to create your custom initializer. Later, you will call this initializer from another initializer defined within this same type. For now, add the following initializer to your **Town** type.

Listing 17.4 Adding a memberwise initializer (Town.swift)

```
...
var numberOfStoplights: Int

init(region: String, population: Int, stoplights: Int) {
    self.region = region
    self.population = population
    numberOfStoplights = stoplights
}

enum Size {
    case small
    case medium
    case large
}
...
```

The **init(region:population:stoplights:)** initializer takes three arguments, one for each of the stored properties on the **Town** type other than world, which has a default value. In the body of the initializer, you take the values given to the arguments and pass them to the actual properties of the type.

Because the parameter names for region and population are the same as the property names, you need to explicitly access those properties via self. The numberOfStoplights property does not have this issue, so you simply set the value of the initializer's argument for stoplights to the numberOfStoplights property.

Notice that you set the value for the region property even though it was declared as a constant. The Swift compiler allows you to set a value for a constant property one time during initialization. Remember, the goal of initialization is to ensure that a type's properties have values after initialization completes.

At this point, you may be noticing that Xcode's issue navigator has opened on the left, informing you of errors (Figure 17.1). (If the issue navigator does not open automatically, open it by clicking the fifth icon from the left above the navigator area (⚠). If no errors appear in the navigator, try to run the program.) You will see that the issues are located in main.swift and relate to the initializer that the compiler was giving you by default.

Figure 17.1 Showing errors in the issue navigator

There are two issues, both in main.swift, where you create an instance of **Town** using the memberwise initializer:

```
var myTown = Town(population: 10_000, numberOfStoplights: 6)
```

The memberwise initializer you used to create myTown used the property name numberOfStoplights as its parameter name. In **Town**'s new initializer, you shortened this parameter name to stoplights, so the compiler no longer recognizes the numberOfStoplights argument. Also, the new region argument is missing.

Switch back to main.swift. (To get back to the project navigator, click the leftmost icon above the navigator area.) Fix the problems by including all the parameters, using the names the compiler is expecting. (We have put each parameter on its own line to fit this page; you can leave them on one line or break them as shown.)

Listing 17.5 Making sure the parameters align (main.swift)

```
var myTown = Town(region: "West",
                  population: 10_000,
                  numberOfStoplights stoplights: 6)
...
```

Build and run the program. The errors should disappear, and you should see console log output beginning with Population: 10000; number of stoplights: 6; region: West.

Initializer delegation

You can define initializers to call other initializers on the same type. This procedure is called *initializer delegation*. It is typically used to provide multiple paths for creating an instance of a type.

In value types (enumerations and structures), initializer delegation is relatively straightforward. Because value types do not support inheritance, initializer delegation only involves calling another initializer defined on the type. It is somewhat more complicated for classes, as you will soon see.

Switch to `Town.swift` to write a new initializer on this type that uses initializer delegation.

Listing 17.6 Using initializer delegation (`Town.swift`)

```
...
init(region: String, population: Int, stoplights: Int) {
    self.region = region
    self.population = population
    numberOfStoplights = stoplights
}

init(population: Int, stoplights: Int) {
    self.init(region: "N/A", population: population, stoplights: stoplights)
}

enum Size {
    case small
    case medium
    case large
}
...
```

Here, you define a new initializer on the **Town** type. But this initializer only takes two arguments: `population` and `stoplights`. What about the `region` property? How is that getting set?

Look at this new initializer's implementation. You call **Town**'s other initializer on `self` in the line `self.init(region: "N/A", population: population, stoplights: stoplights)`. You pass in the supplied arguments for `population` and `stoplights`. Because you do not have an argument for `region`, you supply a value - in this case, the string `"N/A"` - to signify that there was no region information given to the initializer.

Initializer delegation helps avoid duplication of code. Instead of retyping the same code to assign the values passed in to the initializer's arguments to the type's properties, you can simply call across to another initializer on the type.

Avoiding duplication of code does more than save you from typing the same thing twice. It can also help avoid bugs. When you have the same code in two places, you have to remember to change both places any time you make a change.

We say that initializer delegation "defines a path" by which a type creates an instance. One initializer calls across to another on a given type to provide specific pieces that are needed to create an instance. Eventually, initializer delegation ends up in an initializer that has all it needs to fully prepare an instance for use.

Because you defined your own memberwise initializer, the compiler will give you no free initializers. This is not all that limiting; it can even be a benefit. For example, you might want to use this new initializer if there is no region information available for a given town that you would like to create. In that case, you would use your handy new initializer with arguments for `population` and `stoplights` to set the corresponding properties while also giving `region` a value so that initialization can complete.

Try out this new initializer in `main.swift`.

Listing 17.7 Using the new initializer (`main.swift`)

```
var myTown = Town(region: "West", population: 10_000, stoplights: 6)
myTown.printDescription()
...
```

Build and run your application. You are no longer setting the instance's `region` to anything specific, so you will see `N/A` logged to the console for `region`'s value.

Class Initialization

The general syntax for initialization in classes looks very similar to initialization in value types. However, there are some different rules for classes that must be observed. These additional rules are mainly due to the fact that classes can inherit from other classes, which adds some complexity to initialization.

In particular, classes add the concepts of *designated* and *convenience* initializers. An initializer on a class is either one or the other. Designated initializers are responsible for making sure that an instance's properties all have values before initialization completes, thus making the instance ready to use. Convenience initializers supplement designated initializers by calling across a class to its designated initializer. The role of convenience initializers is typically to create an instance of a class for a very specific use case.

Default initializers for classes

You have already seen examples of using a class's default initializer. Classes get a default empty initializer if you provide default values to all properties and do not write your own initializer. This explains why you gave your classes default values before: It allowed you to take advantage of the free empty initializer. Thus, you were able to get an instance of the **Zombie** class with code like `let fredTheZombie = Zombie()`, with the empty parentheses indicating that you were using the default initializer.

(As we said before, classes do not get a free memberwise initializer like structs.)

Initialization and class inheritance

Open `Monster.swift` and modify the class to give it an initializer. Also, remove the default value of "Monster" from the name property.

Listing 17.8 Initializing **Monster** (Monster.swift)

```
class Monster {
    ...
    var town: Town?
    var name = "Monster"
    var name: String
    var victimPool: Int {
        get {
            return town?.population ?? 0
        }
        set(newVictimPool) {
            town?.population = newVictimPool
        }
    }

    init(town: Town?, monsterName: String) {
        self.town = town
        name = monsterName
    }

    func terrorizeTown() {
        if town != nil {
            print("\(name) is terrorizing a town!")
        } else {
            print("\(name) hasn't found a town to terrorize yet...")
        }
    }
}
```

This initializer has two arguments: one for an optional instance of the **Town** type and another for the name of the monster. The values for these arguments are assigned to the class's properties within the initializer's implementation. Once again, note that the argument for the town in the initializer matches the property name on the class, so you have to set the property's value by accessing it through `self`. You do not have to do this for name because the initializer's parameter has a different name.

Now that you have added this initializer, you may notice that the toolbar is indicating that there is a compiler error. (As before, if the error does not appear automatically, try to run the program.) Click on the error icon to jump to the issue navigator, and you will find that it is in `main.swift`. Switch to this file to examine the error.

Your previous use of `Zombie()` to get an instance of this class is no longer satisfying the compiler. The error states: `Missing argument for parameters 'town', 'monsterName' in call`, signifying that the compiler is expecting **Zombie**'s initializer to include parameters for town and monsterName.

This expectation may seem strange, because you did not provide an initializer to the **Zombie** class that required those parameters. In fact, you have provided no initializer to this class whatsoever. Instead, you have been relying on the empty initializer the compiler gives you for free when your properties have default values.

That is the source of the error: **Zombie** no longer gets the free empty initializer that you were using earlier. Why not? *Automatic initializer inheritance.*

Automatic initializer inheritance

Classes do not typically inherit their superclass's initializers. This feature of Swift is intended to prevent subclasses from inadvertently providing initializers that do not set values on all the properties of the subclass type, because subclasses frequently add properties that do not exist in the superclass. Requiring subclasses to have their own initializers helps prevent types from being partially initialized with incomplete initializers.

Nonetheless, there are circumstances in which a class *does* automatically inherit its superclass's initializers. If your subclass provides default values for all new properties it adds, then there are two scenarios in which it will inherit its superclass's initializers:

- If the subclass does not implement any designated initializers, it will inherit its superclass's designated initializers.

- If the subclass provides all its superclass's designated initializers – either by overriding or by inheriting them – it will inherit all the superclass's convenience initializers.

Your **Zombie** type falls within the first of these two scenarios. It is inheriting the **Monster** type's sole designated initializer because it provides default values for all new properties it adds and does not define its own designated initializer. And because the **Zombie** type is inheriting an initializer, the compiler is no longer providing the free empty initializer you were using before.

The signature for the initializer **Zombie** inherits is `init(town:monsterName:)`, with parameters for `town` and `monsterName`. Update `fredTheZombie`'s initialization in `main.swift` to include these parameters and remove the error.

Listing 17.9 Updating `fredTheZombie`'s initialization (`main.swift`)

```
...
let fredTheZombie = Zombie(town: myTown, monsterName: "Fred")
fredTheZombie.town = myTown
fredTheZombie.terrorizeTown()
fredTheZombie.town?.printDescription()
...
```

Now, when you create an instance of the **Monster** or **Zombie** type, you give the instance a value for its `town` and `name` properties. Build and run the application. The errors should be gone, and the results are the same as before.

Designated initializers for classes

Classes use designated initializers as their primary initializers. As part of this role, designated initializers are responsible for ensuring that the class's properties are all given values before initialization is ended. If a class has a superclass, then its designated initializer must also call its superclass's designated initializer.

You have already written a designated initializer for the **Monster** class:

```
init(town: Town?, monsterName: String) {
    self.town = town
    name = monsterName
}
```

The **Monster** class's initializer ensures that all its properties are given values before initialization completes. Currently, the **Zombie** type gives default values to all its properties (except the ones inherited from **Monster**). So the initializer you defined for **Monster** works fine for **Zombie**.

Still, it would be better if **Zombie** defined its own initializer so that you could customize its initialization.

In Zombie.swift, start by removing the default values for **Zombie**'s properties.

Listing 17.10 Removing default values (Zombie.swift)

```
class Zombie: Monster {
    override class var spookyNoise: String {
        return "Brains..."
    }
    var walksWithLimp = true
    var walksWithLimp: Bool
    private(set) var isFallingApart = false
    private(set) var isFallingApart: Bool
    ...
}
```

Removing these default values triggers a compiler error: Class 'Zombie' has no initializers. With no default values assigned, the **Zombie** class needs an initializer to give its properties values before initialization completes.

Add a new initializer to the **Zombie** class to solve this problem.

Listing 17.11 Adding a zombie initializer (Zombie.swift)

```
class Zombie: Monster {
    override class var spookyNoise: String {
        return "Brains..."
    }
    var walksWithLimp: Bool
    private(set) var isFallingApart: Bool

    init(limp: Bool, fallingApart: Bool, town: Town?, monsterName: String) {
        walksWithLimp = limp
        isFallingApart = fallingApart
        super.init(town: town, monsterName: monsterName)
    }

    func regenerate() {
        walksWithLimp = false
    }
    ...
}
```

Your new initializer takes care of the error, because you are now ensuring that the **Zombie**'s properties have values by the end of initialization. There are two parts to what you have added here. First, the new initializer sets the values of the walksWithLimp and isFallingApart properties via the limp and fallingApart arguments. These properties are specific to the **Zombie** class, so the designated initializer initializes them with appropriate values.

Second, you call the designated initializer of **Zombie**'s superclass. As you saw in Chapter 15, super points to a subclass's superclass. So the syntax super.init(town: town, monsterName: monsterName) passes the values of the parameters town and monsterName from the initializer on the **Zombie** class to the designated initializer on the **Monster** class. This, in turn, calls the designated initializer on **Monster**, which will ensure that the **Zombie**'s properties for town and name will be set.

Figure 17.2 shows this relationship graphically.

Figure 17.2 Calling **super.init**

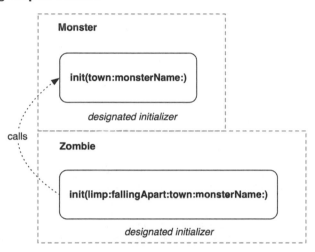

You might be wondering why you called the superclass's initializer last. Because **Zombie**'s initializer is the designated initializer on the **Zombie** class, it is responsible for initializing all the properties it introduced. After these properties have been given values, the designated initializer of a subclass is responsible for calling its superclass's initializer so that it can initialize *its* properties.

There is a new error to fix in main.swift. Switch to this file, and you will see that the compiler is telling you that the initializer for **Zombie** is missing an argument. Fix this by updating fredTheZombie's initializer to include all the arguments in the initializer you added to **Zombie**.

Listing 17.12 Does Fred walk with a limp? Is he falling apart? (main.swift)

```
...
let fredTheZombie = Zombie(
    limp: false, fallingApart: false, town: myTown, monsterName: "Fred")
...
```

fredTheZombie is now getting initialized with all the information that it needs to be ready for use.

Convenience initializers for classes

Unlike designated initializers, convenience initializers are not responsible for making sure all of a class's properties have a value. Instead, they do the work that they are defined to do and then hand off that information to either another convenience initializer or a designated initializer.

All convenience initializers call across to another initializer on the same class. Eventually, a convenience initializer must call through to its class's designated initializer. The relationship between convenience and designated initializers defines a path by which a class's stored properties receive initial values.

Make a convenience initializer on the **Zombie** type. This initializer will provide arguments for whether the **Zombie** instance walks with a limp and whether the instance is falling apart. It will omit parameters for town and monsterName; callers of this initializer will only be responsible for providing arguments to this initializer's parameters.

Listing 17.13 Using a convenience initializer (Zombie.swift)

```
...
init(limp: Bool, fallingApart: Bool, town: Town?, monsterName: String) {
    walksWithLimp = limp
    isFallingApart = fallingApart
    super.init(town: town, monsterName: monsterName)
}

convenience init(limp: Bool, fallingApart: Bool) {
    self.init(limp: limp, fallingApart: fallingApart, town: nil, monsterName: "Fred")
    if walksWithLimp {
        print("This zombie has a bad knee.")
    }
}
...
```

You mark an initializer as a convenience initializer with the convenience keyword. This keyword tells the compiler that the initializer will need to delegate to another initializer on the class, eventually calling to a designated initializer. After this call, an instance of the class is ready for use.

Here, the convenience initializer calls the designated initializer on the **Zombie** class. It passes in the values for the parameters it received: limp and fallingApart. For town and monsterName, the parameters that the convenience initializer did not receive values for, you pass nil and "Fred" to **Zombie**'s designated initializer.

After the convenience initializer calls the designated initializer, the instance is fully prepared for use. That means you can check the value of the walksWithLimp property on the instance. If you had tried to do this check before calling across to the **Zombie**'s designated initializer, the compiler would have issued an error: Use of 'self' in delegating initializer before self.init is called. This error tells you that the delegating initializer is trying to use self, which is needed to access the walksWithLimp property, before it is ready for use.

Figure 17.3 shows the relationships between the convenience and designated initializers.

Figure 17.3 Initializer delegation

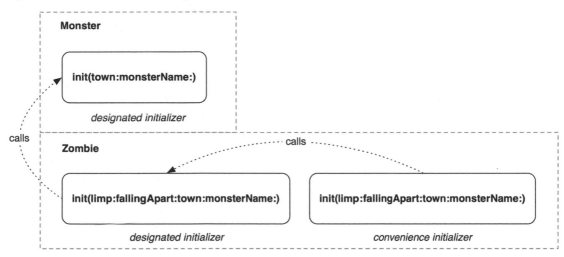

You can now create instances of the **Zombie** type with this convenience initializer. But remember that instances of **Zombie** created with this convenience initializer will have nil for the town property and "Fred" for the name property. Switch to main.swift and use it to create an instance.

Listing 17.14 Creating a convenient zombie (`main.swift`)

```
...
let fredTheZombie = Zombie(
    limp: false, fallingApart: false, town: myTown, monsterName: "Fred")
fredTheZombie.terrorizeTown()
fredTheZombie.town?.printDescription()

var convenientZombie = Zombie(limp: true, fallingApart: false)
...
```

Build and run your program, and you will see that convenientZombie has a bad knee, but fredTheZombie does not.

Required initializers for classes

You have learned that sometimes an initializer is inherited by a subclass, and sometimes it is not, depending on which other initializers the subclass may have implemented. But what if you want to be able to create instances of a class and all its subclasses with the same initializer? You can require that subclasses provide a specific initializer, if it is not inherited.

For example, suppose you want all subclasses of the **Monster** class to provide an initializer that takes values for the monster's name and the town it is terrorizing (or nil, if the monster has not yet found a town). To do so, you mark the initializer with the keyword required to indicate that all subclasses of this type must provide the given initializer, either by overriding or inheriting it.

Switch to Monster.swift to make this change.

Listing 17.15 Making town and monsterName required (Monster.swift)

```
class Monster {
    ...
    required init(town: Town?, monsterName: String) {
        self.town = town
        name = monsterName
    }
    ...
}
```

The sole designated initializer on the **Monster** class is now required. Subclasses must override or inherit this initializer.

Build your program to check for errors. This change creates a compiler error, as revealed by Xcode's toolbar. Select the red icon to display the issue navigator and see what is wrong. The error reads 'required' initializer 'init(town:monsterName:)' must be provided by subclass of 'Monster'. It is telling you that you are not yet implementing the required initializer on the **Zombie** class.

Because **Zombie** defines its own designated initializer, it does not inherit any of its superclass's designated initializers, including required ones. You must now override it yourself. Navigate to Zombie.swift to implement the initializer.

Listing 17.16 Adding the required initializer (Zombie.swift)

```
...
convenience init(limp: Bool, fallingApart: Bool) {
    self.init(limp: limp, fallingApart: fallingApart, town: nil, monsterName: "Fred")
    if walksWithLimp {
        print("This zombie has a bad knee.")
    }
}

required init(town: Town?, monsterName: String) {
    walksWithLimp = false
    isFallingApart = false
    super.init(town: town, monsterName: monsterName)
}
...
```

To implement a superclass's required initializer, you prefix the subclass's implementation of the initializer with the `required` keyword. Unlike other functions that you must override if you inherit them from your superclass, you do not mark `required` initializers with the `override` keyword. It is implied by marking the initializer with `required`.

Your implementation of this `required` initializer makes it a designated initializer for the **Zombie** class. Why, you ask? Good question.

Recall that designated initializers are responsible for initializing the type's properties and for delegating up to the superclass's initializer. This implementation does exactly those two things. You can therefore use this initializer to instantiate the **Zombie** class.

At this point, you might be wondering, "How many designated initializers does **Zombie** have?" The answer is two: `init(limp:fallingApart:town:monsterName:)` and `init(town:monsterName:)`. Having more than one designated initializer is completely fine and is not uncommon.

Deinitialization

Deinitialization is part of the process of removing instances of a class from memory when they are no longer needed. Conceptually, it is the opposite of initialization. Deinitialization is limited to reference types; it is not available for value types.

In Swift, a deinitializer provides an opportunity to do any final maintenance before the instance is deallocated. It is called automatically, immediately prior to the removal of an instance from memory. If the class is a subclass, then the superclass's deinitializer will execute next, and on up the chain, before the instance's deallocation.

The details of memory management are covered in greater detail in Chapter 24, but it makes sense to introduce the idea of deinitialization while we are discussing initialization.

A class can only have one deinitializer. Deinitializers are written with **deinit**; they do not use the `func` keyword or an argument list, as they are not like methods - you cannot call them directly. Let's see a deinitializer in action in the **Zombie** class.

Listing 17.17 One less zombie (Zombie.swift)

```
...
required init(town: Town?, monsterName: String) {
    walksWithLimp = false
    isFallingApart = false
    super.init(town: town, monsterName: monsterName)
}

deinit {
    print("Zombie \(name) is no longer with us.")
}
...
```

Your new deinitializer simply logs a farewell to the **Zombie** instance that is about to be deallocated from memory. Notice that the deinitializer accesses the **Zombie**'s name. Deinitializers have full access to an instance's properties and methods.

Open `main.swift`. To exercise the **Zombie**'s **deinit** method, you are going to set `fredTheZombie` to be `nil` at the end of the file. Doing so will trigger the process of removing this instance from memory.

There are some other changes you will need to make before you can wave goodbye to fredTheZombie. You need to declare fredTheZombie with var instead of let so that the instance can become nil. Also, because only optional types can be or become nil in Swift, you have to declare fredTheZombie as an optional – **Zombie?**. And this change means that you have to use optional chaining to unwrap the optional's value.

Listing 17.18 Fred, we hardly knew ye (main.swift)

```
...
let var fredTheZombie: Zombie? = Zombie(
    limp: false, fallingApart: false, town: myTown, monsterName: "Fred")
fredTheZombie fredTheZombie?.terrorizeTown()
fredTheZombie fredTheZombie?.town?.printDescription()

var convenientZombie = Zombie(limp: true, fallingApart: false)

print("Victim pool: \(fredTheZombie String(describing: fredTheZombie?.victimPool))")
fredTheZombie fredTheZombie?.victimPool = 500
print("Victim pool: \(fredTheZombie String(describing: fredTheZombie?.victimPool))")
print(Zombie.spookyNoise)
if Zombie.isTerrifying {
    print("Run away!")
}
fredTheZombie = nil
```

You created new strings using the **String(describing:)** method when printing here. This is because the **print()** function does not like to accept optional input, but optional chaining produces optional return values. The **String(describing:)** string initializer safely creates a new string for the **print()** function.

Build and run the program now to double-check that your parentheses are balanced correctly after the last change. You will see that you bid fredTheZombie farewell when the instance is deallocated.

Failable Initializers

Sometimes it is useful to define a type whose initialization can fail at runtime. For example, imagine defining a struct to model a combination lock, such as what someone might put on their luggage. You would want to ensure that every new instance was initialized with a four-digit integer combination, 0000 through 9999, as its argument.

Checking that the passed-in combination is valid must happen when the program is running. What should the initializer do if the combination is invalid? One solution is to return nil from the initialization process.

In these cases, you need a way to report to the caller that you were not able to initialize the instance. You use *failable initializers* to handle these scenarios.

A failable Town initializer

Failable initializers return an optional instance of the type. To indicate that an initializer is failable, you add a question mark to the init keyword: init?.

You can also use an exclamation point after init to create a failable initializer that returns an implicitly unwrapped optional: init!. Returning an implicitly unwrapped optional allows you to avoid optional unwrapping syntax - but remember that Swift provides that syntax to make optionals safe to use. So be cautious about returning implicitly unwrapped optionals.

If an instance of **Town** is being created with a population of 0, then initialization should fail – you cannot have a town without a population. Open main.swift and change the initialization of myTown to have a value of 0 for its population parameter.

Listing 17.19 myTown, population zero (main.swift)

```
var myTown = Town(population: 10_000 0, stoplights: 6)
myTown.printDescription()
...
```

This does not cause an error – yet. Switch to Town.swift to give the **Town** struct a failable initializer.

Town has two initializers. Remember that you delegated from the **init(population:stoplights:)** initializer to the **init(region:population:stoplights:)** initializer in this type. For now, just make the **init(region:population:stoplights:)** failable.

Listing 17.20 Using a failable initializer (Town.swift)

```
struct Town {
...
    init init?(region: String, population: Int, stoplights: Int) {
        guard population > 0 else {
            return nil
        }
        self.region = region
        self.population = population
        numberOfStoplights = stoplights
    }
...
}
```

You now use the failable initializer syntax in **init?(region:population:stoplights:)**. After this declaration, you check whether the given value for population is greater than 0. If it is not, then you return nil and the initializer fails. In the context of failable initializers, "fail" means that the initializer will create an optional instance of the **Town** type with a value of nil. This is good. It is preferable to have an instance set to nil rather than an instance with bad data in its properties.

At this point, you should notice a few errors in your program. (Build your program if you do not. You can build without running using Product → Build or Command-B.) Take a moment to consider what is going on before you run the program.

The initializer **init(population:stoplights:)** currently delegates to a failable initializer. This suggests that **init(population:stoplights:)** may get nil back from the designated initializer. Receiving nil back from the designated initializer would be unexpected, because **init(population:stoplights:)** is not failable itself.

233

Fix this problem by also making **init(population:stoplights:)** a failable initializer.

Listing 17.21 Making both **Town** initializers failable (Town.swift)

```
struct Town {
...
    init?(region: String, population: Int, stoplights: Int) {
        guard population > 0 else {
            return nil
        }
        self.region = region
        self.population = population
        numberOfStoplights = stoplights
    }


    init init?(population: Int, stoplights: Int) {
        self.init(region: "N/A", population: population, stoplights: stoplights)
    }
...
}
```

Now try to run the program, and you will see that there are still a number of errors that you have to fix. You can find these errors in main.swift.

The line myTown.printDescription() has an error that reads: Value of optional type 'Town?' must be unwrapped to refer to member 'printDescription' of wrapped base type 'Town'. Remember that making the initializers on the **Town** struct failable means that they now return optionals: **Town?** instead of **Town**. That means you have to unwrap the optionals before using them.

Use optional chaining to fix the errors in main.swift. Also, use **String(describing:)** to print the information about a town instance.

Listing 17.22 Using optional chaining (main.swift)

```
var myTown = Town(population: 0, stoplights: 6)
myTown myTown?.printDescription()
let myTownSize = myTown myTown?.townSize
print(String(describing: myTownSize))
myTown myTown?.changePopulation(by: 1_000_000)
print("Size: \(myTown String(describing: myTown?.townSize));
        population: \(myTown String(describing: myTown?.population))")
...
```

Note that the last **print()** statement should be all on one line in your code.

As you can see, representing nil in Swift tends to have a fairly extensive impact on your code. These changes can add complexity and more code to your project. Both increase the chances of making a troublesome mistake.

We recommend that you minimize your use of optionals to those cases in which you absolutely need them.

Build and run the program now. You removed the errors, so the project runs fine.

Aside from some of your print statements printing nil now, you are also missing a print statement in your output. Because myTown is nil, the optionally chained call to **printDescription()** does not happen at all.

It is time to say farewell to MonsterTown. For the next several chapters, you will move back to Swift playgrounds to focus on a some specific language features. If you are itching to work on more projects, fear not! There are more projects to come.

Initialization Going Forward

"How am I going to remember all this?" We hear you. Initialization in Swift is a very defined process with a lot of rules - rules that even longtime Swift developers frequently forget. Thankfully, the compiler will remind you of what you need to do to comply and write a valid initializer.

Rather than memorizing all the rules of initialization, it is useful to think of Swift initialization in terms of value types and classes.

For value types, such as structs, initialization is principally responsible for ensuring that all the instance's stored properties have been initialized and given appropriate values.

That statement is true for classes as well, but class initialization is a bit more complicated due to classes' inheritance relationships. It can be thought of as unfolding in two sequential phases.

In the first phase, a class's designated initializer is eventually called (either directly or by delegation from a convenience initializer). At this point, all the properties declared on the class are initialized with appropriate values inside the designated initializer's definition.

Next, a designated initializer delegates up to its superclass's designated initializer. The designated initializer on the superclass then ensures that all its own stored properties are initialized with appropriate values, which is a process that continues until the class at the top of the inheritance chain is reached. The first phase is now complete.

The second phase begins, providing an opportunity for a class to further customize the values held by its stored properties. For example, a designated initializer can modify properties on `self` after it calls to the superclass's designated initializer. Designated initializers can also call instance methods on `self`. Finally, initialization reenters the convenience initializer, providing it with an opportunity to perform any customization on the instance.

The instance is fully initialized after these two phases, and all its properties and methods are available for use.

The goal of this very definite initialization process is to guarantee the successful initialization of a class. The compiler secures this procedure and will issue errors if you do not adhere to any step in the process. In the end, it is not important that you remember each step in the process so long as you follow the compiler's guidance. Over time, the details of initialization will become more secure in your mind.

Silver Challenge

Currently, the required initializer on the **Monster** class is implemented as a designated initializer on the **Zombie** subclass. Make this initializer a convenience initializer on the **Zombie** class instead. This change will involve delegating across the **Zombie** class to its designated initializer.

Gold Challenge

The **Monster** class can be initialized with any **String** instance for the monsterName parameter, even an empty **String**. Doing so would lead to an instance of **Monster** with no name. Even though Frankenstein's monster had no name, you want all of yours to be individually identified. Fix this problem in the **Monster** class by ensuring that monsterName cannot be empty.

Your solution will involve giving **Monster** a failable initializer. Note that this change will have an impact on initialization in the **Zombie** subclass. Make the necessary adjustments in this class as well.

For the More Curious: Initializer Parameters

External parameter names distinguish between the parameter names available to callers and the local parameter names used in a function's implementation. Because initializers follow different naming conventions than other functions (initializers are always **init**), the parameters' names and types help determine which initializer should be called. So Swift provides external parameter names for all initializer parameters by default.

You can also provide your own external parameter names as needed. For example, imagine a **WeightRecordInLbs** struct that should be able to be initialized with kilograms.

```
struct WeightRecordInLbs {
    let weight: Double

    init(kilograms kilos: Double) {
        weight = kilos * 2.20462
    }
}
```

This initializer supplies `kilograms` as an explicit external parameter and gives `kilos` as a local parameter. In its implementation, you convert `kilos` to pounds by multiplying it by the conversion factor. You would then use this initializer like so: `let wr = WeightRecordInLbs(kilograms: 84)`.

You can also use _ as an explicit external parameter name if you do not want to expose a parameter name. For example, the **WeightRecordInLbs** struct obviously defines a weight record in terms of pounds. So it would make sense for the initializer to default to taking pounds in its argument.

```
struct WeightRecordInLBS {
    let weight: Double

    init(_ pounds: Double) {
        weight = pounds
    }

    init(kilograms kilos: Double) {
        weight = kilos * 2.20462
    }
}
```

The new initializer can be used like so: `let wr = WeightRecordInLbs(185)`. Because this type explicitly represents a weight record in pounds, there is no need for a named parameter in the argument list. Using _ can make your code more concise and is convenient when it is clear what will be passed in to the argument.

18

Value vs Reference Types

This chapter reviews and builds on the lessons you have been learning about value types (structs and enums) and reference types (classes). You will explore the differences between the two by comparing their differing behaviors in a variety of scenarios. At the end of this chapter, you should have a good understanding of when to use a value type or a reference type.

Value Semantics

Create a new macOS playground called ValueVsRefs. Your playground has the usual template code:

```
import Cocoa

var str = "Hello, playground"
```

You have seen this code many times before: You have a mutable instance of type **String** set to the value "Hello, playground". Make a new string by giving the value of str to another instance.

Listing 18.1 Making a new string

```
import Cocoa

var str = "Hello, playground"                          "Hello, playground"
var playgroundGreeting = str                           "Hello, playground"
```

playgroundGreeting has the same value as str. They both hold the string "Hello, playground", which you can verify in the results sidebar. But what happens when you change the value of playgroundGreeting? Will it also change the value of str? Change playgroundGreeting to find out.

Listing 18.2 Updating playgroundGreeting

```
var str = "Hello, playground"                          "Hello, playground"
var playgroundGreeting = str                           "Hello, playground"
playgroundGreeting += "! How are you today?"           "Hello, playground! How...
str                                                    "Hello, playground"
```

As you can see, even though playgroundGreeting's value has been updated, str's value has not changed. Why not? The answer has to do with value semantics.

To better understand value semantics, Option-click on `playgroundGreeting`. You should see the pop-up shown in Figure 18.1.

Figure 18.1 `playgroundGreeting` information

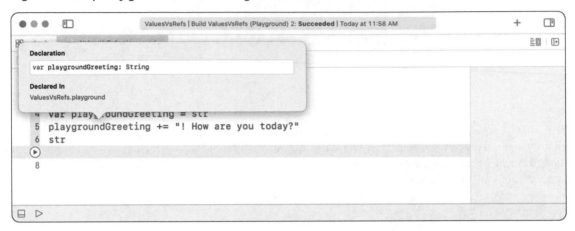

The pop-up shows that `playgroundGreeting` is of type **String** – no surprise there. Click on the word "String" in the pop-up to open the documentation for the **String** type (Figure 18.2).

Figure 18.2 **String** documentation

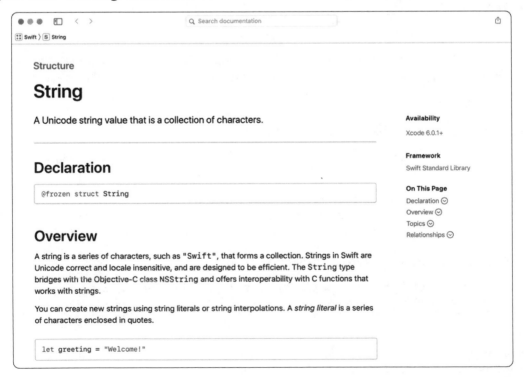

Scroll down to the section called *Modifying and Comparing Strings*, and you will see that **String**s in Swift always have value semantics. And, as you saw in Chapter 15, types with value semantics are copied when they are assigned to an instance or passed as an argument to a function.

When you assigned `str`'s value to be equal to `playgroundGreeting`'s value, you gave a copy of `str`'s value to `playgroundGreeting`. They are not the same instance. So when you changed `playgroundGreeting`'s value, it had no impact on `str`'s value. Figure 18.3 shows this relationship graphically.

Figure 18.3 Value semantics and copy behavior

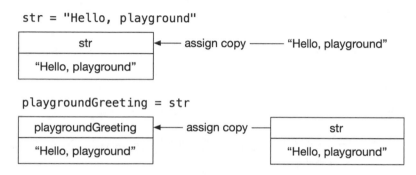

Swift's basic data types – **Array**, **Dictionary**, **Int**, **String**, and so on – are all implemented as structs, so they are all value types. This design choice made at the level of the standard library should indicate to you how important value types are to Swift. You should first consider modeling your data with a struct and only use a class if needed.

Let's look at how reference semantics work to get a better understanding of when it is appropriate to use them.

Reference Semantics

Reference semantics work differently than value semantics. With value types, you get a copy of the instance when you assign it to a new constant or variable. The same is true when you pass an instance of a value type as the argument to a function. But for an instance of a reference type, these two actions create an additional reference to the *same underlying instance*.

To see what this means, you are going to model a company and its employees, who for some reason have a hard time keeping their employee IDs straight. Add a new class to the playground to model a company's employee:

Listing 18.3 Adding an **Employee** class

```
...
playgroundGreeting += "! How are you today?"          "Hello, playground! How...
str                                                    "Hello, playground"

class Employee {
    var id: Int = 0
}
```

The class **Employee** is small – it supplies a single stored property to hold on to the employee's ID number. Make a new instance of this class.

Listing 18.4 Making an employee

```
...
class Employee {
    var id: Int = 0
}
let anika = Employee()                                 Employee
```

You now have a new instance of **Employee** with the id 0.

Some other employees only know Anika as "the boss." Make a new constant called theBoss and assign anika to it.

Listing 18.5 Getting a reference to an employee

```
...
class Employee {
    var id: Int = 0
}
let anika = Employee()                                 Employee
let theBoss = anika                                    Employee
```

Uh oh! Anika's employee ID is 16, not 0. At this point, you have two constants – but they both point to the same instance of the **Employee** class. Update anika's ID to see this.

Listing 18.6 Changing an employee's ID

```
...
let anika = Employee()                                 Employee
let theBoss = anika                                    Employee

anika.id = 16                                          Employee
anika.id                                               16
theBoss.id                                             16
```

The code in Listing 18.6 changes anika's ID and leaves theBoss's ID alone. But the id property for both of them has changed to 16, as shown in the results sidebar.

The code Employee() created an instance of the **Employee** class. When you assign an instance of a class to a constant or variable, as you did with anika, that constant or variable gets a reference to the instance. And, as you can see, a reference works differently than a copy.

With a reference, the constant or variable refers to an instance of the class in memory. And because theBoss is set to equal anika, both constants refer to the *same* instance of the **Employee** class. Figure 18.4 shows this relationship.

Figure 18.4 Reference semantics

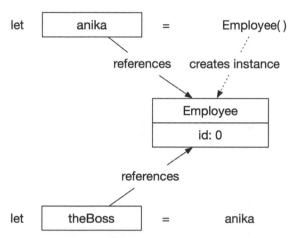

Because anika and theBoss refer to the same instance of **Employee**, you can use either reference to make changes to the shared instance. Using one reference to set the id and the other reference to get the id will access the same ID of the same **Employee**.

This does not mean that *all* references *always* refer to a single, shared instance; you can make more instances and references to them using the constructor syntax (Employee()).

In terms of size, on all modern Apple platforms a reference type variable is always 64 bits (8 bytes), no matter what kind of object it refers to. You might have a reference to a large class instance packed with 500 **Int** properties adding up to 4 kilobytes of memory, but your reference is still only 8 bytes, and the actual 4 kilobyte instance is somewhere else, managed by the system.

Contrast that with a struct instance being passed around with 500 integers inside it. Every time that struct instance is passed, 4 more kilobytes are allocated to hold the new copy of the struct. This might sound like structs are inefficient. But if you can keep them relatively small, they can be much more memory- and processor-efficient than classes. (Also, this is a slightly simplified description of value types' copying behavior. You can learn more of the details in the For the More Curious section at the end of this chapter.)

You will learn more about weighing the use of value and reference types toward the end of this chapter, after you have learned more about their differences.

Constant Value and Reference Types

Value and reference types behave differently when they are constants. To model a list of employees who work together, define a new struct called **Company**.

Listing 18.7 Making the **Company**

```
...
anika.id = 16                                          Employee
anika.id                                               16
theBoss.id                                             16

struct Company {
    var boss: Employee
}
```

Your new **Company** struct has one stored property to reflect the **Employee** in charge. Companies change over time, so you made this property mutable with var.

Create a new instance of **Company** with anika as its boss.

Listing 18.8 Anika's **Company**

```
...
struct Company {
    var boss: Employee
}
let acme = Company(boss: anika)                        Company
```

You now have acme, an instance of **Company** with anika at its head. Note that this instance is created with let, so it is a constant. Try to change acme's boss property.

Listing 18.9 A new boss

```
...
struct Company {
    var boss: Employee
}
let acme = Company(boss: anika)                        Company
let mel = Employee()                                   Employee
acme.boss = mel
```

First, you create a new instance of **Employee** named mel. Second, you assign that new instance to the boss property on acme. You should see a compiler error on that line: Cannot assign to property: 'acme' is a 'let' constant.

This error is telling you that acme is an immutable instance, which means you cannot change it. Value types that are declared as constants cannot have their properties changed, even if those properties are declared with var in the type's implementation. Mel's mutiny has failed.

Remove the assignment to the boss property to silence the compiler error. Leave mel alone; you will be using him in the next example.

Listing 18.10 Demoting Mel

```
...
struct Company {
    var boss: Employee
}
let acme = Company(boss: anika)                    Company
let mel = Employee()                               Employee
acme.boss = mel
```

Mutability works differently for reference types. Imagine that, due to a human resources mix-up, Mel's employee ID must be changed. Try to change the id property on mel.

Listing 18.11 Changing Mel's ID

```
...
struct Company {
    var boss: Employee
}
let acme = Company(boss: anika)                    Company
let mel = Employee()                               Employee
mel.id = 86                                        Employee
mel.id                                             86
```

Despite mel being declared with let, you will see that the compiler is absolutely fine with this id change.

Why can't you change the value of a property on a constant that is an instance of a value type, but you *can* change the value of a property on a constant that is an instance of a reference type?

Because mel is an instance of a reference type, it refers to the instance of **Employee** that was made via this code: Employee(). When you change the value that the id property stores, you are not actually changing the mel variable, because it is just a *reference* to an **Employee**.

Because you made id a mutable stored property when you defined the **Employee** class (via its var declaration), you are free to change id's value however much you like. No matter how many times you change mel's id, mel still refers to the same instance. The thing you cannot do is set the mel variable to refer to a different instance of **Employee**, because that would be changing the variable itself, which is disallowed by your use of let.

Using Value and Reference Types Together

You may be wondering, "Can I put a value type inside a reference type? Can I put a reference type inside a value type?" The answer to both of these questions is "Yes," and you did the latter by adding a property of type **Employee** to **Company**. However, although we led you to do this without warning, you must be very careful about using a reference type inside a value type. (Using a value type inside a reference type does not present any particular problems.)

Suppose that Acme Co. is restructured as Widget Co., and, in the process of reviewing employee records, Anika realizes that she is actually employee number 15, not 16.

Listing 18.12 Fixing Anika's ID

```
...
mel.id = 86                                            Employee
mel.id                                                 86

acme.boss.id                                           16
let widgetCo = acme                                    Company
anika.id = 15                                          Employee
widgetCo.boss.id                                       15
```

When you log the value of `acme.boss.id`, the results sidebar bar shows 16. You next assign a copy of `acme` to a new constant named `widgetCo`. Remember that **Company** is a value type, so you should expect `widgetCo` to receive a copy of `acme`. Then you update `anika`'s ID to 15. Last, you check the `id` of `widgetCo`'s boss and get a surprise.

The `boss`'s ID is now 15, reflecting the change made to `anika`'s ID. How did this happen?

Remember that the `boss` property is of type **Employee**. **Employee** is a class, and is therefore a reference type. Even though **Company** is a value type, it can have properties of reference types like **Employee**, and they are still only references.

This example demonstrates the complications of placing a reference type within a value type. You should expect instances of value types to be copied when they are assigned to a new variable or constant or passed in to a function. But a value type with a reference type in a property will pass a reference to the *same instance* to the new variable or constant. Changes made to that instance via the property of any one of the constants or variables will be reflected in all of them.

To avoid this confusion, you should generally avoid using reference type properties inside value types. If you find yourself needing a reference type property in your struct, then it is best to use an immutable instance.

Copying

The concept of making copies has been lurking behind nearly every topic covered in this chapter. Developers often want to know if copying an instance yields a *shallow* or a *deep* copy. Swift does not provide any language-level support for making a deep copy, which means copies in Swift are shallow.

To get a sense of what these concepts mean, let's look at an example. Imagine that Widget Co. hires a new employee. Create a new instance of **Employee** and put all instances into an array.

Listing 18.13 Adding a new employee

```
...
let juampa = Employee()                          Employee

let employees = [anika, mel, juampa]             [{id 15}, {id 86}, {id 0}]
```

You create a new employee named juampa and add that instance, anika, and mel to a new array. The sidebar shows the array with the three **Employee**s, identified by their ids.

While adding everyone to the invitation list for a company party, Anika discovers that Juampa's ID was not entered correctly. Make a copy of the employees array, update juampa's id, and compare employees to its copy.

Listing 18.14 Copying employees

```
...
let juampa = Employee()

let employees = [anika, mel, juampa]             [{id 15}, {id 86}, {id 0}]
let partyGoers = employees                       [{id 15}, {id 86}, {id 0}]
employees.last?.id = 4                           ()
employees                                        [{id 15}, {id 86}, {id 4}]
partyGoers                                       [{id 15}, {id 86}, {id 4}]
```

The last property refers to the last element in an array. It is optional, because the array may be empty, so you use optional binding to access juampa's id in employees.last?.id = 4.

Arrays are structs, which means that they are value types. So you might expect that partyGoers is a distinct copy of employees. But employees and its copy, partyGoers, have the same contents after you change juampa's id property. Why did changing the ID of the last employee in the employees array change the ID of the last employee in partyGoers?

Remember that employees contains instances of **Employee** (a reference type). So the partyGoers and employees arrays have references to the same instances of **Employee**. This is very similar to acme and widgetCo sharing references to an **Employee**.

Putting it all together, last will get the last element in the employees array, which is juampa – an instance of **Employee**. When you change the ID, you are changing it for the instance of **Employee** that juampa refers to. Thus, the change to juampa is reflected in both arrays.

This form of copying is referred to as shallow copying. Shallow copying does not traverse references: A shallow copy of a value type copies the value. A shallow copy of a reference type copies the reference. This is what you have come to expect of the assignment operator in Swift, and Figure 18.5 is a graphical visualization of it.

Figure 18.5 Shallow copy of an array of employees

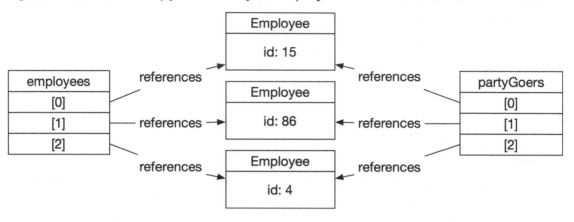

A *deep copy*, on the other hand, would duplicate the instance at the destination of a reference. That would mean that the indices of the partyGoers array would not reference the same instances of **Employee**. Instead, a deep copy of employees would create a new array with references to its own instances of **Employee**. That form of copying would look something like Figure 18.6.

Figure 18.6 Deep copy of an array of employees

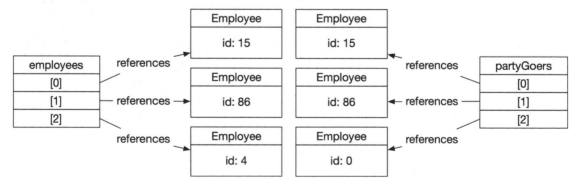

Swift does not supply any means to perform a deep copy, but these are common terms used by developers discussing data modeling needs, so we present the ideas to you here. If you would like this behavior, then you will need to make it yourself.

Equality vs Identity

Now that you understand the difference between value and reference types, you are ready to learn about equality and identity. *Equality* refers to two instances having the same values for their observable characteristics, such as two instances of the **String** type that have the same text. Take a look at this sample code.

```
let x = 1
let y = 1
x == y // true
```

Two constants, x and y, are created. They are both of type **Int** and hold on to the same value, 1. Not surprisingly, the equality check, done via ==, evaluates to true. This makes sense because x and y hold on to exactly the same value.

This is exactly what we want to know from an equality check: Do two instances have the same value? All Swift's basic data types (**String**, **Int**, **Float**, **Double**, **Array**, **Set**, and **Dictionary**) can be checked for equality.

Identity, on the other hand, refers to whether two references point to the same instance in memory. You can check two instances of **Employee** for identity because they are both reference types. In your playground, check for identity on two new instances using the identity operator (===) to see whether they point to the same instance.

Listing 18.15 Checking for identity

```
...
acme.boss === anika                                         true
```

Here, the identity check succeeds, not because the boss of Acme has the same properties as anika, but because the boss of Acme *is* anika. The boss property of the acme **Company** is a reference to the same instance that anika is a reference to.

Now try an identity check between new instances of **Employee**:

Listing 18.16 Another identity check

```
...
acme.boss === anika                                         true
let joe = Employee()                                        Employee
let sam = Employee()                                        Employee
joe === sam                                                 false
```

This identity check fails because joe and sam are not references to the same instance, even though they have the same employee ID (0).

What if you want to check for identity on x and y? You might think you could use the identity operator, as in x === y. But this code will generate an error from the compiler. Why? The === operator exists to check the memory address of instances referred to by reference type variables. Value type variables do not store references, so an identity check would be meaningless.

What if you tried to check for equality on joe and sam, to see if they had the same properties? Try it.

Listing 18.17 Checking for equality on a custom type

```
let joe = Employee()                                    Employee
let sam = Employee()                                    Employee
joe === sam                                             false
joe == sam
```

A compiler error tells you that it does not know how to call the **==** function on the **Employee** class. If you want to check for equality on classes that you make, you have to teach your classes how by implementing the **==** function. Doing so entails conforming to a protocol called **Equatable**, which you will read about in Chapter 25.

You will return to this example in Chapter 25 to do just that. For now, remove the last line.

Listing 18.18 Removing the bad equality check

```
let joe = Employee()                                    Employee
let sam = Employee()                                    Employee
joe === sam                                             false
joe == sam
```

It is important to realize that two constants or variables can be equal (i.e., they have the same values) yet not be identical (i.e., they may point to different instances of a given type). But it does not work the other way around: If two variables or constants point to the same instance in memory, then they will be equal as well.

What Should I Use?

Structures and classes are well suited for defining many custom types. Before Swift, structs were so distinct from classes in macOS and iOS development that the use-cases for both types were obvious. In Swift, however, the functionality added to structs makes their behavior more similar to that of classes. This similarity makes deciding which to use somewhat more complicated.

Still, there are important differences between structs and classes that give some guidance on which to use when. Strict rules are hard to define, because there are many factors to consider, but here are some general guidelines.

- If you want a type to be passed by reference, use a class. Doing so will ensure that the type is referenced rather than copied when assigned or passed in to a function's argument.

- If the type needs to support inheritance, then use a class. Structs do not support inheritance and cannot be subclassed.

- Otherwise, you probably want a struct.

Structs are commonly used when modeling shapes (e.g., rectangles have a width and a height), ranges (e.g., a race has a start and an end), and points in a coordinate system (e.g., a point in a two-dimensional space has an x and y value). They are also great for defining data structures: The **String**, **Array**, and **Dictionary** types are all defined as structs in Swift's standard library.

There are some other cases in which you might want to use a class instead of a struct, but they will be somewhat less common than the need for reference semantics or inheritance. For example, if you want to take advantage of passing a reference around but do not want a class to be subclassed, you might ask yourself whether you should use a struct (to avoid inheritance) or a class (to have reference semantics). The answer here is to use a `final class { ... }`. Marking a class as `final` will prevent the class from being subclassed and will also offer you the desired reference semantics for instances of the class.

In general, we suggest starting out with a struct unless you absolutely know you need the benefits of a reference type. Value types are easier to reason about because you do not need to worry about what happens to an instance when you change values on a copy.

For the More Curious: Copy on Write

You might be wondering about the performance implications of Swift's copying behavior. For example, if you get a new copy of an **Array** every time you pass it in to a function or assign it to a new constant or variable, won't you have a wasteful number of copies floating about? What about very large arrays?

The answers depend on your data and how you are using it.

Swift's standard library types use a strategy called *copy on write* to ensure that working with value types is not wasteful. Copy on write, or COW, refers to the implicit sharing of value types' underlying storage. Instances of a value type do not *immediately* have their own copies of the data. They share their underlying storage, with each instance maintaining its own reference to the store. If an instance needs to mutate the storage, or write to it, *then* the instance gets its own distinct copy.

This allows value types to avoid creating copies of data unnecessarily.

To better understand this idea, you will create a very simple implementation of an array to hold instances of type **Int**. This implementation will illustrate the concepts at hand, but it will fall short of an actual implementation of Swift's **Array** type. You will see how to create a more complete implementation of a custom collection type in Chapter 21.

Figure 18.7 provides a sketch of how your **IntArray** will be implemented to support COW.

Figure 18.7 Diagram of **IntArray**

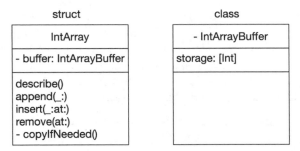

This kind of figure is called a *structure diagram*, and it uses something called Unified Modeling Language (UML). UML provides a standardized language to describe and visualize a system in software engineering. If the diagram is well formed, you should be able to look it and write its corresponding code. Many of the conventions are intuitive, but there are a few special symbols. For example, the – preceding buffer and **copyIfNeeded()** in **IntArray**'s description means that these members of the struct are private.

IntArray will be a struct that has one property named buffer that is of type **IntArrayBuffer**. buffer will be a private property, because you do not want your underlying storage to be visible externally. **IntArrayBuffer** will be a class with one property named storage that is an array of integers. Your buffer type will be private as well, because it is merely an implementation detail of **IntArray**, so it should not be available externally either.

It may feel strange to use an array of integers as the storage. After all, aren't you doing all this to make an array that can store integers? Well, yes, but a more realistic implementation of an array would use concepts covered later in the book. For now, the main point is that **IntArrayBuffer** serves as a reference type modeling **IntArray**'s underlying storage.

IntArray will provide three public methods central to an array's behavior: **append(_:)**, **insert(_:at:)**, and **remove(at:)**. **IntArray** will also have a **describe()** method so that you will be able to observe changes to the underlying storage.

After you set up your initial implementation, you will add the private **copyIfNeeded()** method to **IntArray**. This is where you will implement the COW behavior of your **IntArray** type.

It is time to implement your array and its underlying buffer. Create a new macOS playground and name it IntArray. Begin by implementing your buffer class.

Listing 18.19 Implementing **IntArrayBuffer**

```
import Cocoa

var str = "Hello, playground"

fileprivate class IntArrayBuffer {
    var storage: [Int]

    init() {
        storage = []
    }

    init(buffer: IntArrayBuffer) {
        storage = buffer.storage
    }
}
```

IntArrayBuffer is a fileprivate class. This means that the class would need to locate its implementation within the same file as **IntArray**. Because you are writing this code in a playground, it will be visible to your array implementation.

The variable storage has the type **[Int]** and is initialized to be an empty array in the parameterless initializer. You also supply an initializer that takes an **IntArrayBuffer** instance as an argument. This is only added for convenience, as you will use it inside your **IntArray** implementation.

Now it is time to write your **IntArray** type. Create a struct below your **IntArrayBuffer** class.

Listing 18.20 Initial implementation of **IntArray**

```
fileprivate class IntArrayBuffer {
    var storage: [Int]

    init() {
        storage = []
    }

    init(buffer: IntArrayBuffer) {
        storage = buffer.storage
    }
}

struct IntArray {
    private var buffer: IntArrayBuffer

    init() {
        buffer = IntArrayBuffer()
    }

    func describe() {
        print(buffer.storage)
    }
}
```

IntArray has a fairly small implementation at this point. It has a private property named buffer that is of type **IntArrayBuffer**. This property maintains the backing storage for **IntArray**. You also include a small initializer that takes no arguments and uses the empty initializer on **IntArrayBuffer** to set up the array's storage. Last, you provide a simple **describe()** method to print out the contents of the buffer's storage property. This will help you keep track of changes to the array so that you can see how COW works.

Your implementation of **IntArray** is limited at this point. All it does is set up a buffer as its backing storage. That is important work, but it leaves the array lacking its main features. You need to write some methods to insert, append, and remove data from the array.

Listing 18.21 Defining **IntArray**'s API

```
...
struct IntArray {
    private var buffer: IntArrayBuffer

    init() {
        buffer = IntArrayBuffer()
    }

    func describe() {
        print(buffer.storage)
    }

    func insert(_ value: Int, at index: Int) {
        buffer.storage.insert(value, at: index)
    }

    func append(_ value: Int) {
        buffer.storage.append(value)
    }

    func remove(at index: Int) {
        buffer.storage.remove(at: index)
    }
}
```

The methods **insert(_:at:)**, **append(_:)**, and **remove(at:)** all call through to methods defined on the **Array** type in the standard library. This is another value of using **[Int]** as the backing storage of the buffer: While the buffer's implementation is not quite realistic, it allows you to keep things simple and focus on COW's behavior.

Exercise your new **IntArray** by creating an instance and adding some integers to it.

Listing 18.22 Exercising **IntArray**

```
...
struct IntArray {
    private var buffer: IntArrayBuffer

    init() {
        buffer = IntArrayBuffer()
    }

    func describe() {
        print(buffer.storage)
    }

    func insert(_ value: Int, at index: Int) {
        buffer.storage.insert(value, at: index)
    }

    func append(_ value: Int) {
        buffer.storage.append(value)
    }

    func remove(at index: Int) {
        buffer.storage.remove(at: index)
    }
}

var integers = IntArray()
integers.append(1)
integers.append(2)
integers.append(4)
integers.describe()
```

You create an instance of **IntArray** and use **append(_:)** to give a few values to the array. The console prints the result: [1, 2, 4].

But your implementation of COW is not complete. Make a copy of integers and insert a new value into the copy to see why.

Listing 18.23 Making a copy of **IntArray**

```
...
var integers = IntArray()
integers.append(1)
integers.append(2)
integers.append(4)
integers.describe()
var moreIntegers = integers
moreIntegers.insert(3, at: 2)
integers.describe()
moreIntegers.describe()
```

You create a new instance of **IntArray** named moreIntegers and set it to be equal to integers. Next, you use the **insert(_:at:)** to insert the value 3 at index 2 to complete the sequence. Last, you call **describe()** on both integers and moreIntegers to compare their storage.

Take a look at your console and you will see the problem. The two calls to **describe()** show that the storage for both integers and moreIntegers contains the same data. Why did this happen? After all, you defined **IntArray** to be a struct. Structs are supposed to be copied, right?

The problem is that **IntArray** uses a class as its backing storage. As you learned earlier in this chapter, that means both integers and moreIntegers point to the same reference type holding their data. If you change one of these arrays, the change is reflected in both, because the change is made to the storage they share.

It is fine for copies of integers to point to the same underlying storage as long as none of the copies changes the shared data. But you need to ensure that the array's data is copied when it needs to be mutated. Implement a new method on **IntArray** called **copyIfNeeded()** to create a copy when an instance needs to change.

Listing 18.24 Adding COW to **IntArray**

```
...
struct IntArray {
    private var buffer: IntArrayBuffer

    init() {
        buffer = IntArrayBuffer()
    }

    func describe() {
        print(buffer.storage)
    }

    private mutating func copyIfNeeded() {
        if !isKnownUniquelyReferenced(&buffer) {
            print("Making a copy of \(buffer.storage)")
            buffer = IntArrayBuffer(buffer: buffer)
        }
    }

    func insert(_ value: Int, at index: Int) {
        buffer.storage.insert(value, at: index)
    }

    func append(_ value: Int) {
        buffer.storage.append(value)
    }

    func remove(at index: Int) {
        buffer.storage.remove(at: index)
    }
}
...
integers.describe()
print("copying integers to moreIntegers")
var moreIntegers = integers
print("inserting into moreIntegers")
moreIntegers.insert(3, at: 2)
...
```

Here, you add a new method called **copyIfNeeded()**. This method is declared as mutating because it creates a new instance of **IntArrayBuffer** and assigns it to **IntArray**'s buffer property. To do so, you used the **init(buffer:)** initializer on **IntArray** that you created above. This initializer creates a new buffer instance with the same set of values for its storage property as the previous buffer. You also include a call to **print()** to log some information about the change to the console.

Note that a new buffer is only created if you need one. The conditional (if !isKnownUniquelyReferenced(&buffer)) checks whether the buffer has only one reference to it. (Pay no mind to the requirement that you pass buffer in to the function as an inout parameter. That is only an implementation detail; the function does not actually modify the argument passed to it.)

If the buffer is referenced only once, then the function returns true. In that case, you do not want to create a new instance, because you do not need one; there are no other instances sharing a reference to the underlying data. On the other hand, if the buffer is not uniquely referenced, then that means that the buffer's storage is referenced by more than one instance of **IntArray**. Thus, changes to the buffer will be reflected in all instances of this type. You make a new buffer in this case.

You also add some calls to **print()** so that you can log what is happening to the console. These logs will help keep track of when the underlying buffer is copied. The buffer should only be copied when a new value is inserted into moreIntegers with moreIntegers.insert(3, at: 2).

If you look at your console, you will see that no change has occurred. Both integers and moreIntegers have the same values in their buffers. To see the benefit of **copyIfNeeded()**, you need to call it within the mutating methods. This makes sense, because a mutating method changes the instance it was called on, and you will therefore want to have a unique buffer for this instance.

Listing 18.25 Implementing COW in **IntArray**

```
...
struct IntArray {
    private var buffer: IntArrayBuffer

    init() {
        buffer = IntArrayBuffer()
    }

    func describe() {
        print(buffer.storage)
    }

    private mutating func copyIfNeeded() {
        if !isKnownUniquelyReferenced(&buffer) {
            print("Making a copy of \(buffer.storage)")
            buffer = IntArrayBuffer(buffer: buffer)
        }
    }

    mutating func insert(_ value: Int, at index: Int) {
        copyIfNeeded()
        buffer.storage.insert(value, at: index)
    }

    mutating func append(_ value: Int) {
        copyIfNeeded()
        buffer.storage.append(value)
    }

    mutating func remove(at index: Int) {
        copyIfNeeded()
        buffer.storage.remove(at: index)
    }
}
...
```

You mark the **insert(_:at:)**, **append(_:)**, and **remove(at:)** methods as mutating. These methods now mutate the struct. How exactly could that happen?

You have to use a new buffer when you want to mutate an instance. So every time you make a call to insert, append, or remove some data from the instance's storage, you need to create a new instance of **IntArrayBuffer** if the existing instance is not uniquely referenced. In that case, **copyIfNeeded()** will create a new instance of **IntArrayBuffer** and assign it to the **IntArray**'s buffer property. By adding calls to **copyIfNeeded()** to these methods, you are telling the compiler that the methods can change a property on the struct. (Refer back to Chapter 15 for a discussion on mutating.)

If you check the console, you will see that integers and moreIntegers no longer have the same contents. The beauty of this strategy is that instances will share their underlying storage until they need to be distinct. Copying an instance of **IntArrayBuffer** will not entail much overhead on memory because copies point to the same storage until a change is made and the instances need to refer to their own data.

You do not typically need to write your own COW types. Swift's collections already provide COW. A struct made up of arrays, dictionaries, and strings gets COW behavior for free, because its component parts already implement it via the standard library. This discussion was meant to give you a sense of how COW works and to alleviate any concern about memory pressure resulting from the copy behavior of value types.

Part V
Advanced Swift

Swift provides advanced language features that give developers more sophisticated tools to control their applications. This part of the book introduces concepts that will be essential to the more experienced Swift developer. *Protocols*, *extensions*, and *generics* provide mechanisms for developing idiomatic code that leverages the strengths of Swift.

You will also learn more about customizing your types and about the ways your types interact with one another and the Swift standard library. To do this, you will leverage language features that enable you to write more reusable code and handle runtime problems effectively.

19
Protocols

Your Swift journey has reached the point where you are ready to work with more abstract ideas about writing good code. One such abstraction is the idea of *encapsulation* – separating the implementation details of a system from the visible features of the system.

Rather than writing your MonsterTown program as a pile of global variables and functions, you used structs and classes to encapsulate the details of what it means to be a **Monster** or a **Town**. You improved your encapsulation by hiding certain implementation details with access control keywords like `private`, cleaning up your types' *interfaces* to be as clear and meaningful as possible to developers writing programs with your types. (A type's interface is its set of properties and methods of `internal` or higher visibility – those that allow other types to interface with it.)

Another form of encapsulation in Swift is the *protocol*, which is a list of properties and methods – an interface – that a type must have to fulfill some role. Multiple types can *conform* to a protocol. As long as they have the required properties and methods, the protocol does not care what the concrete type is. Protocols are especially useful when you want to implement a function that only cares about a specific feature of the types that it will work with.

Imagine renting a car. You might say, "I want one with a radio." You probably did not imagine a specific brand or model of radio, but you probably do have in mind some basic requirements that make a device "a radio." If it has buttons to play and stop the music, change the channel, and change the volume, you probably consider it a radio. A Swift developer might say, "It conforms to the **Radio** protocol."

To understand how protocols work, you are going to create a function that formats data into a table. Initially, your function will only accept a specific type as its argument. Then you will codify the list of minimum requirements that your function needs into a protocol and make it flexible enough to accept an argument of any type that conforms to your protocol.

Formatting a Table of Data

macOS and iOS apps often put code for presenting data to the user in a different type from code that stores or manages that data. By separating code into single-purpose types, you can write programs that are easier to maintain and reason about as you fix bugs in the future. In this chapter, you will define a single function to present data to the user and a *data source* type to manage the details of the data to be presented.

Create a new macOS playground called Protocols.

Begin with a function that takes a nested array – an array of arrays, in other words – of strings and prints the data in a table format. Each element of the data array represents a single row in the table, so the total number of rows is data.count. The contents of each column for a single row are the **String**s within each data element.

Listing 19.1 Setting up a table

```
import Cocoa

var str = "Hello, playground"

func printTable(_ data: [[String]]) {
    for row in data {
        // Start the output string
        var out = "|"

        // Append each item in this row to the string
        for item in row {
            out += " \(item) |"
        }

        // Done – print it!
        print(out)
    }
}

let data = [
    ["Eva", "30", "6"],
    ["Saleh", "40", "18"],
    ["Amit", "50", "20"],
]

printTable(data)
```

The console shows a simple table displaying the data:

```
| Eva | 30 | 6 |
| Saleh | 40 | 18 |
| Amit | 50 | 20 |
```

Next, you will add the ability to label the columns. The column names will be passed in separately from the data because they are distinct – you might decide to format the column names differently, for example.

Listing 19.2 Labeling the columns

```
func printTable(_ data: [[String]], withColumnLabels columnLabels: [String]) {
    // Create header row containing column headers
    var headerRow = "|"

    for columnLabel in columnLabels {
        let columnHeader = " \(columnLabel) |"
        headerRow += columnHeader
    }
    print(headerRow)

    for row in data {
        // Start the output string
        var out = "|"

        // Append each item in this row to the string
        for item in row {
            out += " \(item) |"
        }

        // Done – print it!
        print(out)
    }
}

let data = [
    ["Eva", "30", "6"],
    ["Saleh", "40", "18"],
    ["Amit", "50", "20"],
]

printTable(data, withColumnLabels: ["Employee Name", "Age", "Years of Experience"])
```

You should see the column labels as the first row in your debug area.

```
| Employee Name | Age | Years of Experience |
| Eva | 30 | 6 |
| Saleh | 40 | 18 |
| Amit | 50 | 20 |
```

The columns' widths are all different, so the table is very ugly. You can fix this by keeping track of the width of each column label, then padding each data element with extra spaces.

Listing 19.3 Aligning the columns

```
func printTable(_ data: [[String]], withColumnLabels columnLabels: [String]) {
    // Create header row containing column headers
    var headerRow = "|"

    // Also keep track of the width of each column
    var columnWidths = [Int]()

    for columnLabel in columnLabels {
        let columnHeader = " \(columnLabel) |"
        headerRow += columnHeader
        columnWidths.append(columnLabel.count)
    }
    print(headerRow)

    for row in data {
        // Start the output string
        var out = "|"

        // Append each item in this row to the string
        for item in row {
            out += " \(item) |"
        for (j, item) in row.enumerated() {
            let paddingNeeded = columnWidths[j] - item.count
            let padding = repeatElement(" ", count:
                            paddingNeeded).joined(separator: "")
            out += " \(padding)\(item) |"
        }

        // Done - print it!
        print(out)
    }
}
...
```

As you are constructing the header row, you also record the width of each column header in the columnWidths array. Then, when you append each item to the output row, you calculate how much shorter the item is than the column header and store that in paddingNeeded. You construct a string with paddingNeeded spaces by using **repeatElement(_:count:)**, which creates a collection of individual spaces, and use that collection's **joined(separator:)** method to join them into a single string.

Check your debug area again. You now have a well-formatted table of data.

```
| Employee Name | Age | Years of Experience |
|           Eva |  30 |                   6 |
|         Saleh |  40 |                  18 |
|          Amit |  50 |                  20 |
```

However, there is at least one major problem with the **printTable(_:withColumnLabels:)** function: It is very difficult to use! You have to have separate arrays for the column labels and the data, and you have to manually make sure that the number of column labels matches the number of elements in the data array.

You are much more likely to want to represent information like this using structures and classes.

To begin, replace the part of the code where you call **printTable(_:withColumnLabels:)** with some *model objects*, which are types that represent the data your app works with.

Listing 19.4 Using model objects

```
...
let data = [
    ["Eva", "30", "6"],
    ["Saleh", "40", "18"],
    ["Amit", "50", "20"],
]

printTable(data, withColumnLabels: ["Employee Name", "Age", "Years of Experience"])
struct Person {
    let name: String
    let age: Int
    let yearsOfExperience: Int
}

struct Department {
    let name: String
    var people = [Person]()

    init(name: String) {
        self.name = name
    }

    mutating func add(_ person: Person) {
        people.append(person)
    }
}

var department = Department(name: "Engineering")
department.add(Person(name: "Eva", age: 30, yearsOfExperience: 6))
department.add(Person(name: "Saleh", age: 40, yearsOfExperience: 18))
department.add(Person(name: "Amit", age: 50, yearsOfExperience: 20))
```

You now have a **Department**, and you would like to be able to print out the details of its people using the **printTable(_:withColumnLabels:)** function. You could modify the function to take a **Department** instead of the two arguments it takes now. However, the current implementation of **printTable(_:withColumnLabels:)** could be used to print any kind of tabular data, and it would be nice to keep that feature. A protocol can help preserve this functionality.

Protocols

A protocol allows you to define the interface you want a type to satisfy. A type that satisfies a protocol is said to "conform to" the protocol. You can think of a protocol like a contract that every conforming type agrees to. This allows you to code against that contract without concerning yourself with specific types.

Define a protocol that specifies the interface you need for the **printTable(_:withColumnLabels:)** function. The function needs to know how many rows and columns there are, what the label for each column is, and what data should be displayed in each cell.

It does not matter to the Swift compiler where in your playground file you put this protocol. But it probably makes the most sense to put it at the top, just before **printTable(_:withColumnLabels:)**, because you are going to use the protocol in the function.

Listing 19.5 Defining a protocol

```
import Cocoa

protocol TabularDataSource {
    var numberOfRows: Int { get }
    var numberOfColumns: Int { get }

    func label(forColumn column: Int) -> String

    func itemFor(row: Int, column: Int) -> String
}
func printTable(_ data: [[String]], withColumnLabels columnLabels: [String]) {
    ...
}
...
```

The syntax for a protocol should look familiar to you. It is very similar to defining a structure or a class, except that all the computed property and function definitions are omitted.

The **TabularDataSource** protocol states that any conforming type must have two properties: numberOfRows and numberOfColumns. The syntax { get } signifies that these properties can be read. If the property were intended to be read/write, you would use { get set }. Note that marking a protocol property with { get } does not exclude the possibility that a conforming type might have a property that is read/write. It only indicates that the protocol requires it to be readable. This is also why the var keyword is always used rather than let for properties in a protocol definition.

Finally, **TabularDataSource** specifies that a conforming type must have the two methods listed – **label(forColumn:)** and **itemFor(row:column:)** – with the exact types that are listed.

A protocol defines the minimum set of properties and methods a type must have. The type can have more than what the protocol lists – extra properties and methods are fine as long as all the requirements of the protocol are present.

Make **Department** conform to the **TabularDataSource** protocol. Begin by declaring that it conforms.

Listing 19.6 Declaring that **Department** conforms to **TabularDataSource**

```
...
struct Department: TabularDataSource {
    ...
}
...
```

The syntax for conforming to a protocol is to add : ProtocolName after the name of the type. (This looks the same as declaring a superclass. We will cover how protocols and superclasses can be used together later.)

Your playground file now has an error. You have claimed that **Department** conforms to **TabularDataSource**, but **Department** is missing all the properties and methods that **TabularDataSource** requires. Add implementations of them all.

Listing 19.7 Adding required properties and methods

```
...
struct Department: TabularDataSource {
    let name: String
    var people = [Person]()

    init(name: String) {
        self.name = name
    }

    mutating func add(_ person: Person) {
        people.append(person)
    }

    var numberOfRows: Int {
        return people.count
    }

    var numberOfColumns: Int {
        return 3
    }

    func label(forColumn column: Int) -> String {
        switch column {
        case 0: return "Employee Name"
        case 1: return "Age"
        case 2: return "Years of Experience"
        default: fatalError("Invalid column!")
        }
    }

    func itemFor(row: Int, column: Int) -> String {
        let person = people[row]
        switch column {
        case 0: return person.name
        case 1: return String(person.age)
        case 2: return String(person.yearsOfExperience)
        default: fatalError("Invalid column!")
        }
    }
}
...
```

A **Department** has a row for each person, so its numberOfRows property returns the number of people in the department. Each person has three properties that should be displayed, so numberOfColumns returns 3. **label(forColumn:)** and **itemFor(row:column:)** are a little more interesting: You use a switch statement to return one of the three column headers. (Why is there a default case? Refer back to Chapter 5 if you are unsure.)

The error in your playground is gone now that **Department** conforms to **TabularDataSource**. You still need to modify **printTable(_:withColumnLabels:)** to acccpt and work with a **TabularDataSource**, because now you do not have any way of calling this function with your department.

Protocols do not just define the properties and methods a conforming type must supply. They can also be used as types themselves: You can have variables, function arguments, and return values that have the type of a protocol.

Change **printTable(_:withColumnLabels:)** to take a data source of type **TabularDataSource**, now that the protocol provides all the same data as the old arguments did (including all the column labels and the amount of data available).

Listing 19.8 Making **printTable(_:)** take a **TabularDataSource**

```
...
func printTable(_ data: [[String]], withColumnLabels columnLabels: [String]) {
func printTable(_ dataSource: TabularDataSource) {
    // Create header row containing column headers
    var headerRow = "|"

    // Also keep track of the width of each column
    var columnWidths = [Int]()

    for columnLabel in columnLabels {
    for i in 0 ..< dataSource.numberOfColumns {
        let columnLabel = dataSource.label(forColumn: i)
        let columnHeader = " \(columnLabel) |"
        headerRow += columnHeader
        columnWidths.append(columnLabel.count)
    }
    print(headerRow)

    for row in data {
    for i in 0 ..< dataSource.numberOfRows {
        // Start the output string
        var out = "|"

        // Append each item in this row to the string
        for (j, item) in row.enumerated() {
        for j in 0 ..< dataSource.numberOfColumns {
            let item = dataSource.itemFor(row: i, column: j)
            let paddingNeeded = columnWidths[j] - item.count
            let padding = repeatElement(" ", count:
                         paddingNeeded).joined(separator: "")
            out += " \(padding)\(item) |"
        }

        // Done - print it!
        print(out)
    }
}
...
```

The **Department** type now conforms to **TabularDataSource**, and **printTable(_:)** has been modified to accept a **TabularDataSource**. Therefore, you can print your department. Add a call to **printTable(_:)**.

Listing 19.9 Printing **Department**

```
...
var department = Department(name: "Engineering")
department.add(Person(name: "Eva", age: 30, yearsOfExperience: 6))
department.add(Person(name: "Saleh", age: 40, yearsOfExperience: 18))
department.add(Person(name: "Amit", age: 50, yearsOfExperience: 20))

printTable(department)
```

Confirm in the debug area that the output once again reflects the department you created:

```
| Employee Name | Age | Years of Experience |
|           Eva |  30 |                   6 |
|         Saleh |  40 |                  18 |
|          Amit |  50 |                  20 |
```

Protocol Conformance

As noted earlier, the syntax for protocol conformance looks exactly the same as the syntax you use to declare a class's superclass, as seen in Chapter 15. This brings up a few questions:

1. What types can conform to protocols?

2. Can a type conform to multiple protocols?

3. Can a class have a superclass and still conform to protocols?

All types can conform to protocols. You made a structure (**Department**) conform to a protocol. Enums and classes can also conform to protocols. The syntax for declaring that an enum conforms to a protocol is exactly the same as it is for a struct: the declaration of the type is followed by a colon and the protocol name. (Classes can be a little more complicated. We will get to them in a moment.)

It is also possible for a type to conform to multiple protocols. One of the protocols defined by Swift is **CustomStringConvertible**, which types can implement when they want to control how their instances are converted into string representations for use in debugging. Other functions, like **print()**, will check whether the values being printed conform to **CustomStringConvertible** when deciding how to display them. **CustomStringConvertible** has a single requirement: The type must have a gettable property named description that returns a **String**.

Modify **Department** so that it conforms to both **TabularDataSource** and **CustomStringConvertible**, using a comma to separate the protocols.

Listing 19.10 Conforming to **CustomStringConvertible**

```
...
struct Department: TabularDataSource, CustomStringConvertible {
    let name: String
    var people = [Person]()

    var description: String {
        return "Department (\(name))"
    }
...
}
```

Here, you declare **Department**'s conformance to **CustomStringConvertible** and implement description as a read-only, computed property. You can now see the name of your department when you print it.

Listing 19.11 Printing the department's name

```
...
printTable(department)
print(department)
```

Note that it is not enough to merely implement a description property. You must both declare conformance to a protocol and implement the required methods and properties to fully conform.

CustomStringConvertible lets the developer of a type describe instances of the type to other developers who will use those instances in their code. When you pass **print()** an argument of a type that is not **CustomStringConvertible**, the output is generated by the compiler and is often not very useful. By making your types – especially types that model data – conform to **CustomStringConvertible**, you give other developers the important information about that type that they will need to know when printing its instances.

Finally, classes can also conform to protocols. If the class does not have a superclass, the syntax is the same as for structs and enums:

```
class ClassName: ProtocolOne, ProtocolTwo {
    // ...
}
```

If the class does have a superclass, the name of the superclass comes first, followed by the protocol (or protocols).

```
class ClassName: SuperClass, ProtocolOne, ProtocolTwo {
    // ...
}
```

Protocol Inheritance

Swift supports *protocol inheritance*. A protocol that inherits from another protocol requires conforming types to provide implementations for all the properties and methods required by both itself and the protocol it inherits from. This is different from class inheritance, which defines a close relationship between the superclass and subclass. Protocol inheritance merely adds any requirements from the parent protocol to the child protocol. For example, modify **TabularDataSource** so that it inherits from the **CustomStringConvertible** protocol.

Listing 19.12 Making **TabularDataSource** inherit from **CustomStringConvertible**

```
protocol TabularDataSource: CustomStringConvertible {
    var numberOfRows: Int { get }
    var numberOfColumns: Int { get }

    func label(forColumn column: Int) -> String

    func itemFor(row: Int, column: Int) -> String
}
...
```

Now, any type that conforms to **TabularDataSource** must also conform to **CustomStringConvertible**, meaning it has to supply all the properties and methods listed in **TabularDataSource** as well as the description property required by **CustomStringConvertible**. Use this in **printTable(_:)** to print a heading on the table. You will no longer need the declared conformance you added in Listing 19.10, nor the call to **print()** from Listing 19.11.

Listing 19.13 Printing a table heading

```
...
func printTable(_ dataSource: TabularDataSource) {
    print("Table: \(dataSource)")
    ...
}
...
struct Department: TabularDataSource, CustomStringConvertible {
    ...
}
...
printTable(department)
print(department)
```

Now the printout in your debug area includes a description of the table.

```
Table: Department (Engineering)
| Employee Name | Age | Years of Experience |
|          Eva  | 30  |                  6  |
|        Saleh  | 40  |                 18  |
|         Amit  | 50  |                 20  |
```

Protocols are allowed to inherit from multiple other protocols, just as types can conform to multiple protocols. The syntax for multiple protocol inheritance is what you probably expect – separate additional parent protocols with commas, like so:

```
protocol MyProtocol: MyOtherProtocol, SomeThirdProtocol {
    // Requirements of MyProtocol
}
```

Protocols as Types

Your ability to pass an instance of any **TabularDataSource**-conforming type (like **Department**) in to **printTable(_:)** may look familiar. It is an example of polymorphism similar to the subclass polymorphism that you learned about in Chapter 15.

As with the subclassing example, you can declare a variable of protocol type:

Listing 19.14 Creating an instance of a protocol type

```
...
printTable(department)

let operationsDataSource: TabularDataSource = Department(name: "Operations")
```

Here, you assign an instance of **Department** into a variable of type **TabularDataSource**. As you might expect, the compiler will now insist that you can only access properties and methods required by the **TabularDataSource** protocol on operationsDataSource. This is because the compiler knows that you might replace the **Department** instance stored in the variable with an instance of another type that conforms to **TabularDataSource** at any time, so it would be unsafe to allow you to access **Department**-only properties like people.

The **as** keyword (and its forcible and conditional variants) are also available for casting between protocol types and the concrete types that conform to them. Declare a new variable of type **TabularDataSource** to put a copy of your engineering department into.

Listing 19.15 Casting a concrete type to a protocol type

```
...
let operationsDataSource: TabularDataSource = Department(name: "Operations")
let engineeringDataSource = department as TabularDataSource
```

Because the compiler can verify that department's type, **Department**, conforms to **TabularDataSource**, this is a safe cast, and the compiler will infer the type of engineeringDataSource to be **TabularDataSource**. Casting a variable of type **TabularDataSource** to be of type **Department** would be unsafe, since there might be other types that conform to **TabularDataSource**, and the compiler would not know which of them is in the variable at any given time.

Last, the **is** keyword can be used to check for protocol conformance:

Listing 19.16 Asking a variable whether its type conforms to a protocol

```
...
let operationsDataSource: TabularDataSource = Department(name: "Operations")
let engineeringDataSource = department as TabularDataSource

let mikey = Person(name: "Mikey", age: 37, yearsOfExperience: 10)
mikey is TabularDataSource
```

Here you ask the program, "Hey, is the value stored in this variable of a type that conforms to **TabularDataSource**?" The **Person** type does not, which is reflected in your sidebar: false.

It is important to remember that when you declare a variable or function argument to be of a protocol type, you are stating to the compiler, "The actual instance inside this variable may be of any type that conforms to this protocol, and an instance of a different concrete type that conforms to this protocol might be used instead at any time." You will learn more about variables and function arguments of protocol types in Chapter 21.

Protocol Composition

Protocol inheritance is a powerful tool that lets you easily create a new protocol to add requirements to an existing protocol or set of protocols. Nevertheless, using protocol inheritance can potentially lead you to make poor decisions in creating your types.

In fact, that is exactly what has happened with **TabularDataSource** when you made it inherit from **CustomStringConvertible** because you wanted to be able to print a description of the data source. (In fairness, you did it because we told you to.)

There is no correlation between the requirements of **CustomStringConvertible** and **TabularDataSource**, making them a poor candidate for inheritance. In a moment you will see how you can accomplish the same results without conflating the two protocols. First, go back and fix that misguided attempt to print data sources.

Listing 19.17 **TabularDataSource** should not be **CustomStringConvertible**

```
protocol TabularDataSource: CustomStringConvertible {
    ...
}
```

Unfortunately, **Department**, while still printed to the console, is now anything but pretty.

```
Table: Department(name: "Engineering", people: [__lldb_expr_3.Person(name: "Eva",
age: 30, yearsOfExperience: 6), __lldb_expr_3.Person(name: "Saleh",
age: 40, yearsOfExperience: 18), __lldb_expr_3.Person(name: "Amit",
age: 50, yearsOfExperience: 20)])
    ...
```

The **print()** function will use the description property if the type to be printed conforms to **CustomStringConvertible**, but it falls back to a more raw representation if it does not. That raw representation is what you are seeing in the console.

The output from the **printTable(_:)** function looks terrible unless the dataSource conforms to the **CustomStringConvertible** protocol, so you need a way to make the function's parameter ensure that incoming data meets this requirement. *Protocol composition* to the rescue: This syntax allows you to state that a type must conform to multiple protocols. Make the following change:

Listing 19.18 Making **printTable**'s argument conform to **CustomStringConvertible**

```
...
func printTable(_ dataSource: TabularDataSource & CustomStringConvertible) {
    print("Table: \(dataSource)")
    ...
}
```

The syntax for protocol composition uses the & infix operator to signal to the compiler that you are combining multiple protocols into a single requirement. Here, you require that dataSource conform to both **TabularDataSource** and **CustomStringConvertible**.

The compiler rightly gives you an error indicating that **Department** does not conform to
CustomStringConvertible. Explicitly declare this conformance and run the playground to see that
everything is back to normal.

Listing 19.19 Declaring conformance to **CustomStringConvertible**

```
...
struct Department: TabularDataSource, CustomStringConvertible {
    ...
}
...
```

Consider another possibility. You could create a new protocol that inherits from both
TabularDataSource and **CustomStringConvertible**, like so:

```
protocol PrintableTabularDataSource: TabularDataSource, CustomStringConvertible {
}
```

You could then use that protocol as the type of the argument to **printTable(_:)**.

In short, you have a few options for ensuring that a function like **printTable(_:)** correctly constrains
its arguments:

- Make **TabularDataSource** inherit from **CustomStringConvertible**. A solution like this could
  be appropriate if the two protocols are naturally related. But in this case, they are pretty different
  from one another.

- Define a new protocol like **PrintableTabularDataSource** that inherits from both
  TabularDataSource and **CustomStringConvertible**. There is nothing wrong with this approach,
  but its real utility would be if you had additional requirements to add to the new protocol or
  needed many functions to use it as a parameter type. Here, it would be empty and would likely be
  the argument type of only one function, so it would not add much meaning to your program.

- Compose the two protocols at the call site, as you have done. This signifies to developers that the
  requirement is particular to this function, is unlikely to be used elsewhere, and requires very little
  code elsewhere.

As with many questions in programming, there is not always a clear correct choice in this situation,
or any singularly correct choice at all. All three of these approaches would solve the needs of the
printTable(_:) function, and all three could be the best choice for certain situations. In the future, it
will be up to you to decide how to proceed. It is acceptable and even common to choose one solution
and then change your mind later as you learn more about the problem.

It is also possible to use composition to combine a protocol with a class. Say your **Person** type was a class, instead of a struct, with an **Employee** subclass. You could use a composition of **CustomStringConvertible** and **Person** to create a function that only accepts subclasses of **Person** that are also **CustomStringConvertible**:

```
class Person {
    let name: String
    let age: Int
    let yearsOfExperience: Int
}

class Employee: Person, CustomStringConvertible {
    let employeeID: Int

    var description: String {
        return "Name: \(name) ID: \(employeeID)"
    }
}

func printResource(_ resource: Person & CustomStringConvertible) {
    print("Resource: \(resource)")
}
```

Swift is an expressive language with lots of syntactically legal ways to accomplish most goals, including using protocols to codify type requirements. As you get more practice, you will start to get a sense for when certain strategies are more appropriate or more readable than others.

Mutating Methods

Recall from Chapter 14 and Chapter 15 that methods on value types (enums and structs) cannot modify self unless the method is marked as mutating. For example, in the **LightBulb** enum from Chapter 14, the **toggle()** method was mutating.

```
enum LightBulb {
    case on
    case off
    ...
    mutating func toggle() {
        switch self {
        case .on:
            self = .off

        case .off:
            self = .on
        }
    }
}
```

Methods in protocols default to nonmutating. Suppose you want to define a protocol to describe an object that is "toggleable":

```
protocol Toggleable {
    func toggle()
}
```

Declaring that **LightBulb** conforms to **Toggleable** would result in a compiler error. The error message includes a note that explains the problem:

```
error: type 'LightBulb' does not conform to protocol 'Toggleable'

note: candidate is marked 'mutating' but protocol does not allow it
mutating func toggle() {
              ^
```

The note points out that in **LightBulb**, the **toggle()** method is marked as mutating, but the **Toggleable** protocol expects a nonmutating function. You can fix this problem by marking **toggle()** as mutating in the protocol definition:

```
protocol Toggleable {
    mutating func toggle()
}
```

With this change, value types implementing **Toggleable** would now be required to make their **toggle()** methods mutating. But a class that conforms to the **Toggleable** protocol would not need to mark its **toggle()** method as mutating, because methods on reference types are always allowed to change properties of self.

You have seen several different protocols now, and you may see a naming pattern emerging. Protocol names tend to follow one of two conventions, set by the Swift standard library:

- The name is a noun, such as **TabularDataSource**, when the protocol describes the baseline behavior or meaning of a conforming type.

- The name is an adjective with one of the suffixes "-able," "-ible," or "-ing," such as **Equatable** or **CustomStringConvertible**, when the protocol describes a subset of a conforming type's capabilities.

In the coming chapters, you will see and define many more protocols and see the different ways that they lend flexibility to the types in your programs.

Bronze Challenge

The `printTable(_:)` function has a bug: It crashes if any of the data items are longer than the label of their column. Try changing Eva's age to 1,000 to see this happen. Fix the bug. Your solution will likely result in incorrect table formatting; that is fine for now. You will fix the formatting in the gold challenge, below.

Silver Challenge

Create a new type, `BookCollection`, that conforms to `TabularDataSource`. Calling `printTable(_:)` on a book collection should show a table of books with columns for titles, authors, and average reviews on Amazon. (Unless all the books you use have very short titles and author names, you will need to have completed the previous challenge!)

Electrum Challenge

This challenge will exercise your understanding of multiple topics that you have studied so far.

Sometimes protocols are used to add behavior to existing types, as you will explore in Chapter 22 on protocol extensions. One such protocol can be used to let you loop over the cases of any enum that does not have associated values: `CaseIterable`.

Open your Enumerations.playground file and declare your `ProgrammingLanguage` enum to conform to the `CaseIterable` protocol. Using a loop, print all the enum's cases. Your output should look like this:

```
swift
objective-c
c
c++
java
```

You will need to explore the `CaseIterable` protocol reference in the developer documentation.

To turn this into a gold challenge, do not use a loop. Instead, use what you learned about `map(_:)` in Chapter 13 to make your output look like this:

```
["swift", "objective-c", "c", "c++", "java"]
```

Gold Challenge

After you fixed the crashing bug in the bronze challenge above, the table rows and columns were likely misaligned. Fix your solution to correctly align the table rows and columns. Verify that your solution does not crash with values longer than their column labels.

20
Extensions

Imagine that you are developing an application that uses a particular type in the Swift standard library – say the **Double** type – quite frequently. Based on how you are using it in your app, it would make your development easier if the **Double** type supported some additional methods.

Unfortunately, you do not have **Double**'s implementation available, so you cannot add functionality directly to it yourself. What can you do?

Swift provides a feature called *extensions* that is designed for just these cases. Extensions allow you to add functionality to an existing type. You can extend structs, enums, and classes.

You can use extensions on types to add:

- computed properties
- new initializers
- protocol conformance
- new methods
- embedded types

In this chapter, you will use extensions to add functionality to an existing type whose definition and implementation details are not available to you. You will also use extensions to add functionality to a custom type of your own creation. In both cases, you will add functionality to the type in a modular fashion, meaning that you will group similar functionality in a single extension.

Extending an Existing Type

Create a new macOS playground named Extensions.

Consider the example above involving **Double**. Imagine that you might regularly be computing the square of a number: a number times itself. This is a common thing to do with numbers, but not quite common enough to be included as its own feature of the Swift standard library. Instead, if you need to square a number, you currently use the multiplication operator to do it yourself: 25 * 25.

In your playground, create an extension on the **Double** type:

Listing 20.1 Extending an existing type

```
import Cocoa

var str = "Hello, playground"

extension Double {
    var squared: Double { return self * self }
}

let sideLength: Double = 12.5
let area = sideLength.squared
```

The extension keyword signifies that you are extending the **Double** type. Inside the scope of the extension, you can create new declarations such as computed properties or methods, and all your program's instances of the type now benefit from the additions. In this case, your newly added squared property shows the result, 156.25, in the results sidebar.

Extending Your Own Type

You can also extend your own types. You might wonder why you would want to do that – if you created the type, why add an extension to it instead of editing the type itself? You will mostly use extensions on your own types for code organization. As you will see, extensions provide a convenient way to group related methods and behaviors, such as those required by a protocol.

You will need to create a new type before you can extend it. Make a new struct to represent a **Car** type and create an instance of it.

Listing 20.2 A **Car** struct

```
...
struct Car {
    let make: String
    let model: String
    let year: Int
    var fuelLevel: Double {
        willSet {
            precondition(newValue <= 1.0 && newValue >= 0.0,
                        "New value must be between 0 and 1.")
        }
    }
}

let firstCar = Car(make: "Benz",
                    model: "Patent-Motorwagon",
                    year: 1886,
                    fuelLevel: 0.5)
```

Here you define and instantiate a new struct called **Car**. The **Car** type defines a number of stored properties that will be specific to a given instance. All the properties are constants, with one exception: fuelLevel.

fuelLevel is a mutable stored property with a property observer. The willSet observer will be called every time you are going to set a new value for fuelLevel. These values indicate how full an instance's fuel tank is in terms of percentage.

You use the **precondition(_:_:)** function to ensure that the newValue being assigned to the fuelLevel property is between 0 and 1. This function takes a Boolean expression and a string message. If the Boolean expression resolves to false, then the application will trap and log the provided message to the console.

To a user, watching an app trap or crash is a bad time, so as a developer you must weigh whether you can deal elegantly with bad input or if continuing execution would be meaningless. You will learn more about Swift's features for dealing with runtime errors in Chapter 23.

Using extensions to add protocol conformance

Extensions are great for grouping related chunks of functionality, like conforming to a protocol. Extend the **Car** type to conform to **CustomStringConvertible**.

Listing 20.3 Extending **Car** to conform to **CustomStringConvertible**

```
...
let firstCar = Car(make: "Benz",
                   model: "Patent-Motorwagon",
                   year: 1886,
                   fuelLevel: 0.5)

extension Car: CustomStringConvertible {
    var description: String {
        return "\(year) \(make) \(model), fuel level: \(fuelLevel)"
    }
}
```

Your new extension declares that **Car** conforms to **CustomStringConvertible** and implements the required property to do so. The syntax for conforming to a protocol is the same as when the conformance is declared in the definition of the type, and you implement the protocol's required property inside the extension's body.

By declaring the protocol conformance in an extension, you keep the base definition of your type uncluttered. When another developer – possibly you, later – is learning about your type, the first thing they want to see is the essential list of properties and methods that show what your type is and what it can do. They do not care about auxiliary behavior, like whether it is **CustomStringConvertible**.

By the way, extensions are an important exception to the access control rules you learned in Chapter 16: An extension can access the private declarations within a type as long as the extension and type are defined in the same file. So if **Car** had private properties, you could still use them in your extension.

Adding an initializer with an extension

Recall that structs give you a free memberwise initializer if you do not provide your own. If you want to write a new initializer for your struct but do not want to lose the free memberwise or empty initializer, you can add the initializer to your type with an extension.

Add an initializer to **Car** in a new extension on the type.

Listing 20.4 Extending **Car** with an initializer

```
...
extension Car: CustomStringConvertible {
    var description: String {
        return "\(year) \(make) \(model), fuel level: \(fuelLevel)"
    }
}

extension Car {
    init(make: String, model: String, year: Int) {
        self.init(make: make,
                  model: model,
                  year: year,
                  fuelLevel: 1.0)
    }
}
```

The new extension on the **Car** type adds an initializer that accepts arguments only for an instance's make, model, and year. This new initializer's arguments are passed in to the free memberwise initializer on the **Car** struct, along with a default value for fuelLevel. The combination of these two initializers ensures that an instance of the **Car** type will have values for all its properties.

The memberwise initializer is preserved on **Car** because the new initializer is defined and implemented on an extension. This pattern can be quite helpful.

To see the initializer defined in the extension work, create an instance of **Car**.

Listing 20.5 Creating an instance of **Car**

```
...
extension Car {
    init(make: String, model: String, year: Int) {
        self.init(make: make,
                  model: model,
                  year: year,
                  fuelLevel: 1.0)
    }
}

var currentCar = Car(make: "Honda", model: "Civic", year: 2008)
firstCar.fuelLevel
currentCar.fuelLevel
```

You create a new instance, currentCar, with the initializer defined in an extension on **Car**. Take a look in the results sidebar. You should see that the fuelLevel of firstCar is 0.5, the value you passed in to the compiler-synthesized initializer in Listing 20.2. However, the fuelLevel of currentCar is 1.0, the default value provided by the initializer you implemented in your extension.

Nested types and extensions

Swift's extensions can also add nested types to an existing type. Say, for example, that you want to add an enumeration to your **Car** struct to classify the era an instance is from. Create a new extension on the **Car** type to add a nested type.

Listing 20.6 Creating an extension with a nested type

```
...
var currentCar = Car(make: "Honda", model: "Civic", year: 2008)
firstCar.fuelLevel
currentCar.fuelLevel

extension Car {
    enum Era {
        case veteran, brass, vintage, modern
    }
    var era: Era {
        switch year {
        case ...1896:
            return .veteran
        case 1897...1919:
            return .brass
        case 1920...1930:
            return .vintage
        default:
            return .modern
        }
    }
}
...
```

This new extension on **Car** adds a nested type called **Era**. **Era** is an enumeration that has four cases: veteran, brass, vintage, and modern. Notice the simplified syntax for declaring the cases of an enumeration: all on one line, separated by commas. This syntax is especially convenient for simple enums that do not need raw values or associated values.

The extension also adds a computed property on **Car** called era, which determines the car's era based on its year. Exercise the extension's nested type by accessing the era property on the instance you created earlier.

Listing 20.7 Accessing era

```
...
firstCar.era
```

You should see veteran logged to the results sidebar.

Extensions with methods

You can also use an extension to give an existing type a new method. For example, you may have noticed that **Car** does not have any functionality to adjust the fuel level. Make an extension to add this functionality to **Car**.

Listing 20.8 Using an extension to add methods

```
...
firstCar.era

extension Car {
    mutating func emptyFuel(by amount: Double) {
        precondition(amount <= 1 && amount > 0,
                     "Amount to remove must be between 0 and 1.")
        fuelLevel -= amount
    }

    mutating func fillFuel() {
        fuelLevel = 1.0
    }
}
```

Your new extension adds two methods to the **Car** type: **emptyFuel(by:)** and **fillFuel()**. Note that both methods are marked with the mutating keyword. Why? Remember that the **Car** type is a struct. If a method wants to change the value of any of the struct's properties, then it must be declared with the mutating keyword.

The **emptyFuel(by:)** method takes one argument: the amount of fuel to remove from the tank. You use a **precondition(_:_:)** inside the **emptyFuel(by:)** method to ensure that the amount removed from the tank is between 0 and 1. The implementation of the **fillFuel()** method simply sets the fuelLevel property on the **Car** to be full, or 1.0.

Exercise these new methods on your existing type.

Listing 20.9 Lowering and filling the fuel tank

```
...
extension Car {
    mutating func emptyFuel(by amount: Double) {
        precondition(amount <= 1 && amount > 0,
                     "Amount to remove must be between 0 and 1.")
        fuelLevel -= amount
    }

    mutating func fillFuel() {
        fuelLevel = 1.0
    }
}

currentCar.emptyFuel(by: 0.3)
currentCar.fuelLevel
currentCar.fillFuel()
currentCar.fuelLevel
```

After you use the **emptyFuel(by:)** function, you should see in the sidebar that the fuel level is 0.7. After you fill the fuel level, the fuel level is 1.0.

Extensions are an incredibly flexible tool for enhancing the organization of your code and adding useful behavior to existing types. One caveat on something you might see in the wild: While extensions are primarily used to add new functionality, they can sometimes be used to replace existing functionality by implementing a method or computed property that already exists on a type. This is different from overriding a method in a subclass, and it is an advanced topic with limited utility and inherent risks. It is out of scope for this book.

Bronze Challenge

In Chapter 19, you made the **Department** type conform to the **CustomStringConvertible** protocol. Refactor your playground from that chapter to move **CustomStringConvertible** conformance into an extension.

Silver Challenge

Give the **Int** type a nested enum with cases even and odd. Also give **Int** a property of that type to correctly report whether an integer is even or odd.

21

Generics

When we introduced optionals and collection types earlier in this book, we briefly showed you the "long-form" syntax for each type, like:

- `Optional<String>`
- `Array<String>`
- `Dictionary<String>`
- `Set<String>`

Most of these types have a preferred shorthand syntax, like **String?** or **[String]**, and we did not really discuss the angle bracket syntax except to show you that it exists.

We also told you that, for example, **Array<String>** is not the same type as **Array<Int>**. And that is true – but the Swift standard library only defines one **Array**. So what is the deal with the **Array<String>** type and others like it? You are ready to find out.

Optional and the collection types like **Array** are what we call *generic* types, because they are designed to work with *any* type (with some limitations, as we will discuss). The angle brackets are the *generic syntax*, and they (along with the shorthand equivalent some generic types have) allow you to specify the type that the generic type will work with.

In this chapter, you will investigate how to define your own generic types. You will also learn how to use generics to write flexible functions and explore how generics are related to protocols.

Generic Data Structures

You are going to create a generic *stack*, which is a venerable data structure in computer science. A stack is a last-in, first-out data structure. It supports two basic operations. You can *push* an item onto the stack, which adds the item to the stack, and you can *pop* to remove the most recently pushed item off of the stack.

Create a new macOS playground called Generics and make a **Stack** structure that only stores integers.

Listing 21.1 Setting up a **Stack**

```
import Cocoa

var str = "Hello, playground"

struct Stack {
    var items = [Int]()

    mutating func push(_ newItem: Int) {
        items.append(newItem)
    }

    mutating func pop() -> Int? {
        guard !items.isEmpty else { return nil }
        return items.removeLast()
    }
}
```

This struct has three elements of interest. The items stored property is an array you are using to hold on to the items currently in a stack. The **push(_:)** method pushes a new item onto the stack by appending it to the end of the items array. Finally, the **pop()** method pops the top item off of the stack by calling the **removeLast()** method of an array, which simultaneously removes the last item and returns it. Note that **pop()** returns an optional **Int**, because the stack might be empty (in which case there is nothing to pop).

Create a **Stack** instance to see it in action.

Listing 21.2 Creating an instance of **Stack**

```
...
var intStack = Stack()
intStack.push(1)
intStack.push(2)

print(String(describing: intStack.pop()))
print(String(describing: intStack.pop()))
print(String(describing: intStack.pop()))
```

You create a new **Stack** instance, push two values on, then try to pop three values off. As expected, the console reports that the **pop()** calls return the integers you pushed in reverse order, and then **pop()** returns nil when the stack no longer has any items:

```
Optional(2)
Optional(1)
nil
```

Your **Stack** is useful for storing **Int**s, but it is currently limited to that type. It would be better if **Stack** were more general. Modify **Stack** to be a generic data structure that can hold any type, not just **Int**.

Listing 21.3 Making **Stack** generic

```
struct Stack<Element> {
    var items = [Int Element]()

    mutating func push(_ newItem: Int Element) {
        items.append(newItem)
    }

    mutating func pop() -> Int? Element? {
        guard !items.isEmpty else { return nil }
        return items.removeLast()
    }
}
...
```

You define a *placeholder type*, named **Element**, in the declaration of **Stack**. Swift's syntax for declaring a generic uses angle brackets (<>) immediately following the name of the type to enclose the name of the placeholder type: <Element>.

The placeholder type **Element** can be used inside the **Stack** structure anywhere a concrete type could be used. By defining the placeholder type **Element** and then using it in place of **Int**, you have made your **Stack** generic. Now, you can have a stack of any type at all, not just integers.

There is now a compiler error where you instantiate a **Stack**, because you have not specified what concrete type should be substituted for the placeholder type **Element**. The process of the compiler substituting a concrete type for a placeholder is called *specialization*. The full details of specialization are outside the scope of this book, but the short summary is that it allows the compiler to make your app faster, because the compiler is able to output code knowing the specific type in use.

Fix the error by specifying that intStack should be an instance of **Stack** specialized for **Int**. You will use the same angle bracket syntax to do this.

Listing 21.4 Specializing intStack

```
...
var intStack = Stack<Int>()
...
```

This resolves the compiler error.

You can create a stack of any type. Create a **Stack** of **String**s.

Listing 21.5 Creating a **Stack** of strings

```
...
print(String(describing: intStack.pop()))
print(String(describing: intStack.pop()))

var stringStack = Stack<String>()
stringStack.push("this is a string")
stringStack.push("another string")

print(String(describing: stringStack.pop()))
```

The console prints Optional("another string").

It is important to note that while intStack and stringStack are both **Stack** instances, they do not have the same type. intStack is a **Stack<Int>**; it would be a compile-time error to pass anything other than an **Int** to **intStack.push(_:)**. Likewise, stringStack is a **Stack<String>**, which is distinct from **Stack<Int>**. This is true even though you have defined only one **Stack** type.

Generic data structures are both common and extremely useful. Classes and enumerations can also be made generic using the same syntax you used here for structures. In addition, types are not the only element of Swift that can be generic. Functions and methods can also be generic.

Generic Functions and Methods

Think about the **map(_:)** method that you learned about in Chapter 13 on closures. **map(_:)** applies a closure to each element in an array and returns an array of the results. Given what you just learned about generics, you can now implement a version of this function yourself.

Add the following code to your playground. Some of it may seem unfamiliar; we will walk through it after you have entered it.

Listing 21.6 Your own map function

```
...
func myMap<T,U>(_ items: [T], _ txform: (T) -> (U)) -> [U] {
    var result = [U]()
    for item in items {
        result.append(f(item))
    }
    return result
}
```

The declaration of **myMap(_:_:)** may look pretty ugly if you have not been exposed to generics in other languages. Instead of the concrete types you are familiar with, it just has **T** and **U**, and there are more symbol and punctuation characters than letters! But the only new thing is that it declares two placeholder types, **T** and **U**, instead of just one.

Figure 21.1 shows a breakdown of the function declaration.

Figure 21.1 **myMap** declaration

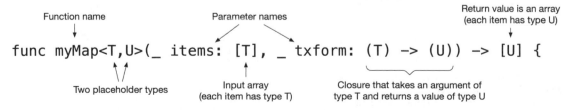

When defining a generic type or function, you should give your placeholder types descriptive, meaningful names if you can. **Array** uses **Element** as its placeholder type name. **Optional** uses **Wrapped**. It is common to use **T** (short for "Type"), **U**, and so on if you require brevity or if there are not more meaningful names to use.

myMap(_:_:) can be used the same way **map(_:)** is used. Create an array of **String**s, then map it to an array of **Int**s representing the strings' lengths.

Listing 21.7 Mapping an array

```
...
func myMap<T,U>(_ items: [T], _ txform: (T) -> (U)) -> [U] {
    ...
}

let strings = ["one", "two", "three"]
let stringLengths = myMap(strings) { $0.count }
print(stringLengths)
```

The closure passed to **myMap(_:_:)** must take a single argument that matches the type contained in the items array, but the type of its return value can be anything. In this call to **myMap(_:_:)**, **T** is replaced by **String** and **U** is replaced by **Int**. The console confirms the result: [3, 3, 5]. (Note that in real projects there is no need to declare your own mapping function – just use the built-in **map(_:)**.)

Methods can also be generic, even inside types that are already themselves generic. The **myMap(_:_:)** function you wrote only works on arrays, but it also seems reasonable to want to map a **Stack**. Create a **map(_:)** method on **Stack**.

Listing 21.8 Mapping on a **Stack**

```
struct Stack<Element> {
    var items = [Element]()

    mutating func push(_ newItem: Element) {
        items.append(newItem)
    }

    mutating func pop() -> Element? {
        guard !items.isEmpty else { return nil }
        return items.removeLast()
    }

    func map<U>(_ txform: (Element) -> U) -> Stack<U> {
        var mappedItems = [U]()
        for item in items {
            mappedItems.append(f(item))
        }
        return Stack<U>(items: mappedItems)
    }
}
...
```

This **map(_:)** method only declares one placeholder type, **U**, but it uses both **Element** and **U**. The **Element** type is available because **map(_:)** is inside the **Stack** structure, which makes the placeholder type **Element** available. The body of **map(_:)** is almost identical to **myMap(_:_:)**, differing only in that it returns a new **Stack** instead of an array.

Try out your new method.

Listing 21.9 Using **Stack.map(_:)**

```
...
var intStack = Stack<Int>()
intStack.push(1)
intStack.push(2)
var doubledStack = intStack.map { 2 * $0 }

print(String(describing: intStack.pop()))
print(String(describing: intStack.pop()))
print(String(describing: intStack.pop()))

print(String(describing: doubledStack.pop()))
print(String(describing: doubledStack.pop()))
...
```

The new **print()** calls show the doubled values in doubledStack:

```
Optional(2)
Optional(1)
nil
Optional(4)
Optional(2)
Optional("another string")
[3, 3, 5]
```

The output from all these **print()** calls is not needed in the rest of this chapter, so if you want you can comment them out to keep things tidy.

Type Constraints

When writing generic functions and data types, by default, you do not know anything about the concrete type that is going to be used. You created stacks of **Int** and **String**, but you can create stacks of any type. The practical impact of this lack of knowledge is that there is very little you can do with the value of a placeholder type. For example, you cannot check whether two of them are equal; this code would not compile:

```
func checkIfEqual<T>(_ first: T, _ second: T) -> Bool {
    return first == second
}
```

This function could be called with any type, including types for which equality does not make sense, such as closures. (It is hard to imagine what it would mean for two closures to be "equal." Swift does not allow the comparison.)

Generic functions would be relatively uncommon if you were never able to assume *anything* about the placeholder types. To solve this problem, Swift allows the use of *type constraints*, which place restrictions on the concrete types that can be passed to generic functions. There are two kinds of type constraints: You can require that a type be a subclass of a given class, or you can require that a type conform to a given protocol (or protocol composition).

For example, **Equatable** is a Swift-provided protocol that states that two values can be checked for equality. (You will read more about **Equatable** in Chapter 25.) To see how type constraints work, write a **checkIfEqual(_:_:)** function including a constraint that **T** must be **Equatable**.

Listing 21.10 Using a type constraint to allow checking for equality

```
...
func checkIfEqual<T: Equatable>(_ first: T, _ second: T) -> Bool {
    return first == second
}

print(checkIfEqual(1, 1))
print(checkIfEqual("a string", "a string"))
print(checkIfEqual("a string", "a different string"))
```

You use the same `: Protocol` syntax you saw in Chapter 19 to declare that the placeholder **T** must conform to **Equatable**. This allows you to check the instances passed in to the function for equality. As the console shows, the first two checks evaluate to true and the third to false.

To prove that the **Equatable** type constraint works, try it with instances of **Stack**:

Listing 21.11 Breaking the constraint

```
...
print(checkIfEqual(1, 1))
print(checkIfEqual("a string", "a string"))
print(checkIfEqual("a string", "a different string"))
print(checkIfEqual(intStack, doubledStack)
```

This code emits a new error: global function 'checkIfEqual' requires that 'Stack' conform to 'Equatable'. Sure enough, the compiler is enforcing the rules that you gave it. Remove the failing check:

Listing 21.12 Rolling back the failure

```
...
print(checkIfEqual(1, 1))
print(checkIfEqual("a string", "a string"))
print(checkIfEqual("a string", "a different string"))
print(checkIfEqual(intStack, doubledStack)
```

Every placeholder type (**T**, **U**, etc.) can have its own constraints. For example, write a function that checks whether two **CustomStringConvertible** values have the same description.

Listing 21.13 Using a type constraint to check **CustomStringConvertible** values

```
...
func checkIfDescriptionsMatch<T: CustomStringConvertible, U: CustomStringConvertible>(
    _ first: T, _ second: U) -> Bool {
    return first.description == second.description
}

print(checkIfDescriptionsMatch(Int(1), UInt(1)))
print(checkIfDescriptionsMatch(1, 1.0))
print(checkIfDescriptionsMatch(Float(1.0), Double(1.0)))
```

The constraint that both **T** and **U** are **CustomStringConvertible** guarantees that both first and second have a property named description that returns a **String**. (If they do not, the compiler will issue an error.) Even though the two arguments may have different types, you can still compare their descriptions. The console shows that the first and last comparisons evaluate to true and the second to false.

Your playground is getting chatty again; you might want to comment out some of your **print()** calls to make future output easier to read. You will not need any of them again.

Associated Types

Now that you know that types and functions (including methods) can be made generic, it is natural to ask whether protocols can be made generic as well. The answer is "no." However, protocols support a similar and related feature: *associated types*.

Let's explore associated types by examining a couple of protocols defined by the Swift standard library. The two protocols you will examine are **IteratorProtocol** and **Sequence**, which together allow you to make your own types that can be iterated over in for-in loops.

These protocols already exist in the Swift standard library, so you should not type them in. First, have a look at the definition of **IteratorProtocol**:

```
protocol IteratorProtocol {
    associatedtype Element
    mutating func next() -> Element?
}
```

IteratorProtocol requires a single mutating method, **next()**, which returns a value of type **Element?**. With **IteratorProtocol**, you can call **next()** repeatedly and it will produce a new value each time. If the iterator is no longer able to produce new values, **next()** returns nil.

Inside a protocol, associatedtype Element states that conforming types must provide a concrete type that will be used as the **Element** type. Conforming types specify what **Element** should be by providing a typealias for **Element** inside their definitions. At the top of your playground, create a new struct called **StackIterator** that conforms to **IteratorProtocol**.

Listing 21.14 Creating **StackIterator**

```
import Cocoa

struct StackIterator<T>: IteratorProtocol {
    typealias Element = T

    var stack: Stack<T>

    mutating func next() -> Element? {
        return stack.pop()
    }
}

struct Stack<Element> {
    ...
}
...
```

StackIterator wraps up a **Stack** and generates values by popping items off of the stack. The type of the **Element** that **next()** returns is **T**, so you set the typealias appropriately.

Create a new stack, add some items, and then create an iterator and loop over its values to see **StackIterator** in action.

Listing 21.15 Using **StackIterator**

```
...
var myStack = Stack<Int>()
myStack.push(10)
myStack.push(20)
myStack.push(30)

var myStackIterator = StackIterator(stack: myStack)
while let value = myStackIterator.next() {
    print("got \(value)")
}
```

In the console, you will see that the three values pop off in last-in, first-out order.

StackIterator is a little more verbose than it needs to be. Swift can infer the type of a protocol's associated types, so you can remove the explicit typealias by indicating that **next()** returns a **T?**.

Listing 21.16 Tightening up **StackIterator**

```
struct StackIterator<T>: IteratorProtocol {
    typealias Element = T

    var stack: Stack<T>

    mutating func next() -> Element? T? {
        return stack.pop()
    }
}
...
```

The next associated type protocol you will examine is **Sequence**. Remember, it already exists in the Swift standard library, so do not add it to your playground. The definition of **Sequence** is large, but the critical part is small:

```
protocol Sequence {
    associatedtype Iterator: IteratorProtocol
    associatedtype Element where Element == Iterator.Element
    func makeIterator() -> Iterator
}
```

Sequence has two associated types. The first is named **Iterator**. The : IteratorProtocol syntax is a type constraint on the associated type. It has the same meaning as type constraints on generics: For a type to conform to **Sequence**, it must have an associated type **Iterator** that conforms to the protocol **IteratorProtocol**.

The second associated type, named **Element**, is the type your iterator returns from the **next()** function. This associated type also uses a type constraint to ensure the **Element** here matches the one supplied in the **IteratorProtocol**.

Sequence also requires conforming types to implement a single method, **makeIterator()**, which returns a value of the associated type **IteratorProtocol**. Because you already have a suitable iterator for stacks, modify **Stack** to conform to **Sequence**.

Listing 21.17 Making **Stack** conform to **Sequence**

```
...
struct Stack<Element>: Sequence {
    var items = [Element]()
    ...
    func map<U>(_ txform: (Element) -> U) -> Stack<U> {
        var mappedItems = [U]()
        for item in items {
            mappedItems.append(f(item))
        }
        return Stack<U>(items: mappedItems)
    }

    func makeIterator() -> StackIterator<Element> {
        return StackIterator(stack: self)
    }
}
...
```

You use Swift's type inference to avoid having to explicitly state typealias Iterator = StackIterator<Element>, although it would not be an error to do so.

The **Sequence** protocol is what Swift uses internally for its for-in loops. Now that **Stack** conforms to **Sequence**, you can loop over its contents.

Listing 21.18 Looping through myStack

```
...
var myStackIterator = StackIterator(stack: myStack)
while let value = myStackIterator.next() {
    print("got \(value)")
}

for value in myStack {
    print("for-in loop: got \(value)")
}
```

StackIterator pops values off of its stack every time **next()** is called, which is a fairly destructive operation. When a **StackIterator** returns nil from **next()**, its stack property is empty. However, you were able to create an iterator from myStack and then use myStack again in a for-in loop. This reuse is possible because **Stack** is a value type, which means every time a **StackIterator** is created, it gets a copy of the stack, leaving the original untouched.

(Note that the order of items you see from the for-in loop is the same as if you popped items off the top of the stack – the reverse of the order the items were pushed on.)

Type Constraints in where Clauses

You have seen the powerful where keyword used to apply constraints to each iteration of a loop or a case of a switch statement. You can also use a where clause to further constrain generic arguments or return types in a function declaration.

Write a new method on **Stack<Element>** that takes every element of an array and pushes it onto a stack.

Listing 21.19 Pushing items from an array onto a stack

```
...
struct Stack<Element>: Sequence {
    ...
    mutating func pushAll(_ array: [Element]) {
        for item in array {
            self.push(item)
        }
    }
}
...
for value in myStack {
    print("for-in loop: got \(value)")
}

myStack.pushAll([1, 2, 3])
for value in myStack {
    print("after pushing: got \(value)")
}
```

Here, your **pushAll(_:)** method pushes 1, 2, and 3 onto the stack and then prints the contents of the stack (which also includes three values from Listing 21.15).

pushAll(_:) is useful, but it is not as general as it could be. You now know that any type that conforms to **Sequence** can be used in a for-in loop, so why should this method require an array? It should be able to accept any kind of sequence – even another **Stack**, now that **Stack** conforms to **Sequence**.

However, a first attempt at this will produce a compile-time type error where you call self.push(_:).

Listing 21.20 Close, but no cigar

```
...
struct Stack<Element>: Sequence {
    ...
    mutating func pushAll(_ array: [Element]) {
    mutating func pushAll<S: Sequence>(_ sequence: S) {
        for item in array sequence {
            self.push(item)
        }
    }
}
...
```

You made **pushAll(_:)** generic with placeholder type **S**, which is some type that conforms to the **Sequence** protocol. The constraint on **S** guarantees that you can loop over it with the for-in syntax.

However, this is not sufficient. To push the items you get from `sequence` onto the stack, you need to guarantee that the type of the items coming from the sequence matches the type of the stack's elements.

That is, you need to add a constraint that the elements produced by **S** are themselves of type **Element**.

Swift supports constraints of this kind using a `where` clause.

Listing 21.21 Using a `where` clause to guarantee type

```
...
struct Stack<Element>: Sequence {
    ...
    mutating func pushAll<S: Sequence>(_ sequence: S) where S.Element == Element {
        for item in sequence {
            self.push(item)
        }
    }
}
...
```

Now, the placeholder type **S** must conform to the **Sequence** protocol *and* meet the requirements of the `where` clause. S.Element refers to the **Element** type associated with the sequence **S**. The constraint S.Element == Element requires that the concrete type used for the **Element** associated type must match the concrete type used for your **Stack**'s **Element** placeholder.

(Keep in mind that because it is a method on **Stack**, which is itself generic with placeholder type **Element**, pushAll(_:) also has access to the **Element** placeholder type.)

The syntax for generic `where` clauses can be difficult to read at first, but an example should make it clearer. If your stack is holding **Int**s, the argument to **pushAll(_:)** must be a sequence that produces **Int**s. Two types you already know that are **Int**-producing sequences are **Stack<Int>** and **[Int]**. Try them out.

Listing 21.22 Pushing items to the stack

```
...
var myOtherStack = Stack<Int>()
myOtherStack.pushAll([1, 2, 3])
myStack.pushAll(myOtherStack)
for value in myStack {
    print("after pushing items onto stack, got \(value)")
}
```

You created a new, empty stack of integers: myOtherStack. Next, you pushed all the integers from an array onto myOtherStack. Finally, you pushed all the integers from myOtherStack onto myStack. You were able to use the same generic method in both cases because arrays and stacks both conform to **Sequence**.

The elements that were added to myStack are 1, 2, and 3, which might feel counterintuitive. If it does, think through the sequence of events. You pushed 1, 2, and 3 onto myOtherStack, so 3 ended up on top of the stack. Then you popped them off of myOtherStack, which grabs the topmost element (3) first, and pushed them onto myStack. The result is that the top three elements of myStack are 1, 2, and 3, in that order.

Side note: If a protocol has an associated type, you currently cannot use that protocol as a type in a variable or function declaration. For example, since **Sequence** has an associated type **Element**, this would not compile:

```
func printElements(from sequence: Sequence) {
    for item in sequence {
        print(item)
    }
}
```

However, you may use the protocol as a generic type constraint:

```
func printElements<S: Sequence>(from sequence: S) {
    for element in sequence {
        print(element)
    }
}
```

Similarly, you cannot declare `let mySequence: Sequence`.

The reasons for these limitations are not intrinsic to associated types or protocols that declare them; they are implementation details of the current Swift compiler that are outside the scope of this book. That said, the generic solution above is effective and, once you get more practice with generics, equally clear.

Generic Composition and Opaque Types

Generic data structures can *compose* with one another using protocols to build systems of types that elegantly describe more complex ideas. For example, think of an array of dictionaries, which might have a composed type like **Array<Dictionary<String,Int>>**. Sometimes, you might want to hide some of the gritty implementation details of your compositions.

To see what this looks like in practice, you will model a hungry human ordering toast at a restaurant. Begin with a **Food** protocol and a food that conforms to it.

Listing 21.23 Defining some food

```
...
protocol Food {
    var menuListing: String { get }
}

struct Bread: Food {
    var kind = "sourdough"
    var menuListing: String {
        "\(kind) bread"
    }
}
```

Using a protocol to define the menuListing requirement allows you to write a function to accept any **Food**, as you learned about in Chapter 19. Define such a function:

Listing 21.24 Eating some bread

```
...
func eat<T: Food>(_ food: T) {
    print("I sure love \(food.menuListing).")
}

eat(Bread())
```

To keep things simple, the **eat(_:)** function will accept any type that conforms to the **Food** protocol.

Your console output should show the customer's reaction:

```
I sure love sourdough bread.
```

With this groundwork laid, things start to get interesting. Define a struct to model a restaurant and some nested structs to define the preparations of food it might create.

Listing 21.25 Restaurants are all about sliced, cooked foods

```
...
eat(Bread())

struct Restaurant {

    struct SlicedFood<Ingredient: Food>: Food {
        var food: Ingredient
        var menuListing: String {
            "a slice of \(food.menuListing)"
        }
    }

    struct CookedFood<Ingredient: Food>: Food {
        var food: Ingredient
        var menuListing: String {
            "\(food.menuListing), cooked to perfection"
        }
    }
}
```

Nested within **Restaurant**, you define new structs **SlicedFood** and **CookedFood**, data structures that are generic over an **Ingredient** that must conform to **Food**. Nesting these structs within **Restaurant** in this example provides a nested scope for access modifiers, which you will apply later, and models the idea that knowledge of cooking is in the domain of the restaurant staff, rather than the public.

To complete the metaphor and let the restaurant take orders, implement some methods for creating sliced bread and toast:

Listing 21.26 Restaurants know how to slice and toast bread

```
...
struct Restaurant {
    ...
    func makeSlicedBread() -> SlicedFood<Bread> {
        return SlicedFood(food: Bread())
    }

    func makeToast() -> CookedFood<SlicedFood<Bread>> {
        let slicedBread = SlicedFood(food: Bread())
        return CookedFood(food: slicedBread)
    }
}
```

Your **makeSlicedBread()** function returns a specialization of the **SlicedFood** generic structure for which the **Ingredient** is **Bread**. Your **makeToast()** function, in turn, returns a composed type, a cooked slice of bread.

Now your restaurant-goer can order toast for breakfast:

Listing 21.27 Let them eat toast

```
...
let restaurant = Restaurant()
let toast = restaurant.makeToast()
eat(toast)
```

Your console output should show the customer enjoying `toast` after the bread they ate previously:

```
I sure love a slice of sourdough bread, cooked to perfection.
```

You have modeled the ability for a customer to eat a slice of **Bread**, plain or cooked, by way of the restaurant's generic **CookedFood** type.

As programs become more complex, the complexity of generic data structures can increase. The number of types in this exercise is limited to respect your time (and your typing), but at each step you should keep in mind the compounding complexity you would face if you needed to model other foods – such as **Butter**, **Egg**, or a composed **CombinedFood<Ingredient>** – or functions, like `makeFrenchToast()`.

A `makeFrenchToast()` function might return an even more deeply composed generic type, such as **CookedFood<CombinedFood<CombinedFood<Bread,Egg>,Butter>>**. Such compositions are not far-fetched.

What would happen if the restaurant changed its toast recipe to cook the bread first and then slice it? Make this change:

Listing 21.28 Who would make such an abomination?

```
...
struct Restaurant {
    ...
    func makeToast() -> CookedFood<SlicedFood<Bread>> SlicedFood<CookedFood<Bread>> {
        let slicedBread = SlicedFood(food: Bread())
        return CookedFood(food: slicedBread)
        let cookedBread = CookedFood(food: Bread())
        return SlicedFood(food: cookedBread)
    }
}
```

The signature of your function has changed, but the meaning of its output has not. Eating the returned food has the same result:

```
I sure love a slice of sourdough bread, cooked to perfection.
```

Changing the order of the steps in `makeToast()`, even to one that yields a food with the same `menuListing`, has resulted in a different return type for the function. This could cause cascading changes to other functions unfortunate enough to be relying on the return type of `makeToast()`, such as some imaginary `makeButteredToast()` function.

This brings us to the crux of the problem: The composition of the type of `toast` is an implementation detail of **Restaurant**. Other functions do not, and should not, need to know about the precise composition of this type. After all, the `eat(_:)` function is happy with any argument that conforms to **Food**.

The solution is to not expose the type at all. This can be done in two ways. First, you can declare your functions as returning **Food**, rather than their precise types. Go ahead and make this change. While you are at it, restore the implementation of **makeToast()** so the bread is sliced first:

Listing 21.29 Any food will do

```
...
struct Restaurant {

    private struct SlicedFood<Ingredient: Food>: Food {
        ...
    }

    private struct CookedFood<Ingredient: Food>: Food {
        ...
    }

    func makeSlicedBread() -> SlicedFood<Bread> Food {
        ...
    }

    func makeToast() -> SlicedFood<CookedFood<Bread>> Food {
        let cookedBread = CookedFood(food: Bread())
        return SlicedFood(food: cookedBread)
        let slicedBread = SlicedFood(food: Bread())
        return CookedFood(food: slicedBread)
    }
}
...
```

Codifying the idea that **SlicedFood** and **CookedFood** are implementation details of the **Restaurant** type means marking them `private`. You allow this by removing them from the signatures of non-`private` methods and instead declaring the return types of those methods as **Food**.

A return type of **Food** means that **makeSlicedBread()** and **makeToast()** could return any kind of **Food**. Different calls to the function could return instances of different **Food**-conforming types. That means that a hypothetical variant **makeToast()** function could decide whether to slice the bread twice:

```
func makeToast() -> Food {
    var slicedBread = SlicedFood(food: Bread())
    if Bool.random() {
        slicedBread = SlicedFood(food: slicedBread)
    }
    return CookedFood(food: slicedBread)
}
```

This sample implementation would either return a **SlicedFood<Bread>** or a **SlicedFood<SlicedFood<Bread>>**, based on a `Bool.random()`. This is a flexible approach, but it may or may not be what you want. Right now, a caller of this function must account for the possibility that **makeToast()** might return items with different menu listings from one call to the next. Two diners ordering toast together might be surprised when one of them gets toast made with doubly sliced bread.

The second way to hide the method's return type is to return an *opaque type*, which is denoted by the some keyword:

Listing 21.30 I sure love some food

```
...
func makeSlicedBread() -> some Food {
    return SlicedFood(food: Bread())
}

func makeToast() -> some Food {
    let slicedBread = SlicedFood(food: Bread())
    return CookedFood(food: slicedBread)
}
...
```

By returning the opaque type some Food, you instruct the compiler to figure out what the function's return type will be – which requires that your function will always return the same type – and to hide that type information from humans writing code that calls the function. This way, visitors to the restaurant can rest assured that makeToast() will always return the exact same kind of toast, without needing to actually know about its composition.

Opaque types can only be used as the declared return type of a function or computed variable (and not as a function argument), but in this capacity, they give you the simplicity and privacy of a protocol type with the specificity of generic programming. They are especially useful for framework developers who want to use complex type compositions without exposing that complexity to users of the framework. You will see a concrete example of this strategy in Chapter 28.

Generics are an extremely powerful feature of Swift, and this flexibility comes at a cost of syntactical complexity. If generics have not sunk in, do not fret – they are an abstract concept, and they take lots of exposure to truly appreciate. Take your time, go back over the **Stack** class you wrote in this chapter, and try your hand at the challenges. It is also perfectly OK to move on and return to this chapter later.

Bronze Challenge

Add a `filter(_:)` method to your **Stack** structure. It should take a single argument, a closure that takes an **Element** and returns a **Bool**, and return a new **Stack<Element>** that contains any elements for which the closure returns `true`.

Silver Challenge

Write a generic function called `findAll(_:_:)` that takes an array of any type **T** that conforms to the **Equatable** protocol and a single element (also of type **T**). `findAll(_:_:)` should return an array of integers corresponding to every location where the element was found in the array. For example, `findAll([5,3,7,3,9], 3)` should return `[1,3]` because the item 3 exists at indices 1 and 3 in the array. Try your function with both integers and strings.

Gold Challenge

Modify the `findAll(_:_:)` function you wrote for the silver challenge to accept a generic **Collection** instead of an array. Hint: You will need to change the return type from **[Int]** to an array of an associated type of the **Collection** protocol.

For the More Curious: Understanding Optionals

Optionals are a mainstay of all nontrivial Swift programs, and the language has a lot of features that make it relatively easy to work with them. Under the hood, however, there is nothing particularly special about the **Optional** type. It is a generic enum with two cases:

```
enum Optional<Wrapped> {
    case none
    case some(Wrapped)
}
```

As you probably expect, the none case corresponds to an optional that is nil. In fact, nil is just another name for Optional.none. It is a value of type **Optional** in the same way that true is a value of type **Bool**, which is why you cannot assign nil to variables of non-optional type.

The some case corresponds to an optional that has a value of type Wrapped. Because the associated value of the some case is a generic placeholder, you are able to create instances of **Optional** to wrap any type.

Most of your interactions with optionals will use optional binding and optional chaining, but you can also treat them like any other enumeration. For example, you could switch over the two cases of an **Int?**:

```
let maybeAnInt: Int? = 10
switch maybeAnInt {
case .none:
    print("maybeAnInt is nil")

case let .some(value):
    print("maybeAnInt has the value \(value)")
}
```

This is not usually necessary, but it is nice to know that optionals are not magic. They are built on top of the same Swift features that are available to you.

22

Protocol Extensions

A dominant software programming paradigm of the past few decades has been *object-oriented programming* (OOP). OOP is powerful and well known, and developers have an intuition for what this style means for code. Traditionally, OOP uses classes to model data and methods to modify and process that data and communicate with instances of other classes. Swift supports OOP, though its approach to this paradigm is nontraditional given that enums and structs can replace many typical uses of classes in OOP.

Swift's value types are powerful and flexible, but they cannot inherit from one another. While you can create a subclass of a class, there are no such things as "sub-structs" or "sub-enums." This limits the ability for value types to substitute for one another and share behavior in the way that a class and its subclass might.

On the other hand, Swift can add power and flexibility to all types via protocols and *protocol extensions*. If you want multiple types – even value types – to have shared behavior, you can make them conform to a shared protocol; no direct inheritance needed. And, as you will see in this chapter, you can even provide a default implementation of your desired behavior using a protocol extension.

This chapter will explore using protocol extensions to add new behavior to all types that conform to a given protocol, to customize the behavior of the Swift standard library, and to add default implementations of protocol requirements to your types.

Modeling Exercise

Before you can begin exploring protocol extensions, you need a protocol and some conforming types to experiment with. You are going to write some very basic code that will let you track workout data.

Create a new macOS playground called ProtocolExtensions. Begin with an **Exercise** protocol.

Listing 22.1 The **Exercise** protocol

```
import Cocoa

var str = "Hello, playground"

protocol Exercise {
    var caloriesBurned: Double { get set }
    var minutes: Double { get set }
}
```

The **Exercise** protocol has two read/write properties to model the number of calories burned and the minutes spent performing the exercise.

Create two structs to track workouts: one for using an elliptical trainer and a second for running.

Listing 22.2 **EllipticalWorkout** and **RunningWorkout** exercises

```
protocol Exercise {
    var caloriesBurned: Double { get set }
    var minutes: Double { get set }
}

struct EllipticalWorkout: Exercise {
    var caloriesBurned: Double
    var minutes: Double
}

struct RunningWorkout: Exercise {
    var caloriesBurned: Double
    var minutes: Double
    var meters: Double
}
```

You define two new structs that both conform to **Exercise**. Each has caloriesBurned and minutes properties that will be set when the instance is created. **RunningWorkout** also has a meters property to keep track of the distance run. meters is not required by **Exercise**, but recall from Chapter 19 that extra properties or methods are perfectly acceptable.

Create an instance of each of these new types.

Listing 22.3 Instances of **EllipticalWorkout** and **RunningWorkout**

```
...
struct EllipticalWorkout: Exercise {
    var caloriesBurned: Double
    var minutes: Double
}

let ellipticalWorkout = EllipticalWorkout(caloriesBurned: 335, minutes: 30)

struct RunningWorkout: Exercise {
    var caloriesBurned: Double
    var minutes: Double
    var meters: Double
}

let runningWorkout = RunningWorkout(caloriesBurned: 350, minutes: 25, meters: 5000)
```

Now that you have a protocol and some conforming types, you can start to add more functionality to these types.

Extending Exercise

A natural question to ask about an instance of **Exercise** is how many calories were burned per minute of exercise. You can use your knowledge of generics and type constraints to write a function that will perform that calculation.

Listing 22.4 Computing calories burned per minute, generically

```
...
func caloriesBurnedPerMinute<E: Exercise>(for exercise: E) -> Double {
    return exercise.caloriesBurned / exercise.minutes
}

print(caloriesBurnedPerMinute(for: ellipticalWorkout))
print(caloriesBurnedPerMinute(for: runningWorkout))
```

caloriesBurnedPerMinute(for:) is a generic function whose placeholder type must conform to the **Exercise** protocol. You made **caloriesBurnedPerMinute(for:)** generic so that you can call it with an instance of any type that conforms to **Exercise**, including **EllipticalWorkout** and **RunningWorkout**. The body of the function uses two of **Exercise**'s properties to compute the calories burned per minute.

There is nothing wrong with **caloriesBurnedPerMinute(for:)**. But if you have an instance of **Exercise**, you have to remember that the **caloriesBurnedPerMinute(for:)** function exists. It would be more natural if every **Exercise** had a caloriesBurnedPerMinute property – but you do not want to have to copy and paste the same implementation into both **EllipticalWorkout** and **RunningWorkout** (and any new **Exercise**s you might create).

You cannot add the property definition to the protocol, as protocols themselves do not define the implementations of properties and methods.

Instead, write an extension on the **Exercise** protocol to add this new property.

Listing 22.5 Adding `caloriesBurnedPerMinute` to **Exercise**

```
...
func caloriesBurnedPerMinute<E: Exercise>(for exercise: E) -> Double {
    return exercise.caloriesBurned / exercise.minutes
}
extension Exercise {
    var caloriesBurnedPerMinute: Double {
        return caloriesBurned / minutes
    }
}
...
```

Protocol extensions use the same `extension` keyword as extensions on other types. Protocol extensions can add new computed properties and methods that have implementations, but they cannot add new requirements to the protocol. Protocol extensions also cannot add stored properties, as extensions in general do not support stored properties.

Properties and methods added in a protocol extension become available on all types that conform to the protocol.

Much like the restrictions on generic functions, the implementations inside a protocol extension can only access other properties and methods that are guaranteed to exist, as `caloriesBurned` and `minutes` are in this case.

Now that you have deleted the **caloriesBurnedPerMinute(for:)** function, your playground is showing errors where you call the nonexistent function. Delete the function calls and instead access the new `caloriesBurnedPerMinute` property on `ellipticalWorkout` and `runningWorkout`.

Listing 22.6 Accessing `caloriesBurnedPerMinute`

```
...
print(caloriesBurnedPerMinute(for: ellipticalWorkout))
print(caloriesBurnedPerMinute(for: runningWorkout))
print(ellipticalWorkout.caloriesBurnedPerMinute)
print(runningWorkout.caloriesBurnedPerMinute)
```

The results are the same.

This ability to use a protocol extension to add features to all types conforming to the protocol is incredibly powerful, and it drives many features of the Swift standard library. You will learn more about standard library usage of protocol extensions in Chapter 25.

Self Types and Type Values

Methods that have implementations on multiple types sometimes need to know the specific type they are being called on. There is a special type, **Self**, that you can use for this purpose. Add and test another extension to **Exercise** to create a modified duplicate of whatever exercise it gets called on:

Listing 22.7 Adding a method that returns **Self**

```
...
print(ellipticalWorkout.caloriesBurnedPerMinute)
print(runningWorkout.caloriesBurnedPerMinute)

extension Exercise {
    func adding(calories: Double) -> Self {
        var dupe = self
        dupe.caloriesBurned += calories
        return dupe
    }
}

let ellipticalCopy = ellipticalWorkout.adding(calories: 50)
let runningCopy = runningWorkout.adding(calories: 100)
```

Why not add this function to the existing extension? Using multiple extensions is common. Organizationally, an extension can help define a logical grouping of behavior, and **adding(calories)** is not very closely related to caloriesBurnedPerMinute.

Self (with a capital S) can be used as the return type of a method or computed property when you are returning an instance of the same type as the one whose code is executing. This could be because your code returns a new instance (as it does in Listing 22.7) or because it returns the same instance, such as with return self.

How might you interpolate the **Self** type into a string, such as to print out the kind of object returned from **adding(calories:)**? Every type has a type property that you can use to access the type as a value. And if you are guessing that the property is called self, then you are right. Print the type of the duplicated object in your playground:

Listing 22.8 Accessing a type as a value

```
...
extension Exercise {
    func adding(calories: Double) -> Self {
        var dupe = self
        dupe.caloriesBurned += calories
        print("Creating a new \(Self.self) with \(dupe.caloriesBurned)cal burned.")
        return dupe
    }
}
...
```

The use of .self on a type is not limited to the **Self** type. In Chapter 28, you will encounter functions that you must pass types in to as arguments, such as functions that ask questions like, "The server sent some data; what type of data is it?" You might want to answer, "It is a string," and you would do so by passing **String.self** as the argument to that function.

Do not worry – this is the last new context in which the word "self" will have special meaning.

Protocol Extension where Clauses

Extensions allow you to add new methods and computed properties to any type, not just types you have defined. Likewise, protocol extensions allow you to add new methods and computed properties to any protocol. However, as we said earlier, the properties and methods you add in a protocol extension can only use other properties and methods that are guaranteed to exist.

Do you remember the **IteratorProtocol** from Chapter 21? It has an associatedtype named Element that indicates the type of elements produced by the generator. That generator, and the elements returned, are used by the **Sequence** protocol to produce values you can iterate over in a loop.

When writing a protocol extension on **Sequence**, there are not very many properties and methods that would be useful. You can use a where clause to restrict the protocol extension to only **Sequence**s whose Element is a particular type.

Write a protocol extension on **Sequence**, constraining it to sequences with elements of type **Exercise**.

Listing 22.9 Extending **Sequence**s containing **Exercise**s

```
...
extension Sequence where Element == Exercise {
    func totalCaloriesBurned() -> Double {
        var total: Double = 0
        for exercise in self {
            total += exercise.caloriesBurned
        }
        return total
    }
}
```

The where clause syntax for protocol extensions is the same as the where clause syntax for generics. You add a **totalCaloriesBurned()** method to compute the total number of calories burned in all exercises contained in the sequence. In the implementation, you loop over every exercise in self, which is allowed because self is some kind of **Sequence**. You then access the caloriesBurned property of each element, which is allowed because the where clause restricts this method to sequences whose elements are **Exercise**.

To use your extension, create an array of **Exercise**s. **Array** conforms to **Sequence**, so you can call your new **totalCaloriesBurned()** method.

Listing 22.10 Calling **totalCaloriesBurned()** on an array of **Exercise**s

```
...
extension Sequence where Element == Exercise {
    func totalCaloriesBurned() -> Double {
        var total: Double = 0
        for exercise in self {
            total += exercise.caloriesBurned
        }
        return total
    }
}

let mondayWorkout: [Exercise] = [ellipticalWorkout, runningWorkout]
print(mondayWorkout.totalCaloriesBurned())
```

The **totalCaloriesBurned()** method is available on this array because it is of type **[Exercise]**, so you get the result 685.0. If you were to create an array of type **[Int]**, on the other hand, the **totalCaloriesBurned()** method would not be available. It would not show up in Xcode's autocompletion, and if you were to type it in manually your program would not compile.

Default Implementations with Protocol Extensions

Both of the protocol extensions you have written so far add new properties or methods to protocols. You can also use protocol extensions to provide default implementations for the protocol's own requirements.

Recall from Chapter 19 that the **CustomStringConvertible** protocol has a single requirement: a readable **String** property named description. Change **Exercise** to inherit from **CustomStringConvertible**, meaning it also requires the description property.

Listing 22.11 Making **Exercise** inherit from **CustomStringConvertible**

```
protocol Exercise: CustomStringConvertible {
    var caloriesBurned: Double { get set }
    var minutes: Double { get set }
}
...
```

Your playground now has two errors because neither **EllipticalWorkout** nor **RunningWorkout** has the required description property.

You could go back and modify both types to add a description, but that seems silly when **Exercise** already has enough properties to provide a reasonable **String** representation. Use a protocol extension to add a default implementation of description to all types that conform to **Exercise**.

Listing 22.12 Adding a default implementation of description to **Exercise**

```
protocol Exercise: CustomStringConvertible {
    var caloriesBurned: Double { get set }
    var minutes: Double { get set }
}

extension Exercise {
    var description: String {
        return "Exercise(\(Self.self), burned \(caloriesBurned) calories
                in \(minutes) minutes)"
    }
}
...
```

The playground no longer has any errors. Your extension provides a default implementation of description, so types that conform to **Exercise** do not have to provide it themselves.

Print out both of your **Exercise** instances to see their descriptions.

Listing 22.13 Seeing the default `description` implementation

```
...
print(ellipticalWorkout.caloriesBurnedPerMinute)
print(runningWorkout.caloriesBurnedPerMinute)

print(ellipticalWorkout)
print(runningWorkout)
...
```

In the debug area of your playground, you should see the following output; it is exactly as you would expect from your implementation of `description`.

```
...
Exercise(Elliptical Workout, burned 335.0 calories in 30.0 minutes)
Exercise(Running Workout, burned 350.0 calories in 25.0 minutes)
```

When a protocol provides a default implementation for a property or method via a protocol extension, conforming types are not required to implement that requirement themselves – but they can. If they do, the compiler will use the conforming type's implementation instead of the default implementation.

Your **RunningWorkout** type also knows how many meters were run, but that information is not included in the description. Implement the `description` property on **RunningWorkout** to include distance information. This implementation will take precedence over the default supplied by your extension on **Exercise**.

Listing 22.14 Overriding a protocol's default implementation

```
...
struct RunningWorkout: Exercise {
    var caloriesBurned: Double
    var minutes: Double
    var meters: Double

    var description: String {
        return "RunningWorkout(\(caloriesBurned) calories and
                \(meters)m in \(minutes) minutes)"
    }
}
...
```

Now that **RunningWorkout** implements `description` itself, you should see in the output that the default implementation is only used when printing `ellipticalWorkout`.

```
...
Exercise(Elliptical Workout, burned 335.0 calories in 30.0 minutes)
RunningWorkout(350.0 calories and 5000m in 25.0 minutes)
```

Implementation Conflicts

As you have seen, the compiler will select a concrete protocol-conforming type's implementation of a method or property over any default implementation provided by a protocol extension. But there is a case where this does not *seem* to be true, and you should be aware of it to help prevent frustration in the future.

Let's look at an example.

Use a protocol extension to implement a `title` property on **Exercise**. Create two identical running workouts and print their titles.

Listing 22.15 Extending **Exercise** to add a `title`

```
...
extension Exercise {
    var title: String {
        return "\(Self.self) – \(minutes) minutes"
    }
}

let tenKRun: RunningWorkout = RunningWorkout(caloriesBurned: 750,
                                             minutes: 60,
                                             meters: 10000)

let workout: Exercise = tenKRun

print(tenKRun.title)
print(workout.title)
```

Note that you declare one of the instances as being of concrete type **RunningWorkout** and the other as being of protocol type **Exercise**. You should see the following output:

```
    ...
    RunningWorkout – 60.0 minutes
    RunningWorkout – 60.0 minutes
```

This makes sense. They are equal runs, after all. Now go back and implement a `title` property on **RunningWorkout**.

Listing 22.16 Adding a `title` to **RunningWorkout**

```
...
struct RunningWorkout: Exercise {
    let title = "Gotta go fast!"
    var caloriesBurned: Double
    ...
}
...
```

Check the output again. Both should change to `Gotta go fast!`, right?

```
    ...
    Gotta go fast!
    RunningWorkout – 60.0 minutes
```

Wait, what? Why are their titles different? They are equal objects and are both instances of **RunningWorkout**!

When a protocol declares a requirement and a type conforms to that protocol, the compiler follows a rigorous series of steps to find the conforming type's implementation to use at every call site. This is the case with your `description` property, which is required by **CustomStringConvertible**.

Behavior that is added using a protocol extension, and *not* listed in the protocol's interface, does not get this priority treatment. The compiler treats the protocol extension's implementation as having equal weight with other implementations provided by the program, rather than as a default implementation to be overridden by concrete types.

At each call site, as with a generic function, the compiler will select the best implementation it can with the information available. Specifically, the compiler will rely on the declared type of the variable or argument being used to access the property or method.

In Listing 22.15, tenKRun is declared as being of type **RunningWorkout**, so the compiler will select the struct's implementation of the `title` property. Since workout is declared as an **Exercise**, the compiler will select the implementation available on the **Exercise** protocol, which is provided by your protocol extension.

Find your declaration of the **Exercise** protocol at the top of your playground and add `title` as a protocol requirement:

Listing 22.17 Adding `title` as a protocol requirement

```
protocol Exercise: CustomStringConvertible {
    var caloriesBurned: Double { get set }
    var minutes: Double { get set }
    var title: String { get }
}
...
```

Look at the output once more.

```
...
Gotta go fast!
Gotta go fast!
```

Since `title` is now listed in the **Exercise** protocol, the compiler interprets the protocol extension's implementation as a default implementation to be overridden by concrete implementations. It will always search for a concrete implementation and give preference to any that it finds.

This is a strange artifact of protocol extensions, and it is OK if it feels counterintuitive. For now, when adding behavior to concrete types using a protocol extension, consider also declaring that behavior in the protocol itself to remove potential confusion over which implementation will be used at the call site.

Of course, if allowing selection of an implementation based on variable type is your desired behavior, that is fine. The standard library does this, as you will see in Chapter 23.

You previously learned that the two major differences between value types and reference types are inheritance and value/reference semantics. Now you know that while inheritance is not available to value types, many of its benefits are available via protocols and protocol extensions. This means that value types can fulfill your needs more frequently than you might previously have thought.

Bronze Challenge

Add a method called **count(where:)** to all collections to count the number of elements that pass a provided test.

You should be able to call it like this:

```
let workouts: [Exercise] = [ellipticalWorkout, runningWorkout, tenKRun]
let hardWorkoutCount = workouts.count(where: { $0.caloriesBurned >= 500})    // 1
```

Look at the documentation for the **Sequence** and **Collection** protocols. Why is **Collection** the better protocol to add this extension to?

Silver Challenge

Sometimes you have a sequence of integers and want to add them up. You can do that by calling **reduce(_:_:)**, but that is ugly and counterintuitive. (Feel free to take time to review the **reduce(_:_:)** method in Chapter 13 on closures.)

To make summing sequences of number more convenient, add a computed property called sum to all sequences of numbers. You should be able to use it like this:

```
[4, 8, 15, 16, 23, 42].sum      // 108
[80.5, 9.6].sum                 // 90.1
```

To solve this challenge, you will need to be able to answer a deeper question: What is a number? Look at the documentation for the **Int** and **Double** types. What protocols do they conform to? What protocols do those protocols inherit from? Do **Int** and **Double** have any protocols in common that would be a good place to add your extension?

Gold Challenge

This challenge is unique in that it does not have a specific problem or solution. Instead, it is an encouragement to spend some time reading interfaces written by the Swift team at Apple. Remember that you can Command-click on a type, function, method, or even operator to jump to a view in Xcode that shows you how the element is declared.

You first encountered the **map(_:)** method in Chapter 13, where you called it on arrays. **map(_:)** is not just a method on arrays, though. It is defined in a protocol extension on all **Sequence**s by the Swift standard library.

The Swift standard library contains many properties and methods provided by protocol extensions. And many of them include where clauses that restrict their use based on various criteria.

The Swift standard library can be difficult to read, especially at first – and especially if Swift is your first exposure to programming or generics. But it is worth investing some time to look at how the library is organized.

Try Command-clicking on **Sequence** in your playground and skimming through some of the extensions defined there. See if you can figure out what some of the where clauses mean. Do some experiments and explore!

Can anything that you learn there help you refine your solutions to the bronze or silver challenges?

For the More Curious: Polymorphism and Protocol-Oriented Programming

In Chapter 15, you learned about class inheritance and that any function that expects an argument of some class can also accept arguments that are subclasses of that class. We said that this ability to accept either a class or any subclass of it is sometimes referred to as *polymorphism*. Polymorphism, meaning "having many forms," allows you to write a single function that can accept different types.

That particular flavor of polymorphism is more precisely known as *runtime polymorphism* or *subclass polymorphism*. Using protocol types as function arguments or return values is another example of runtime polymorphism.

Runtime polymorphism is a powerful tool, and the frameworks Apple provides for development use it frequently. Unfortunately, it also has drawbacks. Classes that are related by inheritance are tied together tightly: It can be difficult to change a superclass without affecting its subclasses. Also, there is a small but observable performance penalty to runtime polymorphism due to how the compiler must implement functions that accept class arguments.

Swift's ability to add constraints to generics allows you to use another form of polymorphism, called *compile-time polymorphism* or *parametric polymorphism*. Generic functions with constraints are still true to the definition of polymorphism: You can write a single function that accepts different types.

Compile-time polymorphic functions address both of the issues listed above that plague runtime polymorphism. Many different types can conform to a protocol, allowing them to be used as constraints in any generic function that requires a type conforming to that protocol – but the types can be otherwise unrelated, making it easy to change any one of them without affecting the others. Additionally, compile-time polymorphism generally does not have a performance penalty.

In Chapter 21, you called your generic **pushAll(_:)** function once with an array and once with a stack. The compiler actually produced two different versions of **pushAll(_:)** behind the scenes, one for each argument type used in the program, so that the function itself does not have to do anything at runtime to handle the different argument types.

Swift's emphasis on value types using protocols for shared behavior, rather than reference types using inheritance for shared behavior, has given popularity to an additional programming paradigm: *protocol-oriented programming*. But despite their names, object-oriented programming and protocol-oriented programming are not mutually exclusive approaches.

At the beginning of this chapter, we said that Swift's approach to OOP is a little different than most other languages', because Swift's value types are very robust and lend themselves well to modeling complex data. In traditional OOP applications, developers define shared behavior using classes, allowing that behavior to be overridden by subclasses that add or augment a type's behavior. Protocol-oriented programming borrows this idea, but makes it work with value types by using protocol hierarchies and protocol extensions to provide behavior to any conforming type.

In a protocol-oriented approach, when you need to define a type to fulfill some role, you start by defining a protocol whose interface reflects the requirements of the role. Then you can write code that uses that role without having to write any concrete implementations. And *then* you can write concrete types that actually conform to your protocol, when you are ready.

By writing your code like this, interface first, you reduce the risk of a concrete type's implementation details cluttering its interface.

As an example, suppose you need to implement an app's login flow. While you are working on your **LoginSession** class, you realize that you need a type to model a logged-in user.

```
class LoginSession {
    var lastLogin: Date?
    // Need a var for current user
    // Need a function to log them in
}
```

For now, all you care about is that every user instance has a name and an ability to validate its credentials. Rather than immediately defining a struct or class, you might define a **User** protocol:

```
protocol User {
    var name: String { get }
    func validatePassword(_ pw: String) -> Bool
}
```

Now you can finish up your **LoginSession** class – without caring about any of the implementation details of whatever type ends up conforming to **User**.

```
class LoginSession {
    var lastLogin: Date?
    var currentUser: User?

    func login(_ user: User, with password: String) {
        if user.validatePassword(password) {
            currentUser = user
        }
        print("\(user.name) logged in!")
    }
}
```

Without even having any concrete data types to conform to **User**, this is already code that would compile. Then you could get around to implementing a concrete user model:

```
struct AppUser: User {
    var name: String
    private var password: String

    func validatePassword(_ pw: String) -> Bool {
        #warning("This whole login flow is really insecure, by the way.")
        return password == pw
    }
}
```

Having designed the interface in advance, using a protocol, you now have an idea of what the central features of this type are – and also which features should probably be marked as private, since their absence from the protocol implies that the rest of your program does not need to know about them. This approach often lends itself well to designing types that are responsibly decoupled from one another, focused, and testable.

23
Error Handling

How often has a piece of software you have been using crashed or done something it was not supposed to do? The majority of the time, these issues are caused by incorrect error handling. Error handling is one of the unsung heroes of software development: Nobody thinks of it as a priority, and if it is done correctly nobody notices. But it is absolutely critical – users of your software will certainly notice (and complain!) if it is done poorly.

In this chapter, you will explore the tools that Swift provides to catch and handle errors.

Classes of Errors

There are two broad categories of errors that can occur: *recoverable errors* and *nonrecoverable errors*.

Recoverable errors are typically events you must be ready for and handle. Common examples of recoverable errors are:

- trying to open a file that does not exist
- trying to communicate with a server that is down
- trying to communicate when a device does not have an internet connection

Swift provides you with a rich set of tools for dealing with recoverable errors. You have become accustomed to Swift enforcing safety rules at compile time, and handling errors is no different. When you call a function that might fail with a recoverable error, Swift will require you to acknowledge and deal with that possibility.

Nonrecoverable errors are just a special kind of bug. You have already encountered one: force-unwrapping an optional that contains `nil`. Another example is trying to access an element past the end of an array. These nonrecoverable errors will cause your program to trap.

A trap is a command to the OS to immediately stop the currently executing program. If you are running the program from Xcode, it will stop in the debugger and show you where the error occurred. For a user running your program, a trap looks the same as a crash – the program immediately shuts down.

Why is Swift so heavy handed with this class of error? The name gives a hint: These errors are not recoverable, meaning there is nothing your program could do to fix the problem.

Think about unwrapping an optional, for example. When you force-unwrap an optional, Swift quietly checks whether it has a value before trying to access that value. If the optional is `nil`, Swift will trap. If it did not, the application might crash anyway – or it might try to continue with invalid or possibly corrupt data.

In this chapter, you will build a very simple two-phase compiler. In doing so, you will implement a function that can evaluate basic mathematical expressions. For example, if you provide the input string "10 + 3 + 5", the function will return the integer 18. Along the way, you will use Swift's facilities for dealing with both recoverable and nonrecoverable errors.

Lexing an Input String

The first phase of your expression-evaluating compiler is *lexing*. In computer science, lexing is the process of turning some input into a sequence of *tokens*. A token is something with meaning, like a number or a plus sign (the two tokens your compiler will recognize). Lexing is sometimes referred to as "tokenizing" because you are turning some input that is meaningless to the compiler (like a string) into a sequence of meaningful tokens.

Create a new macOS playground named ErrorHandling. Define an enumeration that has cases for the two kinds of token.

Listing 23.1 Declaring the **Token** type

```
import Cocoa

var str = "Hello, playground"

enum Token {
    case number(Int)
    case plus
}
```

When building something like a lexer, logging your progress can help with debugging later. You will start by logging tokens as your lexer encounters them. You can define how the tokens are printed by adding the **CustomStringConvertible** protocol to your **Token** type. Update your **Token** enum to conform to it:

Listing 23.2 Adding a debug description

```
enum Token: CustomStringConvertible {
    case number(Int)
    case plus

    var description: String {
        switch self {
        case .number(let n):
            return "Number: \(n)"
        case .plus:
            return "Symbol: +"
        }
    }
}
```

Next, start building your lexer. To lex an input string, you will need to access the individual characters in the input string one by one. You will need to keep track of your current position in **String** as well. Create the **Lexer** class and give it two properties to track these pieces of information.

Listing 23.3 Creating **Lexer**

```
enum Token: CustomStringConvertible {
    case number(Int)
    case plus

    var description: String {
        switch self {
        case .number(let n):
            return "Number: \(n)"
        case .plus:
            return "Symbol: +"
        }
    }
}

class Lexer {
    let input: String
    var position: String.Index

    init(input: String) {
        self.input = input
        self.position = input.startIndex
    }
}
```

Recall from Chapter 7 that strings are collections of **Character**s. **String**s have startIndex and endIndex properties that let you step through the characters. Here, you initialize the input property with the passed-in **String** and initialize the position property to the **String**'s startIndex.

Lexing the input characters is a straightforward process. The steps you will implement are outlined in Figure 23.1.

Figure 23.1 Lexing algorithm

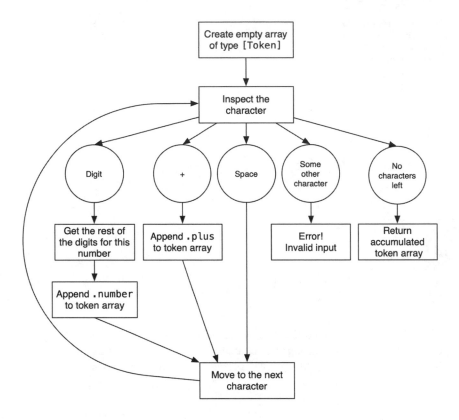

You begin by creating an empty array to hold **Token**s. You then inspect the first character. If it is a digit, you continue to scan forward through the input string, collecting all the subsequent digits into a single number, then appending a .number to the token array. If the character is a +, you append a .plus to the **Token** array. If the character is a space, you ignore it.

In all three of those cases, you then move on to the next character in the input string, repeating the same decision-making process. At any point as you are scanning through the input string, encountering a character that does not fall into one of the three cases above is considered an error: The input is invalid. When you reach the end of the input string, the lexing phase is finished.

To implement this algorithm, **Lexer** will need two basic operations: a way to peek at the next character from the input and a way to advance the current position. Peeking at the next character requires a way to indicate that the lexer has reached the end of its input, so make it return an optional.

Listing 23.4 Implementing **peek()**

```
...
class Lexer {
    let input: String
    var position: String.Index

    init(input: String) {
        self.input = input
        self.position = input.startIndex
    }

    func peek() -> Character? {
        guard position < input.endIndex else {
            return nil
        }
        return input[position]
    }
}
```

You use a guard statement to ensure that you have not reached the end of the input, returning nil if you have. If there is input remaining, you return the character at the current position.

Now that the lexer can peek at the current character, it also needs a way to advance to the next character. Advancing is very simple. position is an index from the input collection, and every collection knows how to compute new indices relative to old ones. Get the index after the current value of position using input's **index(after:)** method and assign that back into position.

Listing 23.5 Implementing **advance()**

```
...
class Lexer {
    ...
    func peek() -> Character? {
        guard position < input.endIndex else {
            return nil
        }
        return input[position]
    }

    func advance() {
        position = input.index(after: position)
    }
}
```

Before moving on, there is an opportunity here to introduce a check for a nonrecoverable error. As you implement the rest of **Lexer**, you will be calling **peek()** and **advance()**. **peek()** can be called any time, but **advance()** should only be called if you are not already at the end of the input. Add an *assertion* to **advance()** that checks for this condition.

Listing 23.6 Adding an assertion to **advance()**

```
...
class Lexer {
    ...
    func advance() {
        assert(position < input.endIndex, "Cannot advance past endIndex!")
        position = input.index(after: position)
    }
}
```

The **assert(_:_:)** function's first argument is a condition to check. If the condition evaluates to true, nothing happens. But if the condition evaluates to false, your program will trap in the debugger with the message you provide as the second argument.

Calls to **assert(_:_:)** will only be evaluated if your program is built in *debug mode*. Debug mode is the default when you are working in a playground or running a project in Xcode. *Release mode* is what Xcode uses when you build an app for submission to the App Store. Among other things, building in release mode turns on a number of compiler optimizations and removes all calls to **assert(_:_:)**.

If you want to keep your assertions around even in release mode, you can use **precondition(_:_:)** instead. It takes the same arguments and has the same effect as **assert(_:_:)**, but it is not removed when your app is built for release.

Both **assert(_:_:)** and **precondition(_:_:)** are used to trap if a condition is not met. If you need to unconditionally halt program execution, you can do so with **fatalError(_:)**, which accepts a string argument that will be printed to the console just before trapping.

Why did you use **assert(_:_:)** instead of **guard** or some other error-handling mechanism? **assert(_:_:)** and its partner **precondition(_:_:)** are tools to help you catch nonrecoverable errors. As you are implementing your lexing algorithm, you are advancing an index from the beginning of the input to the end. You should never attempt to advance past the input's endIndex.

Adding this assertion will help you catch any mistake you make that introduces a bug of this kind, because the assertion will cause the debugger to stop execution at this point, helping you identify the error. The alternatives to this assertion are to not advance the lexer's position or send an error back to the user of your lexer, neither of which makes sense.

Now that the **Lexer** class has the building blocks you need, it is time to start implementing the lexing algorithm. The output of lexing will be an array of **Token**s, but it is also possible for lexing to fail. To indicate that a function or method might emit an error, add the keyword `throws` after the parentheses containing the arguments. (This implementation of `lex()` is incomplete and will not compile, but you will finish it shortly.)

Listing 23.7 Declaring the throwing `lex()` method

```
...
class Lexer {
    ...
    func advance() {
        assert(position < input.endIndex, "Cannot advance past endIndex!")
        position = input.index(after: position)
    }

    func lex() throws -> [Token] {
        var tokens = [Token]()

        while let nextCharacter = peek() {
            switch nextCharacter {
            case "0" ... "9":
                // Start of a number - need to grab the rest
                break // TODO: replace this with real work

            case "+":
                tokens.append(.plus)
                advance()

            case " ":
                // Just advance to ignore spaces
                advance()

            default:
                // Something unexpected - need to send back an error
                break // TODO: replace this with real work
            }
        }

        return tokens
    }
}
```

You have now implemented most of the lexing algorithm. You start by creating an array, `tokens`, that will hold every **Token** you lex. You use a `while let` condition to loop until you reach the end of the input. For each character you look at, you go into one of the four cases. And you have implemented what to do if the character is a plus (append `.plus` to `tokens` and then advance to the next character) or a space (ignore it and advance to the next character).

There are two cases left to implement. Let's start with the `default` case. If this case matches, then a character you were not expecting is next. That means you need to *throw* an error. In Swift, you use the `throws` keyword to send, or "throw," an error back to the caller.

What can you throw? You must throw an instance of a type that conforms to the **Error** protocol. Most of the time, errors you want to throw will lend themselves to being defined as enumerations, and this is no exception.

What should you name your **Error**-conforming enumeration? One option would be to name it **LexerError**. **LexerError** would be acceptable, but it also adds another type just for designating lexing errors, which is not ideal. A separate type would suggest that **LexerError** has meaning beyond and outside **Lexer**.

Recall from Chapter 16 that you can nest types. You can use a nested **Lexer.Error** enumeration that makes it clear that the error cases it provides are directly related to **Lexer**.

Declare an enumeration nested inside the **Lexer** class to express lexing errors.

Listing 23.8 Declaring **Lexer.Error**

```
...
class Lexer {
    enum Error {
        case invalidCharacter(Character)
    }

    let input: String
    var position: String.Index
    ...
}
```

Lexer.Error needs to conform to the **Error** protocol. A direct attempt to add this conformance will fail, but try it anyway to see the error.

Listing 23.9 Attempting to make **Lexer.Error** conform to **Error**

```
...
class Lexer {
    enum Error: Error {
        case invalidCharacter(Character)
    }

    let input: String
    var position: String.Index
    ...
}
```

You will get a number of error messages in the console. Find this one:

```
error: ErrorHandling.playground:18:10: error: 'Error' has a raw type that depends
        on itself
enum Error: Error {
^
```

The compiler is confused because it thinks you are trying to declare an **Error** type using itself. How can you tell the compiler that you want to use the **Error** protocol from the Swift standard library?

Swift does not have explicit namespaces, unlike languages such as C++. Instead, all types and functions are implicitly namespaced to the module they are defined in. You typically do not need to think about which module you are working in. If you are writing an iOS app, for example, the entire app lives in one module.

Declaring **Lexer.Error** is one of the rare cases where being aware of modules is useful. Types and functions that are part of the Swift standard library live in the Swift module. You can specify that you want the Swift module's **Error** type by its full name: **Swift.Error**.

Add the module name to fix your declaration of **Lexer.Error**.

Listing 23.10 Making **Lexer.Error** conform to **Error**

```
...
class Lexer {
    enum Error: Swift.Error {
        case invalidCharacter(Character)
    }
    ...
}
```

Command-click on the **Swift.Error** protocol and choose Jump to Definition to see its definition from the Swift standard library. You will find that it is an empty protocol; the behaviors that Swift wants from **Error**-conforming types are added via protocol extensions in the standard library.

This means that any type you write can conform to **Error** just by stating that it does. Enumerations are by far the most common **Error**s. When something fails, you usually have a discrete list of reasons for the failure, which are representable by enum cases.

Click the back arrow in the Xcode toolbar to return to your playground. Now that you have a throwable type, implement the **default** case in the **lex()** method to throw an instance of your new **Error** enum.

Listing 23.11 Throwing an error

```
...
class Lexer {
    ...
    func lex() throws -> [Token] {
        var tokens = [Token]()

        while let nextCharacter = peek() {
            switch nextCharacter {
            case "0" ... "9":
                // Start of a number - need to grab the rest
                break // TODO: replace this with real work

            case "+":
                tokens.append(.plus)
                advance()

            case " ":
                // Just advance to ignore spaces
                advance()

            default:
                // Something unexpected - need to send back an error
                break // TODO: replace this with real work
                throw Lexer.Error.invalidCharacter(nextCharacter)
            }
        }

        return tokens
    }
}
```

Like return, throw causes the function to immediately stop executing and go back to its caller.

Finally, the lexer needs to be able to extract integers from the input. Create a **getNumber()** method that builds up integers one digit at a time using the same **peek()** and **advance()** tools you are using in **lex()**.

Next, update **lex()** by adding a call to **getNumber()** and appending the number to the array of tokens.

Listing 23.12 Implementing **Lexer.getNumber()**

```
...
class Lexer {
    ...
    func getNumber() -> Int {
        var value = 0

        while let nextCharacter = peek() {
            switch nextCharacter {
            case "0" ... "9":
                // Another digit - add it into value
                let digitValue = Int(String(nextCharacter))!
                value = 10*value + digitValue
                advance()

            default:
                // Something unexpected - need to send back an error
                return value
            }
        }

        return value
    }

    func lex() throws -> [Token] {
        var tokens = [Token]()

        while let nextCharacter = peek() {
            switch nextCharacter {
            case "0" ... "9":
                // Start of a number - need to grab the rest
                break // TODO: replace this with real work
                let value = getNumber()
                tokens.append(.number(value))

            case "+":
                tokens.append(.plus)
                advance()

            case " ":
                // Just advance to ignore spaces
                advance()

            default:
                // Something unexpected - need to send back an error
                throw Lexer.Error.invalidCharacter(nextCharacter)
            }
        }

        return tokens
    }
}
```

At this point, all your errors should be gone.

getNumber() loops over input characters, accumulating digits into a single integer value. Note that you do something we have cautioned against – force-unwrapping an optional – in Int(String(nextCharacter))!. However, it is perfectly safe in this case. Because you know that nextCharacter contains a single digit, converting it to an **Int** will always succeed and never return nil. As soon as **getNumber()** encounters a character that is not a digit (or the end of the input), it stops and returns the accumulated value.

Lexer is complete, and it is time to put it to the test. Write a new function at the bottom of your playground that takes an input string and tries to lex it, then call it with a couple of trial inputs. (This function will not work quite yet – as you type it in, try to figure out why.)

Listing 23.13 Evaluating the lexer

```
...
func evaluate(_ input: String) {
    print("Evaluating: \(input)")
    let lexer = Lexer(input: input)
    let tokens = lexer.lex()
    print("Lexer output: \(tokens)")
}

evaluate("10 + 3 + 5")
evaluate("1 + 2 + three")
```

evaluate(_:) takes an input **String**, creates a **Lexer**, and lexes the input into **Token**s. But the compiler does not allow what you have entered. Note the error message on the line where you call **lex()**:

Call can throw, but it is not marked with 'try' and the error is not handled

The compiler is telling you that because the **lex()** method is marked as throws, calls to **lex()** must be prepared to handle an error.

Catching Errors

To handle errors, Swift uses a control construct you have not yet seen: do/catch, with at least one try statement inside the do. We will explain in a moment. First, modify **evaluate(_:)** to use this control flow to handle errors coming from **lex()**.

Listing 23.14 Error handling in **evaluate(_:)**

```
...
func evaluate(_ input: String) {
    print("Evaluating: \(input)")
    let lexer = Lexer(input: input)

    do {
        let tokens = try lexer.lex()
        print("Lexer output: \(tokens)")
    } catch {
        print("An error occurred: \(error)")
    }
}
```

What do these new keywords mean? do introduces a new scope, much like an if statement. Inside the do scope, you can write code as normal, like calling **print()**. In addition, you can call functions or methods that are marked as throws. Each such call must be indicated with the try keyword.

After the do block, you write a catch block. If any of the try calls inside the do block throw an error, the catch block will run, with the thrown error value bound to the constant error.

You should now be seeing the output of running **evaluate(_:)** in the debug area.

```
Evaluating: 10 + 3 + 5
Lexer output: [Number: 10, Symbol: +, Number: 3, Symbol: +, Number: 5]
Evaluating: 1 + 2 + three
An error occurred: Lexer.Error.invalidCharacter("t")
```

The catch block you wrote above did not specify a particular kind of error, so it will catch any thrown **Error**. You can add catch blocks to catch specific kinds of errors. In this case, you know that the lexer could throw a **Lexer.Error.invalidCharacter** error, so add a catch block for it.

Listing 23.15 Catching an **invalidCharacter** error

```
...
func evaluate(_ input: String) {
    print("Evaluating: \(input)")
    let lexer = Lexer(input: input)

    do {
        let tokens = try lexer.lex()
        print("Lexer output: \(tokens)")
    } catch Lexer.Error.invalidCharacter(let character) {
        print("Input contained an invalid character: \(character)")
    } catch {
        print("An error occurred: \(error)")
    }
}
...
```

You add a catch block that is specifically looking for the **Lexer.Error.invalidCharacter** error. catch blocks support pattern matching, just like switch statements, so you can bind the invalid character to a constant for use within the catch block. You should see a more specific error message now:

```
Evaluating: 10 + 3 + 5
Lexer output: [Number: 10, Symbol: +, Number: 3, Symbol: +, Number: 5]
Evaluating: 1 + 2 + three
Input contained an invalid character: t
```

Congratulations, the lexing phase of your compiler is complete! Before moving on to parsing, delete the call to **evaluate(_:)** that is causing an error.

Listing 23.16 Removing bad input

```
...
evaluate("10 + 3 + 5")
evaluate("1 + 2 + three")
```

Parsing the Token Array

Now that your lexer is complete, you can turn an input string into an array of **Token**s, each of which is either a .number or a .plus. The next step is to write a parser whose job is to evaluate a series of tokens delivered to it from the lexer. For example, feeding [.number(5), .plus, .number(3)] through your parser should give you the answer 8. The algorithm to parse this sequence of tokens is more restrictive than the algorithm you used for lexing, because the order the tokens appear in is very important. The rules are:

- The first token must be a number.

- After parsing a number, either the parser must be at the end of input, or the next token must be .plus.

- After parsing a .plus, the next token must be a number.

The setup of your parser will be very similar to the lexer, although a bit simpler. The parser does not need separate **peek()** and **advance()** methods. They can be combined into one **getNextToken()** method that returns the next **Token** or nil if all tokens have been consumed.

Create the **Parser** class with a **getNextToken()** method.

Listing 23.17 Beginning the implementation of **Parser**

```
...
class Lexer {
    ...
}

class Parser {
    let tokens: [Token]
    var position = 0

    init(tokens: [Token]) {
        self.tokens = tokens
    }

    func getNextToken() -> Token? {
        guard position < tokens.count else {
            return nil
        }
        let token = tokens[position]
        position += 1
        return token
    }
}

func evaluate(_ input: String) {
    ...
}
...
```

A **Parser** is initialized with an array of tokens and begins with a position of 0. The **getNextToken()** method uses guard to check that there are more tokens remaining and, if there are, returns the next one, advancing position past the token it returns.

Two of the three rules for our parser used the phrase "must be a number." A good place to start implementing the parser is with a method to get a number. If the next token must be a number, there are two error cases that need to be considered. The parser might be at the end of the token array, which means there is no number left. Or the next token might be a .plus instead of a number. For example, the input string could be "10 +" or "10 + + 5".

Define an error enumeration conforming to **Error** for both of these cases.

Listing 23.18 Defining possible **Parser** errors

```
...
class Parser {
    enum Error: Swift.Error {
        case unexpectedEndOfInput
        case invalidToken(Token)
    }

    let tokens: [Token]
    var position = 0
    ...
}
...
```

Now that you can express the possible errors you might encounter when trying to get a number, add a method that gets the value of the next `.number` token or throws an error if it cannot.

Listing 23.19 Implementing **Parser.getNumber()**

```
...
class Parser {
    ...
    func getNextToken() -> Token? {
        guard position < tokens.count else {
            return nil
        }
        let token = tokens[position]
        position += 1
        return token
    }

    func getNumber() throws -> Int {
        guard let token = getNextToken() else {
            throw Parser.Error.unexpectedEndOfInput
        }

        switch token {
        case .number(let value):
            return value
        case .plus:
            throw Parser.Error.invalidToken(token)
        }
    }
}
...
```

The **getNumber()** method has the signature `() throws -> Int`, so you know it is a function that normally returns an **Int** but could throw an error.

You use a `guard` statement to check that there is at least one more token available. Note that inside the `else` block of a `guard`, you can use `throw` instead of `return`. This is because `guard` just requires that its `else` block causes the function to stop executing and return to its caller.

After ensuring that you have a token, you use a `switch` statement to either extract the number's value (if the token is a `.number`) or throw an **invalidToken** error (if it is a `.plus`).

Now that you have **getNumber()**, implementing the rest of the parsing algorithm is straightforward. Add a **parse()** method that does just that.

Listing 23.20 Implementing **Parser.parse()**

```
...
class Parser {
    ...
    func parse() throws -> Int {
        // Require a number first
        var value = try getNumber()

        while let token = getNextToken() {
            switch token {

            // Getting a plus after a number is legal
            case .plus:
                // After a plus, we must get another number
                let nextNumber = try getNumber()
                value += nextNumber

            // Getting a number after a number is not legal
            case .number:
                throw Parser.Error.invalidToken(token)
            }
        }

        return value
    }
}
...
```

Your implementation of **parse()** matches the algorithm outlined above for parsing. The input must start with a number (the initialization of value). After parsing a number, you enter a loop over the rest of the tokens. If the next token is .plus, then you require that the *next* token is a .number. When you get to the end of the tokens, the while loop ends and you return value.

There is something new here: You mark the calls to **getNumber()** with the try keyword, which Swift requires because **getNumber()** is a throwing method. However, you do not use a do/catch block. Why does Swift allow you to use try here without a do block?

Swift requires that any call marked with try "handles the error." It would be easy to assume that "handling the error" means catching the error, as in **evaluate(_:)**. But there is another perfectly reasonable way to handle an error: Throw it again. That is what happens in this case.

Because **parse()** is itself a throwing method, you are allowed to try calls inside it without using do/catch. If any of the try calls fail, the error is thrown out of **parse()**.

Your parser is now complete. Update **evaluate(_:)** to call the parser and to handle the specific errors that **Parser** might throw.

Listing 23.21 Updating **evaluate(_:)** to use **Parser**

```
...
func evaluate(_ input: String) {
    print("Evaluating: \(input)")
    let lexer = Lexer(input: input)

    do {
        let tokens = try lexer.lex()
        print("Lexer output: \(tokens)")

        let parser = Parser(tokens: tokens)
        let result = try parser.parse()
        print("Parser output: \(result)")
    } catch Lexer.Error.invalidCharacter(let character) {
        print("Input contained an invalid character: \(character)")
    } catch Parser.Error.unexpectedEndOfInput {
        print("Unexpected end of input during parsing")
    } catch Parser.Error.invalidToken(let token) {
        print("Invalid token during parsing: \(token)")
    } catch {
        print("An error occurred: \(error)")
    }
}
...
```

You should now see your two-phase compiler successfully evaluating the input expression:

```
Evaluating: 10 + 3 + 5
Lexer output: [Number: 10, Symbol: +, Number: 3, Symbol: +, Number: 5]
Parser output: 18
```

Try changing the input. Add more or fewer numbers. Try some inputs that will pass your lexer (i.e., that only contain legal tokens) but should cause your parser to throw errors. A couple of simple examples are "10 + 3 5" and "10 +".

Handling Errors by Sticking Your Head in the Sand

You have seen that every call to a function that might throw an error must be marked with `try` and that any call with `try` must either be inside a do/catch block or inside a function that itself is marked with `throws`. These rules work together to make sure you are handling any potential errors. Try modifying your **evaluate(_:)** function to break one of these rules.

Listing 23.22 Modifying **evaluate(_:)** illegally

```
...
func evaluate(_ input: String) {
    print("Evaluating: \(input)")
    let lexer = Lexer(input: input)
    let tokens = try lexer.lex()

    do {
        let tokens = try lexer.lex()
        print("Lexer output: \(tokens)")

        let parser = Parser(tokens: tokens)
        let result = try parser.parse()
        print("Parser output: \(result)")
    } catch Lexer.Error.invalidCharacter(let character) {
        print("Input contained an invalid character: \(character)")
    } catch Parser.Error.unexpectedEndOfInput {
        print("Unexpected end of input during parsing")
    } catch Parser.Error.invalidToken(let token) {
        print("Invalid token during parsing: \(token)")
    } catch {
        print("An error occurred: \(error)")
    }
}
...
```

You moved the `try lexer.lex()` call outside the do block, so now the compiler is giving you an error. The compiler error says that `Errors thrown from here are not handled`. It is possible to tell the Swift compiler that you do not want to handle potential errors. Change `try` to `try!`.

Listing 23.23 Using `try!` in **evaluate(_:)**

```
...
func evaluate(_ input: String) {
    print("Evaluating: \(input)")
    let lexer = Lexer(input: input)
    let tokens = try try! lexer.lex()
    ...
}
...
```

Your code now compiles, but you should be concerned. What is Swift going to do if an error is thrown by `lexer.lex()`? The exclamation mark at the end of the `try!` keyword should be a big hint. Just like force-unwrapping an optional, using the forceful keyword `try!` will cause your program to trap if an error is thrown.

Earlier, you had a call to **evaluate(_:)** that caused the lexer to throw an error. Add that call back in and see what happens.

Listing 23.24 Lexing bad input with try!

```
...
evaluate("10 + 3 + 5")
evaluate("1 + 2 + three")
```

Instead of seeing the invalid token error message, your program now traps on the try! lexer.lex() line.

We recommended avoiding force-unwrapped and implicitly unwrapped optionals. We even more strongly recommend avoiding try!. You should only use try! when there is no way for your program to handle an error and you really do want your program to trap (or crash, if it is running on a user's device) if an error occurs.

There is a third variant of try that lets you ignore the error without trapping if an error occurs. You can call a throwing function with try?, getting a return value that is an optional of whatever type the function usually returns. This means you need to use something like guard to check that the optional really contains a value.

Change your trapping try! into a combination of guard and try?.

Listing 23.25 Using try? in **evaluate(_:)**

```
...
func evaluate(_ input: String) {
    print("Evaluating: \(input)")
    let lexer = Lexer(input: input)
    let tokens = try! lexer.lex()
    guard let tokens = try? lexer.lex() else {
        print("Lexing failed, but I don't know why")
        return
    }
    ...
}
...
```

The real power of do/catch error handling is that a throws function can communicate to its caller the exact reason for the failure. This allows the caller to decide what to do next, such as present an alert to the user or try something else. If you do not care why the error occurred, only that it occurred at all, you can convert a throws function into an optional-returning function by calling it with try?.

evaluate(_:) *does* care about the error – it prints different messages to the user depending on what went wrong. So it is not a good candidate for try?, and you should restore the call site to use the regular try syntax.

Listing 23.26 Restoring **evaluate(_:)**

```
...
func evaluate(_ input: String) {
    print("Evaluating: \(input)")
    let lexer = Lexer(input: input)
    guard let tokens = try? lexer.lex() else {
        print("Lexing failed, but I don't know why")
        return
    }

    do {
        let tokens = try lexer.lex()
        print("Lexer output: \(tokens)")

        let parser = Parser(tokens: tokens)
        let result = try parser.parse()
        print("Parser output: \(result)")
    } catch Lexer.Error.invalidCharacter(let character) {
        print("Input contained an invalid character: \(character)")
    } catch Parser.Error.unexpectedEndOfInput {
        print("Unexpected end of input during parsing")
    } catch Parser.Error.invalidToken(let token) {
        print("Invalid token during parsing: \(token)")
    } catch {
        print("An error occurred: \(error)")
    }
}
...
```

Swift Error-Handling Philosophy

Swift is designed to encourage safe, easy-to-read code, and its error-handling system is no different. Any function that could fail must be marked with throws. This makes it obvious from the type of a function whether you need to handle potential errors.

Swift also requires you to mark all calls to functions that might fail with try. This gives a great benefit to anyone reading Swift code. If a function call is annotated with try, you know it is a potential source of errors that must be handled. If a function call is not annotated with try, you know it will never emit errors that you need to handle.

If you have used C++ or Java, it is important to note the differences between Swift error handling and exception-based error handling. Even though Swift uses some of the same terminology, particularly try, catch, and throw, Swift does not implement error handling using exceptions. When you mark a function with throws, that effectively changes its return type from whatever type it normally returns to "either whatever type it normally returns or an instance of the **Error** protocol."

Finally, there is one other important philosophical error-handling decision built into Swift. A function that throws does *not* state what kinds of errors it might throw. This has two practical impacts. First, you are always free to add more potential **Error**s that a function might throw without changing the API of the function. Second, when you are handling errors with catch, you must always be prepared to handle an error of some unknown type.

The compiler enforces this second point. Try modifying **evaluate(_:)** by removing the final catch block.

Listing 23.27 Avoiding handling unknown **ErrorTypes** in **evaluate(_:)**

```
...
func evaluate(_ input: String) {
    print("Evaluating: \(input)")
    let lexer = Lexer(input: input)

    do {
        let tokens = try lexer.lex()
        print("Lexer output: \(tokens)")

        let parser = Parser(tokens: tokens)
        let result = try parser.parse()
        print("Parser output: \(result)")
    } catch Lexer.Error.invalidCharacter(let character) {
        print("Input contained an invalid character: \(character)")
    } catch Parser.Error.unexpectedEndOfInput {
        print("Unexpected end of input during parsing")
    } catch Parser.Error.invalidToken(let token) {
        print("Invalid token during parsing: \(token)")
    } catch {
        print("An error occurred: \(error)")
    }
}
...
```

The compiler is now giving you errors on both lines in the do block where you made try calls. The error message reads Errors thrown from here are not handled because the enclosing catch is not exhaustive. As it does for switch statements, Swift performs exhaustiveness checks on your do/catch blocks, requiring you to handle any potential **Error**.

Fix **evaluate(_:)** by restoring the catch block that will handle any error.

Listing 23.28 Exhaustive error handling in **evaluate(_:)**

```
...
func evaluate(_ input: String) {
    print("Evaluating: \(input)")
    let lexer = Lexer(input: input)

    do {
        let tokens = try lexer.lex()
        print("Lexer output: \(tokens)")

        let parser = Parser(tokens: tokens)
        let result = try parser.parse()
        print("Parser output: \(result)")
    } catch Lexer.Error.invalidCharacter(let character) {
        print("Input contained an invalid character: \(character)")
    } catch Parser.Error.unexpectedEndOfInput {
        print("Unexpected end of input during parsing")
    } catch Parser.Error.invalidToken(let token) {
        print("Invalid token during parsing: \(token)")
    } catch {
        print("An error occurred: \(error)")
    }
}
...
```

Bronze Challenge

Your expression evaluator currently only supports addition. That is not very useful! Add support for subtraction. You should be able to call `evaluate("10 + 5 - 3 - 1")` and see it output 11.

Silver Challenge

The error messages printed out by **evaluate(_:)** are useful, but not as useful as they could be. Here are a couple of erroneous inputs and the error messages they produce:

```
evaluate("1 + 3 + 7a + 8")
> Input contained an invalid character: a

evaluate("10 + 3 3 + 7")
> Invalid token during parsing: .number(3)
```

Make these messages more helpful by including the character position where the error occurred. After completing this challenge, you should see error messages like this:

```
evaluate("1 + 3 + 7a + 8")
> Input contained an invalid character at index 9: a

evaluate("10 + 3 3 + 7")
> Invalid token during parsing at index 7: 3
```

Hint: You will need to associate error positions with your existing error cases. To convert a **String.Index** into an integral position, you can use the **distance(from:to:)** method on the string. For example, if input is a **String** and position is a **String.Index**, the following will compute how many characters separate the beginning of the string and position.

```
let distanceToPosition = input.distance(from: input.startIndex, to: position)
```

Gold Challenge

Time to step it up a notch. Add support for multiplication and division to your calculator. If you think this will be as easy as adding subtraction, think again! Your evaluator should give higher precedence to multiplication and division than it does to addition and subtraction. Here are some sample inputs and their expected output.

```
evaluate("10 * 3 + 5 * 3") // Should print 45
evaluate("10 + 3 * 5 + 3") // Should print 28
evaluate("10 + 3 * 5 * 3") // Should print 55
```

If you get stuck, try researching "recursive descent parsers." That is the kind of parser you have been implementing. Here is a hint to get you started: Instead of parsing a single number and then expecting a .plus or .minus, try parsing a term computed from numbers and multiplication/division operators, and *then* expecting a .plus or .minus.

For the More Curious: Storing Failable Results for Later

You have spent a great deal of time now writing and thinking about functions that do failable work. You have studied three ways that a function can let its caller know that it cannot produce its intended return value:

- Trap with **assert(_:_:)**, **precondition(_:_:)**, or **fatalError(_:)** if you want to indicate a nonrecoverable error state.

- Return an **Optional**, which is nil on failure, when the caller does not need to know why the failure occurred.

- Throw an **Error** in case the caller might want to react differently to different reasons for failure.

One downside to error-throwing functions is that they force you to handle the success or failure immediately, using a catch block. If you are not ready to process the result of the function call, your only option is to convert the result to an optional with try? (or trap on failures with try!, but that is an exceptional case). Converting a throwing function's output to an optional is a convenient way to capture your desired data on success, but it loses error information on failure.

Swift provides a data type that you can use to store the entire result of a throwing function for future use, whether the function succeeded and returned a value or failed and threw an error. That type is **Result**. Here is what it looks like to use **Result** to capture a throwing function's output:

```
let lexer = Lexer(input: "1 + 3 + 3 + 7")
let tokensResult = Result { try lexer.lex() }
```

The closure is using trailing closure syntax to call **Result(catching:)**, an initializer for **Result** that takes a throwing closure, calls it, and then stores the output. How does it store the output, if the output could be either a **[Token]** or an **Error**?

Result looks a lot like **Optional**. Here is the declaration of **Result** in the Swift standard library:

```
enum Result<Success, Failure> where Failure : Error {
    case .success(Success)
    case .failure(Failure)
}
```

Where **Optional** is a generic enum whose cases represent the presence or absence of a value, **Result** is a generic enum whose cases represent the success or failure of some operation. Its success case stores the ideal return type of the function (such as **[Token]**), and its failure case stores a thrown error. Notice that **Result** has a generic type constraint that whatever type fills in **Failure** must conform to **Error**.

Now the function's output has been tucked into a single enum that you can pass around in your program or store as a property of an object. You can also process it later using a switch statement:

```
switch tokensResult {
case let .success(tokens):
    print("Found \(tokens.count) tokens: \(tokens)")
case let .failure(error):
    print("Couldn't lex '\(lexer.input)': \(error)")
}
```

Result has several features for working with its cases. You could use its **map(_:)** method to transform the success value if there is one:

```
let numbersResult: Result<[Int],Error> = tokensResult.map {
    tokens.compactMap { token in
        switch token {
        case let .number(digit): return digit
        default: return nil
        }
    }
}
```

If the result is storing an error, the new result will store the same error. But if the result is storing data, the new result will store the transformed data. Note that **Optional** also has an implementation of **map(_:)**. Try it out!

Last, if you have a **Result** and you want to either return its data or throw its error, you can use its throwing **get()** method:

```
func extractNumbers(from result: Result<[Int],Error>) throws -> [Int] {
    return try result.get()
}
```

The **Result** type is a flexible way to store success/failure states that you need to cache or are not ready to process yet. As you grow as a Swift developer and explore asynchronous programming, you will encounter many frameworks that use **Result** for passing around the results of background work. For now, it is enough that you will recognize it when you see it in the wild.

24

Memory Management and ARC

This chapter brings together several topics from earlier in the book, especially Chapter 13 on closures and Chapter 15 on structs and classes, that all relate to managing the memory used by your programs.

All computer programs use memory, and most use memory dynamically: As a program runs, it allocates and deallocates memory as needed. An important role of any memory management system is managing object lifetimes, in particular ensuring that memory is not deallocated too soon or too late. Programming languages use different tools to manage memory; Java, for example, uses a garbage collector.

Swift uses *reference counting* to manage object lifetimes. In this chapter, you will investigate how the reference counting system works and learn what you can do to avoid memory leaks.

Memory Allocation

The allocation and deallocation of memory for value types – enumerations and structures – is handled for you. When you create a variable to store an instance of a value type, an appropriate amount of memory is automatically set aside for your instance, and your variable contains the entire value. Anything you do to pass the instance around, including passing it to a function and storing it in a property, creates a copy of the instance.

When a variable containing a value type instance is destroyed, such as when a function that creates one returns, Swift reclaims the memory that was occupied by the instance. Each copy lives an independent lifetime and is automatically destroyed when the variable holding it goes away. You do not have to do anything to manage the memory of value types.

You will need to know a little more about the memory management of reference types – specifically, class instances. When you create a new class instance, memory is allocated for the instance to use, just as it is for value types. The difference is in what happens when you pass the class instance around.

As you learned in Chapter 18 on value and reference types, passing a class instance to a function or storing it in a property creates an additional reference to the same memory, rather than copying the instance itself. Having multiple references to the same memory means that when any one of them changes the class instance, that change is apparent through any of its references.

This distinction raises an important question: When should a class instance deallocate? The answer is: when all the references to it are gone. Every class instance knows its *reference count*: the number of existing references to the instance. The instance remains allocated as long as its reference count is greater than 0. When the last reference to an instance is destroyed and the instance's reference count becomes 0, the system deallocates the instance and runs its **deinit** method.

The Swift compiler handles incrementing and decrementing instance reference counts so that you do not have to. This *Automatic Reference Counting* (ARC) feature helps ensure that class instances are destroyed at the correct time. However, logic errors in your program can cause objects to not deallocate when you are done with them. This is called a *memory leak*, and in this chapter you will learn how to prevent such errors by instructing the compiler to use variant memory management rules where appropriate.

To demonstrate these features, you are going to build a small program to model interacting with a storage vault. Create a new macOS command-line tool (as you did in Chapter 15) named CyclicalAssets.

Strong Reference Cycles

To start, you will define the types you will be interacting with: **Vault** and **Asset**. You will create one vault and multiple assets to put into the vault, and then you will observe how your code affects their lifetimes.

You are going to create a new file to model your vault. First, in the project navigator on the left side of the Xcode screen, click the yellow CyclicalAssets folder. This will ensure that the file appears in the correct location in your project. Next, create a new Swift file, Vault.swift, and define a **Vault** class that conforms to the **CustomStringConvertible** protocol:

Listing 24.1 Defining the **Vault** class (Vault.swift)

```
import Foundation

class Vault {
    let number: Int

    init(number: Int) {
        self.number = number
    }

    deinit {
        print("\(self) is being deallocated")
    }
}

extension Vault: CustomStringConvertible {
    var description: String {
        return "Vault(\(number))"
    }
}
```

The **Vault** class has a single property, which you set in its initializer. It conforms to the **CustomStringConvertible** protocol by implementing the description computed property in an extension. You add an implementation of **deinit** so you can see when a vault is being deallocated – that is, when its memory is being reclaimed because its reference count has dropped to 0.

In main.swift, define a class whose single method will be where you do the rest of your work, and create a **Vault** in it:

Listing 24.2 Creating the simulation (`main.swift`)

```
import Foundation

print("Hello, World!")

class Simulation {
    func run() {
        let vault13 = Vault(number: 13)
        print("Created \(vault13)")
    }
}

let simulation = Simulation()
simulation.run()
```

The **run()** method of the **Simulation** class is where all your experimentation will happen. You might be wondering why you are using this method, instead of just working at the top level of `main.swift`, like you did with MonsterTown.

You did this for two reasons: First, to define a *scope*, which you first learned about in Chapter 12 on functions. Scopes, as you might recall, are defined by pairs of braces ({ }). Functions and closures, conditionals, loops, and do/catch blocks all define scopes where their work is done.

Variables defined inside a scope (such as vault13, defined within **run()**'s scope) are reclaimed when that scope ends at the }. If the variable contained a value type instance, the end of the enclosing scope is where the instance is deallocated. If the variable contained a reference, the end of the enclosing scope is where the instance's reference count is decremented, possibly leading to its deallocation.

Instances that deallocate at the end of a program, on the other hand, do not execute their deinitializers. They do not need to; all the application's memory is being reclaimed anyway. So an instance method of a class, like **Simulation**'s **run()** method, provides an observable scope where you can model the memory management issues that can plague more complicated apps.

The second reason is related to tooling. In this chapter, you will use Xcode's Memory Graph Debugger to find and fix certain memory-related issues. If all you wanted to do was demonstrate object allocation and destruction, a do {} scope in `main.swift` would be plenty. But the Memory Graph Debugger is adept at finding memory issues in more complex applications built from relationships between types. So – for the sake of this exercise, to simulate an object graph more in line with the tool's expectations – you will run your experiments from within an instance method of a class.

Build and run your program. You should see the following output:

```
Created Vault(13)
Vault(13) is being deallocated
Program ended with exit code: 0
```

The vault13 variable contains a class instance – a reference type. By default, all references that you create are *strong references*, which means they increment the reference count of the instance they refer to for the duration of the existence of the reference. Therefore, the **Vault** instance has a reference count of 1 after it is created and a reference to it is stored in the vault13 variable.

When **run()** finishes executing, the vault13 variable falls out of scope and is destroyed, so the instance's reference count is decremented. You then see the Vault(13) is being deallocated message, because its reference count has dropped to 0.

Next, create a new Swift file called `Asset.swift` and define an **Asset** class that also conforms to **CustomStringConvertible**.

Listing 24.3 Defining the **Asset** class (`Asset.swift`)

```
import Foundation

class Asset {
    let name: String
    let value: Double
    var container: Vault?

    init(name: String, value: Double) {
        self.name = name
        self.value = value
    }

    deinit {
        print("\(self) is being deallocated")
    }
}

extension Asset: CustomStringConvertible {
    var description: String {
        if let container = container {
            return "Asset(\(name), worth \(value), in \(container))"
        } else {
            return "Asset(\(name), worth \(value), not stored anywhere)"
        }
    }
}
```

The **Asset** class is very similar to the **Vault** class so far. **Asset** has some useful properties, conforms to **CustomStringConvertible**, and prints a message when it is deallocated. It also has a variable stored property, `container`, which will refer to the **Vault** containing the asset. `container` is optional because it is reasonable for an asset to exist in the world without being in a vault.

Create a few assets in `main.swift`:

Listing 24.4 Creating assets (`main.swift`)

```
...
func run() {
    let vault13 = Vault(number: 13)
    print("Created \(vault13)")

    let coin: Asset = Asset(name: "Rare Coin", value: 1_000.0)
    let gem: Asset = Asset(name: "Big Diamond", value: 5_000.0)
    let poem: Asset = Asset(name: "Magnum Opus", value: 0.0)

    print("Created some assets: \([coin, gem, poem])")
}
...
```

Build and run your program. As with vault13, the three **Asset** instances deallocate when their only references are reclaimed at the end of **run()**:

```
Created Vault(13)
Created some assets: [Asset(Rare Coin, worth 1000.0, not stored anywhere),
    Asset(Big Diamond, worth 5000.0, not stored anywhere),
    Asset(Magnum Opus, worth 0.0, not stored anywhere)]
Asset(Magnum Opus, worth 0.0, not stored anywhere) is being deallocated
Asset(Big Diamond, worth 5000.0, not stored anywhere) is being deallocated
Asset(Rare Coin, worth 1000.0, not stored anywhere) is being deallocated
Vault(13) is being deallocated
Program ended with exit code: 0
```

Now you will make things interesting. It is time to fill the vault with assets and see what happens. Go back to Vault.swift and add a property and method for storing assets.

Listing 24.5 Letting a **Vault** store assets (Vault.swift)

```
class Vault {
    let number: Int

    private(set) var assets = [Asset]()

    init(number: Int) {
        self.number = number
    }

    deinit {
        print("\(self) is being deallocated")
    }

    func store(_ asset: Asset) {
        asset.container = self
        assets.append(asset)
    }
}
...
```

You add **assets**, an array of **Asset** instances that the vault contains, and **store(_:)**, a method to put an asset in a vault. **store(_:)** adds the asset passed in to it to the **assets** array and sets the asset's container property to refer back to the vault that the method is called on.

In `main.swift`, put a couple of the assets in your vault:

Listing 24.6 Vault 13 is storing assets (`main.swift`)

```
...
func run() {
    let vault13 = Vault(number: 13)
    print("Created \(vault13)")

    let coin: Asset = Asset(name: "Rare Coin", value: 1_000.0)
    let gem: Asset = Asset(name: "Big Diamond", value: 5_000.0)
    let poem: Asset = Asset(name: "Magnum Opus", value: 0.0)

    vault13.store(coin)
    vault13.store(gem)

    print("Created some assets: \([coin, gem, poem])")
}
...
```

Build and run again. The output may be surprising:

```
Created Vault(13)
Created some assets: [Asset(Rare Coin, worth 1000.0, in Vault(13)),
    Asset(Big Diamond, worth 5000.0, in Vault(13)),
    Asset(Magnum Opus, worth 0.0, not stored anywhere)]
Asset(Magnum Opus, worth 0.0, not stored anywhere) is being deallocated
Program ended with exit code: 0
```

The only instance being deallocated now is poem – its reference count dropped to 0 as expected at the end of the scope. coin and gem (which are in the vault) and the vault itself are no longer being deallocated. Why not?

Take a look at Figure 24.1, which shows the reference relationships before any of the variables are destroyed in **run()**.

Figure 24.1 CyclicalAssets before

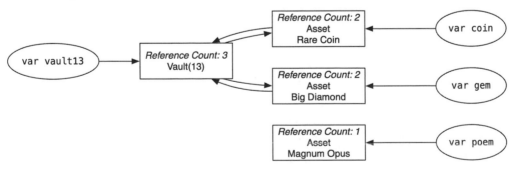

Each instance of **Vault** and **Asset** is depicted within a rectangle labeled with its current reference count. Remember, vault13 is not the instance itself, but is instead a *reference* to an instance of the **Vault** class. The reference count in the rectangle is exactly the number of arrows pointing to the instance – the number of references to the instance.

As your **run()** function returns, those references go away, leaving what you see in Figure 24.2.

Figure 24.2 CyclicalAssets after

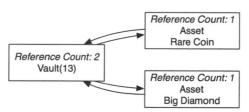

You have created two *strong reference cycles*, which is the term for when two instances have strong references to each other. Vault 13 has a reference to the coin (via its `assets` property), and the coin has a reference to Vault 13 (via its `container` property). Same for Vault 13 and the gem. The memory for these instances is no longer reachable – all the variables containing references to them are gone – but the memory will never be reclaimed because each instance still has a reference count greater than 0.

Strong reference cycles are one kind of memory leak. Your application allocated the memory necessary to store Vault 13 and its two assets, but it did not return that memory to the system, even after your program no longer needed it.

Without the console, how could you have known about these memory leaks? Xcode can show them to you directly.

Xcode has several built-in tools that you can use to try to identify leaked objects and the references to them. You will take a look at one of these tools, the Memory Graph Debugger, in a moment. But first, to allow it to examine your program, you need your application to keep running when it reaches the end of `main.swift`. Add this line to `main.swift`:

Listing 24.7 Keeping the app running (`main.swift`)

```
...
let simulation = Simulation()
simulation.run()
dispatchMain()
```

The **dispatchMain** function starts an infinite loop. It is intended to be used by event-driven applications to check for user input or other events, but it is a handy trick to use here to keep your program running after your code is done executing.

Build and run your program again and observe the output:

```
Created Vault(13)
Created some assets: [Asset(Rare Coin, worth 1000.0, in Vault(13)),
    Asset(Big Diamond, worth 5000.0, in Vault(13)),
    Asset(Magnum Opus, worth 0.0, not stored anywhere)]
Asset(Magnum Opus, worth 0.0, not stored anywhere) is being deallocated
```

Notice that the message `Program ended with exit code: 0` is missing, because the program is still running. There is also a message confirming this in the Xcode main toolbar (Figure 24.3):

Figure 24.3 CyclicalAssets is running

In the debug area, just above your output console, find and click the button for the Memory Graph Debugger (⅏), indicated in Figure 24.4.

Figure 24.4 Using the Memory Graph Debugger

Your source code will disappear and be replaced after a few seconds by a diagram of objects in your application, which should look something like Figure 24.5. (If the diagram does not load, you may need to relaunch Xcode. If a graph loads but looks different than the one shown here, hang on – we will explain in a moment how to view the graphs for different instances.)

Figure 24.5 Memory graph for an **Asset**

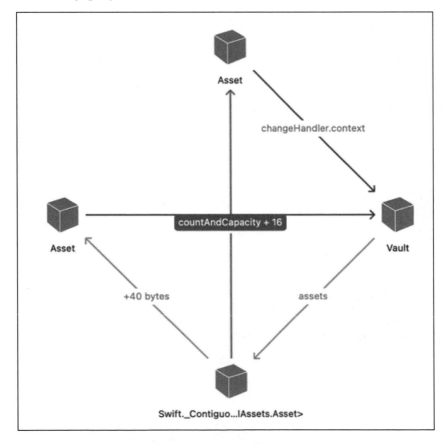

Look at the debug navigator on the left side of the Xcode window. The Memory Graph Debugger has listed all the allocations from all the frameworks and modules in your application. You only care about those from your own code, which are conveniently at the top of the list (Figure 24.6):

Figure 24.6 Allocations in CyclicalAssets

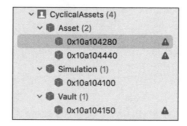

Each item in this list is an instance of the type that it is listed under. If the editor area does not look like the graph in Figure 24.5, select the first **Asset** in the list to see the graph.

Notice the purple triangles (⚠)? They are like the symbol Xcode uses to indicate a warning in your code, but a different color. These symbols indicate instances that have leaked. Sure enough, your program has leaked two instances of **Asset** and one of **Vault**.

In your graph, you should see four allocations: Two called Asset, one called Vault, and one called something like _ContiguousAr...torage<Asset>. The last one begins with an underscore (_) to let you know that it is one of Apple's private types; it represents the assets array.

If you follow the arrows in this diagram, you will see that they represent the same thing as Figure 24.2: A pair of reference cycles, one between each **Asset** and the **Vault**, with the assets array making up the third node in each cycle.

In short: The vault owns an array, which contains references to the assets, which have references back to the vault.

Whew! That was a lot to parse. The Xcode Memory Graph Debugger is a great tool to use when you want to look for memory leaks. It will show you the shape of the leak (the other objects and references involved), which can help you figure out how to fix them. (You will fix this leak shortly.)

If this tool feels intimidating at first, that is normal. It can sometimes show you useful data quickly – but if you look at it and do not find the graph helpful, you can always use other strategies, like adding **print()** statements to your **deinit** methods.

Click the Continue button (▷) in the debug toolbar to exit the Memory Graph Debugger and return to your code.

Breaking Strong Reference Cycles with weak

The solution to a strong reference cycle is to break the cycle. You could manually break the cycles by looping over each asset and setting its container to nil while you have access to those variables (before the function ends), but that would be tedious and error prone.

Instead, Swift provides a keyword to get the same effect automatically. Modify **Asset** to make the container property a *weak reference* instead of a strong reference.

Listing 24.8 Making the container property a weak reference (Asset.swift)

```
class Asset {
    let name: String
    let value: Double
    weak var container: Vault?
    ...
}
```

A weak reference is not included in the reference count of the instance it refers to. In this case, making container a weak reference means that when you assign Vault 13 as the container of the coin and the gem, Vault 13's reference count does not increase. The only strong reference to Vault 13 is the vault13 variable in main.swift.

Now, when the vault13 variable is destroyed at the end of **run()**, the reference count on Vault 13 drops to 0, so it is deallocated. When Vault 13 is deallocated, it no longer holds a strong reference to its assets, so their reference counts drop to 0 as well.

Run your program again. (Xcode will ask you whether you want to stop CyclicalAssets, because it is already running. Click Stop to terminate the old instance and launch a new one.) Confirm that all the objects are deallocated:

```
Created Vault(13)
Created some assets: [Asset(Rare Coin, worth 1000.0, in Vault(13)),
    Asset(Big Diamond, worth 5000.0, in Vault(13)),
    Asset(Magnum Opus, worth 0.0, not stored anywhere)]
Asset(Magnum Opus, worth 0.0, not stored anywhere) is being deallocated
Vault(13) is being deallocated
Asset(Rare Coin, worth 1000.0, not stored anywhere) is being deallocated
Asset(Big Diamond, worth 5000.0, not stored anywhere) is being deallocated
```

You can check the Memory Graph Debugger again to verify that there are no vaults or assets remaining in memory. Only the **Simulation** that you defined in main.swift remains.

What happens to a weak reference if the instance it refers to is deallocated? The weak reference is set to nil as soon as the instance begins to deallocate. You can see this by looking closely at your console output:

```
...
Vault(13) is being deallocated
Asset(Rare Coin, worth 1000.0, not stored anywhere) is being deallocated
Asset(Big Diamond, worth 5000.0, not stored anywhere) is being deallocated
```

Your log statements show that the **Vault** begins deallocating (logging its **deinit**) first. It then destroys its properties, including the assets array (which is a value type, so the whole array is destroyed). When the array deallocates, so do the references it contains, which causes the **Asset** reference counts to fall to 0, allowing them to begin deallocating. As each asset begins deallocating, its own **deinit** executes, showing that, since the vault has already begun to deallocate, the weak container references to it have already been set to nil.

There are two requirements for weak references:

- Weak references must always be declared as var, not let.

- Weak references must always be declared as optional.

Both of these requirements are the result of weak references being changed to nil if the instance they refer to is deallocated. The only types that can become nil are optionals, so weak references must be optional. And instances declared with let cannot change, so weak references must be declared with var.

In most cases, strong reference cycles like the one you just resolved are easy to avoid. **Vault** is a class that stores assets, so it makes sense that it would keep strong references to the assets. **Asset** is a class that is contained by a **Vault**. If it wants a reference to its container, that reference should be weak. When faced with two types that want references to each other, try to determine which one is the "parent" object in the relationship. That is the object that should "own" the other object with a strong reference.

Not all strong reference cycles are caused by objects with explicit properties referring to one another. Recall from Chapter 13 that closures can capture variables from their surrounding scope. By default, closures also keep strong references to any class instances that they capture.

Reference Cycles with Closures

Sometimes assets appreciate or depreciate in value. To demonstrate some closure-related memory management behavior, you will teach **Asset** instances to react to changes in their value using a provided closure.

In your **Asset** type, allow value to be mutable and react to value changes by executing a stored closure of type **(Asset) -> Void**.

Listing 24.9 Reacting to changes in asset value (Asset.swift)

```swift
class Asset {
    let name: String
    let value: Double
    var value: Double {
        didSet {
            changeHandler(value - oldValue)
        }
    }
    weak var container: Vault?

    typealias ValueChangeHandler = (Double) -> Void
    var changeHandler: ValueChangeHandler = {_ in}

    init(name: String, value: Double) {
        self.name = name
        self.value = value
    }

    deinit {
        print("\(self) is being deallocated")
    }
}
...
```

Asset now defines a typealias, **ValueChangeHandler**, which is a closure that takes a **Double** (the amount by which the value has changed) and returns nothing. **Asset** also has a new property, changeHandler, which stores a **ValueChangeHandler** closure. The default value of this property is an empty closure that discards its argument by using an underscore for the local parameter name.

Any other object, such as a vault that contains an asset, can give the asset a new changeHandler closure. The asset will execute this closure every time its value changes using a didSet property observer. This strategy allows other objects to react to changes in an asset's value by telling the asset what to do in response to changes in value.

But the strategy must be implemented with care, as you will see.

Update Vault.swift to report its net worth every time an asset's value changes.

Listing 24.10 Reporting total value when an asset changes (Vault.swift)

```swift
class Vault {
    let number: Int

    private(set) var assets = [Asset]()

    var totalValue: Double = 0
    #warning("Implement totalValue as a computed property")
    ...
}
```

To report your vault's total value, you need a totalValue property to report. It should be a computed property, calculated by summing the values of the assets. But that is a distraction; you are busy right now and focused on changeHandler, so for now you just tell the compiler to warn you about this unfinished business.

The #warning expression is special. It causes a compiler warning with the specified message. There is also an #error expression to force a compiler error. These expressions are very handy when you are deep in code and need to leave yourself a reminder to come back and fix or finish something.

Sometimes, when warnings have popped up during exercises in this book, we have told you to ignore them for the moment. Our goal was to minimize distraction and move on with the exercise. But when you are writing production code, you should not leave warnings unaddressed. Even though a program with warnings will compile to allow you to run and test your code, a warning means that there is probably a logic error in the program that will have runtime consequences.

Since you, as a conscientious programmer, will never have unintended warnings hanging out in your code, the #warning expression can be a useful tool to keep track of issues you know you need to fix. In Chapter 23 you used a // TODO: comment for this purpose. Compiler warnings are a more in-your-face way to accomplish the same goal. Which you prefer is up to you.

Now, update your **store(_:)** to set a new changeHandler on the new asset. This change will introduce an error, which you will fix in the next step.

Listing 24.11 Setting the changeHandler on new assets (Vault.swift)

```
...
func store(_ asset: Asset) {
    asset.container = self
    asset.changeHandler = { (change) in
        print("An asset has changed value by \(change).
            New total value: \(totalValue)")
    }
    assets.append(asset)
}
...
```

Also update your simulation to account for your coin appreciating in value:

Listing 24.12 Rare coins gaining value (main.swift)

```
...
func run() {
    let vault13 = Vault(number: 13)
    print("Created \(vault13)")

    let coin: Asset = Asset(name: "Rare Coin", value: 1_000.0)
    let gem: Asset = Asset(name: "Big Diamond", value: 5_000.0)
    let poem: Asset = Asset(name: "Magnum Opus", value: 0.0)

    vault13.store(coin)
    vault13.store(gem)

    print("Created some assets: \([coin, gem, poem])")

    coin.value += 137
}
...
```

Try to build your program now. You will get an error message reading Reference to property 'totalValue' in closure requires explicit use of 'self' to make capture semantics explicit.

By default, any variable or constant of reference type is a strong reference. Closure-captured references are no different, and the strong reference exists as long as the closure does.

Look again at the closure in **store(_:)**. At first glance, it appears that the closure only captures value types: Both change and totalValue are **Double**s. However, since the compiler cannot be sure that the value of a property like totalValue will not change after the closure is created, the closure instead captures the object that *owns* the property, so that it can access the property and read any fresh or computed value it may have.

Since totalValue is a property on **Vault**, which is the type of self within the scope of the closure, a strong reference to the **Vault** instance itself is captured. Swift wants you to notice this capture, hence the error. By requiring you to explicitly reference self, Swift makes you consider whether you are creating a strong reference cycle – and therefore a memory leak.

Fix the error:

Listing 24.13 Explicitly accessing `self` in a closure (`Vault.swift`)

```
...
func store(_ asset: Asset) {
    asset.container = self
    asset.changeHandler = { (change) in
        print("An asset has changed value by \(change).
                New total value: \(self.totalValue)")
    }
    assets.append(asset)
}
...
```

Build and run your program. Your output should look like this:

```
Created Vault(13)
Created some assets: [Asset(Rare Coin, worth 1000.0, in Vault(13)),
    Asset(Big Diamond, worth 5000.0, in Vault(13)),
    Asset(Magnum Opus, worth 0.0, not stored anywhere)]
An asset has changed value by 137.0. New total value: 0.0
Asset(Magnum Opus, worth 0.0, not stored anywhere) is being deallocated
```

The coin's value is changing, but the coin, gem, and vault are failing to deallocate again.

The fact that the closure strongly captures the vault explains why you are leaking memory: The **Asset** actually *does* have a strong reference back to **Vault**. The **Vault** owns an array of **Asset**s, and each **Asset** has a changeHandler closure that has captured a strong reference back to the **Vault**. This cycle is shown in Figure 24.7.

Figure 24.7 Closure-capture strong reference cycle

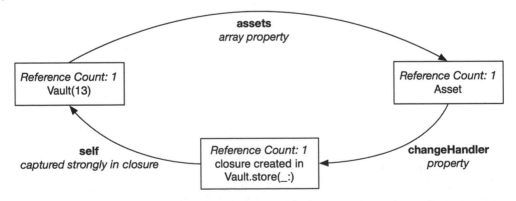

Think about the error message you saw: `...requires explicit use of 'self'...`. Swift could allow you to use `self` implicitly in closures, but doing so would make it very easy to accidentally create strong reference cycles. Instead, the language usually requires you to be explicit about your use of `self`, forcing you to consider whether a reference cycle is a possibility.

In cases where the compiler knows a reference cycle is impossible, such as when `self` is a value type (and therefore is copied rather than referenced by the closure), you do not need to be explicit with `self`.

To change the capture semantics of a closure to capture references weakly, you can use a *capture list*. Modify `Vault.swift` to use a capture list when creating the closure.

Listing 24.14 Using a capture list (`Vault.swift`)

```
...
func store(_ asset: Asset) {
    asset.container = self
    asset.changeHandler = { [weak self] (change) in
        print("An asset has changed value by \(change).
            New total value: \(self.totalValue)")
            New total value: \(String(describing: self?.totalValue))")
    }
    assets.append(asset)
}
...
```

The capture list syntax is a list of variables inside square brackets (`[]`) immediately before the list of the closure arguments. The capture list you wrote here tells Swift to capture `self` weakly instead of strongly. Now that the **Asset**'s closure no longer strongly references the **Vault**, the strong reference cycle is broken.

Do not miss the new use of `self?` in the body of the closure. Because `self` is captured weakly, and all weak instances must be optional, `self` inside the closure is optional.

As an aside, you can also use a capture list to acknowledge an intentional strong capture of self, eliminating the need for explicitly referencing `self` throughout the closure. Do not change your code, but here is what it would look like:

```
asset.changeHandler = { [self] (change) in
    print("An asset has changed value by \(change).
            New total value: \(totalValue)")
}
```

You should only do this if you have code elsewhere in your program that will break the reference cycle another way, such as making `changeHandler` optional and setting it to `nil` later in the program. Your program does not have any special handling of this closure relationship to make the reference cycle temporary, so ensuring that `self` is only captured weakly is the safe move.

Run your program again and confirm that all the instances are being deallocated appropriately:

```
...
An asset has changed value by 137.0. New total value: Optional(0.0)
Asset(Magnum Opus, worth 0.0, not stored anywhere) is being deallocated
Vault(13) is being deallocated
Asset(Rare Coin, worth 1137.0, not stored anywhere) is being deallocated
Asset(Big Diamond, worth 5000.0, not stored anywhere) is being deallocated
```

Once again, the strong reference cycle is broken, and all your objects are deallocating when you expect them to.

Escaping and Non-Escaping Closures

Imagine that – rather than using an empty closure as the default value of **Asset**'s changeHandler property – you wanted to let its initializer take an initial value. In Asset.swift, remove the default value from the property and add it as the default value of an initializer argument:

Listing 24.15 Accepting a changeHandler argument (Asset.swift)

```
...
typealias ValueChangeHandler = (Double) -> Void
var changeHandler: ValueChangeHandler = { _ in }

init(name: String, value: Double, changeHandler: ValueChangeHandler = { _ in }) {
    self.name = name
    self.value = value
    self.changeHandler = changeHandler
}
...
```

Because the empty closure is the default value for the changeHandler argument of your initializer, current call sites that are not passing this new argument remain valid.

But you now have a new error: Assigning non-escaping parameter 'changeHandler' to an @escaping closure. What do @escaping and *non-escaping* mean?

You have seen that the compiler helps look for possible strong reference cycles. When you assign a closure to a property of another object, you know that closure might exist for a while, and that objects that have been strongly captured by the closure cannot deallocate before the closure itself does. Setting a closure property always means that you must be on the lookout for possible reference cycles.

But passing a closure as a function argument can be less risky. If the function will execute the closure before the function returns, never passing the closure anywhere else, then there is no possibility of a strong reference cycle. The closure might still strongly capture its scope, but it does not matter, because the closure will be destroyed when the function returns – also destroying any strong references it captured.

A closure argument like this that will not escape the function's own scope is called *non-escaping*. You do not need to worry about closure-captured strong reference cycles with non-escaping closure arguments.

On the other hand, when a function accepts a closure argument that it might store in a property or pass to another function, the closure is called *escaping*. Swift wants developers to be aware of escaping closure arguments so they know to look out for strong reference cycles and consider using a capture list to change strong captures into weak ones. Swift enforces this warning by requiring that escaping closure arguments be marked with the @escaping attribute.

An *attribute* – a keyword prefixed with @ – gives the compiler extra information about a variable or function declaration. In this case, @escaping communicates that the closure can escape its scope, which affects which other warnings and errors you might get related to the closure. You will see more attributes later in this book.

Now you know how to fix the error:

Listing 24.16 Marking escaping closures with @escaping (Asset.swift)

```
...
init(name: String, value: Double,
     changeHandler: @escaping ValueChangeHandler = {_ in}) {
    self.name = name
    self.value = value
    self.changeHandler = changeHandler
}
...
```

ARC is an amazing feature of Swift that protects you from lots of possible memory problems. Still, you should always be vigilant when working with reference types – and especially with closures – to ensure that you do not create memory leaks.

Having said that, do not worry about memory leaks causing problems with your computer. When a program like CyclicalAssets stops running, all memory (including any leaked memory) is reclaimed by the OS. However, memory leaks are still serious, and even more so in iOS than in macOS. iOS tracks how much memory each app uses and will terminate apps that use too much. When an app leaks memory, that memory still counts as part of the app's total memory usage, even though it is no longer needed or useful.

Tin Challenge

It feels like we forgot to get back to something. What could it be?

Hint: Check your warnings. See how useful that was?

Bronze Challenge

The idea of asset containment by a **Vault** is incomplete. **Vault** has a way to store an asset, but no way to remove an asset. Update **Vault** to allow asset removal and use this feature in **run()**.

Gold Challenge

What if you want to be able to access other properties of the asset that changed? In Vault.swift, print the details of the changing asset in the new changeHandler:

Listing 24.17 Logging the changed asset (Vault.swift)

```
...
func store(_ asset: Asset) {
    asset.container = self
    asset.changeHandler = { [weak self] change in
        print("An asset \(asset) has changed value by \(change).
                New total value: \(String(describing: self?.totalValue))")
    }
    assets.append(asset)
}
...
```

Notice that the asset is now being interpolated into the printed string.

Does this introduce any new strong reference cycles? If so, fix them.

For the More Curious: A Bit of History

Prior to the introduction of Swift in 2014, macOS and iOS applications were written in Objective-C, with some C and possibly even C++.

ARC was introduced for Objective-C in 2011. Prior to ARC, developers were responsible for manual reference counting: manually incrementing and decrementing the reference counts of class instances. Every class had an instance method to *retain* the instance (increment its reference count) and a method to *release* the instance (decrement its reference count).

The rules for knowing when to retain and release an instance were relatively straightforward in theory, but easy to mess up in practice. As you can probably imagine, manual reference counting was the source of many bugs: If you retained an instance too many times, it would never get deallocated (causing a memory leak), and if you released an instance too many times, a crash would usually result.

Imagine an instance method responsible for updating the value of a private stored property of a class. Manual reference counting code, if it could be written with Swift, might look something like this:

```
class SomeClass {
    private var someObject: SomeOtherClass()

    func setSomeObject(newObject: SomeOtherClass) {
        // Increment ref count of new instance to keep it alive
        newObject.retain()
        // Decrement ref count of old instance; it might deallocate
        someObject.release()
        // Actually assign our property to refer to the new instance
        someObject = newObject
    }
}
```

We are happy to say that Swift's ARC feature not only takes care of this for you automatically but also does so in an efficient way that increases the performance of your application. It does not just insert calls to methods like **retain()** and **release()** behind the scenes – nothing like these methods actually exists in Swift. Instead, the compiler does reference counting work much more aggressively and at a much lower level than your code.

For the More Curious: Do I Have the Only Reference?

Unfortunately, Swift does not give you access to the actual reference count of any instances. (Although recall from Chapter 18 that you can ask if a variable is the *only* reference to an instance via the `isKnownUniquelyReferenced(_:)` function.)

Even if you could ask an instance what its reference count was, the answer you got might not be what you expected. Throughout this chapter, we said things like, "At this point, the reference count is 2." That was an innocent lie.

Conceptually, it is perfectly reasonable and even helpful for you to think of reference counts the way we described. Under the hood, the compiler is free to insert additional changes to the reference count wherever it decides that your code can be optimized. As long as it does its job correctly, there is no harm to your program. If you could ask what the actual reference count of an instance is, the answer would depend on what sort of analysis the compiler had done at that point. Additionally, there are some classes in Apple's system libraries that behave in strange ways when it comes to reference counting (the details of which are beyond the scope of this book).

The important things for you to remember are how to recognize the potential for strong reference cycles and how to use weak to break them.

25

Equatable, Comparable, and Hashable

You have spent a lot of time now learning to model data. You have explored value types and reference types and the "free" features that you can sometimes get from them, such as compiler-synthesized empty initializers.

You have also seen useful behaviors that are enabled for you when you conform to certain protocols from the Swift standard library. For example, conforming to **CustomStringConvertible** and implementing its required `description` property lets you customize how instances of your types will print to the console. Conforming to **Error** allows instances of your types to be thrown as errors from functions that do failable work.

There are other common behaviors that you can unlock by conforming to standard library protocols. In this chapter, you will learn about three important protocols and the features that they offer your custom types.

Equatable

Create a new playground called Comparison to work in. The first feature you will examine is the ability to compare two instances of a type using the == operator. Begin by creating a new struct and two equal instances of it.

Listing 25.1 Defining **Point**

```
import Cocoa

var str = "Hello, playground"

struct Point {
    let x: Int
    let y: Int
    let label: String? = nil
}

let a = Point(x: 3, y: 4)                                   Point
let b = Point(x: 3, y: 4)                                   Point
```

The struct above defines a **Point** type. **Point**'s x and y properties describe a location on a two-dimensional plane. Its label is an optional string that might tell a user what the point is used for.

You know that these two points are equal; you created them with the same x, y, and label values. However, the **Point** type does not know how to determine whether one instance is equal to another. Try asking your program whether they are equal using the == operator.

Listing 25.2 Is a the same as b?

```
...
let a = Point(x: 3, y: 4)                                Point
let b = Point(x: 3, y: 4)                                Point
let abEqual = (a == b)
```

This check for equality does not work. In fact, it generates an error from the compiler. This error stems from the fact that you have not yet taught your **Point** struct how to test for equality between two instances.

To tell the compiler "I intend to equate two instances of this type," you start by declaring that your type wants to conform to the **Equatable** protocol.

Listing 25.3 Adding a protocol conformance declaration

```
struct Point: Equatable {
    let x: Int
    let y: Int
    let label: String? = nil
}

let a = Point(x: 3, y: 4)                                Point
let b = Point(x: 3, y: 4)                                Point
let abEqual = (a == b)                                   true
```

The errors are gone, and the results sidebar shows that your test for equality between a and b succeeds. The two points are equal because their x, y, and label values are the same.

(Try changing just the x values so that they do not match. You should see that the two points are no longer equal. Make sure to change the values back before proceeding.)

Wait, is that really it?

Mostly, yes. You have already seen behavior that Swift implements on your behalf, such as the free initializers you learned about in Chapter 17. Swift and its compiler are doing work for you here as well.

The **Equatable** protocol has one requirement: an implementation of the == function. You have not implemented this function for **Point** – but just as the compiler can synthesize initializers, it can synthesize some other common function implementations. Among them, the compiler can synthesize == for an **Equatable** struct whose properties are all also **Equatable**. It will do the same for **Equatable** enums whose raw values or associated values are **Equatable**. (It cannot synthesize == for classes.)

The free implementation of ==, which you are taking advantage of for **Point**, checks the equality of every property on the two instances and returns true only if all the properties are equal.

You can also provide your own implementation of ==. Do so now, making sure to add the function definition inside the **Point** struct's definition.

Listing 25.4 Providing an implementation of ==

```
struct Point: Equatable {
    let x: Int
    let y: Int
    let label: String? = nil

    static func ==(lhs: Point, rhs: Point) -> Bool {
        return (lhs.x == rhs.x) && (lhs.y == rhs.y) && (lhs.label == rhs.label)
    }
}
...
```

Operator implementations can be written either as global functions or as static methods on the types they operate on. Protocols cannot require global functions, so the **Equatable** protocol declares its requirement in the form of a static method. In either case, the operator is the name of the function.

The == function takes two arguments of type **Point**. Called lhs and rhs, they represent the values that appear on the lefthand side and righthand side of the operator when it is used. Your implementation returns true only if the x, y, and label properties of both instances are all equal. This is identical to the implementation that the compiler previously synthesized for you.

For a type that is not eligible for **Equatable** synthesis (such as a class or a struct with non-**Equatable** properties), you must implement == yourself. And sometimes you just do not want the free implementation. Suppose you do not care about points' labels. In that case, two instances of Point having equal values for x and y would be enough for you to consider them equal and interchangeable. You would write your own implementation that only tests the values of x and y.

You have seen that organizing your code by implementing protocol conformance in an extension is common. Move your implementation of == into an extension and update it to disregard the labels:

Listing 25.5 Moving protocol conformance to an extension

```
struct Point: Equatable {
    let x: Int
    let y: Int
    let label: String? = nil

    static func ==(lhs: Point, rhs: Point) -> Bool {
        return (lhs.x == rhs.x) && (lhs.y == rhs.y) && (lhs.label == rhs.label)
    }
}

extension Point: Equatable {
    static func ==(lhs: Point, rhs: Point) -> Bool {
        return (lhs.x == rhs.x) && (lhs.y == rhs.y)
    }
}
...
```

Your instances are still equal, and **Point** is now a well-organized **Equatable** type.

Infix operators

It may feel strange to declare == as a static method. In Chapter 15, you learned that static methods are defined on a type. But you do not call this method on the **Point** type, like Point.==(a, b).

Indeed, operators like == are declared at the global level in Swift. The == operator is declared like this in the Swift standard library:

```
precedencegroup ComparisonPrecedence {
    higherThan: LogicalConjunctionPrecedence
}

infix operator == : ComparisonPrecedence
```

Do not worry about what a precedencegroup is right now; that is discussed in the section called *For the More Curious: Custom Operators* at the end of this chapter.

But do note that the == operator is declared as an infix operator. This means that its implementation is executed by placing the operator between the two instances it will operate on. Hence, you called **Point**'s implementation of == via this code in the example above: (a == b).

The Swift compiler knows to check both in the global scope and inside types for implementations of operators. Placing them inside types as static methods is the more stylish approach.

Buy one method, get another free!

Your **Point** struct now conforms to **Equatable**, so you can test **Point**s for equality. And it turns out that you can check for inequality, too. Try it out:

Listing 25.6 Is a not the same as b?

```
...
let a = Point(x: 3, y: 4)                                          Point
let b = Point(x: 3, y: 4)                                          Point
let abEqual = (a == b)                                             true
let abNotEqual = (a != b)                                          false
```

As the results sidebar shows, this test for inequality yields false (because the points are, in fact, equal).

Swift's standard library provides a default implementation of the != function via an extension to the **Equatable** protocol. This default implementation uses the definition of == and negates the result. So if your type conforms to **Equatable**, then it also has a working implementation of the != function – whether it uses the default implementation of == or its own version.

Comparable

Now that your **Point** type conforms to the **Equatable** protocol, you may be interested in more nuanced forms of comparison. For example, perhaps you want to know if one point is less than another point. As with equality, types must define for themselves what it means for one instance to be "less than" another. You define this functionality by conforming to the **Comparable** protocol.

Start by reviewing the documentation for **Comparable**. You have not typed it anywhere yet, so you cannot Option-click its name. Instead, open Xcode's Help menu and select Developer Documentation.

Search the documentation for "Comparable" and select the result for the **Comparable** protocol in the Swift standard library. Under "Conforming to the Comparable Protocol," you will find that you need to implement the < infix operator as well as the == operator. Update the extension on your struct to make it conform to **Comparable**:

Listing 25.7 Conforming to **Comparable**

```
...
extension Point: Equatable, Comparable {
    static func ==(lhs: Point, rhs: Point) -> Bool {
        return (lhs.x == rhs.x) && (lhs.y == rhs.y)
    }

    static func <(lhs: Point, rhs: Point) -> Bool {
        return (lhs.x < rhs.x) && (lhs.y < rhs.y)
    }
}
...
```

Your implementation of the < function works similarly to your implementation of the == function. It checks whether the point passed in on the lefthand side is less than the point passed in on the righthand side. If the x and y values for the point on the lefthand side are both smaller than the values on the righthand side, the function will return true. Otherwise, the function will return false, indicating that the point on the lefthand side is not less than the righthand side.

Create two new points to test this function.

Listing 25.8 Testing the < function

```
...
let abEqual = (a == b)                                    true
let abNotEqual = (a != b)                                 false

let c = Point(x: 2, y: 6)                                 Point
let d = Point(x: 3, y: 7)                                 Point
let cdEqual = (c == d)                                    false
let cLessThanD = (c < d)                                  true
```

You create two new points with different values for x and y. You check whether c and d are equal, which returns false: The two points are not the same. Then, you exercise your < function to determine whether c is less than d. The comparison evaluates to true; c is less than d because both its x and y values are smaller than d's values.

As with implementing == to conform to **Equatable**, implementing < to conform to **Comparable** gives you bonus functionality. The Swift standard library defines the >, >=, and <= operators in terms of the < and == operators. This is why **Comparable** only requires that you overload the < and == operators. If your type conforms to **Comparable**, then it will get implementations of the other operators for free.

Note that – unlike for == and **Equatable** – the compiler cannot synthesize the required < function for you. You must provide your own implementation, carefully considering what it means for your program for one instance to be less than another. Should it mean that all properties are less? Or something else? For example, should it mean that one point is closer to the origin (0,0) than the other? Your implementation should reflect your decision.

Test your free functionality by adding a series of new comparisons.

Listing 25.9 Exercising comparisons

```
...
let cdEqual = (c == b)                                    false
let cLessThanD = (c < d)                                  true

let cLessThanEqualD = (c <= d)                            true
let cGreaterThanD = (c > d)                               false
let cGreaterThanEqualD = (c >= d)                         false
```

These last three comparisons check whether:

- c is less than or equal to d
- c is greater than d
- c is greater than or equal to d

As anticipated, these comparisons evaluate to true, false, and false, respectively.

You can also make a **Range** of any **Comparable** type. Add this to your playground:

Listing 25.10 Ranges of comparable types

```
...
let cLessThanEqualD = (c <= d)                            true
let cGreaterThanD = (c > d)                               false
let cGreaterThanEqualD = (c >= d)                         false

let pointRange = c..<d                                    {{x 2, y 6, nil},...
pointRange.contains(a)                                    true
pointRange.contains(Point(x: -1, y: -1))                 false
```

Here you define a range of points and then check whether two specific points exist within that range. How does this work?

Swift does not need to compute all possible values that would fall within a range. An instance of **Range** only stores the lower bound and the upper bound. When you ask a range if it contains a value, the range compares the value to its bounds, with the exact comparison depending on its type. A half-open range like this one returns true if the value is greater than or equal to the lower bound and less than the upper bound.

Since conforming to **Comparable** means that you have defined what it means for one **Point** to be less than another, this check can be performed.

Protocol inheritance

Comparable inherits from **Equatable**. You may be able to guess the implication of this inheritance. To conform to the **Comparable** protocol, you must also conform to the **Equatable** protocol (including, as you have seen, by supplying an implementation of the == operator). This relationship also means that a type does not have to explicitly declare conformance to **Equatable** if it declares conformance to **Comparable**. Remove the explicit declaration of conformance to **Equatable** from your **Point** struct.

Listing 25.11 Removing the unnecessary conformance declaration

```
...
extension Point: Equatable, Comparable {
    static func ==(lhs: Point, rhs: Point) -> Bool {
        return (lhs.x == rhs.x) && (lhs.y == rhs.y)
    }

    static func <(lhs: Point, rhs: Point) -> Bool {
        return (lhs.x < rhs.x) && (lhs.y < rhs.y)
    }
}
...
```

You should see that the playground works just as it did before.

A note on style: While it is not wrong to explicitly declare conformance to both **Equatable** and **Comparable**, it is unnecessary. If your type conforms to **Comparable**, then it must conform to **Equatable** as well. This point is a detail listed in the documentation, which makes it an expected consequence of conforming to **Comparable**. Adding the explicit conformance to **Equatable** does not really add any information.

On the other hand, it may make sense to have a type explicitly conform to all protocols involved when conforming to a custom protocol that inherits from another protocol. Although it is still unnecessary, it may make your code more readable and easier to maintain, because your custom protocol is not listed in the official documentation.

Hashable

When you learned about the **Dictionary** and **Set** types in Chapter 10 and Chapter 11, you learned that in order for a type to be included in a **Set** or used as the key type in a **Dictionary**, it must be *hashable*. A type is hashable when it conforms to the **Hashable** protocol. Hashability has a straightforward purpose: the ability of a type to generate an integer based on its content. But why is that useful? You will explore hashing in this section.

Put some **Point** instances to work in a set and a dictionary to see the error that you get:

Listing 25.12 Verifying **Hashable** conformance

```
...
let pointRange = c..<d                           {{x 2, y 6, nil},...
pointRange.contains(a)                           true
pointRange.contains(Point(x: -1, y: -1))         false

let points: Set = [a, b, c]
points.intersection([b, c, d])

let pointNames: [Point:String] = [
    Point(x: 0, y: 0): "origin",
    a: "a",
]
```

Here you define a **Set** of **Point** instances and call its **intersection(_:)** method. You also create a dictionary whose keys are **Point**s and use it to give names to some points. The compiler emits two errors: Generic struct 'Set' requires that 'Point' conform to 'Hashable' and Type 'Point' does not conform to protocol 'Hashable'.

That is straightforward enough. You must make **Point** conform to **Hashable** for either of these uses of the type to be legal.

Similar to **Equatable**, the compiler will happily synthesize implementations of **Hashable**'s requirements for structs with all hashable stored properties and enums with no associated values (or all hashable associated values). Update **Point** to conform to **Hashable**:

Listing 25.13 Conforming to **Hashable**

```
...
extension Point: Comparable, Hashable {
    static func ==(lhs: Point, rhs: Point) -> Bool {
        return (lhs.x == rhs.x) && (lhs.y == rhs.y)
    }

    static func <(lhs: Point, rhs: Point) -> Bool {
        return (lhs.x < rhs.x) && (lhs.y < rhs.y)
    }
}
...
```

Because **Point** is **Hashable** now, the compiler can understand all these uses of **Point**.

Custom hashing

Unfortunately, the free implementation that the compiler has synthesized for **Point** is problematic. To understand why, you need to learn a little bit about *hashes*.

In Swift, the hash of an instance is an integer that is generated from the instance's data. Comparing the hashes of two instances of a type can be a very fast way to check whether the instances are different – often much faster than comparing the instances using the == operator.

Consider how long it could take to compare two instances of **String** for equality: The program must advance along the complete length of at least one of the strings, comparing the **Character** at each index to the **Character** at the same index of the other string. If the program gets to the very end of the strings without encountering a difference, the strings are the same. By contrast, comparing two integers is blazing fast, and modern CPUs are often designed to make it even faster.

If you want to know whether two strings are equal, you can first check their hashes, which takes nearly no time at all. If their hashes are different, then you know the strings are different.

But, because strings can be larger and more complex than integers, it is possible for two different strings to have the same hash. So, if two strings' hashes are the same, you have not learned anything, and you must proceed with a complete equality check to be sure.

(As an aside: Because an equality check is a necessary backup plan when comparing the hashes of instances, **Hashable** inherits from **Equatable**.)

An ideal hashing algorithm is one that is fast to compute and unlikely to collide with another instance's hash – but does not need to guarantee that two hashes will never be the same.

To make lookups and comparisons as fast as possible, dictionaries use hashes as an initial check to ensure that dictionary keys are unique, and sets use hashes as an initial check to ensure the uniqueness of their contents. Adding lots of instances with the same hash value would force these types to fall back on equality checks to ensure uniqueness, which can be much slower.

Fortunately, Swift has a safe, fast hashing algorithm built in. All you have to do is tell Swift which properties of an instance should participate in the computation of its hash. Swift calls these properties that contribute to an equality comparison the instance's *essential components*.

Your current implementation of the == operator uses only the x and y properties of a **Point**. However, the compiler-synthesized hash of a **Point** uses all the instance's stored properties. And that is the source of the problem: If one property is not relevant to an instance's uniqueness, then it should not be an essential component for hashing.

To control which properties of an instance will contribute to its hash, you must provide your own implementation of the **Hashable** requirement. That requirement is an implementation of a method called **hash(into:)**. Implement it in your **Point** extension:

Listing 25.14 Producing your own hash

```
extension Point: Comparable, Hashable {
    static func ==(lhs: Point, rhs: Point) -> Bool {
        return (lhs.x == rhs.x) && (lhs.y == rhs.y)
    }

    static func <(lhs: Point, rhs: Point) -> Bool {
        return (lhs.x < rhs.x) && (lhs.y < rhs.y)
    }

    func hash(into hasher: inout Hasher) {
        hasher.combine(x)
        hasher.combine(y)
    }
}
```

When Swift needs to compute your object's hash, it will call **hash(into:)** and pass in a reference to an instance of the **Hasher** struct as its argument. **Hasher** implements Swift's hashing algorithm, and your job is to tell it which properties to include by passing them to its **combine(_:)** method.

That is all! **Point** is now stylishly **Hashable**.

Bronze Challenge

Make it possible to add two points. The addition of two points should return a new **Point** that adds the given points' x values and y values. You will need to provide an implementation of the + operator that takes two **Point** instances.

Silver Challenge

In Chapter 21 on generics, you created a **Stack** type. It would be handy to be able to tell whether two instances of **Stack** are equal. Implement **Equatable** for **Stack** at the bottom of your Generics.playground.

The conformance should only apply to stacks of also-equatable types. Add some comparisons to the bottom of the playground to test your solution:

Listing 25.15 Conditional conformance to **Equatable**

```
...
let myTasks = Stack(items: ["Clean up"])
let yourTasks = Stack(items: ["Master Swift"])
myTasks == yourTasks                    // Result should be false

class Pancake { }
let breakfast = Stack(items: [Pancake(), Pancake()])
let lunch = Stack(items: [Pancake()])
breakfast == lunch                      // Compiler error: Pancake is not Equatable
```

Hint: Use an extension to add **Equatable** conformance, but use a where clause to allow the extension to apply only to stacks of types that are, themselves, equatable.

Gold Challenge

Create a new **Person** class with two properties: name and age. For convenience, create an initializer that provides arguments for both these properties.

Next, create two new instances of the **Person** class. Assign those instances to two constants named p1 and p2. Also create an array named people to hold these instances and then put them inside the array.

You will occasionally need to find the index of an instance of a custom type within an array. Call the **firstIndex(of:)** method on your array to do so. The argument takes the value of some element in the collection whose index you would like to find. Use the method to find the index of p1 inside the people array.

You will get an error. Take some time to understand the error, then resolve it. You should be able to assign the result of **firstIndex(of:)** to a constant named p1Index. Its value should be 0.

Platinum Challenge

Point's current conformance to **Comparable** yields some confusing results.

```
let e = Point(x: 3, y: 4)
let f = Point(x: 2, y: 5)

let eGreaterThanF = (e > f) // false
let eLessThanF = (e < f)    // false
let eEqualToF = (e == f)    // false
```

As the example above demonstrates, the trouble arises in comparing two points when one point's x and y properties are not both larger than the other point's properties. In actuality, it is not reasonable to compare two points in this manner.

Fix this problem by changing **Point**'s conformance to **Comparable**. Calculate each point's Euclidean distance from the origin instead of comparing x and y values. This implementation should return true for a < b when a is closer to the origin than b.

Use the formula shown in Figure 25.1 to calculate a point's Euclidean distance.

Figure 25.1 Euclidean distance

$$distance(a, b) = \sqrt{(a_x - b_x)^2 + (a_y - b_y)^2}$$

For the More Curious: Custom Operators

Swift allows developers to create custom operators. This feature means that you can create your own operator to signify, for example, that one instance of the **Person** type has married another instance. Say, for example, you want to create a **+++** function to marry one instance to another.

Create a new **Person** class, like so:

Listing 25.16 Setting up a **Person** class

```
...
class Person {
    var name: String
    weak var spouse: Person?

    init(name: String, spouse: Person?) {
        self.name = name
        self.spouse = spouse
    }
}
```

The class has two properties: one for a name and another for a spouse. It also has an initializer that will give values to those properties. Note that the spouse property is an optional, to indicate that a person may not have a spouse.

Next, create two instances of this class.

Listing 25.17 Creating two instances of **Person**

```
...
class Person {
    var name: String
    weak var spouse: Person?

    init(name: String, spouse: Person?) {
        self.name = name
        self.spouse = spouse
    }
}

let matt = Person(name: "Matt", spouse: nil)
let drew = Person(name: "Drew", spouse: nil)
```

Now, declare your new infix operator. It has to be declared at global scope. Also, define how the new operator function will work.

Listing 25.18 Declaring a custom operator

```
...
class Person {
    var name: String
    weak var spouse: Person?

    init(name: String, spouse: Person?) {
        self.name = name
        self.spouse = spouse
    }
}

let matt = Person(name: "Matt", spouse: nil)
let drew = Person(name: "Drew", spouse: nil)

infix operator +++

func +++(lhs: Person, rhs: Person) {
    lhs.spouse = rhs
    rhs.spouse = lhs
}
```

The new operator +++ will be used to marry two instances of the **Person** class. As an infix operator, it will be used between two instances. The implementation of +++ will assign each instance to the other's spouse property. +++ does not state a precedencegroup, which means it is assigned to the DefaultPrecedence group.

```
precedencegroup DefaultPrecedence {
    higherThan: TernaryPrecedence
}
```

So, what does higherThan refer to in the code above? higherThan defines the priority of the operator's relative relationship to another precedencegroup. In this case, DefaultPrecedence has a priority that is higher than TernaryPrecedence. This is the precedencegroup for the ternary operator (see Chapter 3 for a discussion of the ternary operator). That means your new operator, +++(lhs:rhs:), will have higher priority than – and will be executed before – the ternary operator.

Think of how multiplication has higher priority than addition in expressions like 4 + 3 * 3 - 1. Because multiplication has higher priority, 4 + 3 * 3 - 1 is 12. If addition had higher priority than multiplication, then the answer would be 20.

precedencegroups offer a number of other options to define the custom operator. In addition to higherThan, another important option that you will often see is associativity.

associativity defines how operations of the same priority group together. It takes one of two values, left or right. For example, the operators + and – both use the same precedencegroup (AdditionPrecedence) and therefore have the same priority. Both are also left associative. The associativity and precedence for the mathematical operators mean that the order of execution in the equation above is (4 + (3 * 3)) - 1. That is, 3 * 3 is evaluated first, because it has the highest priority, and its product associates to the left. That yields (4 + 9) - 1, which is 13 - 1, which is 12.

Because +++ is intended to marry two **Person** instances together, it does not need to be chained together with multiple calls. For example, you would not see this code: matt +++ drew +++ someOtherInstance. Thus, you can take advantage of the default values for precedence and associativity.

Exercise your new operator.

Listing 25.19 Using the custom operator

```
...
class Person {
    var name: String
    weak var spouse: Person?

    init(name: String, spouse: Person?) {
        self.name = name
        self.spouse = spouse
    }
}

let matt = Person(name: "Matt", spouse: nil)
let drew = Person(name: "Drew", spouse: nil)

infix operator +++

func +++(lhs: Person, rhs: Person) {
    lhs.spouse = rhs
    rhs.spouse = lhs
}

matt +++ drew
matt.spouse?.name
drew.spouse?.name
```

The code matt +++ drew serves to marry the two instances. Check that this process worked by examining the playground's results sidebar.

While this operator works, and it is not too difficult to determine what is going on by looking at it, we generally recommend that you avoid declaring custom operators. It is good practice to only create custom operators for your own types when the operator will be recognizable to anyone who may read your code. That typically means restricting your custom operators to the realm of well-known mathematical operators.

In fact, Swift only allows you to use a well-defined collection of mathematical symbols to create custom operators. For example, you cannot rename the +++ operator to be the emoji "face throwing a kiss" (i.e., U+1F61A).

Someone reviewing your code in the future may not know exactly what you meant by +++. (You might even forget, yourself.) Moreover, it is not as though this custom operator is more elegant or efficient than a marry(_:) method would be:

```
func marry(_ spouse: Person) {
    self.spouse = spouse
    spouse.spouse = self
}
```

This code is far more readable, and it is quite clear what the code is doing. These qualities will make it easier to maintain in the future.

26

Property Wrappers

Manipulating data as it is stored into or retrieved from a property is a common task in programming. In Chapter 20, you saw an implementation of a `fuelLevel` property; as fuel is added and used up, the fill percentage of a car's fuel tank changes – but it must always stay between 0.0 and 1.0.

The `fuelLevel` property you wrote earlier used **precondition()** to check a provided value and trap if the value was outside the allowed range. In Chapter 23, you learned about other ways to handle runtime errors like invalid inputs.

But what if you want your code to simply replace values less than 0.0 with 0.0 and values greater than 1.0 with 1.0? You could implement a computed property coupled with a private stored property, where the `get` and `set` blocks of the computed property change the stored property's data. That might look like this:

```
struct Car {
    private var fuelLevelStorage: Double = 1.0
    var fuelLevel: Double {
        set {
            fuelLevelStorage = max(min(newValue, 1), 0)
        }
        get {
            return fuelLevelStorage
        }
    }
}
```

Here, the internal `fuelLevel` computed property allows users of the **Car** type to set and retrieve a value that is secretly stored in the `fuelLevelStorage` private variable. The `set` block *clamps* to the range of `0.0` through `1.0` by storing a value of `1.0` when the value is too high or storing a value of `0.0` when the value is too low.

Unfortunately, this approach clutters the defining type. It also is not reusable. What if you need to store the percentage completion of a task? What if you need to store the percentage brightness of a light bulb? Despite the formulaic nature of the code above, you would need to repeat it everywhere you need to clamp a value between 0.0 and 1.0.

In this chapter, you will learn to use a *property wrapper* to define a reusable abstraction for manipulating data coming into and out of your properties. A property wrapper is a specialized enum, struct, or class that you define to hold and manipulate a *wrapped* value that uses computed properties internally. You can wrap a stored property of any other type in an instance of your wrapper type – and your code becomes much less cluttered and more readable as a result. To understand this process, get started with an example.

Defining a Property Wrapper

Create a new macOS playground named PercentageClamping and define a simple **Car** struct:

Listing 26.1 Preparing your playground (`PercentageClamping`)

```
import Cocoa

var str = "Hello, playground"

struct Car {
    var fuelLevel: Double = 1.0
}

var myCar = Car()
myCar.fuelLevel = 1.1
print("Fuel:", myCar.fuelLevel)
```

There is nothing special about this type. You define and create an instance of **Car** and overfill its fuel tank by trying to put 110% of a tank's worth of fuel into it.

In real life, the extra would spill out, leaving your tank 100% full. But your playground output reflects a fuelLevel value of 1.1. This is no good.

Open up the navigator area using the Show Navigator button (⊞) near Xcode's top-left corner. Select the Sources group, then create a new Swift file, either by right-clicking Sources and choosing New File or by selecting File → New → File from Xcode's menu bar. Name your new file `Percentage.swift`. The result should look like Figure 26.1.

Figure 26.1 Adding to your playground sources

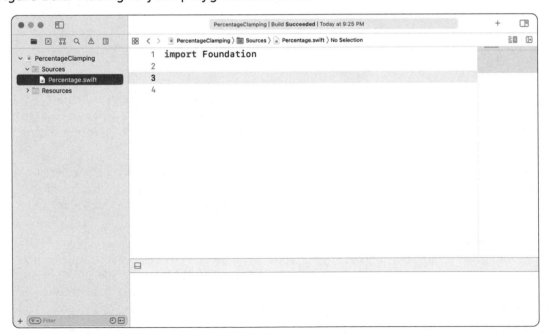

When you are working in a playground and want to separate some of your code into other files like you do in a project, you can do it by adding those files to the Sources group like this. Note that when you do this, any declarations in your Sources are compiled into a separate module from your main playground content, so they must be declared `public` to be usable by the playground.

Now it is time to define your property wrapper. In `Percentage.swift`, define a property wrapper struct to encapsulate logic that uses a computed property to set and retrieve the value of a private variable, similar to the sample code you saw earlier.

Listing 26.2 Defining a property wrapper (`Percentage.swift`)

```
import Foundation

@propertyWrapper public struct Percentage {

    private var storage: Double

    public init(wrappedValue: Double) {
        storage = max(min(wrappedValue, 1), 0)
    }

    public var wrappedValue: Double {
        set {
            storage = max(min(newValue, 1), 0)
        }
        get {
            return storage
        }
    }
}
```

There is very little new syntax here. You define a **Percentage** struct with a private variable along with an initializer and a computed property that both set a value on the private property. The new syntax is the `@propertyWrapper` attribute. This attribute marks your type as a property wrapper, which can now be used as the wrapping type for any other property.

The only requirements for a property wrapper are a variable named `wrappedValue` and an initializer whose first argument is called `wrappedValue`, which must be of the same type as the variable. Since a property wrapper exists to manipulate data coming into or out of a property, the `wrappedValue` is generally a computed property, and the property wrapper will often have a private property to store a value between accesses.

Switch back to your playground by clicking PercentageClamping at the top of the navigator area. Use your property wrapper to see the benefit it brings:

Listing 26.3 Using your property wrapper (`PercentageClamping`)

```
struct Car {
    @Percentage var fuelLevel: Double = 1.0
}

var myCar = Car()
myCar.fuelLevel = 1.1
print("Fuel:", myCar.fuelLevel)
```

Look at your playground output: `Fuel: 1.0`! Your property wrapper is successfully clamping the `fuelLevel` to be between 0.0 and 1.0. How?

When you declare a data structure as a `@propertyWrapper`, that type can then be used with the `@` symbol as a custom attribute. Then, when you declare a property using a property wrapper attribute such as `@Percentage`, the compiler rewrites your property declaration to use an instance of the wrapper type (**Percentage**) to handle the storage and transformation of its value.

In this case, the compiler takes your `fuelLevel` property declaration:

```
@Percentage var fuelLevel: Double = 1.0
```

And rewrites it at compile time to something more like this:

```
private var _fuelLevel = Percentage(wrappedValue: 1.0)
var fuelLevel: Double {
    get { return _fuelLevel.wrappedValue }
    set { _fuelLevel.wrappedValue = newValue }
}
```

First, the compiler synthesizes storage for an instance of **Percentage**, using `fuelLevel`'s default value of 1.0 as the argument to the wrapper's **init(wrappedValue:)** initializer. Then, the compiler rewrites the `fuelLevel` property as a computed variable, whose setter and getter store and retrieve its value using the `wrappedValue` property of the **Percentage** instance.

When you set the `fuelLevel` property of `myCar` to `1.1`, its synthesized setter assigns `1.1` to the `wrappedValue` of the wrapping instance of **Percentage**, which clamps and stores the value in its own `storage` property.

When you read from a **Car**'s `fuelLevel`, its getter reads the `wrappedValue` of the **Percentage** instance.

The effect is that now, at your usage site, you get a simple-looking `fuelLevel` property, and the **Percentage** machinery behind the scenes handles its storage and value clamping. If you store a value outside the range of 0.0 to 1.0, the value will be clamped into the range – but, in this file, you do not have to look at or think about the logic that manages that behavior. The presence of the `@Percentage` property wrapper attribute also serves as a visual reminder to you that this property will clamp its value using an instance of **Percentage**.

That is a lot of free work! Your data manipulation needs have now been cleanly abstracted into a property wrapper that you can use to wrap any **Double** property. Add another wrapped property to your **Car**:

Listing 26.4 Wrapping another property (`PercentageClamping`)

```
struct Car {
    @Percentage var fuelLevel: Double = 1.0
    @Percentage var wiperFluidLevel: Double = 0.5
}
```

Now you have two properties, both clamped to values between 0.0 and 1.0, and the compiler handles the rest. There are two hidden instances of **Percentage**, one for storing and clamping values assigned to `fuelLevel` and one to do the same for `wiperFluidLevel`.

Additional configuration

Sometimes bosses or coaches ask you to give 110%. Some amplifiers go up to 11. Your property wrapper should support scenarios where the developer using it wants to allow the upper bound to be a value greater than 1.0.

Switch back to `Percentage.swift` and add an `upperBound` property to **Percentage**. You will need to update your initializer and `wrappedValue` to account for it.

Listing 26.5 Adding customization to **Percentage** (`Percentage.swift`)

```
@propertyWrapper public struct Percentage {

    private var storage: Double
    private var upperBound: Double

    public init(wrappedValue: Double, upperBound: Double = 1) {
        storage = max(min(wrappedValue, 1), 0)
        self.upperBound = upperBound
    }

    public var wrappedValue: Double {
        set {
            storage = max(min(newValue, ⨮ upperBound), 0)
        }
        get {
            return storage
        }
    }
}
```

Here, you add a new property, `upperBound`, that will be used as the highest value that can be stored in a `@Percentage` variable. You update the initializer to accept and store a value for the `upperBound`, with a default value of 1. Last, you update the `wrappedValue` setter to compare new values to the provided `upperBound`.

Return to the main playground content and add a new wrapped property, this time with an upper bound.

Listing 26.6 Adding another wrapped property (`PercentageClamping`)

```
struct Car {
    @Percentage var fuelLevel: Double = 1.0
    @Percentage var wiperFluidLevel: Double = 0.5
    @Percentage(upperBound: 2.0) var stereoVolume: Double = 1.0
}
...
```

Now you have an upgraded stereo whose volume can be turned up to 200%. More to the point, the declaration @Percentage(upperBound: 2.0) highlights more of what happens behind the scenes of a property wrapper.

When Swift creates the wrapping instance of **Percentage**, the initializer's first parameter (wrappedValue) is implicit and takes the property's default value as its argument. Any other parameters to the property wrapper's initializer must be passed explicitly at the site of the property wrapper's custom attribute, which is what you do here when passing the value 2.0 as an argument to the wrapper's initializer.

Now you can test this wrapped property to see its behavior:

Listing 26.7 Pushing your boundaries (`PercentageClamping`)

```
...
var myCar = Car()
myCar.fuelLevel = 1.1
print("Fuel:", myCar.fuelLevel)
myCar.stereoVolume = 2.5
print("Volume:", myCar.stereoVolume)
```

Your playground output should end with the correct value: Volume: 2.0.

Accessing the Wrapper Itself

A type with a wrapped property, such as **Car** and its fuelLevel, can access the wrapper object directly – rather than its wrappedValue – by prefixing the wrapped property name with an underscore (_). Demonstrate this feature by making **Car** conform to **CustomStringConvertible** and logging the wrapper from the description property:

Listing 26.8 Printing the wrapper to the console (PercentageClamping)

```
struct Car {
    @Percentage var fuelLevel: Double = 1.0
    @Percentage var wiperFluidLevel: Double = 0.5
    @Percentage(upperBound: 2.0) var stereoVolume: Double = 1.0
}

extension Car: CustomStringConvertible {
    var description: String {
        return "fuelLevel: \(fuelLevel), wrapped by \(_fuelLevel)"
    }
}

var myCar = Car()
print(myCar)
myCar.fuelLevel = 1.1
print("Fuel:", myCar.fuelLevel)
...
```

The first line of your output should show the truth of your wrapper:

```
fuelLevel: 1.0, wrapped by Percentage(storage: 1.0, upperBound: 1.0)
```

Inside the implementation of **Car** – and even in an extension on **Car** in the same file – you can access the **Percentage** instance that is wrapping the fuelLevel property via its underscore-prefixed version, _fuelLevel. But note that it is private to the **Car** type. For example, you would not be able to print myCar._fuelLevel from outside the struct or its extension (try it).

Projecting Related Values

While debugging a program that uses your **Percentage** property wrapper, you might want to find out, at any given point, what the last assignment to a variable's value was – *before* it was clamped into the allowed range.

Change the behavior of the initializer and wrapped value to store any value and to do its clamping work when the property is read, instead of written.

Listing 26.9 Clamping when reading instead of writing (`Percentage.swift`)

```
@propertyWrapper public struct Percentage {

    private var storage: Double
    private var upperBound: Double

    public init(wrappedValue: Double, upperBound: Double = 1) {
        storage = max(min(wrappedValue, 1), 0)
        storage = wrappedValue
        self.upperBound = upperBound
    }

    public var wrappedValue: Double {
        set {
            storage = max(min(newValue, upperBound), 0)
            storage = newValue
        }
        get {
            return storage
            return max(min(storage, upperBound), 0)
        }
    }
}
```

Now an instance of **Percentage** stores the last value assigned to its wrappedValue, regardless of magnitude. At any given time, the storage contains a value that may or may not be within range, but reading the wrappedValue will produce the clamped value. To the call site in the main playground content, nothing has changed. Storing a too-large value and then reading it will still report the clamped value.

Now, to give users of your property wrapper access to the un-clamped value, your property wrapper can *project* an additional value related to its wrapped value. You do this by implementing a projectedValue property:

Listing 26.10 Projecting a value from a wrapper (`Percentage.swift`)

```
@propertyWrapper public struct Percentage {
    ...
    public var projectedValue: Double {
        get {
            return storage
        }
    }
}
```

Here, you project the value of storage without clamping it. That value can be accessed by prefixing a wrapped variable's name with $. Test your ability to access this projected value in the main playground:

Listing 26.11 Accessing the projected value (`PercentageClamping`)

```
...
var myCar = Car()
print(myCar)
myCar.fuelLevel = 1.1
print("Fuel:", myCar.fuelLevel)
myCar.stereoVolume = 2.5
print("Volume:", myCar.stereoVolume)
print("Projected volume:", myCar.$stereoVolume)
```

When you access a wrapped property on an object, prefixing the property name with $ gives you access to the projectedValue instead of the wrappedValue. Your final playground output should be:

```
fuelLevel: 1.0, wrapped by Percentage(storage: 1.0, upperBound: 1.0)
Fuel: 1.0
Volume: 2.0
Projected volume: 2.5
```

Note that a property wrapper's projectedValue can have both a getter and a setter and can represent any value related to the wrappedValue. It does not even have to be the same type. For example, you could have implemented projectedValue to return a **Bool** indicating whether the value in storage is within the allowed range.

It is up to the implementer of a property wrapper to decide whether to project an additional value and what that value might be, so check the documentation of any property wrapper you adopt in your own programs to understand whether you will find its projected value useful.

Property wrappers are a flexible way to define custom behaviors that should be executed when a property is accessed, and they make it easy to define those behaviors in an abstract and reusable way. You will see some of Apple's property wrappers from the SwiftUI framework in Chapter 28.

Bronze Challenge

Open the completed MonsterTown project that you worked on from Chapter 15 to Chapter 17.

Define a property wrapper type in that project called **Logged** that logs changes to a wrapped property and logs when a property's value gets too low. Its wrappedValue should be an **Int**. Its initializer should take and store a second **Int** argument called warningValue.

Every time a @Logged property's value changes, a message should print to the console containing the old value and the new value. If the value drops below the warningValue, an additional message should be logged indicating that the value is getting too low.

Mark the population property of the **Town** type as @Logged with a warningValue of 50. Now, every time a town's population changes, the change is printed to the console – and if a town's population drops below 50, the additional warning message is printed.

This means that you can get rid of the didSet property observer of the population property. (It also means that any time you want to make any property log its changes, you can make it a @Logged property.)

Test that your property wrapper works by assigning different values to a town's population in main.swift.

Silver Challenge

The syntax max(min(someValue, 1), 0) is not very intuitive. It takes a moment of reading to understand that this is clamping a value to be between 0 and 1.

In a new file in your PercentageClamping playground's Sources, define an extension to give all floating-point numbers a **clamped(to:)** method. The method should accept an instance of **ClosedRange**, so that it can be called like someValue.clamped(to: 0...1).

Update your **Percentage** struct to use it instead of the current, difficult-to-read formula.

Hint: You may need to refer back to what you learned about **Self** in Chapter 22 on protocol extensions.

Gold Challenge

The majority of property wrappers are generic. Since the point of defining a property wrapper is to make a reusable tool, you will usually want to make your property wrappers generic so that they are as broadly useful as possible.

Right now, the **Percentage** property wrapper can only accept values of type **Double**. That is limiting; what if someone wants to store a **Float**?

Modify **Percentage** to allow its wrapped value to be any floating-point number.

Hint: This will require you to define **Percentage** as a generic data structure, which you learned about in Chapter 21. Look closely at the documentation for the **Float** and **Double** types. Do they have anything in common that you could use as a constraint on your generic type?

For bonus points, upgrade your solution to the bronze challenge by eliminating the warningValue feature and instead allowing @Logged to wrap a property of any type that conforms to **CustomStringConvertible**.

Part VI

Writing Applications

After learning the syntax, grammar, and features of Swift, you are ready to begin learning how to write real apps. In this part of the book, you will apply your knowledge of Swift to develop more robust applications for the macOS command line and for iOS devices, and you will whet your appetite for the next step in your learning journey.

27

Command-Line Utilities

Earlier in this book, you used the macOS command-line tool template to create two projects: MonsterTown and CyclicalAssets. Those exercises were designed to give you a place to explore the Swift language; they were not real, useful tools.

As a Swift developer, you now have the ability to create command-line tools that you can use to automate common tasks, perform calculations, transform data, and more. In this chapter, you will build a tool that can process command-line options and arguments, interactively accept user input, and be run outside of Xcode.

Introduction to the Command Line

Command-line tools are so named because users interact with them using a *command-line interface* (CLI), often via the Terminal application. (And, by the way, they are often called "tools" and "applications" interchangeably.) We will begin with some basic information about the command line. If you are already comfortable with navigating and using the command line on a Mac, feel free to move on to the next section.

There are lots of CLI commands and tools already available on your Mac, and in your career as a Swift developer you will end up relying on several. To see some of them in action, open up the Terminal application in your /Applications/Utilities directory. It should look something like Figure 27.1.

Figure 27.1 Opening a new Terminal window

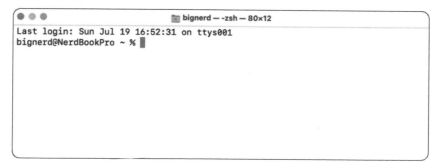

The portion that reads: bignerd@NerdBookPro ~ % ▓ may look very different for you. The important parts will be there, but they might be in a different order – and they will certainly be personalized based on your system.

Figure 27.2 breaks it down. The most important pieces to identify are the directory (~, here) and the prompt, which is the last character before the cursor.

Figure 27.2 The command prompt

Here are the constituent parts:

user	The username of the computer's current user.
host	The host name of the system. You can set this for your Mac in the Sharing pane of System Preferences.
directory	The current working directory name. The symbol ~ represents the user's home directory, such as /Users/*username*/, which is usually the default directory for a new Terminal session.
prompt	The command prompt. The command that you type appears after this symbol. On some systems it might be a different symbol, such as $ or >. Throughout this chapter, we will use the % symbol before text that you should enter at a command prompt.
cursor	The current text insertion point. Yours might look different, but it usually appears as a line or box.

As noted above, by default a new Terminal session opens with the path of your home directory. Use the cd ("change directory") command to move to your desktop directory (Listing 27.1). (Unless we specify otherwise, assume that you should press Return after entering a command.)

Listing 27.1 Changing directory to the desktop (Terminal)

```
% cd ~/Desktop
```

The text after the command is its *argument*, and, like the argument to a function, it tells the command what object to operate on. Some commands can take multiple arguments. In the case of the cd command, the expected argument is a path to the directory to change to, such as the Desktop subdirectory of the user's home directory.

You should see that the command prompt now lists Desktop as its current directory. Use the ls ("list") command to list the files in the current directory. If you get a pop-up requesting permission for Terminal to access the directory, click OK.

Listing 27.2 Listing a directory's contents (Terminal)

```
% ls
```

The contents of each user's desktop will be different, but you should see output something like Figure 27.3.

Figure 27.3 Desktop directory

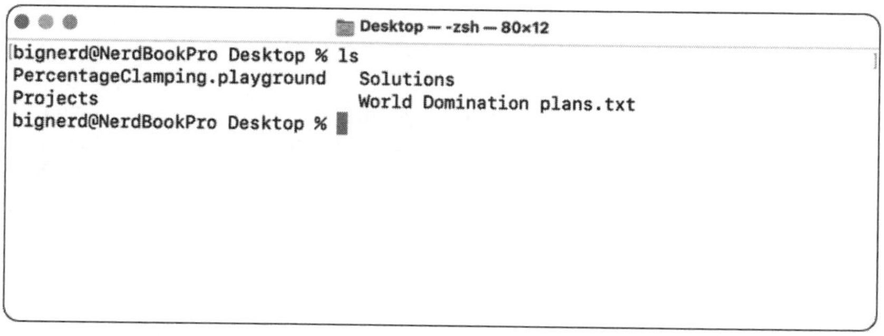

```
● ● ●                        📁 Desktop — -zsh — 80×12
bignerd@NerdBookPro Desktop % ls
PercentageClamping.playground    Solutions
Projects                         World Domination plans.txt
bignerd@NerdBookPro Desktop % ▊
```

Some commands take *options*, usually represented by letters or words prefixed with a hyphen (–), that change the way the command will behave. Change back to your home directory, then list the contents of a different directory by passing its path as an argument to the ls command. This time, use the –l option to instruct the ls command to list the directory contents in a detailed list format:

Listing 27.3 Commands, options, and arguments, oh my (Terminal)

```
% cd ..
% ls -l /usr/share/dict/
```

Here, you change to the .. *pseudo-directory*. This is not truly a directory at all, but a reference to the current directory's parent directory. So, cd .. will move you up one directory in the hierarchy of directories – in this case, to your home directory.

Then you execute the ls command with an option (–l, to specify a detailed list output format) and an argument (/usr/share/dict/, to specify the directory whose contents you want to list). The /usr/share/dict/ directory is a location on every Mac where files with common words are stored. You will use these files in the exercise later.

Your output should look something like Figure 27.4.

Figure 27.4 Passing an option and an argument to the ls command

```
● ● ●                        📁 bignerd — -zsh — 80×12
bignerd@NerdBookPro Desktop % cd ..
bignerd@NerdBookPro ~ % ls -l /usr/share/dict/
total 2928
-r--r--r--  1 root  wheel     1311 Jan  1  2020 README
-r--r--r--  1 root  wheel      706 Jan  1  2020 connectives
-r--r--r--  1 root  wheel     8546 Jan  1  2020 propernames
-r--r--r--  1 root  wheel  2493109 Jan  1  2020 web2
-r--r--r--  1 root  wheel  1012731 Jan  1  2020 web2a
lrwxr-xr-x  1 root  wheel        4 Jan  1  2020 words -> web2
bignerd@NerdBookPro ~ % ▊
```

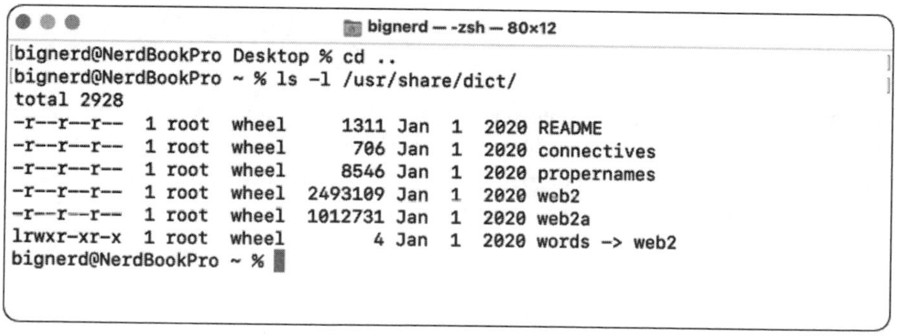

Most command-line tools expect options first and arguments at the end of the command.

Finally, many command-line tools are willing to teach you how to use them with a –h or ––help option. Here is the help available for the xcode-select tool, for example:

```
% xcode-select --help

Usage: xcode-select [options]

Print or change the path to the active developer directory. This directory
controls which tools are used for the Xcode command line tools (for example,
xcodebuild) as well as the BSD development commands (such as cc and make).

Options:
-h, --help                    print this help message and exit
-p, --print-path              print the path of the active developer directory
-s <path>, --switch <path>    set the path for the active developer directory
--install                     open a dialog for installation of the command [...]
-v, --version                 print the xcode-select version
-r, --reset                   reset to the default command line tools path
```

You can see in the list of options that most have a short form (like –h) and a long form (like ––help) for the same command. This is as a convenience to the user; when running command-line utilities, use whichever form of the option you like.

This is just an example of command-line tool help output. You will probably not need to use xcode-select anytime soon; it is useful for developers who need to have multiple installations of some of Xcode's tools installed.

You are going to move on now to writing a robust command-line app. If you want to learn more about using the command line, there are lots of free resources on the internet to learn about using the Mac Terminal and its default command shell, zsh.

Building the Word Finder

The tool you are about to build, wordlasso, is a word-finding application that could be used to help you with crossword puzzles and other word-based games. The user will be able to execute it like so:

```
% wordlasso -i la..o
lacto
Lanao
Lango
largo
lasso
latro
```

wordlasso will accept a few different options and will take as its argument a string template with periods for wildcards. It will produce a list of words that fit the provided template. In the example above, with the template la..o, the tool outputs a list of all five-letter words that begin with "la" and end in "o." Note that in this example the search is not case sensitive – wordlasso will support both case-sensitive and case-insensitive searches.

In Xcode, create a new macOS command-line tool called wordlasso. Notice that the name is all lowercase; this is typical for command-line tool names.

First, you will need a type able to compare a list of known words against a template string. Add a new Swift file called WordFinder.swift. In it, define a **WordFinder** struct with a couple properties:

Listing 27.4 Defining the **WordFinder** struct (WordFinder.swift)

```
import Foundation

struct WordFinder {
    static let wildcard: Character = "."
    let wordList: [String]
}
```

The wildcard gives a name to your wildcard character so that you do not need to repeat the **Character** literal throughout the program. Your wordList is where you will store the list of known words to compare against the provided template string.

Implement a private helper method to determine whether a given word matches a template:

Listing 27.5 Identifying a match (WordFinder.swift)

```
struct WordFinder {
    static let wildcard: Character = "."
    let wordList: [String]

    private func isMatch(template: String, with word: String) -> Bool {
        guard template.count == word.count else { return false }

        return template.indices.allSatisfy { index in
            template[index] == WordFinder.wildcard || template[index] == word[index]
        }
    }
}
```

You start by comparing the template's length to the candidate word's length; if they are different lengths, they cannot possibly be a match. Then you use the **allSatisfy(_:)** higher-order function to iterate over every index in the template string and figure out whether the character at that index in the template matches either the wildcard character or the character at the same index in the candidate word.

Now you can implement the method that other types will use to interact with this one: a method to filter the wordList to only words that are matches for the template.

Listing 27.6 Filtering wordList for matches (WordFinder.swift)

```
struct WordFinder {
    static let wildcard: Character = "."
    let wordList: [String]

    private func isMatch(template: String, with word: String) -> Bool {
        guard template.count == word.count else { return false }

        return template.indices.allSatisfy { index in
            template[index] == WordFinder.wildcard || template[index] == word[index]
        }
    }

    func findMatches(for template: String) -> [String] {
        return wordList.filter { candidate in
            isMatch(template: template,
                    with: candidate)
        }
    }
}
```

Take a moment to be proud of how far you have come. The **WordFinder** implementation is relatively complex, but you have studied all of it before: type definitions, property declarations, functions, and closures.

If any of it feels uncomfortable, that is OK. Take your time and consider reviewing the relevant chapters. This is not a race. If the code above feels good to you – even better! Either way, you are making solid headway toward becoming a stylish Swift programmer.

As you work on a larger application, it is important to periodically test small pieces of it as you build them. Double-check that your **WordFinder** works by defining a word list and a template in main.swift. For reasons that will become clear later in this chapter, define a struct to encapsulate this behavior.

Listing 27.7 Testing **WordFinder** (main.swift)

```swift
import Foundation

print("Hello, World!")

struct Wordlasso {
    func run() throws {
        let wordList = ["Wolf", "wolf", "word", "works", "woo"]
        let wordFinder = WordFinder(wordList: wordList)

        let template = "wo.."

        let matches = wordFinder.findMatches(for: template)
        print("Found \(matches.count) \(matches.count == 1 ? "match" : "matches"):")
        for match in matches {
            print(match)
        }
    }
}

do {
    try Wordlasso().run()
} catch {
    fatalError("Program exited unexpectedly. \(error)")
}
```

You create a list of known words and use it to initialize an instance of **WordFinder**. Then you define a four-letter word template with two letters and two wildcards, and you plug it in. You implement this behavior inside the **run()** method on a new struct, **Wordlasso**.

Finally, you create a **Wordlasso** instance and call its **run()** method to kick off the rest of your code. You use your do/catch block to trap the app and log any thrown errors. A **fatalError(_:)** call is not the usual way to exit a command-line utility. You will replace it with a more robust solution later.

Build and run your program. Your output in the console (which is also a CLI) should look like this:

```
Found 2 matches:
wolf
word
Program ended with exit code: 0
```

This is correct, but possibly unexpected. All-lowercase "wolf" (the animal) matched. Capitalized "Wolf" (the proper name) did not. A user of wordlasso might want the option to perform a case-insensitive search, so that both "Wolf" and "wolf" match. Add a Boolean property to **WordFinder** to let it know whether to ignore case. Add a helper method to produce a case-corrected version of a string if your Boolean is true. Also, update **findMatches(for:)** to use this helper method.

Listing 27.8 Supporting case-insensitivity (`WordFinder.swift`)

```
struct WordFinder {
    static let wildcard: Character = "."
    let wordList: [String]
    let ignoreCase: Bool

    private func caseCorrected(_ value: String) -> String {
        ignoreCase ? value.lowercased() : value
    }
    ...
    func findMatches(for template: String) -> [String] {
        return wordList.filter { candidate in
            isMatch(template: caseCorrected(template),
                    with: caseCorrected(candidate))
        }
    }
}
```

Now, if ignoreCase is true, then **findMatches(for:)** will use lowercase versions of both the template and the candidate words, so that their original cases do not prevent a match. Update main.swift to match your updated **WordFinder**:

Listing 27.9 Testing case-insensitivity (`main.swift`)

```
...
func run() throws {
    let wordList = ["Wolf", "wolf", "word", "works", "woo"]
    let wordFinder = WordFinder(wordList: wordList, ignoreCase: true)
    ...
}
...
```

Build and run. Now your output should reflect a case-insensitive comparison:

```
Found 3 matches:
Wolf
wolf
word
Program ended with exit code: 0
```

Loading the words from disk

Your **WordFinder** is almost complete. The last step is to give it a larger pool of known words to use for comparison. Fortunately, every Mac ships with word lists that you can draw from. One of the files in the /usr/share/dict/ directory, simply named words, is a file that contains nearly a quarter-million words, one per line.

Replace the compiler-synthesized initializer in **WordFinder** with an initializer that accepts the path of a word list file and loads the words from it.

Listing 27.10 Loading a word list from disk (WordFinder.swift)

```swift
struct WordFinder {
    static let wildcard: Character = "."
    let wordList: [String]
    let ignoreCase: Bool

    init(wordListPath: String, ignoreCase: Bool) throws {
        let wordListContent = try String(contentsOfFile: wordListPath)
        wordList = wordListContent.components(separatedBy: .newlines)
        self.ignoreCase = ignoreCase
    }

    ...
}
```

The **String(contentsOfFile:)** initializer is a failable initializer that synchronously loads a file from disk into an instance of **String**. It will fail if the file does not exist, if the program does not have permission to access the file, or if the file cannot be successfully decoded into text.

The **components(separatedBy:)** method explodes a **String** into a **[String]** by using its argument – which can be another string or a **CharacterSet** – as a delimiter. Here, you specify the character set of new line characters.

To test your shiny new **WordFinder**, update main.swift to use your new initializer.

Listing 27.11 Testing the completed **WordFinder** (main.swift)

```swift
...
func run() throws {
    let wordList = ["Wolf", "wolf", "word", "works", "woe"]
    let wordFinder = WordFinder(wordList: wordList, ignoreCase: true)
    let path = "/usr/share/dict/words"
    let wordFinder = try WordFinder(wordListPath: path, ignoreCase: true)

    let template = "wo.."
    ...
}
...
```

Build and run. Your output should print about 30 matches.

Retrieving Command-Line Arguments

Up to now, this project has not felt very different from MonsterTown. The application is still dependent on a hardcoded input template. It can read strings from the disk, but there is nothing for the user to do yet.

There are two ways to receive user input in a command-line app. The first is what you saw earlier when you typed commands at the prompt and Terminal performed them. That works well for short, discrete tools that do their work, produce some output, and are done.

The second way to receive user input is to interact with the user while the program is running, allowing them to enter text that the app can react to – possibly in a repeating cycle.

You are going to set wordlasso up for both kinds of user interaction. The first step is to accept some command-line input. In main.swift, print the command-line arguments to your program.

Listing 27.12 Arguments at the command line (`main.swift`)

```
...
func run() throws {
    let path = "/usr/share/dict/words"
    let wordFinder = try WordFinder(wordListPath: path, ignoreCase: true)

    let args = CommandLine.arguments
    print("Command-line arguments: \(args)")

    let template = "wo.."
    ...
}
...
```

The **CommandLine** enum from the Swift standard library has no cases. It serves as a memorable namespace for static properties, including arguments, that would otherwise be global variables. If you need to declare several related global variables, declaring them as static properties of a caseless enum is a solid strategy for collecting them under an umbrella type with a name that is meaningful to your program.

Build and run, and you should see something new at the top of your output:

```
Command-line arguments:
    ["/Users/bignerd/Library/Developer/Xcode/DerivedData/wordlasso-hgifsfesye
    cfmaeaznyxzbfqdlmq/Build/Products/Debug/wordlasso"]
Found 30 matches:
    ...
```

The arguments static property of **CommandLine** stores an array of strings, each of which is one of the arguments to your program. The zeroth argument is the full path to your program's executable (which can be quite long.) The remaining arguments are ones that were passed in when the program was executed.

Because your program ran with no supplied arguments, only the zeroth argument (the program's own path) was printed. How can you supply additional arguments? By configuring how Xcode will run your program in the scheme editor.

Find the scheme editor control in the Xcode toolbar and click on its lefthand component, pictured in Figure 27.5. Select Edit Scheme... from the drop-down menu that appears.

Figure 27.5 Opening the scheme editor

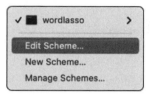

In the pop-up, select the Run group in the lefthand sidebar, then switch to its Arguments tab.

Under Arguments Passed On Launch, click the plus button (+) to add a new argument. Type in the wo.. template you used earlier and press Return. Figure 27.6 shows the result.

Figure 27.6 Adding command-line arguments via the scheme editor

Click Close. When you build and run your program, Xcode will pass it any arguments in this list, in order, as though you had done it yourself:

```
% wordlasso wo..
```

Later, you will see how to export your program so that you can execute it yourself in Terminal. For now, return to `main.swift` and extract the provided template, if one exists. If one does not, you will ask the user for a template interactively – but not yet. You should test what you have first. For now, satisfy the compiler with an empty string and leave yourself a warning as a reminder to finish implementing interactive mode.

Listing 27.13 Getting the template from the command line (`main.swift`)

```
...
let args = CommandLine.arguments
print("Command-line arguments: \(args)")

let template = "wo.."
let template: String
if args.count > 1 {
    template = args[1]
} else {
    template = ""
    #warning("Ask the user for input interactively")
}

let matches = wordFinder.findMatches(for: template)
...
```

Recall that `args[0]` is the path to the program itself. Here, you access `args[1]` to retrieve the first passed argument *if* you know there is one. Otherwise, you provide an error message.

Build and run your program. You should get the same output as before – but now, your program is accepting the template as a command-line argument rather than a hardcoded value. Your app is growing up!

Receiving Input Interactively

Now you will update wordlasso to get its input from the user. To do this, you will change the program to have two modes, depending on whether the user provides a template argument when they run the tool:

- If the user passes a template as a command-line argument, wordlasso will find and print matches for it, then exit.

- If the user does not provide a template as a command-line argument, wordlasso will ask for one. Then, if the user enters a template, the program will find and print matches for it and ask for another template. This will continue until the user tells the program to stop.

Start with the second mode: If the user does not provide a template via a command-line argument, ask them for one.

Listing 27.14 Accepting text input with **readLine()** (main.swift)

```
...
let template: String
if args.count > 1 {
    template = args[1]
} else {
    template = ""
    #warning("Ask the user for input interactively")
    print("Enter word template: ", terminator: "")
    template = readLine() ?? ""
}
...
```

The function commonly known as **print()** actually has a more elaborate signature: **print(_:separator:terminator:)**. Its separator and terminator parameters are not often used, but they can come in handy. Here, you provide an argument to the terminator parameter, which tells the function what to put at the end of your text. The default value is a new line; by passing an empty string here, you ensure that no new line will appear after the printed text. You do this so that your Enter word template: prompt will be on the same line as the user's input.

The **readLine()** function pauses a command-line app to wait for the user to type text and press Return. The return value of **readLine()** is the entered text, or nil if the user presses Return without typing any text.

Since your program is now asking the user for a template, it should not receive one as a command-line argument. Open the scheme editor again and disable the argument by unchecking the box next to it, as pictured in Figure 27.7.

Figure 27.7 Disabling a command-line argument in the scheme editor

Close the scheme editor, then build and run your program. The prompt Enter word template: should appear in the console. Click to place your cursor after the colon, type the template word war., and press Return. Your console should look like this:

```
Command-line arguments:
    ["/Users/bignerd/Library/Developer/Xcode/DerivedData/wordlasso-hgifsfesye
    cfmaeaznyxzbfqdlmq/Build/Products/Debug/wordlasso"]
Enter word template: war.
Found 10 matches:
ward
ware
...
Program ended with exit code: 0
```

Now for the next step. wordlasso, remember, should have two process flows: If the user passes a template as a command-line argument, wordlasso will provide the matches and exit. If the user does not include a template as an argument, the program should continue asking for templates and returning results until the user tells it to quit.

To make this work, you should do some minor refactoring so that you can access your match-finding code from multiple code paths or loops. Move your match-finding code into its own helper method that you can call from anywhere:

Listing 27.15 Moving match-finding code into a method (`main.swift`)

```
struct Wordlasso {
    func run() throws {
        ...
        let matches = wordFinder.findMatches(for: template)
        print("Found \(matches.count) \(matches.count == 1 ? "match" : "matches"):")
        for match in matches {
            print(match)
        }
    }

    private func findAndPrintMatches(for template: String,
                                     using wordFinder: WordFinder) {
        let matches = wordFinder.findMatches(for: template)
        print("Found \(matches.count) \(matches.count == 1 ? "match" : "matches"):")
        for match in matches {
            print(match)
        }
    }
}
...
```

Now you can clean up your conditional argument-parsing code and call
`findAndPrintMatches(using:)` when appropriate.

Listing 27.16 Cleaning up (`main.swift`)

```
...
let template: String
if args.count > 1 {
    let template = args[1]
    findAndPrintMatches(for: template, using: wordFinder)
} else {
    print("Enter word template: ", terminator: "")
    let template = readLine() ?? ""
    findAndPrintMatches(for: template, using: wordFinder)
}
...
```

It feels good to clean up crufty conditionals. Now you are ready to move on. The last step to
implementing wordlasso's interactive mode is wrapping your user interaction in an infinite loop, so
wordlasso will keep asking the user for input until they press Return without typing text.

Listing 27.17 Infinitely looping until there is no input (`main.swift`)

```
...
if args.count > 1 {
    let template = args[1]
    findAndPrintMatches(for: template, using: wordFinder)
} else {
    while true {
        print("Enter word template: ", terminator: "")
        let template = readLine() ?? ""
        if template.isEmpty { return }
        findAndPrintMatches(for: template, using: wordFinder)
    }
}
...
```

Build and run your program. Try a few different templates. When you are done, press Return without
typing a template, and your program will exit.

Congratulations! It is time to test your program in Terminal.

Running Your App from the Command Line

In Xcode's navigator area, click the disclosure arrow next to the Products group to reveal the compiled wordlasso application, as shown in Figure 27.8.

Figure 27.8 Revealing wordlasso

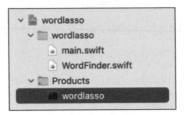

Option-drag the wordlasso application from the Products group onto your Mac's desktop. (Make sure you Option-drag by holding down the Option key while dragging; this copies the application, rather than merely making a shortcut to it.)

Launch a new terminal session. Change the directory to your desktop.

```
% cd ~/Desktop
```

Execute wordlasso and give it a template.

```
% ./wordlasso awes...
Command-line arguments: ["./wordlasso", "awes..."]
Found 1 match:
awesome
```

The . at the beginning of a path is a pseudo-directory, like the .. you saw earlier. Where .. means "parent directory," . means "this directory." So ./wordlasso means "execute the wordlasso in this directory." Without the ./ prefix, Terminal would look for a wordlasso tool in a small list of mostly system-owned directories referred to as your $PATH.

Run wordlasso again, but this time with no template. It will ask you for one – and keep asking until you press Return without typing anything.

Congratulations! You have built and executed a simple CLI app. You could stop here … but do not. wordlasso can – and will – support more features.

But before you expand on wordlasso's functionality, give some thought to what it could mean to try to parse complex command-line input. A command-line app can have many different options, and the user can generally pass them in any order. Consider the complexity of the conditional and switch statements you would need to process a command like this:

```
% ./wordlasso -c 4 -i --word-list /usr/share/dict/propernames Mik..
```

Right now, you are accessing the command-line argument by its index, using args[1]. It is time to bring in a specialized framework to ensure that you can correctly parse all the command-line options and arguments as your program grows.

Parsing Command-Line Arguments with ArgumentParser

The idea of importing frameworks is not new to you. You learned a little bit about the Foundation framework while working on the MonsterTown project in Chapter 15. As you continue your Swift development career, you will encounter lots of frameworks that can offer your program features for everything from modeling data to presenting user interfaces.

The next feature that you will add to wordlasso will use the ArgumentParser framework, an open-source framework developed by Apple. ArgumentParser does not ship as part of Xcode, like Foundation does, so you will need to download the framework and add it to your project before you can import it in a file and start using it. You will do this with the Xcode package manager.

Adding ArgumentParser to your project

From Xcode's File menu, select Swift Packages → Add Package Dependency.... A new window will appear, shown in Figure 27.9.

Figure 27.9 Choose Package Repository window

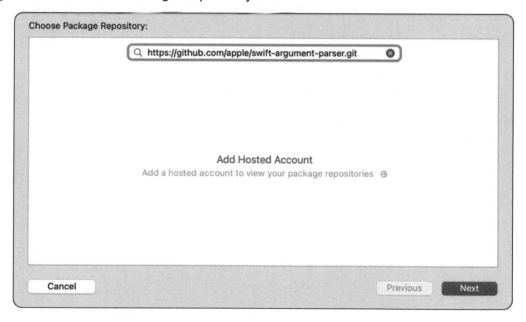

"Repository" is a fancy name for a place where the source code of a project lives, especially if it is under control of a *version control system* such as git. If you are unfamiliar with git, do not worry. It is something that you can add to your goals list to research later; you will not need to know about it to complete this book.

In the package repository URL bar, enter the address of the Swift Argument Parser repository: `https://github.com/apple/swift-argument-parser.git`. Click Next. You will be asked to set or confirm some package options (Figure 27.10).

Figure 27.10 Choose Package Options window

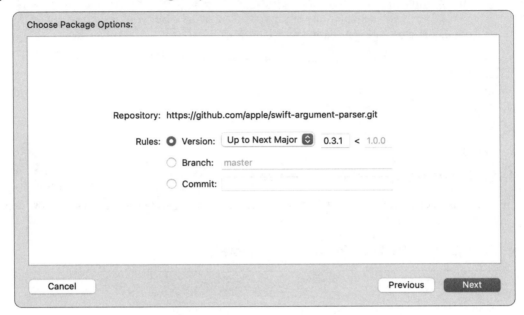

Whatever version you are offered should be fine for this project. Click Next, and you will be asked to confirm the package products you want to add to your project (Figure 27.11).

Figure 27.11 Add Package window

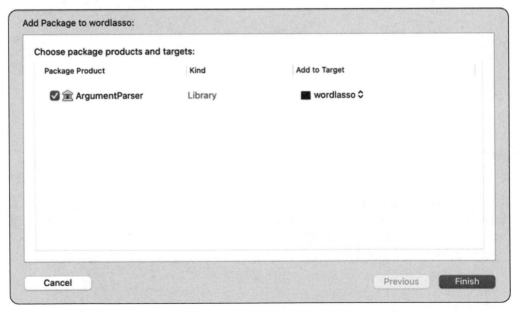

Again, the default settings here are what you want. Click Finish, and you will see a progress bar while Xcode downloads and adds ArgumentParser to your project. When it is done, you will see swift-argument-parser in the Xcode project navigator, below the rest of your project files (Figure 27.12).

Figure 27.12 swift-argument-parser

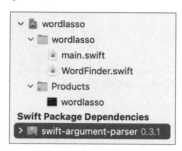

Now it is time to put ArgumentParser to work. Return to `main.swift` and import it.

Listing 27.18 Importing ArgumentParser (`main.swift`)

```
import Foundation
import ArgumentParser

struct Wordlasso {
    ...
}
...
```

Now you will see why you defined **Wordlasso** as a struct. The ArgumentParser framework defines a **ParsableCommand** protocol, which requires a throwing method called **run()**. The body of your program is – or is called by – code in this method. ArgumentParser defines a robust suite of types and property wrappers (which you learned about in Chapter 26) to automatically parse command-line arguments for you and store them into properties of your **ParsableCommand**-conforming type.

Declare that **Wordlasso** conforms to **ParsableCommand**.

Listing 27.19 Conforming to **ParsableCommand** (`main.swift`)

```
import Foundation
import ArgumentParser

struct Wordlasso: ParsableCommand {
    ...
}
...
```

`ParsableCommand` has a protocol extension that adds a free static **main()** method to parse your command-line arguments and call your **run()** function for you. Replace the manual execution of your **run()** function with a call to **main()** instead.

Listing 27.20 Calling **main()** instead of **run()** (main.swift)

```
...
do {
    try Wordlasso().run()
} catch {
    fatalError("Program exited unexpectedly. \(error)")
}

Wordlasso.main()
```

Notice that this is now your only line of top-level code in the entire program. Calling **main()** on **Wordlasso** kicks off everything else your program does. Modern iOS and macOS apps have surprisingly little top-level code.

Build and run your program in Xcode's console. Everything should work just as it did before adding ArgumentParser to your project.

Now it is time to put ArgumentParser to work for you by declaring the arguments that you want it to parse.

Declaring arguments for ArgumentParser to parse

ArgumentParser uses property wrappers to implement its parsing behaviors on your behalf. When you want to identify an argument or option for ArgumentParser to look for at the command line, you select and configure the appropriate property wrapper and use it to declare a property of your `ParsableCommand`-conforming type.

The first argument that you will parse is `template`, to let the user provide the template string for you to match. Add the following property declaration to `Wordlasso`:

Listing 27.21 Adding a `template` argument (`main.swift`)

```swift
struct Wordlasso: ParsableCommand {
    @Argument(help: """
        The word template to match, with \(WordFinder.wildcard) as \
        placeholders. Leaving this blank will enter interactive mode.
        """)
    var template: String?

    func run() throws {
        ...
    }
    ...
}
...
```

The `@Argument` property wrapper is used to declare a property that will store the primary argument to the program. In a moment you will use other property wrappers to declare properties that ArgumentParser will store your program's options into. All ArgumentParser property wrappers take a `help` argument to their initializer that is used to autogenerate your tool's documentation.

Refer back to Chapter 7 if you need a refresher on using multiline strings. This one uses an escape sequence that you have not seen before: a backslash followed by only whitespace at the end of a line. This instructs Swift not to hard-wrap the string at this location, but to pretend that the string is not broken.

Update your **run()** function to use this template property instead of pulling the template out of the **CommandLine** enum.

Listing 27.22 Using the parsed template (main.swift)

```
...
i̶f̶ ̶a̶r̶g̶s̶.̶c̶o̶u̶n̶t̶ ̶>̶ ̶1̶ ̶{̶
    l̶e̶t̶ ̶t̶e̶m̶p̶l̶a̶t̶e̶ ̶=̶ ̶a̶r̶g̶s̶[̶1̶]̶
if let template = template {
    findAndPrintMatches(for: template, using: wordFinder)
} else {
    ...
}
...
```

Build your program and Option-drag it to your desktop again. Run it from a Terminal session to check its documentation:

```
% ./wordlasso --help

USAGE: wordlasso [<template>]
ARGUMENTS:
  <template>              The word template to match, with . as placeholders.
                          Leaving this blank will enter interactive mode.
OPTIONS:
  -h, --help              Show help information.

Program ended with exit code: 0
```

This output was autogenerated for you by ArgumentParser's inspection of the **Wordlasso** type and its properties. Notice that an option to print the tool's documentation is built in, with both a long form and a short form, as you saw with the xcode-select utility at the beginning of this chapter.

Now try it with a template:

```
% ./wordlasso ranc.

Command-line arguments: ["./wordlasso", "ranc."]
Found 2 matches:
rance
ranch
Program ended with exit code: 0
```

What about options? ArgumentParser has those also. An option that does not need an argument of its own, like −l for the `ls` command, is also called a *flag*. Declare a flag to let the user enable case-insensitive matching.

Listing 27.23 Adding a flag for `ignoreCase` (`main.swift`)

```
struct Wordlasso: ParsableCommand {
    @Argument(help: """
        The word template to match, with \(WordFinder.wildcard) as \
        placeholders. Leaving this blank will enter interactive mode.
        """)
    var template: String?

    @Flag(name: .shortAndLong, help: "Perform case-insensitive matches.")
    var ignoreCase: Bool = false

    func run() throws {
        ...
    }
    ...
}
...
```

Here you declare a flag using the `@Flag` property wrapper, which takes a `name` argument of type **ArgumentParser.NameSpecification** and the `help` argument to describe its usage to the user.

While the primary argument of your program comes at the end of the command and is unnamed, options and flags have names. Sometimes the names are short, like −h, and sometimes they are long, like −−help. Passing the value `.shortAndLong` indicates that you want both and that ArgumentParser should infer their names from the property name. ArgumentParser's inferred names default to the first letter for the short form and a hyphen-separated lowercase spelling for the long form.

The result is that your program now has a new flag, which can be passed as −i or −−ignore−case. When this new flag is included in the options list when wordlasso is executed, `ignoreCase` will be `true`.

Update **run()** to use your new flag.

Listing 27.24 Honoring the −i flag (`main.swift`)

```
...
func run() throws {
    let path = "/usr/share/dict/words"
    let wordFinder = try WordFinder(wordListPath: path, ignoreCase: true ignoreCase)
    ...
}
...
```

Now add one more declaration, an option to let the user specify a word list other than the default.

Listing 27.25 Parsing a word list path argument (`main.swift`)

```
struct Wordlasso: ParsableCommand {
    @Argument(help: """
        The word template to match, with \(WordFinder.wildcard) as \
        placeholders. Leaving this blank will enter interactive mode.
        """)
    var template: String?

    @Flag(name: .shortAndLong, help: "Perform case-insensitive matches.")
    var ignoreCase: Bool = false

    @Option(name: .customLong("wordfile"),
            help: "Path to a newline-delimited word list.")
    var wordListPath: String = "/usr/share/dict/words"

    func run() throws {
        ...
    }
    ...
}
...
```

Can you guess the usage of this option?

Unlike a flag, an `@Option` property is parsed with an accompanying value. For example, your `wordListPath` option could be passed as `--wordfile /path/to/list`. If no word list path is specified, the value will default to `/usr/share/dict/words`.

It would be illegal usage of the tool to pass `--wordfile` without also passing a string after it, in which case the program would exit and log its usage documentation.

Ensure that **run()** uses the provided word list if there is one:

Listing 27.26 Opting for a different word list (`main.swift`)

```
...
func run() throws {
    let path = "/usr/share/dict/words"
    let wordFinder = try WordFinder(wordListPath: path wordListPath,
                                    ignoreCase: ignoreCase)
    ...
}
...
```

Build your program again and export it to your desktop. Play with wordlasso in your Terminal session. Try different combinations of your flags and options. Try it with a different word list, such as `/usr/share/dict/propernames` – or create your own.

As a Swift developer, you are now equipped to write tools that can be used at the command line to automate tasks on your Mac. You should be proud of this milestone! In the next chapter, you will dip your toe into the waters of iOS app development.

Silver Challenge

Sometimes wordlasso returns a lot of matches, but sometimes it returns only a few. Add an option to wordlasso to let the user specify a maximum number of results.

Its usage should look like this:

```
% ./wordlasso -i -c 4 ne..
Found 31 matches; listing the first 4:
Neal
neal
neap
neat
Program ended with exit code: 0
```

Gold Challenge

In this exercise, you used the ArgumentParser library to parse command-line options and arguments. And, when you learned about error handling in Chapter 23, you wrote code to lex and parse a string containing an arithmetic formula.

Now, write a command-line tool called calc based on your Chapter 23 solution to allow the user to execute basic arithmetic operations in a Terminal session. Copy over as much code as you want from ErrorHandling.playground.

The user should be able to enter a command like this:

```
% ./calc 11+11+7+13
```

And get the correct numerical output printed to the console.

28

iOS and macOS Apps

Swift is a versatile language that is used to develop apps for all Apple devices, from iPhone to Mac. As you saw in the last chapter, you can use it to write tools for use at the command line. In this chapter, you will write an app for iOS and macOS using the SwiftUI framework, which comes with Xcode.

SwiftUI includes types used to describe visual elements like buttons, colors, text, and images. It also provides the machinery for reacting to user input, such as the user typing text or tapping a button.

SwiftUI is a large framework, and iOS and macOS application development are large topics deserving of their own books. This chapter aims to whet your appetite to continue your learning journey by showing you how far you have come and what you are ready for.

To keep you on track in your journey, you will build a multiplatform to-do list app called TahDoodle (Figure 28.1). Running it on macOS requires macOS Big Sur (10.16). However, most of this chapter is focused on the iOS version, which you can run in the Simulator app that also comes with Xcode.

Figure 28.1 TahDoodle

Getting Started with TahDoodle

Begin by creating a new Xcode project. Unlike previous projects, this will use the Multiplatform App template (Figure 28.2). Name it TahDoodle. Leave the Use Core Data and Include Unit Tests options unchecked.

Figure 28.2 Creating a multiplatform app

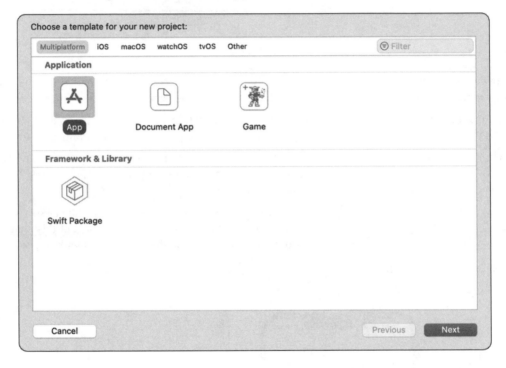

As with the other projects that you have created, you will find that the template populates your navigator area with some files. In addition to some supporting files for managing app metadata and supplemental assets such as icons, there are two Swift files, TahDoodleApp.swift and ContentView.swift.

At the heart of SwiftUI app development is the idea of a *view*: a visual element. SwiftUI defines many types of views for displaying text, images, and even groups of other views. You will define some of your own.

Because views are so central to SwiftUI, Xcode changes its interface when you are editing a view type. Open ContentView.swift and click on the line of code that contains Text("Hello, world!"). The graphical representation on the righthand side of the editor should update to reflect the selected object, as illustrated in Figure 28.3. (If you do not see the graphical representation, click the Resume button, indicated in the screenshot. If you see an error message reading Cannot preview in this file, make sure the scheme selector, above the editor, is set to TahDoodle (iOS).)

Figure 28.3 Xcode user interface

You have already encountered many of the important parts of Xcode's interface, such as the navigator area, editor, run button, and scheme selector. As you dive into app development with SwiftUI, there are some additional areas you should know about.

- The *canvas* provides a live-updating rendering of your views. You can show and hide the canvas with the Editor Options button (▤▯) above the editor area (Figure 28.4). Check or uncheck Canvas in the pop-up menu. The Layout option in the same menu allows you to set whether the canvas is to the right of the editor or below it.

- When you make large changes to your code, the canvas will pause updates to the preview. When it does, you can click the Resume button to begin updating the preview again.

- If your preview is uncomfortably small or large, you can resize it with a pinch/zoom gesture on your track pad or with the zoom control in the bottom-right corner of the canvas.

- The attributes inspector (the right-most tab of the inspector area, with an icon that looks like ≛) allows you to configure the currently selected view. We encourage you to experiment with the attributes inspector (and the other inspectors), but most of this chapter will focus on code. You can hide the inspector area anytime with the ▣▯ button at the top right of the Xcode window.

Figure 28.4 Editor options

In the editor's code area, change the string text from Hello, world! to Hello, SwiftUI! and watch the canvas update. (You may need to click the Resume button at the top-right corner of the canvas.)

Your app will run in both iOS and macOS environments, but for now, you will test your application in Simulator, a program that ships with Xcode to simulate the experience of using an iOS (or watchOS, etc.) device.

From the scheme drop-down menu, move to the TahDoodle (iOS) submenu and select an iPhone to simulate (Figure 28.5):

Figure 28.5 Selecting an iOS simulator

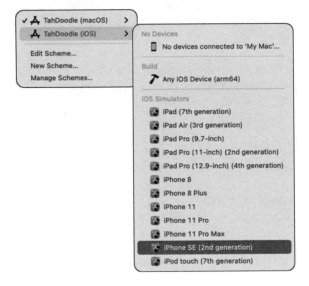

Build and run your program, and Xcode will launch the Simulator app. If this is the first time you have launched Simulator, it may take a while to initialize. Eventually, you should see the app launch (Figure 28.6).

Figure 28.6 Hello, SwiftUI!

Right now, TahDoodle does not do much. It is time to fix that.

That is some View

To explore the components of a view, you will create your own. You will start with the view responsible for displaying the title of a task in the task list. Create a new file using File → New → File... or Command-N. Select the Swift File template, name the file `TaskView.swift`, and make sure it will be saved in the `Shared` group.

The file opens with the familiar import statement `import Foundation`. You will need to import the SwiftUI framework so that you can work with the elements it provides.

The SwiftUI framework imports the Foundation framework for its own use, so you do not need to manually import both. Replace `import Foundation` with `import SwiftUI`, then define a struct that conforms to the **View** protocol. Ignore the error that arises for now.

Listing 28.1 Importing SwiftUI (`TaskView.swift`)

```
import Foundation
import SwiftUI

struct TaskView: View {

}
```

A view is an instance of a value type that conforms to the **View** protocol, which has only two requirements:

```
public protocol View {
    associatedtype Body : View
    @ViewBuilder var body: Self.Body { get }
}
```

When you learned about generics in Chapter 21, you learned that protocols can have associated types that must be defined by the conforming type. **View** requires an associated type called **Body** that also conforms to **View**. This associated type is inferred by the compiler based on the type of the protocol's other, primary requirement: a property called body.

You can ignore the @ViewBuilder attribute for now; you will learn about it later.

Add a body property to satisfy the protocol requirements.

Listing 28.2 Adding a body (TaskView.swift)

```
struct TaskView: View {
    var body: some View {
        Text("Take out the trash")
    }
}
```

The **Text** type is a **View**-conforming struct defined in the SwiftUI framework. It displays non-editable text to the user and supports all the text features that you might expect, such as fonts, weights, and colors.

Every view has a body that is also a view, and you build a SwiftUI app by composing a *view hierarchy* of SwiftUI views, your own views, and the relationships among them.

A hierarchy of views, with each of their bodies returning an instance of a different **View**-conforming associated type, can get very deep and complex. To spare you the gritty details of deep view hierarchy types, the body property is declared as returning the **some View** opaque type.

Recall from Chapter 21 that an opaque return type allows an API developer to hide implementation details of the actual return type behind a protocol that it conforms to, while promising that the actual return type is stable across calls to the function.

To allow the canvas to display a preview of your view type, define a new **PreviewProvider**-conforming struct at the bottom of TaskView.swift, outside the **TaskView**'s definition:

Listing 28.3 Adding a **PreviewProvider** (TaskView.swift)

```
...
struct TaskCell_Previews: PreviewProvider {

    static var previews: some View {
        TaskView()
    }
}
```

PreviewProvider enables a type to be rendered in Xcode's preview canvas. Xcode will search your file for a type conforming to **PreviewProvider** and use it to generate a preview of the view returned by its static previews property. Here, you return an instance of your **TaskView** type.

If the preview has paused, resume it to see the results. (And if it is not visible at all, click the Editor Options button and check Canvas. If it is already checked, try toggling it off and back on.)

To change how a view appears, you can apply a *modifier* to it. Add some modifiers to your **Text** instance to change its appearance.

Listing 28.4 Adding modifiers to the **Text** (TaskView.swift)

```
struct TaskView: View {
    var body: some View {
        Text("Take out the trash")
            .padding(.vertical, 50)
            .background(Color.yellow)
            .font(.title3)
    }
}
...
```

Modifiers are methods that return a new type of view, creating a nested hierarchy. Here, you apply the **padding(_:_:)** modifier to the **Text** instance, which creates and returns a new view that contains the **Text** as its child view, with 50 points of padding above and below the **Text**. Then, you apply the **background(_:)** modifier to the padding view, which paints the entire padding view and its child view (the **Text**) with a yellow background.

Last, you apply the **font(_:)** modifier to the background view, which creates and returns yet another view, applying the title3 font style to strings in all its children recursively, all the way down to the **Text** instance.

Figure 28.7 breaks down what you see in the preview. Note that the righthand edges of the diagram rectangles have been artificially expanded to make it easier for you to tell them apart.

Figure 28.7 A hierarchy of views

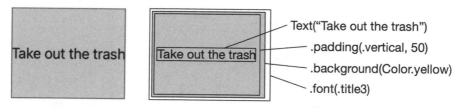

The order of modifiers is important, because it affects the resulting hierarchy. Move the **background(_:)** modifier to be applied before the **padding(_:_:)** modifier.

Listing 28.5 Reordering modifiers (TaskView.swift)

```
struct TaskView: View {
    var body: some View {
        Text("Take out the trash")
            .background(Color.yellow)
            .padding(.vertical, 50)
            .background(Color.yellow)
            .font(.title3)
    }
}
...
```

Now that the background is applied first, the padding view adds padding around the background view rather than just around the text, as depicted in Figure 28.8.

Figure 28.8 A reordered hierarchy of views

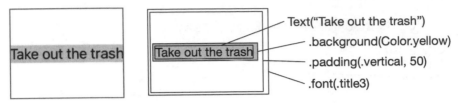

In both these hierarchies, the outermost view that is being returned by your body is the one returned by the `font(_:)` modifier.

You can delete the background modifier and decrease the severity of the vertical padding, as both have served their illustrative purposes. Also, since **TaskView** is intended to display the title of any task, not just taking out the trash, give it a `title` property to display in the **Text**.

Listing 28.6 Completing **TaskView** (TaskView.swift)

```swift
struct TaskView: View {

    let title: String

    var body: some View {
        Text("Take out the trash" title)
            .background(Color.yellow)
            .padding(.vertical, 50 4 )
            .font(.title3)
    }
}

struct TaskCell_Previews: PreviewProvider {

    static var previews: some View {
        TaskView(title: "Take out the trash")
    }
}
```

Since **TaskView** has a new property, its compiler-synthesized initializer has changed to take `title` as an argument, so you also update the **TaskView** initialization in the **TaskCell_Previews** struct.

Displaying Dynamic Data

It is fine to see previews that display hardcoded strings, but eventually TahDoodle should display user-generated tasks – and not just one task, but a whole list of them. You need to define a type to model a task and a place to store a collection of them.

Define a **Task** type in a new Swift file called `Task.swift`.

Listing 28.7 Defining **Task** (`Task.swift`)

```
import Foundation

struct Task {

    let title: String

}
```

Your **Task** type is very bare-bones right now, but it will grow over time as the needs of your program evolve.

Next, define a type in a new file named `TaskStore.swift` that will hold and manage a collection of tasks. Your code will emit an error, which you will fix in a subsequent step.

Listing 28.8 Defining **TaskStore** (`TaskStore.swift`)

```
import Foundation

class TaskStore {

    private(set) var tasks: [Task] = []

    func add(_ task: Task) {
        tasks.append(task)
    }

    func remove(_ task: Task) {
        guard let index = tasks.firstIndex(of: task) else { return }
        tasks.remove(at: index)
    }
}
```

When building more robust programs, it is common to build an abstraction around the collection of data that you will manage. One way to do this is with a *store* type.

There is nothing special about a store. It is just a name used to say, "This is a type that encapsulates and protects data. The type's users can only access the data the way I want them to, and they don't know where I got the data from." For example, an even more complex app might abstract a networking layer and a disk persistence layer behind a store, so that users of the store do not have to think about the source of the data they are accessing. This strategy, or pattern, is a stylish way to ensure that the data is never manipulated in unexpected ways.

TaskStore is a simple store type that owns an array of **Task** instances and makes the setter for that property `private`. This ensures that the only way for another type to change the list of tasks is through the store's **add(_:)** and **remove(_:)** methods.

This code produces an error: Referencing instance method 'firstIndex(of:)' on 'Collection' requires that 'Task' conform to 'Equatable'. The reason is that **firstIndex(of:)** will perform an equality check to compare its argument to each instance in the collection, and it will return the index of the first instance for which the check returns true. Fair enough. Make your **Task** struct **Equatable**.

Listing 28.9 Making **Task** conform to **Equatable** (Task.swift)

```
struct Task: Equatable {

    let title: String

}
```

As you learned in Chapter 25, merely declaring conformance to **Equatable** is enough if you want the compiler to implement the required == operator for you.

You have not developed any views to allow a user to enter tasks yet, but it would be nice to see some sample data in your previews and when you run the app during development. At the bottom of TaskStore.swift, outside the class's definition, use an extension to define a static property holding a sample instance of a **TaskStore** populated with hardcoded data.

Listing 28.10 Providing sample data (TaskStore.swift)

```
...
#if DEBUG
extension TaskStore {
    static var sample: TaskStore = {
        let tasks = [
            Task(title: "Add features"),
            Task(title: "Fix bugs"),
            Task(title: "Ship it")
        ]
        let store = TaskStore()
        store.tasks = tasks
        return store
    }()
}
#endif
```

Very little of this is new. You have defined extensions. You have worked with static properties. You have created variables whose initial values are assigned to the result of calling an inline closure. You do all these things here to create a sample instance of **TaskStore** that you can use as dummy data during development.

The new syntax is #if DEBUG and #endif. These *compiler control statements* allow you to specify chunks of code that should only be compiled into your program under certain conditions. Notice that the compiler control statements do not create braced scopes; the conditionally compiled code is between the lines containing #if and #endif.

In this case, the condition is that you are building for debugging, as opposed to building to release your app for distribution. Recall from your error handling work in Chapter 23 that the **assert(_:_:)** function only checks its condition when debugging. Now you know how.

Using these compiler control statements, you can ensure that your sample data does not accidentally ship if you distribute your app to the App Store. Since SwiftUI canvas previews and Simulator both execute your code in debug mode, you can use this sample data as much as you want while you are developing your app. By the way, the #warning and #error expressions that you met in Chapter 24 are examples of another type of compiler control statement called a *compile-time diagnostic*.

Later, you will let the user enter their own tasks, but for now, you have a collection of sample tasks to display in a list.

Now that you have created a SwiftUI view from the ground up and have studied its constituent pieces, you are ready to use Xcode's SwiftUI View file template, which you can access from the File → New → File... menu item or with Command-N (Figure 28.9). Use it to create a new SwiftUI view in a file named TaskListView.swift.

Figure 28.9 Creating a new SwiftUI View

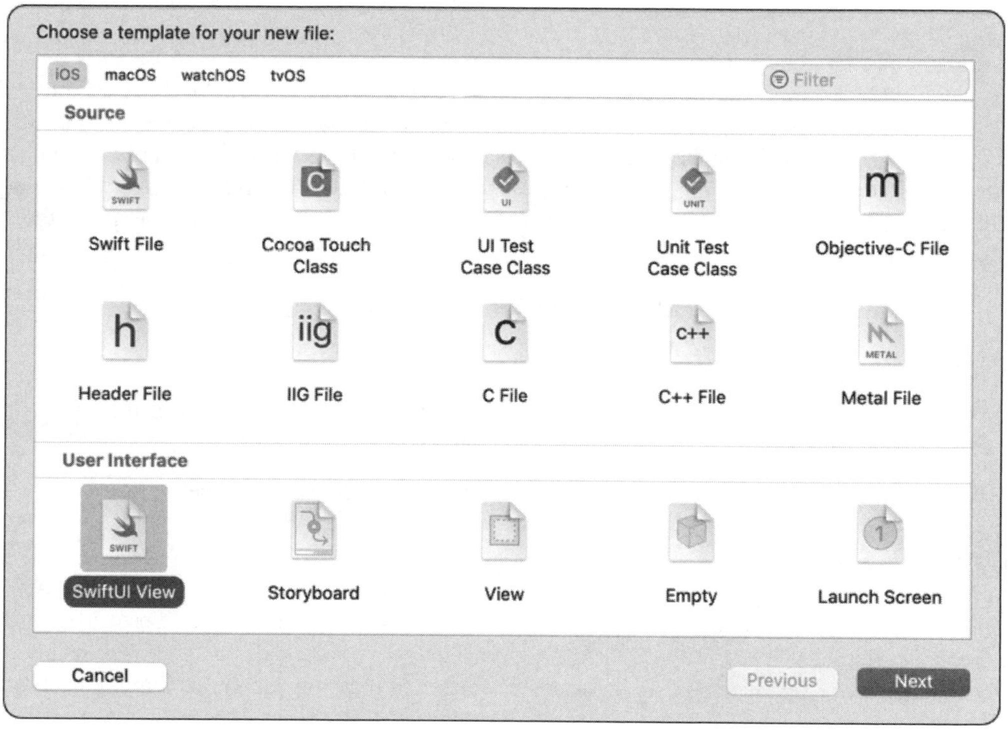

The template sets you up with a struct that includes the required body property as well as a second struct that conforms to **PreviewProvider**.

TaskListView will be responsible for displaying a list of **TaskView** instances. Fortunately, SwiftUI has a built-in view type called **List** that will do nicely. From the body of **TaskListView**, create a **List** and populate it with some **TaskView** instances.

Listing 28.11 Beginning the task list (TaskListView.swift)

```
import SwiftUI

struct TaskListView: View {
    var body: some View {
        Text("Hello, World!")
        List {
            TaskView(title: "Take out the trash")
            TaskView(title: "Do the dishes")
            TaskView(title: "Learn Swift")
        }
    }
}
...
```

That strange **List** creation syntax is using a *view builder*. Remember the @ViewBuilder attribute on the body property in the **View** protocol requirements list? Computed properties and function parameters of closure type can be marked with the @ViewBuilder attribute to allow syntax like what you use here: a newline-delimited (instead of comma-delimited) list of SwiftUI views that are automatically collected as children of the type the closure is passed to. Here, three **TaskView**s are collected and made the children of the **List**.

The complete signature for the **List** initializer that you are using here is:

```
init(@ViewBuilder content: () -> Content)
```

Content is the generic placeholder for the type of the list's content view. You are passing a view builder closure to the **List** initializer using trailing closure syntax.

Your preview should look like the kind of simple list you might have seen in other apps (Figure 28.10):

Figure 28.10 A simple list

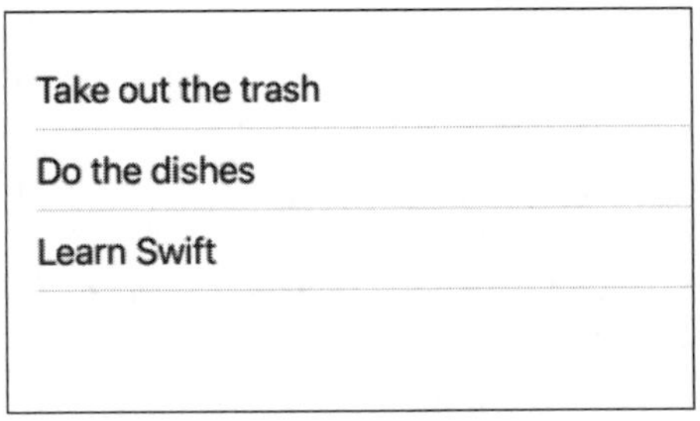

View builder syntax for composing views is very cool, but this data is insufficient. You want to display the tasks from the **TaskStore**. Give **TaskListView** a task store, and give the sample data to the preview provider.

Listing 28.12 Giving the list a task store (`TaskListView.swift`)

```
struct TaskListView: View {

    var taskStore: TaskStore

    var body: some View {
        ...
    }
}

struct TaskListView_Previews: PreviewProvider {
    static var previews: some View {
        TaskListView(taskStore: .sample)
    }
}
```

Now you are ready to iterate over your array of tasks and create views for them. SwiftUI has a view for this as well. Use a **ForEach** instance to unpack your **Task**s into **TaskListView** instances for the **List**. This will generate an error, which you will fix shortly.

Listing 28.13 Using **ForEach** (`TaskListView.swift`)

```
struct TaskListView: View {

    var taskStore: TaskStore

    var body: some View {
        List {
            TaskView(title: "Take out the trash")
            TaskView(title: "Do the dishes")
            TaskView(title: "Learn Swift")
            ForEach(taskStore.tasks) { task in
                TaskView(title: task.title)
            }
        }
    }
}
...
```

While **ForEach** conforms to **View**, it is not designed to be used as a view on its own. Instead, think of it like an object that you use to map an array of data models into views for a view builder. Here, you use it to map your array of tasks into instances of **TaskView** for the **List** view builder.

The **ForEach** type has an unmet need that the compiler wants you to know about (Figure 28.11):

Figure 28.11 **ForEach** requires **Identifiable** data

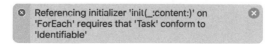

Referencing initializer 'init(_:content:)' on 'ForEach' requires that 'Task' conform to 'Identifiable'

When the **ForEach** is filling the **List**'s view builder, it wants a way to uniquely identify each instance of **Task**, so it can track them even when their properties change. Swift's **Identifiable** protocol exists to fill this need. Make **Task** conform to **Identifiable**:

Listing 28.14 Making **Task Identifiable** (Task.swift)

```
struct Task: Equatable, Identifiable {

    let id: UUID
    let title: String

    init(title: String) {
        id = UUID()
        self.title = title
    }

}
```

You declare conformance to the **Identifiable** protocol and implement its only requirement: a property called id of a **Hashable** type. The id property must be unique for any instance in your program.

The task's title would not work for the id, since a user could enter two tasks with the same title. A random number could work. However, Swift supports a type built for this purpose called **UUID**, which stands for *universally unique identifier*. A **UUID** is like a long random string, and it is generated such that its uniqueness is guaranteed.

Why **Identifiable** and not **Hashable**, like dictionaries and sets use for testing uniqueness? Internally, the list will tie a task's id to a row index for positioning its children. This has two consequences:

- One instance's id must never collide with another, or the **List** might accidentally order its children incorrectly when it updates. Recall from Chapter 25 that hash values are not *guaranteed* to be unique. They are only *likely* to be unique within a sample, to balance the performance of lookups in sets and dictionaries.

- An instance's id must be stable; it should not change when the instance's other properties change. That way, the list can maintain correct ordering. As you have learned, the implementations of equality and hashability are generally data dependent and would produce different results before and after an instance's essential data changed.

Now that **Task** conforms to **Identifiable**, the compiler error is gone. (If it does not disappear on its own, try building your project with Product → Build or Command-B.)

To see the fruits of your labor in Simulator, temporarily adjust TahDoodleApp.swift to create a **TaskListView** and feed it the sample task data.

Listing 28.15 Creating a **TaskStore** (TahDoodleApp.swift)

```
@main
struct TahDoodleApp: App {
    var body: some Scene {
        WindowGroup {
            ContentView()
            TaskListView(taskStore: .sample)
        }
    }
}
```

The @main attribute, the **Scene** and **App** protocols, and the **WindowGroup** view type are out of scope for this chapter – but, as you might imagine, they are collectively responsible for getting your app's interface onto the screen when your app launches. Check them out in the developer documentation if you are curious.

Build and run the app in your selected Simulator to see the sample task list (Figure 28.12).

Figure 28.12 Showing your sample data in Simulator

Accepting User Input

It is time to let the user manage their own list of tasks, rather than only looking at yours. To do this, you will make your view hierarchy even deeper by fleshing out the **ContentView** to contain a **TaskListView**, as well as a place to enter text and a submit button.

You are going to reinstall the **ContentView** as the root view created by the **TahDoodleApp**. Start in ContentView.swift by giving the **ContentView** a store that it will, in turn, pass along to its **TaskListView**. Make sure to update the preview provider to give it your sample data.

Listing 28.16 Giving the **ContentView** a store (ContentView.swift)

```
import SwiftUI

struct ContentView: View {

    let taskStore: TaskStore

    var body: some View {
        Text("Hello, world!")
            .padding()
        TaskListView(taskStore: taskStore)
    }

    struct ContentView_Previews: PreviewProvider {
        static var previews: some View {
            ContentView(taskStore: .sample)
        }
    }
}
```

Now the **ContentView** does nothing more than embed a **TaskListView**, which you can verify by checking the canvas preview. Next, put the **ContentView** back into the hierarchy.

Listing 28.17 Putting the **ContentView** back in the hierarchy (TahDoodleApp.swift)

```
@main
struct TahDoodleApp: App {
    var body: some Scene {
        WindowGroup {
            TaskListView(taskStore: .sample)
            ContentView(taskStore: .sample)
        }
    }
}
```

The fact that you can swap the **TaskListView** and **ContentView** so easily implies – correctly – that there is nothing special about the **ContentView**. It is merely a **View** that comes as a part of the SwiftUI App template, whose name makes it a good top-level view for your hierarchy.

You are ready to create the views that will allow the user to add new tasks. They will appear above the list and will join it as children of the content view.

When you need to compose multiple children of a view (such as a button, a text input field, and a list), it can be useful to factor a subset of the children into a helper property of the owning view. To see what this looks like, add a newTaskView property to the **ContentView**.

Listing 28.18 Adding a helper view property (ContentView.swift)

```
struct ContentView: View {

    let taskStore: TaskStore

    private var newTaskView: some View {
        Text("Placeholder for new task controls")
    }

    var body: some View {
        newTaskView
        TaskListView(taskStore: taskStore)
    }
}
...
```

Factoring potentially complex views into helper properties makes your program more readable in the same way that factoring large methods into groups of smaller ones does. Now you have a single place to focus on your newTaskView hierarchy without thinking about the rest of the body.

Notice that the canvas preview has split your newTaskView and the **TaskListView** instance into two separate previews. (Scroll the preview area down if you do not see them both.) The view builder for your body property does not know how to arrange its child views. Horizontally? Vertically? Deeply? So it does not try.

As you saw previously, the **List** type is designed to arrange any number of child views in a scrolling list. That is not what you want for the newTaskView and **TaskListView**, because you do not want the controls in the newTaskView to ever be offscreen. SwiftUI also offers three *stacking* types that allow you to arrange a few views to fill the available space:

HStack   Arranges its children in a horizontal row, like framed pictures on a shelf.

VStack   Creates a vertical stack similar to a **List**, but without scrolling.

ZStack   Creates a stack of views arranged like cards piled on a table, where those higher in the stack are in front of (and can cover up) views lower in the stack. A **ZStack** is most useful when the views in the stack have different geometries or opacities, to allow those in the back to show.

These types do not support scrolling (though you can put a scrolling element, like a list, inside one); if their content is too large for the available space, some of the content will be unreachable off the edge of the screen. They are useful when you want to arrange views to fit entirely within the visible screen.

You want the newTaskView to appear above the list, so a **VStack** is the most appropriate choice. The **VStack** will keep both the newTaskView and the **TaskListView** onscreen at all times, while the **List** in **TaskListView** will allow the task list to scroll within its space. Nest the contents of the body in a **VStack**.

Listing 28.19 Stacking the contents of the body (ContentView.swift)

```
...
var body: some View {
    VStack {
        newTaskView
        TaskListView(taskStore: taskStore)
    }
}
...
```

Now the preview can render the stacked views correctly (Figure 28.13):

Figure 28.13 **ContentView** with views in a **VStack**

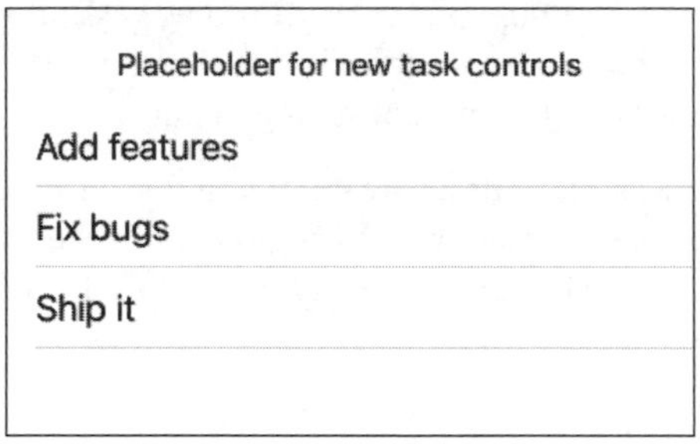

Time to build the newTaskView. Start by adding a button to add new tasks to the taskStore:

Listing 28.20 Adding a button to the newTaskView (ContentView.swift)

```
...
private var newTaskView: some View {
    Text("Placeholder for new task controls")

    Button("Add Task") {
        #warning("The task title is hardcoded")
        let task = Task(title: "Title")
        taskStore.add(task)
    }
}
...
```

You create a new instance of SwiftUI's **Button** type, using its initializer that takes two arguments. The first argument is the title the button will display, and the second is an action – a closure to execute when the button is tapped.

In the closure, you create a new **Task** and add it to the task store. The whole action is passed to the **Button** initializer using trailing closure syntax. The implementation is incomplete, as the task's title is not being provided by the user yet, so you leave yourself a reminder in the form of a #warning.

Sharing references to value-type data

Now you can add a text field for the user to type their new task's title in. Create a **TextField** and embed it, along with the **Button**, in an **HStack**:

Listing 28.21 Creating a **TextField** (ContentView.swift)

```
...
private var newTaskView: some View {
    HStack {
        TextField("Something to do", text: .constant(""))
        Button("Add Task") {
            #warning("The task title is hardcoded")
            let task = Task(title: "Title")
            taskStore.add(task)
        }
    }.padding()
}
...
```

Your preview should look like Figure 28.14, with your padded **HStack** floating above the list.

Figure 28.14 Stacks of stacks of views

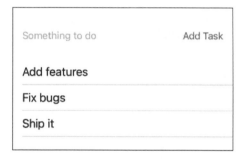

Feel free to play with the **padding** modifier and experiment with its arguments and possible values to see how they affect the preview. To see what the options are, Command-click **padding**, select Jump to Definition, and go spelunking. (You can save this for later, of course; exploring the developer documentation and interfaces is both highly educational and time-consuming.)

The **TextField** type represents a single-line text input control. When the user taps it, a keyboard is presented, allowing them to enter text in the text field. The first argument to this **TextField** initializer is the placeholder text, which appears in a faded color to show the user where they can type. Ignore the .constant("") argument for now; you will come back to it shortly.

As the user types, the text field needs somewhere to put its text where you can access it. Using what you know now, you might be able to build a system using property observers and closures to allow you to store a **String** and let the text field update it for you. But to help you write less code, SwiftUI introduces some property wrappers (which you learned about in Chapter 26) to allow you to declare properties of value types with some special behaviors.

Give your **ContentView** a wrapped **String** property to store text emitted by the **TextField**.

Listing 28.22 Sharing a value type property with child views (ContentView.swift)

```
struct ContentView: View {

    let taskStore: TaskStore
    @State private var newTaskTitle = ""
    ...
}
...
```

Here you declare a new string property, newTaskTitle, that is owned by the **ContentView**.

The newTaskTitle uses an instance of the **State** property wrapper struct to manage its value, as indicated by the @State property wrapper attribute. The property wrapper will store your string in its wrappedValue and return it any time you access your newTaskTitle property.

The @State property wrapper lends your SwiftUI code some very important features. Any time a @State property's value changes, the owning view will *invalidate* itself, which tells SwiftUI to re-create the view and redraw it on the screen. This process re-creates and redraws any of the view's children as well.

Both the text field and the button's action closure will need the newTaskTitle: The text field will update this string, and when the Add Task button is tapped, its action will use this string as the title of a new **Task** instance.

Go ahead and update the button first:

Listing 28.23 Child views are re-created with the latest data (ContentView.swift)

```
struct ContentView: View {

    let taskStore: TaskStore
    @State private var newTaskTitle = ""

    private var newTaskView: some View {
        HStack {
            TextField("Something to do", text: .constant(""))
            Button("Add Task") {
                #warning("The task title is hardcoded")
                let task = Task(title: "Title" newTaskTitle)
                taskStore.add(task)
            }
        }.padding()
    }
    ...
}
...
```

Because newTaskTitle is marked @State, any time its value changes, the **ContentView** will be invalidated and re-created. That process will re-create the **TextField** and **Button** as well – and as the **Button** is re-created, so is its action closure, which captures an up-to-date copy of the newTaskTitle string to use.

So how will the `newTaskTitle` be changed? The **TextField** will need to update it. It is time to look into the second argument that you passed to the **TextField** initializer.

By passing `.constant("")` in Listing 28.21, you told the text field, "I don't have a string property for you to update right now, so just display this constant empty string instead."

In your **ContentView**, tell the text field about your `newTaskTitle`.

Listing 28.24 Sharing a value type property with child views (ContentView.`swift`)

```
struct ContentView: View {

    let taskStore: TaskStore
    @State private var newTaskTitle = ""

    private var newTaskView: some View {
        HStack {
            TextField("Something to do", text: .constant("") $newTaskTitle)
            Button("Add Task") {
                let task = Task(title: newTaskTitle)
                taskStore.add(task)
            }
        }.padding()
    }
    ...
}
...
```

Since **String** is a value type, passing a string to the **TextField** would pass an immutable copy of the value, preventing the **TextField** from updating your `newTaskTitle` as the user types. SwiftUI solves this problem with a type related to the `@State` property wrapper called **Binding**.

Recall from your work with functions in Chapter 12 and structs in Chapter 15 that a function argument can be declared `inout` if it wants to accept a reference to a value-type argument, rather than a copy of the argument. This allows the body of the function to modify the original value owned by the function's caller. **Binding** provides a similar behavior – bidirectional access to a value stored elsewhere – but for stored properties instead of functions. This way, the object with the binding can reach back to the value's owner and modify the original value, rather than a copy of it.

The projected value of a `@State` property (accessed with $, as you saw in Chapter 26) returns an instance of **Binding** holding a reference to the property's wrapped value. So when you pass $newTaskTitle to the text argument of the **TextField** initializer, you are not passing the string itself, but a binding to it. Any time the text in the text field changes, the text field will use this binding to update the value of newTaskTitle.

Convenient, right?

What does the text field actually do with the binding you give it? When a view wants a property to hold a reference to value-type data that it does not own, it can declare its property using the **@Binding** property wrapper attribute, as **TextField** does for its text. For example, the **TextField** type likely declares a property like this:

```
@Binding private var text: String
```

We say "likely" because SwiftUI is not open-source; we cannot see how **TextField** is actually implemented. But this is the code you could write if you wanted a view to have a value-type property whose storage actually belonged to a view higher in the hierarchy. In this case, the string's storage is the newTaskTitle owned by **ContentView**.

The final result of this syntax is this: When you type into the text field, the field will update its text, which is bound to the newTaskTitle of the **ContentView**. The change will update the newTaskTitle of the content view, causing it to invalidate and redraw, which will re-create the button and text field, as you learned previously.

All this required relatively little code on your part.

SwiftUI does a great deal of work to ensure that the invalidation and redrawing process is as fast and lightweight as possible. The @State and @Binding property wrappers give SwiftUI views the best of two worlds: the shared data access of reference types with the optimizations available to value types.

To see an example of views invalidating and redrawing as your data changes, ensure that the Add Task button is disabled when there is no text in the text field. This will prevent the user from creating empty tasks.

Listing 28.25 Disabling the Add Task button when there is no task title (ContentView.swift)

```
...
private var newTaskView: some View {
    HStack {
        TextField("Something to do", text: $newTaskTitle)
        Button("Add Task") {
            let task = Task(title: newTaskTitle)
            taskStore.add(task)
        }.disabled(newTaskTitle.isEmpty)
    }.padding()
}
...
```

The **disabled(_:)** modifier accepts any Boolean expression. If the expression is true, then the modified view will be disabled until it is invalidated and redrawn, evaluating the expression anew.

Your preview should show that the Add Task button is disabled (Figure 28.15), since the default value of newTaskTitle is an empty string.

Figure 28.15 Completed new task view appearance

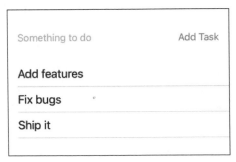

Notice that you did not use a binding to newTaskTitle in the button's action closure in Listing 28.24. The button's action closure, which instantiates the new **Task** instance, does not need persistent bidirectional access to newTaskTitle, like the text field does. When the button is tapped, its action closure will execute once, creating a new task instance with whatever the current value of newTaskTitle happens to be.

Build and run your app in Simulator to play with your beautiful user interface (Figure 28.16).

Figure 28.16 Completed iOS user interface

Tap into the text field, noticing that the Add Task button is disabled. Type some text, and the button is enabled. Because newTaskTitle is marked @State, any changes to its value trigger invalidation of newTaskView, the view that owns the property. That view redraws, re-creating its text field and button. This time, since newTaskTitle is not empty, the new button is not disabled.

Next, tap the Add Task button, and … it just sits there. Why isn't the new task being added to the list?

Interlude: Troubleshooting with property observers

Adding a new task silently fails. No error is produced onscreen or in the console. Did the button fail to add the new task to the task store, or did the list fail to update and show the new task?

To find out, add a property observer to the tasks array in the task store to find out every time it changes:

Listing 28.26 Troubleshooting the task store (TaskStore.swift)

```
class TaskStore {

    private(set) var tasks: [Task] = [] {
        didSet {
            #warning("Remove this when I'm done with it")
            print("There are now \(tasks.count): \(tasks)")
        }
    }
    ...
}
...
```

Build and run again and try adding a task titled "NEW TASK." Watch your console output:

```
There are now 4: [TahDoodle.Task(id: [...], title: "Add features"),
    TahDoodle.Task(id: [...], title: "Fix bugs"),
    TahDoodle.Task(id: [...], title: "Ship it"),
    TahDoodle.Task(id: [...], title: "NEW TASK")]
```

There is your new task, so you can rule out the button and the task store as the source of the problem. That means the list is not updating when the task store does. You will fix this shortly by changing the task store to publish its updates in a way the list can observe, so that the list knows to update as well.

You learned what you came here for, so you can remove the property observer. Adding temporary property observers to properties or local variables is a great way to discover whether values are changing when – and how – you expect them to.

Listing 28.27 Cleaning up after yourself (TaskStore.swift)

```
class TaskStore {

    private(set) var tasks: [Task] = [] {
        didSet {
            #warning("Remove this when I'm done with it")
            print("There are now \(tasks.count): \(tasks)")
        }
    }
    ...
}
...
```

Observing Changes to the Store

You need a way to invalidate the **List** when the task store updates.

But first, think about what it means for the task store to update: The **TaskStore** type is a relatively simple model class. It does not know how to notify other objects when its tasks property changes. Teach it how by marking the tasks property with the @Published property wrapper attribute:

Listing 28.28 Publishing updates to the tasks array (TaskStore.swift)

```
class TaskStore: ObservableObject {
    @Published private(set) var tasks: [Task] = []
    ...
}
...
```

Now, any time the tasks property changes (such as by adding or removing a task), the **TaskStore** instance can publish knowledge of the change to any observing views. By declaring conformance to the **ObservableObject** protocol, **TaskStore** states its willingness to be observed and its intent to publish updates of its @Published properties to observers.

Any views observing an instance of an **ObservableObject**-conforming class will invalidate themselves when the observed instance's @Published properties change their values.

But how does a view actually register to observe changes to the **TaskStore**?

Update the **TaskListView** to observe its own taskStore property:

Listing 28.29 Observing the task store for updated tasks (TaskListView.swift)

```
struct TaskListView: View {

    @ObservedObject var taskStore: TaskStore
    ...
}
...
```

The **ObservedObject** property wrapper sets up the subscription to the @Published properties of an **ObservableObject**-conforming class. When the @Published properties update, the owning view (here, the **TaskListView**) will invalidate itself, just as it would with changes to a @State property.

Why the **TaskListView** and not the **ContentView**? Either would work. But invalidating the entire **ContentView** would be wasteful, as you don't need the button and text field to also invalidate. The **TaskListView** is the closest view to the **List** itself in the hierarchy that has a reference to the **TaskStore**. Invalidating the **TaskListView** invalidates as little of your hierarchy as possible while still getting the desired effect: a **List** refresh.

Build and run, and try adding a task. This time, the task should be added to your list when you tap the Add Task button.

Now you just need to clear the text from the text field when the button is tapped:

Listing 28.30 Clearing the decks (`ContentView.swift`)

```
...
private var newTaskView: some View {
    HStack {
        TextField("Something to do", text: $newTaskTitle)
        Button("Add Task") {
            let task = Task(title: newTaskTitle)
            taskStore.add(task)
            newTaskTitle = ""
        }.disabled(newTaskTitle.isEmpty)
    }.padding()
}
...
```

Note that this assignment to newTaskTitle will, as before, invalidate the content view, causing the button and text field to be redrawn (empty this time).

The user can add tasks and see them populate in the list, which is great. But what should they do when a task is complete? TahDoodle should let users delete tasks when they are done.

Lists of user-editable content in iOS can allow the user to swipe across an item from right to left to reveal a Delete button. Tapping it removes that item from the list. To support this swipe-to-delete behavior, add an **onDelete(_:)** modifier to the **ForEach** that feeds the **List**:

Listing 28.31 Enabling swipe-to-delete in the list (`TaskListView.swift`)

```
...
var body: some View {
    List {
        ForEach(taskStore.tasks) { task in
            TaskView(title: task.title)
        }.onDelete { indexSet in
            indexSet.forEach { index in
                let task = taskStore.tasks[index]
                taskStore.remove(task)
            }
        }
    }
}
...
```

The **onDelete(_:)** modifier takes a closure to execute when a view emitted by the **ForEach** is deleted using the swipe-to-delete gesture.

Build and run, and swipe on a row to reveal its Delete button (Figure 28.17).

Figure 28.17 Swiping to delete

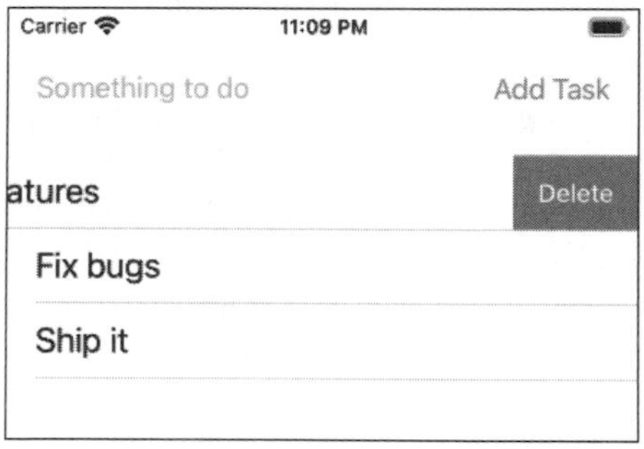

Congratulations! TahDoodle is now nearly feature complete for iOS. There is one glaring omission: When the program quits, all your data is gone. The next time you launch the app, the sample data will be back.

Saving and Loading User Data

The **TaskStore** is not currently saving tasks to disk or loading saved tasks on launch. It is time to fix that so that you can relegate the sample data to the preview providers.

To begin, you will need a **FileManager**. The **FileManager** type allows you to work with the contents of the filesystem, such as generating the local **URL** of a place where you can save data. The **URL** type is basically a specialized string that refers to the location of a resource like a locally stored file or a document on the internet.

Give the **TaskStore** handy access to a local **URL** where it can store your to-do list.

Listing 28.32 Telling the **TaskStore** where to save (TaskStore.swift)

```swift
class TaskStore: ObservableObject {

    private let fileURL: URL = {
        let fileManager = FileManager.default
        let documentDirectories = fileManager.urls(for: .documentDirectory,
                                                    in: .userDomainMask)
        let myDocumentDirectory = documentDirectories.first!
        let tasksFileURL = myDocumentDirectory.appendingPathComponent("tasks.json")
        print("Tasks file is \(tasksFileURL)")
        return tasksFileURL
    }()

    @Published private(set) var tasks: [Task] = []
    ...
}
...
```

You get a reference to the default **FileManager** from the Foundation framework, which is used for working with locations and directories in the filesystem in all kinds of apps, including command-line apps. You can use a **FileManager** to create, move, delete, and learn about files and directories. You could create your own instance, but there is generally no need to, since there is a default instance available.

Next, you call the **urls(for:in:)** method of the file manager to look up a list of document directories that you can access. This method is designed to search for different locations, from system-owned temporary directories to user-owned document directories. The .documentDirectory case of the **FileManager.SearchPathDirectory** enum specifies that you want a directory appropriate for storing documents, as opposed to other types of files such as caches or temporary files. The .userDomainMask case of the **FileManager.SearchDomainMask** enum tells the file manager to look within the user's home folder.

The return value of **urls(for:in:)** is an array of **URL** instances representing the location of local directories where you can store and retrieve data.

The number of directories returned by **urls(for:in:)** depends on its arguments. Since you are searching for the .documentDirectory in the .userDomainMask, there will be exactly one object in the returned array. Finally, you append the tasks.json path component to the **URL** so that the final resulting URL represents the location on disk where you will save and load the tasks.

You are going to store content in the JSON file format, which is a popular text file format for data storage and transmission. The details of JSON are out of scope for this book, but you can find a great summary on Wikipedia at wikipedia.org/wiki/JSON.

Now that the task store knows where to store the tasks, you can teach it *how* to store them. Implement a **saveTasks()** method:

Listing 28.33 Saving tasks to disk (TaskStore.swift)

```
class TaskStore: ObservableObject {
    ...
    func remove(_ task: Task) {
        guard let index = tasks.firstIndex(of: task) else { return }
        tasks.remove(at: index)
    }

    private func saveTasks() {
        do {
            let encoder = JSONEncoder()
            #warning("Finish implementing encoding work.")
        } catch {
            print("Could not save tasks. Reason: \(error)")
        }
    }
}
...
```

Here, you create an instance of **JSONEncoder**, a type that can *encode* instances of various types into instances of **Data** using its throwing **encode(_:)** method. **Data** is a type that encapsulates arbitrary chunks of type-agnostic data: just a pile of ones and zeroes.

When you are transferring data to the disk or across a network, the APIs that handle the transmission generally do not care how your information is encoded. It is up to the saving and loading code – or transmitting and receiving code – to agree on how to interpret and translate the contents of an instance of **Data**. You are using JSON, but there are other formats available.

What types can **JSONEncoder** work with? Any type that conforms to Swift's **Encodable** protocol.

That means the **Task** type must be **Encodable**. You will also want to *decode* instances of **Data** back into an array of tasks; that process will require **Task** to conform to the **Decodable** protocol. So to support both encoding and decoding, **Task** will need to be both **Encodable** and **Decodable**.

To save you some typing, Swift defines a protocol composition (which you learned about in Chapter 19) of **Encodable** and **Decodable** called, simply, **Codable**. Make **Task** conform to **Codable**.

Listing 28.34 Making **Task** conform to **Codable** (Task.swift)

```
struct Task: Equatable, Identifiable, Codable {
    ...
}
```

As with **Equatable** and **Hashable**, the compiler is willing to synthesize the **Codable** protocol requirements for most value types, as long as all non-lazy stored properties are also **Codable**. The compiler will also synthesize **Codable** conformance for classes that meet the same requirement. Nearly all the basic types in the Swift standard library, from **Int** to **URL** and **Data**, conform to **Codable**. And collection types like **Array** are **Codable** as long as their element types are.

Return to the task store and finish encoding and saving data.

Listing 28.35 Encoding and saving tasks (TaskStore.swift)

```
...
private func saveTasks() {
    do {
        let encoder = JSONEncoder()
        #warning("Finish implementing encoding work.")
        let data = try encoder.encode(tasks)
        try data.write(to: fileURL)
        print("Saved \(tasks.count) tasks to \(fileURL.path)")
    } catch {
        print("Could not save tasks. Reason: \(error)")
    }
}
...
```

Here you ask the encoder to encode your array of tasks into an instance of **Data**. Then, you write the encoded data to disk at the location specified by your fileURL.

Both **encode(_:)** and **write(to:)** can fail for reasons related to disk permissions or corrupt data, and they will throw errors if they cannot finish their work. A more robust application would visually notify the app's user that the save had failed, but for your purposes a message logged to the console is enough.

Now implement a **loadTasks()** method:

Listing 28.36 Loading and decoding tasks (TaskStore.swift)

```
class TaskStore: ObservableObject {
    ...
    private func saveTasks() {
        ...
    }

    private func loadTasks() {
        do {
            let data = try Data(contentsOf: fileURL)
            let decoder = JSONDecoder()
            tasks = try decoder.decode([Task].self, from: data)
            print("Loaded \(tasks.count) tasks from \(fileURL.path)")
        } catch {
            print("Did not load any tasks. Reason: \(error)")
        }
    }
}
...
```

You create a new instance of **Data** with the contents of the file located at the fileURL. Then you create a **JSONDecoder** and use it to decode that data into an array of **Task** instances, which you store in the task store's tasks property.

Since the **Data** type does not know anything about the kind of data it contains, the **decode(_:from:)** method of the **JSONDecoder** must be told how to interpret the contents of the **Data**. If the **Data** contains the wrong kind of information, such as an array of integers instead of an array of tasks, **decode(_:from:)** will throw an error.

The task store is now capable of saving and loading tasks. Update the **add(_:)** and **remove(_:)** methods to save changes when they are made.

Listing 28.37 Saving changes (TaskStore.swift)

```
...
func add(_ task: Task) {
    tasks.append(task)
    saveTasks()
}

func remove(_ task: Task) {
    guard let index = tasks.firstIndex(of: task) else { return }
    tasks.remove(at: index)
    saveTasks()
}
...
```

Your task store is almost complete. It can now save and load tasks on behalf of the user.

When the user launches TahDoodle, you should load their saved tasks instead of the sample data. Start by loading any tasks that may be stored when an instance of **TaskStore** is initialized.

Listing 28.38 Adding an initializer that loads stored tasks (TaskStore.swift)

```
class TaskStore: ObservableObject {
    ...
    @Published private(set) var tasks: [Task] = []

    init() {
        loadTasks()
    }

    func add(_ task: Task) {
        tasks.append(task)
        saveTasks()
    }
    ...
}
...
```

The last step is to create a new instance of **TaskStore** rather than using the sample data when the app launches. Update **TahDoodleApp** to create a new **TaskStore** and pass it in to the **ContentView** in place of **TaskStore.sample**.

Listing 28.39 Replacing the sample store (TahDoodleApp.swift)

```
@main
struct TahDoodleApp: App {
    let taskStore = TaskStore()
    var body: some Scene {
        WindowGroup {
            ContentView(taskStore: .sample taskStore)
        }
    }
}
```

Whew! Build and run the app. The list will be empty, since you are not using the sample data. Add a few tasks of your own, then quit Simulator and relaunch your app from Xcode. Your tasks should load up for you.

Congratulations – you have now built a functioning task list app for iOS!

… but what about macOS?

Supporting macOS

The great news is that, as of macOS Big Sur, a single SwiftUI app can be deployed to both iOS and macOS. From the scheme selector at the top of Xcode's window, switch to the TahDoodle (macOS) scheme. Build and run, and TahDoodle will launch on your Mac (Figure 28.18).

Figure 28.18 TahDoodle on macOS

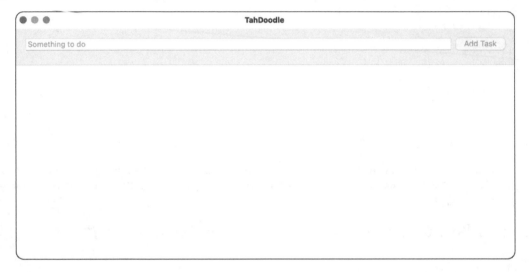

It launches, but it is much wider than necessary.

Unsurprisingly, developing for macOS introduces specific concerns and interaction paradigms that you should take into account. For example, apps can create windows of different sizes. As with any app development project, you would want to work with your users and a designer to help identify the ideal sizes of interface elements.

For now, add some constraints to the window size when the app is running on macOS:

Listing 28.40 Conditionally setting the window's frame (`TahDoodleApp.swift`)

```
...
struct TahDoodleApp: App {
    let taskStore = TaskStore()
    var body: some Scene {
        WindowGroup {
            #if os(macOS)
            ContentView(taskStore: taskStore)
                .frame(minWidth: 200,
                       maxWidth: 300,
                       minHeight: 200)
            #else
            ContentView(taskStore: taskStore)
            #endif
        }
    }
}
```

First, you separate your code into two different versions: one for macOS and one for everything else. ("Everything else" really just means iOS in this case, since this app is only capable of running on macOS and iOS.)

You use the #if compiler control statement to ensure that the lines up to the subsequent #else statement are only compiled when building for macOS. Lines between the #else and the #endif statements will only be included when you are building for a different OS, which in this case would be iOS.

In the macOS-only block, you add a **frame(…)** modifier to specify constraints on the size of the window. The modifier accepts lots of arguments for size restrictions, but you only need to include the ones you want to deviate from the default.

Build and run on macOS again; you will see that the window is smaller (Figure 28.19).

Figure 28.19 Framing the window

Another difference between iOS and macOS is that macOS does not natively use swipe-to-delete to remove rows from lists. Try as you might, you will find that you cannot delete a row from TahDoodle in macOS.

Add a right-click context menu with a Delete option to each **TaskView** created for the **List**.

Listing 28.41 Adding a context menu (TaskListView.swift)

```
...
ForEach(taskStore.tasks) { task in
    TaskView(title: task.title)
        .contextMenu {
            Button("Delete") {
                taskStore.remove(task)
            }
        }
}.onDelete { indexSet in
...
```

The **contextMenu(_:)** modifier accepts a view builder closure containing views that will be used as the menu options for a right-click (or long-press, on iOS) contextual menu.

Build and run, add a task, and then right-click it to show the context menu. Delete the task using the new Delete button (Figure 28.20).

Figure 28.20 Deleting a row on macOS

And there you have it: your shiny, new SwiftUI task list app that works on both macOS and iOS.

There are lots of other features you could add and glitches you could fix. For example, if you open multiple windows on macOS, they edit the same task store. But all that can come later.

For now, take a deep breath, be proud of your accomplishments, and add one more task to TahDoodle:

```
Keep learning
```

Bronze Challenge

Right now, a task can be deleted on iOS in two ways: by swiping the task to show the Delete button or by long-pressing the task to present its context menu.

Context menus have a place in iOS apps, but they are not usually used for deletion, as swipe-to-delete is more idiomatic. Edit your code to restrict the context menu to macOS only.

Silver Challenge

The `ContentView` file has a lot going on, and it could be refactored to improve the readability of your code.

Move the `newTaskView` implementation into the body of its own new SwiftUI View file called `NewTaskView.swift`.

What does this mean for the `newTaskTitle` state variable?

After the refactoring, the body of your **ContentView** should look like this:

```
var body: some View {
    VStack {
        NewTaskView(taskStore: taskStore)
        TaskListView(taskStore: taskStore)
    }.background(Color.white)
}
```

Ensure that your refactor was successful by running TahDoodle in Simulator and checking that nothing has changed visually.

Gold Challenge

It is time to go fishing and learn something on your own.

Right now, when you add a task, it just pops into place at the bottom of the list.

Can this be animated? Search for "SwiftUI" in the developer documentation, and read and browse. Using Apple's developer documentation alone, figure out how to add row animation to the **List** – and then add it.

29
Conclusion

Congratulations! You have finished this introduction to the Swift programming language. Thank you for sticking with us.

Along the way, you covered quite a bit of material, from the basic features of Swift like `let` and `var` to more advanced features like generics and property wrappers. You also saw how to put these pieces together to write complete Swift programs, and you applied your understanding of Swift to write some simple macOS and iOS applications.

You are now a Swift developer. Probably not a very good one – but that is OK, and it will change with time, practice, and continued learning.

Where to Go from Here?

After all your hard work, what should you do next? The truth is that your journey is just beginning. Swift is a rich language, and there is ample opportunity to learn more every day. Swift can be used to develop for any of Apple's platforms using their respective UI frameworks – or even to develop server-side applications. Studying these frameworks for your platform of choice should be your next step.

May we make a recommendation?

Shameless Plugs

If you want to develop iOS apps, we have a book that is a natural follow-up to this one: *iOS Programming: The Big Nerd Ranch Guide*, which is now in its 7th edition.

If you enjoyed this book and want to learn about Android or web development, please take a look at our other Big Nerd Ranch titles at `www.bignerdranch.com/books`.

We also offer in-person training for both open enrollment and corporate environments. Visit `www.bignerdranch.com/training/bootcamps` for more details.

An Invitation to the Community

Your knowledge of Swift will continue to grow with practice. Take the time to begin a project. Make something new. If you do not have a project in mind, visit `developer.apple.com`. This website provides a good overview of the resources available to Mac and iOS developers and also gives some examples that may inspire your creativity.

Consider finding meetup groups for Mac and iOS development in your area. For example, CocoaHeads is a loose organization with chapters all over the world that meet to discuss Apple platform development. You can find your nearest chapter on `CocoaHeads.org`. There are other groups, too! Most major cities have such groups, and they host regular talks. Going to these meetings will help you learn, practice, and get to know your peers.

Also, we would love your feedback! Our Twitter handle is `@bignerdranch`, and Mikey's is `@wookiee`. You can also find us on Facebook at `facebook.com/bignerdranch`.

So, come join us. We're out here making things, and we would love to see what you create.

Index

Symbols

A

Z